TELEVISION AND THE PERFORMING ARTS

TELEVISION AND THE PERFORMING ARTS

A Handbook and Reference Guide to American Cultural Programming

BRIAN G. ROSE

Greenwood Press
New York • Westport, Connecticut • London

Library of Congress Cataloging-in-Publication Data

Rose, Brian Geoffrey.
Television and the performing arts.

Bibliography: p.
Includes index.
1. Television and the performing arts—United States—History. I. Title.
PN1992.66.R67 1986 791.45'09'09357 85-14655
ISBN 0-313-24159-7 (lib. bdg. : alk. paper)

Library of Congress Catalog Card Number: 85-14655
ISBN: 0-313-24159-7

First published in 1986

Greenwood Press, Inc.
88 Post Road West
Westport, Connecticut 06881

Printed in the United States of America

The paper used in this book complies with the Permanent Paper Standard issued by the National Information Standards Organization (Z39.48-1984).

10 9 8 7 6 5 4 3 2 1

Contents

Preface

For nearly five decades, American television and the performing arts have been involved in a complicated relationship. Unlike their widely praised and heavily subsidized counterparts in Europe, TV stations in this country have usually looked at broadcasts of dance, theater, and opera in terms of audience and impact—how many people will watch, will the show make viewers switch to another channel, can a sponsor be found, how much money will it cost. Such types of economic and marketing considerations have played a large role in American cultural programming, not just at ABC, CBS, and NBC but also at PBS and the cable services.

The limited viewership appeal of the performing arts and the high costs involved in their production have generally made it difficult for telecasts of serious music, dance, and drama to find a regular niche on U.S. TV channels. The commercial networks have tended to treat their often distinctive cultural attractions as a form of jewelry—valuable, sometimes glittering ornaments, but too expensive (and too damaging in the ratings) to be displayed more than once or twice a year on ceremonial or prestigious occasions. Public television has proven much more hospitable, finding that certain kinds of mainstream concerts, plays, and ballet lure the very upscale, sophisticated audience its corporate underwriters are most eager to reach.

In addition to problems in funding and scheduling, the performing arts on television have continued to face the fundamental challenges of adaptation and translation. What types of events work best, given the medium's reduced scale? Can large dance movement be captured on the small screen? Does television's inherent intimacy distort the power of grand opera? How can a symphonic concert be made visually dynamic? What happens to a play when viewed in close-up?

These various issues—aesthetic, economic, and historical—are the subject of this book. My goal has been to offer, for both scholars and students of broadcasting, a comprehensive guide to the development, innovations, trials, and achievements of American television and the performing arts, from the 1930s through the close of the 1984–85 TV season. Though they examine different formats, each chapter is united by a common organization and emphasis. They not only chronicle, decade by decade, the evolution and treatment of cultural programming, they also look at how the arts have been transformed by television. What changes are necessary to transplant pieces created for the stage to a two-dimensional medium? Can three-hour works be successfully pared down to 90 minutes? What approaches have television directors used to suggest the vitality of a live performance?

Supplementing the discussion of historical development, each chapter includes a survey of reference material, a catalog of sources, and a videography, listing the production credits of a dozen or so shows cited for their significance and merit.

The chapters vary in length as a result of several factors. Foremost among them is the diversity and ambitiousness of the material produced in that format. The chapter on dance on television is almost twice as long as the chapter on classical music on television not because there were more dance shows aired by the four networks—the number is probably about equal—but because the process of adapting ballet and modern dance to television was approached in so many different and interesting ways. Concert music, on the other hand, was generally offered in only one or two standard methods of presentation. Similarly, there is more available reference material examining the challenges of TV dance, opera, and theater than there is for classical music.

I have tried, in tracing the evolution of cultural programming, to mention most of the major series and specials broadcast by ABC, CBS, NBC, and PBS. My guides in this undertaking were Tim Brooks and Earle Marsh's *The Complete Directory to Prime Time Network TV Shows 1946-Present,* the TV pages of the *New York Times,* listings supplied by the networks' program information departments, and the extensive files relating to the arts on TV available at the Television Information Office. I also relied on critical reviews drawn from *Variety,* the *New York Times,* the *Washington Post, Newsweek, TIME,* the *New Yorker,* and the *Saturday Review* to provide me with useful accounts on the programs discussed in this text.

My study was greatly assisted by the wealth of resources available in New York City. Probably more than any other American entertainment industry, television has had little use for or interest in its past. A good portion of the medium's heritage was never recorded; surviving tapes are often difficult to find. Fortunately, the Museum of Broadcasting and the New York Public Library of the Performing Arts have made a concerted effort to track down and rescue the major programs of American TV history. Thanks to their diligence, I was able to screen dozens of dance, theater, music, and opera telecasts, dating from the late 1940s onwards. Practically every show examined in detail in the pages that follow was viewed at these invaluable institutions.

The staff of both places proved to be especially helpful. Ron Simon of the Museum of Broadcasting was enthusiastic about my project from the start and tipped me off to many programs I might have overlooked. The New York Public Library of the Performing Arts' research staff courteously guided me through the library's vast holdings of rare books, magazines, and clippings files on cultural programming. I was also graciously treated at the Television Information Office, which houses a useful reference center for broadcast-related material.

One of the most pleasurable aspects of working on this project was the opportunity to interview key figures involved in televising the arts. Roger Englander, Jac Venza, Lewis Freedman, Pamela Illott, Schuyler Chapin, Robert Saudek, John Goberman, and Peter Weinberg were generous with their time and insights. Kirk Browning and Curtis Davis were kind enough to meet with me on numerous occasions, and offered worthwhile suggestions on the chapter concerning opera on TV. Talks with Kirsten Beck, John McKinley, and George Heineman supplied interesting background material on industry practices.

Much of the material on recent series and specials was provided by the program information departments at the four networks, who answered my frequent questions on casting and scheduling. My most valuable resource was Tom O'Brien of NBC. Tom cheerfully researched production credits and helped me flesh out my views on network operations.

My colleagues in the Humanities Division at Fordham University, College at Lincoln Center, especially Fred Harris, Margaret Lamb, and Bernard Gilligan, provided me with much needed support and advice. Thanks are also due to Fordham University, who funded my research trips to Washington, D.C., and to the staff of *Great Performances* at WNET–13 and the Media department at the Metropolitan Opera, who arranged for me to view videotapes in their collections. I am indebted as well to James Day, an authority on PBS and a kind friend who suggested several new avenues of inquiry.

This project began in May 1983 when Marilyn Brownstein of Greenwood Press approved my proposal for a reference guide and historical survey of the performing arts on American television. Her recommendations were quite useful in setting up the book's direction and scope. My editor at Greenwood, Cynthia Harris, has been a consistent voice of encouragement, as well as a sharp and penetrating reader, during my two years of research and writing.

Special thanks go to my parents, who introduced me to the performing arts at a very young age, and to my wife Kassie Schwan, who has not only shared with me countless hours at Lincoln Center and in front of the TV set, but made the writing of this book a truly joint project.

TELEVISION AND THE PERFORMING ARTS

1

Introduction

Launched with bold promises in the late 1930s, television in America seemed ready to embrace all types of entertainment. During these early years, performers from folk dancers to ballerinas, from country fiddlers to Metropolitan Opera stars eagerly appeared in front of the cameras, as the few TV stations on the air searched for easy to produce, live programming.

Experimentation was the order of the day, with no one quite certain what formats would work on this new medium. In Schenectady, General Electric's WRGB tried full-length operas and plays by Shakespeare. Dumont and CBS in New York offered dance programs with electronic special effects. NBC presented a series of abridged operas in English.

Numerous contemporary articles and books celebrated television's bright prospects. Writing in 1944, Robert E. Lee hoped "that the flexibility of television will challenge the young imaginations of the musical world to develop a new and freer language of operatic performance," while also producing "its own generation of composers and musical playwrights, to prepare scores and librettos expressly framed for the sweep of sight broadcasting."[1] NBC's Thomas Hutchinson believed "television will do for dance what radio has done for speech."[2]

This enthusiastic spirit continued to surround the medium during the immediate postwar years. As they gradually refined their program formulas, the networks and local stations were also willing to expand the range of their offerings. Since set costs were high, restricting their use originally to the affluent (or to taverns), a variety of cultural material was aired in the hopes of luring the moneyed crowd. ABC televised opening nights at the Metropolitan Opera. CBS broadcast plays direct from Broadway theaters. NBC created its own opera company. Stations in Chicago and Minneapolis presented weekly programs showcasing their local symphony orchestras.

Like most of television's formats, this type of arts programming originated from radio. Symphonic concerts, operatic performances, and classic theater productions had been regular radio features since the 1920s. The New York Philharmonic was a popular attraction on CBS's Sunday afternoon schedule. In order to bring Arturo Toscanini back to America, NBC hired the country's best musicians and formed the NBC Symphony Orchestra. The Metropolitan Opera's Saturday afternoon matinees were heard on NBC's Blue network (and later on ABC). When sponsors could not be found for these programs, they often ran on a "sustaining" basis, their costs paid for by the networks, who could afford the occasional hours of "largesse" while benefitting from the prestige.

The innovative cultural programming on television during the late 1940s and early 1950s coincided with the medium's rapid growth. (Set sales tripled from 1949 to 1952.) Prime-time drama series like *Kraft Television Theatre, Philco Playhouse,* and *Studio One* led the way in testing television's theatrical potential. *Julius Caesar* was staged in modern dress, with unusual video camerawork. There were adaptations of Henrik Ibsen and Luigi Pirandello. NBC's *Cameo Theater* abandoned sets and the proscenium arch, photographing its actors from all sides and angles. *The Hallmark Hall of Fame* presented Maurice Evans in *Hamlet,* the first two-hour network telecast of Shakespeare.

The costs of TV programming, however, no matter what type, were high (up to ten times more than radio); and cultural shows, targeted at only a small portion of the medium's ever expanding mass audience, were especially vulnerable. Despite the support of Texaco, ABC cancelled its opening nights from the Met in 1951. CBS discontinued its *Opera Television Theater* after only two shows. Only NBC was willing to commit itself, without any real hope of financial renumeration, to what emerged as the decade's most ambitious TV arts project—the *NBC Opera Theatre*. Broadcasting up to a half-dozen operas a year, all of them in English, and many of them American premieres or commissions (like Gian-Carlo Menotti's *Amahl and the Night Visitors*), the series proved how television could offer a fresh and vital operatic experience. It also proved how important the personal backing of a company's chief executive (in this case David Sarnoff and later his son Robert) could be in keeping a fairly expensive, virtually sustaining program alive for 15 seasons.

The *Opera Theatre* was not NBC's only effort to include the performing arts in its schedule. In 1952, network executive Sylvester (Pat) Weaver launched "Operation Frontal Lobes," a widely publicized plan to integrate "the cultural, informative, expository and inspirational into existing entertainment patterns."[3] By introducing "some element of culture or information in nearly every program in our schedule," Weaver hoped that his policy of "enlightenment through exposure" would lead to a new era in responsible programming.[4] With characteristic effusiveness, he proclaimed:

> I believe that we must open it [the window of television] so that the greatest numbers of people can look out and see the best, the most rewarding views. We must expose all of our people to the thrilling rewards that come from an understanding of fine

music, ballet, the literary classics, science, art, everything. We could, of course, present cultural events to small audiences who are already mentally attuned to them. But to program for the intellectual alone is easy and duplicates other media. To make us all into intellectuals—there is the challenge of television.[5]

Though never implemented on the large scale Weaver envisioned, NBC did make efforts throughout the 1950s to present a diverse assortment of arts-related programming. There were specials with the Royal Ballet; summer concert series; telecasts with Toscanini and the NBC Symphony; and lively dramatic "spectaculars," such as the fresh-from-Broadway *Peter Pan,* starring Mary Martin and Cyril Ritchard, a musical version of Thornton Wilder's *Our Town* with Frank Sinatra, and an adaptation of *The Petrified Forest,* highlighted by the TV debuts of Humphrey Bogart and Lauren Bacall.

Opera singers, ballet dancers, and classical musicians were also guests on many of the network's variety shows. Daytime audiences for *The Kate Smith Show* saw several performances by members of the New York City Ballet. During prime time, *Your Show of Shows* featured and gently parodied opera and ballet stars. Late-night viewers of *The Tonight Show* witnessed pas-de-deux, piano concerto excerpts, and musical celebrities like Van Cliburn.

But even with its "enlightenment" policies, NBC was, like its two commercial competitors, in the business of reaching mass audiences for its advertisers. Cultural programming, with its comparatively small constituency, held very little clout when directly confronted with the industry's profit-making concerns. Witness the case of NBC's premier weekly forum for the performing arts, *The Voice of Firestone.* Airing first on radio in 1928 and then simulcast on television beginning in 1949, the staid variety series, with a guest roster comprised mostly of opera singers and classical musicians, attracted a loyal audience of two or three million viewers. This was enough for the Firestone Tire Company, its prestige-conscious sponsor, but it was not enough for NBC. Claiming the show's low viewership was dragging down the ratings for the rest of the night, the network in 1954 demanded that the series be moved from its valuable 8:30 P.M. slot on Mondays. "Firestone," according to Tim Brooks and Earle Marsh, "refused to budge, arguing that many of the program's faithful viewers would not be able to watch in a less desirable time period."[6] After 26 seasons on NBC, the show transferred over to ABC that summer, where it held on to its prime Monday night position until the late 1950s.

The Ford Foundation pursued a different approach towards cultural programming and sponsorship. With an initial appropriation of $1.2 million, it created a TV-Radio Workshop in 1951 to put together a program that would, in the words of workshop director Robert Saudek, "have a real impact on the field in terms of originality and experimentation."[7] The result was *Omnibus,* an ambitious 90-minute mixture of everything from the performing arts to the sciences, designed to pay most of its way with advertising. While dubious of its commercial prospects, CBS agreed to air the series on late Sunday afternoons, provided the Workshop guarantee the cost of the programs for a year. *Omnibus* premiered in November 1952, with five sponsors (who had no say in the show's content) and with what would be a characteristic menu of music (a selection from Gilbert and Sullivan), drama (an excerpt from Maxwell Anderson's *The Trial of Ann Boleyn),* dance (an ensemble from Haiti), and the offbeat (the first TV views of x-ray technology).

The show proved to be a success, so much so that by the time the Ford Foundation withdrew its support for the project in 1957, it was able to recoup more than $5 million of the $8 million it originally provided the series in grants. *Omnibus*'s presentations included some of television's most unusual and imaginative cultural experiments. Leonard Bernstein explained the musical architecture of Beethoven's Fifth Symphony while standing on an enormous blow-up of the score. Agnes de Mille demonstrated the art of ballet and choreography by interweaving historical material, personal examples, and live performances. Orson Welles made his television debut in Peter Brook's surprisingly effective 90-minute version of *King Lear.* Gene Kelly revealed the links between classical dancing and athletics.

With its inspired blending of elements, its wide-ranging intellectual curiosity, and its prominent showcase for serious writers, actors, and musicians, *Omnibus* was an important step in charting new possibilities for American television. Yet the show was not without its detractors. The most prominent was Jack Gould of the *New York Times,* who decried the series for its stuffy, snobbish tone and for its willingness to embrace traditional commercial demands. Advertisers, Gould notes, were pretentiously identified as "subscribers," making the show often seem "more commercial than programs which make no pretense to cultural uplift"; selections were sometimes as rigidly scheduled for time as any variety show; and content frequently appeared dictated by ratings concerns.[8] "The [Ford] foundation woefully misjudges its potentiality in television if it regards commercial popularity as an absolute test of success," he wrote. "The workshop's mission should be to stand away from the TV sound and fury and out of real faith and conviction, do those things in the medium that need doing."[9]

For Gould and for other critics, what needed to be done was to carve out a place on the schedule free from the fever of commercialism and its corresponding concern with mass audiences. "Only in television has there been injected the preposterous notion that somehow totally dissimilar attractions can be equated," Gould later remarked when a prime-time broadcast of *Romeo and Juliet* was widely criticized for competing miserably in the ratings against Lucille Ball and George Burns.[10]

The economics of television are, of course, at the root of this cultural evil. The costs run so high that the advertiser feels he must pursue the mob; in other media, he may specialize or deliberately seek out one or more of the limitless groups that together compose the illusory 'mass.'[11]

One solution was to place less than crowd-pleasing attractions in a spot removed from commercial pressures. Out-of-the-way time slots, such as early Sunday mornings and afternoons, when viewership was at a low ebb and ads were hard to sell, became favored locales for cultural programs unconcerned with popularity. As was true on radio, these sustaining shows brought the networks that supported them a sense of prestige at a very small price. The various Sunday series counted as part of ABC, NBC, and CBS's "public affairs" obligation and were usually produced by existing news or religious departments on extremely tight budgets.

CBS's *Camera Three* was the most enterprising and distinguished example of unsponsored Sunday arts programming. Created by WCBS-TV in New York in 1953 and picked up for network transmission in 1956, the show's purpose, as defined by its innovative first producer, Robert Herridge, was to examine television as an original art form. With an initial outlay of less than $1,500 per week, Herridge set out to test the medium's techniques. He abandoned conventional scenery and props, dressed the stage with only a few ladders and stools, limited the illumination to a couple of sharply focused spotlights, and encouraged the cameras to freely roam through the open set. The program, favoring atmosphere and mood over realism, mounted ambitious serializations of *Crime and Punishment, Moby Dick,* and *The Red Badge of Courage,* spread over the course of six or eight weeks. It profiled the activities of authors, musicians, filmmakers, and dancers. It blended informed discussion with demonstration and performance.

During its 25 years on the air, *Camera Three* touched on virtually every aspect of the arts and culture, from dramatizations of the trial of Sacco and Vanzetti to a montage of Krazy Kat cartoons with *Waiting for Godot,* from tributes to jazz greats like Billie Holiday and Bill Evans to explorations of the video choreography of Merce Cunningham. Winner of two Peabody awards and numerous other accolades for programming excellence, the series offered convincing proof that a low budget is not an impediment to creative television. What turned out to be crucial to the show's success was its absence from the commercial fray. Its unrated, often hard to find, time slot (affiliates aired the program whenever they wanted) and its "public affairs" classification gave *Camera Three* an enviable freedom. As one of its producers once remarked, "No one tells us what to do, or even what not to do."[12] The result was a program willing to take challenges and risks prime time would never allow.

But despite its achievements, *Camera Three* and ambitious religious shows like *Look Up and Live* and *Lamp Unto My Feet* were, by economic necessity, restricted to just a few, inconveniently scheduled hours a week. The Sunday "cultural ghetto" was often the only answer for viewers searching for something different from the networks' mainstream orientation during the rest of the time.

Though the audience was certainly not large for these types of programs, it did represent an influential segment of the population concerned about the commercial imperatives of American broadcasting. Comprised of educators, community leaders, and critics, many of its members had been fighting for years to create a viable TV alternative. Pressure applied to the FCC in the early 1950s had helped set aside channel provisions for 242 educational TV stations, but there remained the crucial problem of where the money would come from to get these stations on the air and operating. The pioneering non-commercial outlets established by colleges, community groups, and state boards of education were usually in desperate financial straits. Without the generous grants of the Ford Foundation, who proved to be the system's principal patron for its first decade and a half, few would have survived.

But funding was only one of numerous difficulties educational television faced in its early years. The small number of stations, often assigned a UHF channel number hardly any sets could receive, had little to present in the way of programming. Nighttime proved to be a particularly tough challenge. While a couple of stations were content to rebroadcast their daytime instructional series, those aiming for a broader reach were initially dependent on the vagaries of local resources (live performances by area artists) and the scattered offerings available from the National Educational Television and Radio Center.

Founded in 1952, the Center, which later shortened its name to NET, was originally set up to distribute worthy efforts produced by member stations. Gradually, however, its mission expanded, and with its move to New York City in 1959, it began producing several of its own projects, as well as acquiring shows from independent domestic companies and broadcasters from overseas. By the early 1960s, NET was able to provide its now nearly 100 affiliates with a varied catalog of performing arts programming, ranging from formal academic lectures on music and theater to concert series with American and foreign symphony orchestras, master classes with famous instrumentalists, local opera presentations, and multipart explorations of ballet and modern dance.

Despite its growth, educational television was still far from its goal of being a true "fourth network." Most of NET's initial productions were flat and uninspired, the result of barely adequate budgets and a generally somber approach to the entertainment values of the arts. Livelier cultural telecasts remained the province of the commercial networks who, if nothing else, tended to mount their drama, ballet, and music programs with stylishness and flair. Specials like NBC's *Sleeping Beauty* with the Royal Ballet or CBS's Leonard Bernstein concerts or its broadcasts of *The Nutcracker* with the New York City Ballet were exciting events, custom designed for the scale of the small screen and handsomely produced.

Yet for all their skill in assembling lavish cultural attractions, the networks were scheduling such programs less and less frequently. The shift from New York live productions to the cheaper assembly format of Hollywood in the mid–1950s, and the gradual emergence of ABC as a viable competitor, made it increasingly difficult for expensive, minority-appeal specials to win commercial approval. The climate at the three networks was becoming ever more ferocious and ratings-conscious.

A brief lull occurred in the wake of Newton Minow's "vast wasteland" attack. Speaking before the 1961 convention of the National Association of Broadcasters, the newly appointed chairman of the FCC denounced his well-heeled audience for the vapidity and boredom of most TV programs. Asking "Is there one person in this room who claims that broadcasting can't do better?" Minow angrily warned, "Gentlemen, your trust accounting with your beneficiaries is overdue. Never have so few owed so much to so many."[13]

While the majority of broadcasters tended to dismiss the speech as political rhetoric, there was no question that it struck a nerve, especially among critics and public officials who had been decrying the industry's practices for years. A few seasons earlier, ABC had felt the wrath of this lobby when the network demanded, like NBC before it, that *The Voice of Firestone* shift its time period to avoid damaging the Monday prime-time schedule. Refusing once again to accept a less desirable late-night slot, Firestone found the program cancelled for the second time in five years. Angry protests over the network's decision came from Congress, the press, and the FCC. Hoping to stop the outcry, ABC hastily arranged an alternate, less expensive series, *Music for a Summer Night,* using *Firestone*'s producers, but as Tim Brooks and Earle Marsh observed, "it was not the same."[14]

Minow's address prompted an interest, at least for a while, in reasserting commercial television's cultural vitality. Not only did ABC place *The Voice of Firestone* back on the schedule (for a season), but CBS moved its bimonthly *Young People's Concerts* from weekend afternoons into prime time. Performing arts specials were extensively promoted, none more so than CBS's 1962 broadcast of Igor Stravinsky's *Noah and the Flood.* The show's sponsor, Breck Shampoo, inundated drugstores carrying its products with pamphlets trumpeting the great "creation" which was to come and, thanks to some skillful public relations, managed to receive a commendation in the *Congressional Record* for its "cultural high-mindedness."[15] (Despite the buildup and the $200,000 production costs, the program, with less than half its time actually devoted to Stravinsky's short work, was condemned by most critics as an artistic fiasco.)

Throughout the 1960s, there were continued efforts to televise serious drama, dance, and music in the midst of ever growing economic pressures to reach only majority tastes. Motivated by a sense of public spirit and prestige, advertisers like Xerox, IBM, and several of the oil companies made it a point to sponsor special arts events once or twice a season. More regular support was provided by AT&T, which switched the format of its semi-classical musical program, *The Bell Telephone Hour,* to focus on documentaries of great musicians, and by Hallmark, who while reaching for more popular plays, still turned to the classics occasionally on *The Hallmark Hall of Fame.*

The networks themselves entered into a mini "cultural war" during the middle of the decade, spurred into action, according to *Business Week,* by "increasingly severe attacks from government agencies and Congressional critics on the structure of network broadcasting."[16] Perhaps to make up for years of neglect, ABC's president Leonard Goldenson announced a plan in 1965 to "set aside at least one hour a week of prime time for a new program of some sort. A creative program, a program of innovation—which in and of itself will represent a departure of existing patterns."[17] Admitting later that "I didn't know what was needed. And I didn't know it would cost this much," Goldenson launched *ABC Stage 67,* an experimental, expensive, and wildly uneven weekly series of original dramas, entertainment documentaries, and literary adaptations.[18] Received with little critical enthusiasm and less than expected ratings, the program remained on the air for one season.

The other two commercial networks also offered a fresh supply of cultural attractions. Not wanting to let its "Tiffany" lustre dim, CBS presented David Susskind's celebrated productions of *Death of a Salesman, The Glass Menagerie,* and *The Crucible,* as well as a new series of commissioned dramas, broadcast under the title *CBS Playhouse.* NBC televised several recent Broadway events, including Peter Weiss's *The Investigation,* and began the ambitious *NBC Experiment in Television,* which resembled a somewhat glossier version of *Camera Three.*

There were also independent efforts. The most notable was *Play of the Week,* televised on local New York station WNTA-TV for two seasons in the early 1960s. Produced on a shoestring budget, the series featured top Broadway talents who were willing to work for low wages to appear in a demanding repertory of past and present classics. Threatened with cancellation a few months after its premiere, a campaign organized by the *New York Times*'s influential TV critic, Jack Gould, drew 22,000 letters of protest, and, as a result, the program came under the beneficent sponsorship of Esso. The company, with its strict "hands-off" policy regarding selection and production, later supported several syndicated performing arts series, put together by David Susskind and broadcast on stations on the east coast.

Non-commercial television, meanwhile, reached a watershed when, thanks to pressure from Newton Minow and the FCC, an outlet was finally established in New York City in 1962. By being easily receivable on every TV set in the nation's largest market, WNET-TV helped educational television lose, as Martin Mayer notes, "its state-college, school-system image and become something the New York-based national media started to discuss more seriously."[19] Increased funding from the Ford Foundation for NET, and the first round of government appropriations to set up non-profit stations, also proved important in giving the system greater viability.

With the passage of the Public Broadcasting Act of 1967, educational television (now rechristened "public television") became more of a full-fledged, fourth network, and performing arts programming became one of its centerpieces. Half of NET's Ford Foundation money went to cultural shows, which varied from a series of innovative opera productions (staged by veterans of the *NBC Opera Theatre*) to Off- and Off-Off-Broadway plays, dance concerts, and artist profiles. In the early 1970s, after NET merged with Channel 13 in New York, its long-time producer Jac Venza laid the groundwork for *Theater in America* and *Dance in America,* two of public television's most distinctive enterprises. Venza believed that a central problem with televised dance and drama was the schism between the original creators and the TV personnel who adapted their work for the cameras. Many choreographers and directors had grown increasingly bitter through the years as they watched carefully wrought stage pieces destroyed in the translation to television. Some had simply retreated from any dealings with the medium. It was Venza's hope that the two worlds could be brought together through greater cooperation and understanding.

For *Theater in America* this was achieved by introducing a system of co-direction. Rather than stepping aside once a TV crew came to tape a stage play, the original director would now work closely with an experienced TV counterpart. Frequently, what resulted was an intriguing merger, combining the dramatic vision of the theater production with the freedom and technical possibilities of television. *Dance in America* used a similar approach, letting choreographers decide the best way to reshape their work to the medium's two-dimensional playing area, with the creative assistance of skilled television directors. The series' intelligent and responsive translations of ballet and modern dance have been widely credited with fueling the boom in dance concert attendance during the last decade.

Both *Theater in America* and *Dance in America* were part of *Great Performances,* PBS's longest-running anthology program devoted to the performing arts. At a time when serious music, dance, and theater appeared only spottily on commercial prime time, *Great Performances* provided a weekly showcase for the best in domestic and international productions. American viewers were now able to sample the high quality fare regularly offered on European networks—lavish opera telecasts from Italy and France, concert series with Herbert von Karajan, elegant dramatizations from England. They were also able, thanks to innovative low-light camera technology, to enjoy live music and dance presentations from New York's Lincoln Center. Premiering in 1975 after years of experimentation, *Live from Lincoln Center* captured with surprising success the shared excitement of an actual performance. The alert camerawork and sheer energy of this series-within-a-series often made carefully prepared studio broadcasts seem pale by comparison.

Great Performances depended, like most of PBS's arts programming, on outside funding from corporations eager to be associated with the network's "upscale" image and its audience of opinion makers. Usually this type of support came from the multi-national oil companies, who were always in need of improved public relations. Exxon, Mobil, and Arco contributed millions of dollars for non-controversial cultural shows on PBS, recognizing that the costs of "advertising" were still considerably less on public television than they would be to mount a similar enterprise on the commercial stations.

Even if they had wanted to, public-spirited sponsors looking for suitable performing arts program opportunities on ABC, CBS, or NBC would have found little to choose from. The development and growth of PBS seemed to free the commercial networks from maintaining their previous levels of prime-time cultural offerings. With the elimination in 1973 of the Nielsen Company's "Black Weeks" (the few weeks a year when ratings weren't measured and, consequently, when ABC, NBC, and CBS scheduled most of their prestige events), arts specials became a low priority. NBC's *Live from Studio 8H* was a rare exception. Established in the 1979–80 season by then president Fred Silverman to signal a new direction for the network (and to brighten his own tarnished reputation as a programmer), the once or twice a year events were commercial approximations of PBS's *Great Performances.* An evening of ballets by Jerome Robbins resembled an installment from *Dance in America*; salutes to Toscanini and Enrico Caruso, with the New York Philharmonic conducted by Zubin Mehta, looked like *Live From Lincoln Center* in a more cramped location. Initially heralded with great fanfare, the series disappeared after only four broadcasts during the course of two seasons.

In 1979, another plan to elevate commercial television was proposed, this time from William Paley, CBS's founder and chairman of the board. Announced, suitably enough, in the pages of his autobiography rather than from corporate headquarters, Paley's plan was simple, idealistic, and impractical: each of the three major networks would set aside a few prime-time hours, one night a week "for special high quality programs that would appeal to educated, sophisticated tastes more than to the mass audience. . . . I believe such programs would increase in popularity as time went on and the television audience came to appreciate this kind of fare."[20] Questioning his motives, the other two networks flatly rejected the proposal.

Nevertheless, the idea persisted for Paley, taking shape in greatly altered form two years later with the creation of CBS Cable. This new venture, launched in part to reassure Wall Street of the network's commitment to future technologies, was designed to be the ultimate jewel in CBS's crown—a full-time television service presenting the most prestigious arts programming, supported, it was hoped, by the most prestigious advertisers. As Les Brown observed, its cultural orientation was selected not only "because no one else had yet claimed that turf," but also because "it fit with CBS's image of itself: Culture is class."[21]

CBS Cable was, at first, given the best of everything. The best performing arts producers were hired; the best talent was enlisted for its generously budgeted domestic theater, dance, and music programs; and the best parties and promotional efforts were arranged to woo future sponsors and cable operators. Problems, however, soon began to appear. The network was located on a satellite few cable systems were able to receive. Other companies, including ABC, were entering the cable cultural competition. And, most importantly, advertisers failed to be convinced of the need for a rather high-priced, commercial version of PBS. (Ad sales projected at $40 million for the first season would actually come closer to $8 million.[22])

Sponsors weren't the only ones staying away from the service's enthusiastically praised programming. Despite eventually reaching a potential viewing audience of 5.5 million, only a very small percentage, according to cable operators, tuned in to watch. Costs, meanwhile, were rising, especially since the network, rather than relying on less expensive, imported products, chose the exhorbitant route of producing most of its own shows, hoping for auxiliary sales to overseas broadcasters, which seldom materialized.

Within a few months after CBS Cable's premiere in October 1981, it was clear the service was in serious trouble. Various alternatives were explored—participation in joint operating ventures with other media concerns; converting to a pay-cable operation, instead of being offered free to home subscribers—but none proved workable. Ultimately, the initial error in overestimating CBS Cable's first season revenues, plus the growing red ink and the company's poor performance in other areas, led CBS to cancel their cable experiment less than one year after it began.

The collapse of this highly touted channel, after a loss of nearly $50 million, was a dramatic signal that the cable "cultural explosion" might not turn out as promised. The enthusiastic hymns of the early 1980s to cable television's role as a salvation for the performing arts and as an enterprise "that could erase TV's 'idiot box' image" were appearing less frequently, as the late network's competitors struggled to survive.[23] ARTS, started in April 1981 by ABC and the Hearst Corporation, had an initial advantage—it lacked CBS Cable's extravagant ambitions. Operating only three hours a night on a more easily received satellite, its schedule was comprised largely of inexpensive European programming. The advertiser-supported service did, for several seasons, present many distinctive original productions, but continued deficits, averaging $8 million a year up through 1983, forced it to curtail these activities in favor of mostly imported fare with a few domestic acquisitions. Bravo, the first cable arts network on the air (December 1980), tried a different approach. Its viewers paid an extra eight to ten dollars monthly to receive commercial-free programming. The low number of subscriptions, however, did not cover the costs of a strict performing arts schedule, and the service later switched to a highbrow movie channel concept, mixing scattered foreign music and opera telecasts in between showings of Resnais and Fassbinder films.

The concept of pay cable was also tried by The Entertainment Channel, with results rivaling the disaster of CBS Cable. A cooperative venture of Rockefeller Center and RCA, run by former CBS president Arthur Taylor, The Entertainment Channel showcased a broader program schedule, made up primarily of BBC material and a few Broadway shows. But even with its less rarefied focus, the network's hopeful audience predictions were blocked by the slowdown in new cable system construction and the resistance of cable viewers to pay for any more extras. After only ten months in operation, The Entertainment Channel folded, accumulating losses of $34 million. Its programming resources were later merged with ARTS, creating the somewhat more popularly oriented Arts & Entertainment Network.

The setbacks in cultural cable prompted PBS to drop its own enterprising pay-TV plans, which were based on the idea of a "grand alliance" between the network and the country's major performing arts centers, museums, and universities. Yet, in a sense, cable's problems helped to create a stronger PBS. Besieged just a few years before with powerful competitors, willing to pay more for European product and eager to capture the attention of its corporate underwriters and sophisticated audience, the network emerged from the cable battles in surprisingly healthy shape. It had discovered a new source of co-production deals with several of the cable services. In the face of declining government appropriations, it developed a new spirit of cooperation between its member stations to share the huge expenses of cultural series like *Great Performances*. And, perhaps most significantly, it reestablished its position as the only viable outlet for original arts programming produced in America.

There was little challenge on this score from the commercial networks. By the 1980s, they had virtually abandoned the field of cultural production to PBS, except for an occasional star-studded theatrical revival, such as

ABC's steamy film version of Tennessee Williams's *Streetcar Named Desire* with Ann-Margret. The prime-time variety shows, with their intermittent bows to classical music and dance, were long gone. Even the refuge of the Sunday sustaining series had disappeared, though *Camera Three*'s replacement, the news magazine *Sunday Morning*, featured excellent performing artists' profiles. Sadly, the most consistently scheduled cultural event on commercial TV now took place only once a year, with the CBS broadcast of *The Kennedy Center Honors,* a program that, since 1978, has saluted the achievements of distinguished American composers, choreographers, and musicians.

With the bright promise of cable largely faded and commercial network interest in the arts at an all-time low, PBS remains the chief hope for cultural programming on television. Despite ever-rising production expenses, cutbacks in government funding, and a growing tendency to pursue the safe and the conventional, public television continues to offer its viewers an often glittering showcase for the performing arts. The network, to the regret of its critics, will probably never approach the uniformly high standards of state-supported European systems like the BBC or Italy's RAI—the desperate scramble to win corporate underwriting and entice viewer contributions several times a year makes it inevitable that efforts marked by too much daring, controversy, or expense will rarely be broadcast.

Still, PBS has given the arts the best forum on American television they have ever enjoyed. After many decades of being treated as disruptive elements in the commercial networks' broad flow of programming, the performing arts have at last found one place on television willing to welcome and celebrate their special audience appeal.

NOTES

1. Robert E. Lee, *Television: The Revolution* (New York: Essential Books, 1944), pp. 108, 109.

2. Atholie Bays, "The Seeker Finds," *American Dancer,* October 1939, p. 10.

3. Sylvester L. Weaver, Jr., "Enlightenment Through Exposure," *Television Magazine,* January 1952, p. 31.

4. Sylvester L. Weaver, Jr., "Enlightenment Through Exposure is NBC Technique," *Musical America,* 15 February, 1956, p. 25.

5. Weaver, "NBC Technique," p. 25.

6. Tim Brooks and Earle Marsh, *The Complete Directory to Prime Time Network TV Shows 1946-Present* (New York: Ballantine Books, 1981), p. 799.

7. Christina Adam, "Omnibus," *Emmy,* Fall 1979, p. 40.

8. Jack Gould, "Love That 'Omnibus,' " *New York Times,* 28 November 1954, Section II, p. 13.

9. Gould, "Love," p. 13.

10. Jack Gould, " 'Juliet' Outpointed," *New York Times,* 10 March 1957, Section II, p. 11.

11. Gould, " 'Juliet,' " p. 11.

12. Remark by Clair Roskam in George Gent, "Decade of Progress," *New York Times,* 26 May 1963, Section II, p. 13.

13. Quoted in Erik Barnouw, *The Image Empire: A History of Broadcasting in the United States, 1953-* (New York: Oxford University Press, 1970), p. 198.

14. Tim Brooks and Earle Marsh, *Directory to Prime Time,* p. 800.

15. Arthur Todd, "What went wrong," *Dancemagazine,* August 1962, p. 60.

16. "TV Sets Stage for Quality Shows," *Business Week,* 21 May 1966, p. 84.

17. Quoted in "Networks Take Cue from Stage 67," *Business Week,* 25 February 1967, p. 61.

18. "TV Sets Stage," p. 84.

19. Martin Mayer, *About Television* (New York: Harper and Row, 1972), p. 316.

20. William Paley, *As It Happened* (New York: Doubleday and Company, 1979), pp. 275–276.

21. Les Brown, "Who Killed CBS Cable?," *Channels,* November/December 1982, p. 12.

22. Kirsten Beck, *Cultivating the Wasteland* (New York: American Council for the Arts, 1983), p. 71.

23. James Mann, "TV's Big Leap Forward Into Culture," *U.S. News & World Report,* 23 February 1981, p. 53.

REFERENCES

Any study of the history and practices of American broadcasting should begin with Erik Barnouw's invaluable books, *A Tower in Babel, The Golden Web* and *The Image Empire.* Though Barnouw touches on cultural programming only occasionally, his discussions of network economics and politics are quite useful in tracing the development of arts-oriented shows on radio and television. Other helpful historical studies include Christopher Sterling and John Kittross's *Stay Tuned* and Laurence Bergreen's *Look Now, Pay Later: The Rise of Network Broadcasting,* which contains interesting material on the various cultural wars of NBC and CBS. Tim Brooks and Earle Marsh's general reference guide *The Complete Directory to Prime Time Network TV Shows 1946-Present* is also highly recommended. Listing every single program broadcast by the three commercial networks, with detailed production information and credits, the book offers shrewd insights into the rise and fall of such celebrated arts series as *Omnibus, Studio One,* and *The Voice of Firestone.*

The early years of television marked a period of tremendous enthusiasm concerning the medium's artistic potential. Robert E. Lee's 1944 book *Television: The Revolution*, Thomas Hutchinson's *Here is Television: Your Window to the World* from 1946, and Atholie Bays's effusive "The Seeker Finds" are typical examples of the excitement television provoked in contemporary observers.

As the commercial networks grew and more hardened business practices began to dominate programming decisions, one of the few executives who paid more than lip service to the idea of television's creative possibilities was Sylvester (Pat) Weaver of NBC. His somewhat grandiloquent essays, "Enlightment Through Exposure" and "Enlightment Through Exposure is NBC Technique," describe his ambitious

1952 plan, "Operation Frontal Lobes," to inject some cultural or educational element into every NBC show.

The Ford Foundation also hoped to change the shape of television in the early 1950s with its program *Omnibus.* Though generally well received, the show prompted harsh criticism from the *New York Times*'s Jack Gould, who attacked its snobbish attitudes in his articles "Love That 'Omnibus,' " "The Future of 'Omnibus,' " and "TV Notebook." Christina Adam offers a more balanced view in her 1979 appraisal, "Omnibus." (Discussion of the specific achievements in dance, music, and theater of this and other arts programs is available in later chapters of this book.)

Throughout the 1950s, the mass audience programming philosophy of the commercial networks, which led to the scheduling of increasingly fewer arts specials and the cancellation of programs like *The Voice of Firestone,* provoked constant outcry from critics, educators, and essayists of all persuasions. This was particularly true in the pages of the *New York Times*'s Sunday "Arts and Leisure" section, where the paper's reviewers and outside contributors lambasted ABC, NBC, and CBS for their various cultural sins. TV critic Jack Gould was the most powerful and consistent voice arguing for an alternative to the networks' mercenary attitudes—his 1957 article " 'Juliet' Outpointed" is a characteristic example. Other notable denunciations include music critic Howard Taubman's "Minority Audience" and Arthur Miller's fiery complaints about TV play adaptations, "Mailbag—Arthur Miller on Adaptations."

One area where the networks were not attacked was their Sunday morning and afternoon sustaining programs. The most celebrated of these was CBS's weekly arts show, *Camera Three,* which premiered in 1953 and has been the subject of considerable attention through the years. Raymond J. Schneider's dissertation, "A Study of the Television Program 'Camera Three,' " provides a close analysis of the program's history and production techniques. Granville Hick's "A Weekly View of Reel Fiction," George Gent's "Decade of Progress," and Fabian Bower's "Does It Make Sense to the Man with a Beer Can" are general surveys of *Camera Three*'s activities.

Educational television offered the performing arts a much more congenial environment than ABC, CBS, or NBC. In addition to the previously mentioned broadcast histories of Barnouw and Sterling and Kittross, useful information about non-commercial TV may be found in Martin Mayer's *About Television;* Allen E. Koenig's anthology *The Farther Vision,* which concentrates on NET; and Robert Avery and Robert Pepper's *The Politics of Interconnection,* which focuses on the development of PBS. The network's recent problems and cultural programming practices are discussed in John Jay Iselin's "TV and the Arts—A Great Match," James Roman's "Programming for Public Television," Martin Koughan's "The Fall and Rise of Public Television," and John J. O'Connor's "Are Channel 13's Viewers Being Shortchanged?" and "Old Films vs. Visions." Sally Bedell's "The Man Whose Personality Shapes 'Great Performances' " is a lively profile of Jac Venza, one of public television's key performing arts producers.

Outside of non-commercial television, the creative possibilities of television were rather limited—an issue explored in numerous books like *The Eighth Art,* Charles Steinberg's *Broadcasting: The Critical Challenges,* and Patrick Hazard's *TV as Art.* Other than a few elaborate specials, such as CBS's broadcast of Igor Stravinsky's *Noah and the Flood* (see Arthur Todd's "What went wrong" for a review of the hysterical promotion surrounding this telecast) or a brief period in the 1960s when the networks engaged in a culture war (documented in "TV Sets Stage for Quality Shows" and "Networks Take Cue from Stage 67" in *Business Week*), the arts were becoming an increasingly rare prime-time event on ABC, CBS, and NBC.

With the rapid growth of cable television in the 1970s, however, "A New Era for Cultural Programming on TV," to adopt the title of Les Brown's 1979 article, appeared to be on the horizon. (Martin Mayer's "Cable and the Arts" is one of the earliest examinations written on this issue.) CBS Cable, anticipated in a somewhat different form by William Paley in his autobiography *As It Happened,* was one of many services promising to make the performing arts a staple of their schedule. Gerald Clarke's "Cable's Cultural Crapshoot," Martin Mayer's "Can Culture Channels Survive?," Peter Caranicas's "Can PBS Survive Cable?," and James Mann's "TV's Big Leap Forward Into Culture" capture the prevailing mixture of excitement and caution surrounding the launching of the various arts cable networks. Problems began to surface in the industry within a few months (see Harry F. Walters's "Culture Shock on Cable"), and less than a year after its premiere, CBS Cable collapsed. The reasons behind the costly failure are examined in Jack Loftus's " 'Hang the Cost' Policy Sunk CBS Cable," Les Brown's "Who Killed CBS Cable?," and in Kirsten Beck's *Cultivating the Wasteland,* which offers the best account of the network's rise and fall. Though now somewhat outdated in its utopian vision for cable, *Cultivating the Wasteland* is highly recommended for its thorough accounts of each of the cultural networks and its insights into the problems of adapting the performing arts to television.

The continuing decline of the cultural cable industry has been well covered in newspapers and magazines. Useful accounts include Carl Levine's "Can Culture Survive on Cable?," Steve Knoll's "Culture Struggles for Survival" and "Can Bravo Make Culture Pay?," Peter Kerr's "Is There a Future For Cultural Fare?," Sandra Salmans's "How a Cable Channel Flopped," Bob Brewin's "Bravo for Bravo!," John J. O'Connor's "Where's That Promised New World of Cable?," Joanmarie Kalter's "It Could Be Culture's Last Stand," and Sally Bedell Smith's "Specialized Choices in Cable TV Dwindling."

Broad accounts of the challenges facing the performing arts on television during the last ten years can be found in Maureen Harmonay's anthology *Promise and Performance: ACT's Guide to TV Programming for Children,* which looks at the various ways drama, dance, and music have been translated to the small screen, and the National Endowment for the Arts 1977 study of "prestige" broadcasting and its sponsors, *Arts and Cultural Programs on Radio and Television.*

Books

Arts and Cultural Programs on Radio and Television. Washington, D.C.: National Endowment for the Arts, 1977.

Avery, Robert K., and Pepper, Robert. *The Politics of Interconnection: A History of Public Television at the National Level.* Washington, D.C.: National Association of Educational Broadcasters, 1979.

Barnouw, Erik. *The Golden Web: A History of Broadcasting in the United States, 1933–1953.* New York: Oxford University Press, 1968.

———. *The Image Empire: A History of Broadcasting in the United States, 1953-.* New York: Oxford University Press, 1970.

———. *A Tower in Babel: A History of Broadcasting in the United States to 1933.* New York: Oxford University Press, 1966.

Beck, Kirsten. *Cultivating the Wasteland.* New York: American Council for the Arts, 1983.

Bergreen, Laurence. *Look Now, Pay Later: The Rise of Network Broadcasting.* New York: Doubleday, 1980.

Brooks, Tim, and Earle Marsh. *The Complete Directory to Prime Time Network TV Shows 1946-Present.* Rev. ed. New York: Ballantine Books, 1981.

The Eighth Art. New York: Holt, Rinehart and Winston, 1962.

Harmonay, Maureen, ed. *Promise and Performance: ACT's Guide to TV Programming for Children.* Cambridge: Battinger Publishers, 1979.

Hazard, Patrick, ed. *TV as Art.* Champaign, Illinois: National Council of Teachers of English, 1966.

Hutchinson, Thomas. *Here Is Television: Your Window to the World.* New York: Hastings House, 1946.

Koenig, Allen E., and Ruane B. Hill, eds. *The Farther Vision: Education Television Today.* Madison: University of Wisconsin Press, 1967.

Lee, Robert E. *Television: The Revolution.* New York: Essential Books, 1944.

Mayer, Martin. *About Television.* New York: Harper and Row, 1972.

Paley, William. *As It Happened.* New York: Doubleday and Company, 1979.

Steinberg, Charles S. *Broadcasting: The Critical Challenges.* New York: Hastings, 1974.

Sterling, Christopher, and John Kittross. *Stay Tuned.* Belmont, California: Wadsworth Publishing, 1978.

Articles

Adam, Christina. "Omnibus." *Emmy,* Fall 1979, pp. 40–44.

Bays, Atholie. "The Seeker Finds." *American Dancer,* October 1939, p. 10.

Bedell, Sally. "The Man Whose Personality Shapes 'Great Performances.' " *New York Times,* 3 October 1982, Section II, p. 25.

Bowers, Fabian. "Does It Make Sense to the Man with a Beer Can?" *Saturday Review,* 10 June 1976, pp. 24–26.

Brewin, Bob. "Bravo for Bravo!" *Village Voice,* 10 January 1984, p. 22.

Brown, Les. "A New Era for Cultural Programming on TV." *New York Times,* 15 April 1979, Section II, p. 29.

———. "Who Killed CBS Cable?" *Channels,* November/December 1982, pp. 12–13.

Caranicas, Peter. "Can PBS Survive Cable?" *Saturday Review,* January 1981, pp. 37–38.

Clarke, Gerald. "Cable's Cultural Crapshoot." *TIME,* 26 October 1981, pp. 84–85.

Gent, George. "Decade of Progress." *New York Times,* 26 May 1963, Section II, p. 13.

Gould, Jack. "The Future of 'Omnibus.' " *New York Times,* 24 February 1957, Section II, p. 11.

———. " 'Juliet' Outpointed." *New York Times,* 10 March 1957, Section II, p. 11.

———. "Love That 'Omnibus.' " *New York Times,* 28 November 1954, Section II, p. 13.

———. "TV Notebook." *New York Times,* 6 January 1957, Section II, p. 11.

Hicks, Granville. "A Weekly View of Reel Fiction." *Saturday Review,* 6 July 1963, pp. 21–22.

Iselin, John Jay. "TV and the Arts—A Great Match." *New York Times,* 29 January 1978, Section II, p. 1.

Kalter, Joanmarie. "It Could Be Culture's Last Stand." *TV Guide,* 30 July 1983, p. 31–32.

Kerr, Peter. "Is There a Future For Cultural Fare?" *New York Times,* 6 November 1983, Section II, p. 34.

Knoll, Steve. "Can Bravo Make Culture Pay?" *New York Times,* 26 February 1984, Section II, p. 31.

———. "Culture Struggles for Survival." *New York Times,* 10 June 1984, Section II, p. 26.

Koughan, Martin. "The Fall and Rise of Public Television." *Channels,* May/June 1981, pp. 23–29.

Levine, Carl. "Can Culture Survive on Cable?" *Videopro,* December 1982, pp. 42–45.

Loftus, Jack. " 'Hang the Cost' Policy Sunk CBS Cable." *Variety,* 15 September 1982, pp. 59, 61.

Mann, James. "TV's Big Leap Forward Into Culture." *U.S. News & World Report,* 23 February 1981, pp. 53–54.

Mayer, Martin. "Cable and the Arts." *Urban Review,* November/December 1972, pp. 19–21.

———. "Can Culture Channels Survive?" *American Film,* May 1981, pp. 14, 76.

Miller, Arthur. "Mailbag—Arthur Miller on Adaptations." *New York Times,* 29 November, 1959, Section II, p. 12.

"Networks Take Cue from Stage 67." *Business Week,* 25 February 1967, p. 61.

O'Connor, John J. "Are Channel 13's Viewers Being Shortchanged?" *New York Times,* 18 March 1984, Section II, p. 33.

———. "Old Films vs. Visions." *New York Times,* 3 December, 1979, Section II, p. 37.

———. "Where's That Promised New World of Cable?" *New York Times,* 25 November, 1984, Section II, pp. 1, 22.

Roman, James. "Programming for Public Television." *Journal of Communication,* Volume 30, Number 3, Summer 1980, pp. 150–156.

Salmans, Sandra. "How a Cable Channel Flopped." *New York Times,* 28 February, 1983, Section IV, pp. 1, 5.

Smith, Sally Bedell. "Specialized Choices in Cable TV Dwindling." *New York Times,* 24 November 1983, p. 1.

Taubman, Howard. "Minority Audience." *New York Times,* 21 February 1954, Section II, p. 7.

Todd, Arthur. "What went wrong." *Dancemagazine,* August 1962, pp. 39, 60–61.

"TV Sets Stage for Quality Shows." *Business Week,* 21 May 1966, p. 84.

Walters, Harry F. "Culture Shock on Cable." *Newsweek,* 15 March, 1982, pp. 85–87.

Weaver, Sylvester L., Jr. "Enlightment Through Exposure." *Television Magazine,* January 1952, pp. 28–31.

———. "Enlightment Through Exposure is NBC Technique." *Musical America,* 15 February 1956, p. 25.

Dissertations

Schneider, Raymond J. "A Study of the Television Program 'Camera Three.' " Ph.D. diss., University of Michigan, 1965.

2

Dance on Television

Dance was one of the first arts to be seen on American television, yet its relationship with the medium has remained unusually complicated. No one would dispute that television has provided dance with an enormous forum. The audience for ballet and modern dance has grown steadily over the years, and televised dance has played a large factor in increasing awareness and promoting live concert attendance. Yet many choreographers and critics still regard television with suspicion and distrust. They feel that the medium's inevitable technological distortions transform the very nature of dance, fracturing its lines and robbing it of sweep and form.

The debate over the merits and hazards of dance on television has been going on for more than 50 years, with each decade seeing new terms added to the argument. The issue invariably boils down to one of choreographic intentions versus electronic limitations. How accurately can television capture dance design? How much compromise is necessary to meet the demands of the broadcast studio? Can a two-dimensional medium reproduce a three-dimensional art? And, finally, what type of dance style and method of presentation works best given television's inherent restrictions?

The approaches dancers have taken to the problems of television and the approaches TV producers and directors have taken to the problems of dance have varied considerably through the years. Rarely has either side been completely happy. Still, as TV techniques grow increasingly more sophisticated, televised dance has become one of the medium's most stylistically expressive and widely viewed cultural formats. The history of how dance developed on television through the past five decades offers an interesting case study of the diverse ways a venerable theatrical form has had to come to terms with the challenges and pitfalls of adapting to the electronic screen.

HISTORICAL DEVELOPMENT

The Experimental Years

Maria Gambarelli was the first dancer to appear before a TV camera in America. The date was May 26, 1931, and television was still in its experimental infancy. Sound and picture had to be broadcast on two different stations, and the mechanical scanning disk system of transmission then in use made it difficult to view the small screen with any degree of clarity. The few members of the public able to receive the signal of the Jenkins Television Company's station W2XCR from New York City that day weren't, however, the only ones encountering the obstacles of television. Miss Gambarelli was forced to perform on a stage which was no larger than five feet square. Still, her experience must not have been completely unpleasant, since she travelled to London a year later to participate in the BBC's experimental dance broadcasts and made a point to wear the same costume that marked her U.S. TV debut.

Maria Gambarelli was not the only dancer to appear on American televison in 1931. Yugoslavian modern dancer Tashamira set a record when she began what would turn into 52 consecutive weekly television appearances. All of them were broadcast from a stage only three feet square in area, making, as one critic noted, "a full image of the movement impossible."[1]

As historian Nelson D. Neal has pointed out, the most severe problems affecting TV dance in the 1930s "were space, or the lack of it, and the camera limitations."[2] The prisonlike stage spaces endured by dancers in 1931 were expanded within a few years to handle at least two performers comfortably. Nevertheless, sweeping dance steps and rapid action were almost impossible to capture, given the bulky cameras and cramped studio conditions. A contemporary commentator offered this prescription: "The most suitable dances for television are those that require both a minimum of floor space and vertical movement, such as tossing a partner in the air. For these reasons, Oriental, tap, and rumba routines are ideally suited to the medium."[3]

Solo dances posed similar technical difficulties. The limited range of camera focus and the small screen size forced TV directors to choose between close ups and indistinct full shots. Writing in 1944, producer Worthington Miner remarked, "The director knows that if he is to get the full figure of the dancer on the screen, he must necessarily obscure the facial detail. Under such conditions, the audience might have difficulty distinguishing Katherine Dunham from Sono Osato."[4]

Nevertheless, the period was marked by a tremendous excitement about the future of dance and television. Thomas Hutchinson, the manager of the television department at NBC in 1939 promised, "Television will do for dance what radio has done for speech. . . . Within the next five years, dancing will become more a part of the consciousness of the people, that it has since its first beginnings."[5] A programming executive of CBS in 1946 noted, "Television being a visual medium and dance being a visual art, they simply go hand in glove."[6]

Dance magazines were filled with enthusiastic hymns to television's potential power. Atholie Bays, writing in the *American Dancer* in 1939, rhapsodized over the fact that television "seems to release the inner creativeness, the real person just as it releases in naked simplicity everything that is fine and beautiful in an art, that is perfected through impeccable technique. This is the television that will offer the dance world its opportunity."[7] He concluded with this paean to the new electronic age: "Television is here! The new day has dawned! The seeker finds!"[8] Seven years later, Maurice Stoller proclaimed in *Dancemagazine* that the "outlook for dancing in television is encouraging. Comes the day when eurythmics will replace calisthetics and ballet the soap opera. What a wonderful morning that will be!"[9] Andrew N. McLellan echoed the feelings of many critics of the time when he observed, "There is no other medium which offers the dance art a more promising or challenging and, at the same time, more intimate and personalized channel of expression than television."[10]

The enthusiasm greeting televised dance during the 1930s and 1940s resulted both from the medium's newness and the broadcast industry's willingness to experiment. Unsure of exactly what shape television would take, the networks were more flexible in the kind of programs and performers they chose to put on the air. After RCA launched its dramatic public demonstration of television at the 1939 New York World's Fair, dancers such as Paul Draper, Katherine Dunham, Martha Graham, and Hanya Holm were among the many artists called upon to appear before the cameras.

The Advent of Commercial Broadcasting

When commercial broadcasting was finally authorized on July 1, 1941, both NBC and CBS featured numerous programs devoted to dance. The first group to appear live at CBS Studios was the Country Dance Society, whose debut occurred just three days after authorization was granted. The group had a regularly scheduled show every Sunday that featured a wide variety of international folk dancing as well as guest dancers like Erick Hawkins, the Charles Weidman group, and Agnes de Mille. CBS also broadcast an innovative program entitled *Men At Work*, that examined the difficulties artists faced in adapting their work to television. Dancers appearing included Ruth Page, Edwin Strawbridge, and Eugene Loring, who presented the first of what would be many TV versions of *Billy the Kid*.

Individual stations not affiliated with the networks also experimented with dance telecasts. General Electric's WRGB in Schenectady produced 50 dance programs, as well as the first complete ballet adapted for television, the *Ballet for Americans* in 1942. The Dumont Broadcasting Company's WABD in New York City was widely heralded for creatively using special effects in their dance shows. Producer Bud Gamble's *Sketchbook* series employed a fanciful collection of devices to technologically enhance the programs' dance settings. Utilizing superimpositions, mixtures of live and film action, whirling cameras, and miniature sets, Gamble transported dance on television into a realm of electronic magic, where ballerinas danced on clouds, undersea among live fish, and in the middle of flames and lightning flashes.

Testing the Medium

While Bud Gamble was not a choreographer, his technological interventions represented an interesting approach open to dancers in tackling some of television's considerable problems. Up to this point, the medium's restrictions on space, time, and movement were compounded by the fact that most TV dance was simply a broadcast of a performance done live in the studio. Increasingly, dancers and critics were beginning to recognize that television demanded something altogether new. Commenting on the difficulties of reproducing old choreographic patterns to a new medium, two TV dancers, Pauline Koner and Kitty Doner, observed that

> when these patterns are transferred to a television stage, the movement is hampered, loses its spontaneity and freedom, and the result is mechanical and static. The logical conclusion is that television dance programs should be especially created or revised to conform to the essential demands of television.[11]

For Koner and Doner, these demands were simple. Dances should be restricted to only one area at any given time. Dancers should move slow enough for the camera to follow. Choreographers should remember not to use large groups and always be aware of how something looks through the camera. More importantly, they concluded that "television must not be regarded as outlet only, but as a new kind of theatre."[12]

Pauline Koner, who had studied dance with Mikhail Fokine, and Kitty Doner, an ex-vaudeville headliner, formulated these rules from their experiences at CBS, where they developed and starred in a highly successful dance series in 1945 called *Choreotones*. The program featured popular dancing that took full advantage of television's expressive possibilities. Choreography was created to explore the boundaries of both the TV frame and current TV technology.

Other dancers also experimented with television's special abilities. The most notable was Valerie Bettis, who produced consistently innovative work on television starting in the mid–1940s. One of her first productions was called *Fantasy in Space*, which, according to a review in *Dancemagazine*, employed "novel effects . . . by full use of video dissolve mechanism in superimpositions."[13] This willingness to mix technology and dance continued when Bettis became the staff choreographer for *The Paul Whiteman*

Show a few years later and was called upon to create a new, 15–minute ballet every week.

The Postwar Dance Boom

Perhaps the most ambitious program devoted to TV dance during the immediate postwar period was *Through the Crystal Ball*, which aired on CBS for a couple of months in 1949. Sponsored by the Ford Motor Company and produced by CBS's dance director Paul Belanger, *Through the Crystal Ball* was the first half-hour, all-dance show on television. Each week a different choreographer would be responsible for creating an original TV production. The presentations included a new mounting by George Balanchine of *Cinderella*, danced by Tanaquil LeClercq and Herbert Bliss; a ballet by Todd Bolender called *The Wild West*, danced by LeClercq and Patricia MacBride; and programs conceived by Michael Kidd, Pauline Koner, and Valerie Bettis. Sadly, like most of the live dance shows of the late 1940s, no record remains of any of the five episodes aired in the series.

Beginning in the early 1950s, popular dance programs became one of the few places dancers and choreographers could not only experiment a bit with TV techniques but also find steady work in the medium. Programs such as *The Milton Berle Show*, *The Martha Raye Show*, and *Your Show of Shows* employed a regular staff choreographer and a company of dancers to provide a variety of dance interludes every week. Writing in 1951, Arthur Todd noted, "Today we rarely face a program that doesn't use dance in some form—a ballet, dance sequence or story, a dance-minded song or even a danced comedy."[14]

Dancers lucky enough to work on these New York-based shows faced a grueling schedule. New routines had to be created constantly; there was a very limited rehearsal schedule; and there was no time to correct mistakes in performance, since the programs were broadcast live. Nevertheless, choreographers like Peter Gennaro, who worked on *The Perry Como Show*, Tony Charmoli, who worked on *Your Hit Parade*, and James Starbuck, who worked on *Your Show of Shows* were able to flourish in this pressure-filled environment and helped to create a breezy, sophisticated dance style that often worked beautifully on the small screen. James Starbuck, in particular, was renowned for the diversity of his TV dances. A former soloist with the Ballet Russe de Monte Carlo, he was adept at creating devastating ballet parodies for Imogene Coca on *Your Show of Shows*. He also believed strongly that TV dance was playing an important role in helping the medium explore its own possibilities. "Dance has been responsible for the increasing fluidity of the TV camera," he wrote in 1951, "and has given directors and cameramen a greater scope for their imagination than was ever conceived a few years ago."[15]

While there were few shows devoted exclusively to ballet, many variety programs of the period included ballet excerpts among their offerings. Max Liebman, the producer of *Your Show of Shows*, was a dance and opera enthusiast, and performers from the New York City Ballet and the Metropolitan Opera were regularly featured and often gently lampooned by Imogene Coca later in the show. Alicia Markova, Tamara Toumanova, and Frederick Franklin made several appearances. Kate Smith, who had an afternoon program on NBC, also spotlighted many dancers from the New York City Ballet, including Melissa Hayden, Tanaquil LeClercq, and Andre Eglevsky.

The majority of programs featuring dance in any guise favored a tried-and-true approach, and ballet stars were expected to restrict their dancing to the classical pas de deux. If serious dance was to be presented, it was invariably from a well-known ballet (preferably a late-nineteenth-century Russian classic) or at least pretty to look at. A perfect example of why network executives stuck to this edict was the outcry surrounding the 1954 broadcast of Lew Christensen's modern dress ballet *Filling Station*. The ratings service reported that within minutes after the piece began as part of an *NBC Spectacular*, viewers deserted the channel in large numbers. Newspaper critics, by and large, vilifed the presentation, and, to make matters worse, alarmed sponsors "complained and said, 'no more ballet.' "[16] Reflecting on the flurry his decision to air the ballet generated, producer Max Liebman offered this analysis, as reported by Doris Hering, which has remained remarkably on target at the commercial networks ever since:

> A television audience, which does not see much ballet, somehow thinks of it as symbolic of an ideal world. They prefer works like *Les Sylphides* or *Sleeping Beauty* because they are so completely escapist. He [Liebman] decided that many viewers must have felt uncomfortable about seeing the cartoon-realism of *Filling Station*—of seeing people doing ballet technique in overalls and knickers, instead of tutus and tights.[17]

Network Dance Specials

Given these aesthetic restrictions, the networks did offer several impressive "classical" ballet shows on a special events basis, during television's growth years of the 1950s. NBC pioneered the broadcasting of live ballet performances in 1949 when it presented Ballet Theatre in *Les Sylphides*. A year later, it offered *Giselle*, the first full-length ballet seen on television, danced once again by Ballet Theatre, with a cast headed by Nora Kaye, Igor Youskevitch, and Diana Adams. In 1956, NBC broadcast what was probably the most acclaimed live ballet presentation of the decade: Frederick Ashton's version of Marius Petipa's *The Sleeping Beauty*. The Sadlers Wells Ballet was brought over from London for the telecast, and, to the surprise of everyone, 30 million viewers tuned in. Dance and TV critics were jubilant. The *New York Times*'s TV critic Jack Gould saw the program's ratings success as a victory for viewers of "quality fare," while Lillian Moore, writing in *Dancing Times*, praised the ways TV techniques served the dancing.

> The camera work was effective, and in many scenes a substantial effect of spaciousness was achieved, although the vision scene seemed uncomfortably cramped. In this, however, the resources of the camera were cleverly employed to make the wraith of Aurora appear and disappear, and sometimes one could actually see through her.[18]

Buoyed by the acclaim and the prestige, NBC brought the Sadlers Wells Ballet over again in April 1957, this time for a telecast of Ashton's *Cinderella*. Preparations were much more extensive. NBC directors had flown to London to watch the company in four performances in order to preplan every camera angle and to help pare the work down from 90 minutes to 72 minutes. Ashton was impressed with the results. "TV ballet in America," he remarked, "is much more ambitious than in Britain, thanks to money, time spent, and color. In Britain we've never been on the air for more than 45 minutes."[19]

Like many ballet productions of the period, NBC's 1957 telecast of *Cinderella* employed some special effects, appropriately used here to serve the story's fairy-tale qualities. Superimpositions transformed Cinderella's home into a flower field and merged the clockface reading 12 with the pumpkin and the carriage. When Margot Fonteyn puts on a crown towards the end, the scene magically dissolves into a painted sun, where a beggar woman has been electronically altered into a fairy, dancing alone in the radiance.

Special effects also played a part in CBS's 1958 Christmas night broadcast of Balanchine's *The Nutcracker*, but the 90–minute program's special glow was more the result of inspired performances and responsive direction than any technical wizardry. The chief attraction was Balanchine himself, who, in his only dramatic appearance on American television, played the role of Herr Drosselmeier with great zestiness. Unlike current versions of the ballet, which tend to portray Drosselmeier as a dark, sinister figure (in keeping with its E.T.A. Hoffmann source), Balanchine emphasized the part's waggish qualities, obviously delighting in the chance to have some fun with a character that serves in some ways as a metaphor for the implicit sorcery of any choreographer.

The cast that brought Drosselmeier's spells to life (including Diana Adams as the Sugar Plum Fairy, Allegra Kent as Dewdrop, Arthur Mitchell as Coffee, and Edward Villella as Candy Cane) made it easy to believe in an enchanted kingdom of dancing, and fortunately their efforts were well served by director Ralph Nelson. Rather than cutting from one view to the next as a way of establishing visual variety, Nelson usually preferred to employ a single, crane-mounted camera, which calmly followed the principal dancers, letting their movements suggest appropriate times to sweep in and out. The TV camera was sometimes given a participatory role by Balanchine's choreography as well, with characters occasionally leaning towards its electronic eye, addressing it as if it were a living observer. (In Coffee's dance, Arthur Mitchell approached the camera as a mischievous voyeur, often staring directly into the lens in mock solemnity and, at one point, gently blowing smoke from his pipe to obscure the view.) Despite Balanchine's complaints about network production attitudes, this live broadcast of *The Nutcracker* remains a landmark example of how a ballet's spirit can be successfully transferred to television.

Omnibus

Though broadcasts like *Sleeping Beauty* and *The Nutcracker* brought the networks favorable attention, they were, by necessity, "special" events. The expense and effort involved in their production made it difficult to consider scheduling them as anything but an infrequent occurrence. TV ballet did, however, have one fairly regular forum during the 1950s—the Sunday afternoon cultural magazine series *Omnibus*. Funded by the Ford Foundation and premiering in 1952, *Omnibus* throughout its nine-and-a-half-year run on the commercial networks aired many programs devoted to dance. One of its first presentations was a somewhat trimmed version of Agnes de Mille's *Rodeo*, performed live by a cast that included John Kriza and Jenny Workman. De Mille approached the task of adapting her work for television with characteristic intensity and a sure eye for the pleasing detail. She recognized that television seemed to change everything about the way choreography looked, especially in terms of duration. Dance sequences which gripped an audience in the theater might appear unusually slow and lifeless on a small, black-and-white screen. As associate producer Paul Feigay explained, she not only cut choreography which didn't serve *Rodeo*'s dramatic line, she refashioned how her ballet was seen:

> Under Miss De Mille's watchful eye, new sets were designed more in keeping with the availability of television to create vast space out of very little. Miss De Mille began to think of herself as a camera, and suddenly began to see that although there were distinct limitations of space, there was an added dimension which the camera could supply. This was, that the camera could get close to the dancers and they became people in a story, more actor-dancers, less ballet dancers.[20]

During its first season, *Omnibus* continued to search for standard works which it could, in Feigay's words, "re-mold within the limitations of television."[21] Presentations included William Dollar's *Five Gifts*, de Mille's *Three Virgins and a Devil*, performed by Ballet Theatre, and the Ballet Russe in *Gaite Parisienne*. The program's second season featured several interesting adapted-for-TV dance pieces. To heighten the drama, as well as explain its actions, Jose Limon's ballet *The Moor's Pavanne* was presented with spoken quotations from its source, Shakespeare's *Othello*. The brief snippets of narration, however, were a scarcely noticeable distraction in this well-done TV adaptation. The camera served Limon's choreography with great skill. By emphasizing the ballet's sharp diagonal lines and positioning the dancers at key moments so that they are in an almost intimate contact with the lens, the production revealed some of the ways television could create an interesting dance perspective of its own.

One of the highlights of the early years of *Omnibus* was a November 1953 scaled-down presentation of Eugene Loring's *Billy the Kid*. Unlike the stage version, this *Billy the Kid* featured narration, delivered by Loring himself, that, oddly enough, did little to detract from the ballet's effectiveness. Loring's words helped give his mythological ballet of the Old West a realistic focus as he explained Billy's origins, as well as his own choreographic intentions, at the beginning of each section. Though performed in a small studio, the telecast's moody lighting, with its deep pools of blackness highlighted by dramatic bursts of white, imparted a surprising feeling of spaciousness to a work which uses the sweep of the outdoors as one of its central elements.

An important feature in this *Omnibus* production of *Billy the Kid* was the decision to change portions of the ballet to accommodate the camera. Instead of photographing the piece from the strict perspective of the proscenium stage (the traditional method of most dance telecasts), the TV camera was brought directly into the swirl of activity, almost as a friendly participant. In the second scene, for example, as the frontier town comes to life, characters enter and exit not just from stage left or right but from in front of and behind the camera; the dancers occasionally face the lens as they would the eyes of a bystander, and the can-can girls actively flirt with it.

To increase the production's realism, it was decided that in the opening scene Billy should be played by a child, not by the adult Billy in overalls as is customary on stage. Associate producer Paul Feigay explained how the show handled Billy's leap to maturity:

> Through the magic and flexibility of the television camera, the grown Billy was able to make his first entrance behind the boy. There was no doubt in anyone's mind that the kid had projected himself into the future, and the events which followed were clear to everyone.[22]

Despite its smaller cast, what stands out from this ambitious telecast is how well the ballet's spirit and flavor emerges on the small screen. The larger-than-life drama of Billy the Kid and Pat Garrett as played on stage assumes a chamberlike intensity on television. Commenting in *Dancemagazine*, Ann Barzel praised the production as "the most notable TV ballet we have seen in five years of looking," as well as singling out the ways television enhanced the ballet's drama.

> Close-ups helped establish character and brought in details that were lost on stage. At the other extreme, the impersonality of a line of tiny figures silhouetted against the blurred endlessness of the television background suggest the push westward in a broader way than the proscenium stage could.[23]

A month after the *Billy the Kid* telecast, *Omnibus* broadcast a TV first: the world premiere of Eugene Loring's *Capital of the World*, performed by Ballet Theatre. Though the work was not judged a success, its presentation on the show, where it was preceded by a dramatization of the Ernest Hemingway story on which it was based, was typical of the program's interest in exploring new methods of televising dance. Perhaps the shows which best represent *Omnibus*'s experimental zeal were two 1956 episodes featuring Agnes de Mille. Both were lecture/demonstrations covering hundreds of years of dance history, but their style was anything but dry and academic. De Mille's vivid stage presence (she was a natural TV performer who treated the camera as if it were a dinner party companion) and her choreographic gift for pacing and presentation made her two shows move with a zesty assurance.

In her first program, *The Art of Ballet*, de Mille told the story of ballet's evolution from the French court of the sixteenth century to its integration in Broadway musicals beginning in the 1940s. Her wide-ranging discussion made full use of the studio's resources. Dancers appeared and disappeared out of the darkness to illustrate her examples. The settings dissolved from a ballet class to a dance hall to a quiet performance area for the *Swan Lake*. The effect was one of great fluidity, with Agnes de Mille tying together the disparate elements not only through stage magic but by the quirky magnetism of her personality. Her role on the program was more than that of guide. Sometimes she was a tough-minded instructor, who forcefully directed her dancers. At other moments, she was a performer, who demonstrated steps and, on one occasion, executed a kicky solo in the style of the eighteenth-century French dancer Marie Camargo with considerable aplomb.

De Mille's second *Omnibus* program, *The Art of Choreography*, roughly followed the format of the first. Once again, viewers were given a lively tour through dance history, combining brief demonstrations, informed discussion, and short excerpts from repertory works. This time, the subject matter concerned the difficulties and challenges in creating dance movement. To illustrate her points, de Mille drew from an eclectic range of sources, including folk dances from Africa and Scotland and from the Royal Court of Thailand. Her most effective examples were, not surprisingly, her most personal: how she made the dancers in *Rodeo* look like they were riding horses, and how she worked with her company to put together a new piece. (The program concluded with a fascinating ten-minute sequence showing her creating a section from what would later become *Fall River Legend*.)

Both *The Art of Ballet* and *The Art of Choreography* revealed de Mille's talent for recasting dance in vivid TV terms. The fact that both programs were broadcast live only added to their achievement, since the technique called for tremendous coordination between performers, camera people, and the sound and lighting crew. Every dance was rechoreographed to enhance its TV presentation, with special attention paid to camera positioning and placement. De Mille worked closely with the show's technical staff to determine the most effective methods of capturing performance style without compromising dance intention. As Janet Mason reports, Agnes de Mille had very clear ideas on what TV dance should look like:

> She pointed out to the director, Charles Dubin, that the ideal spot from which to view most dances is center balcony: that this view gives one the floor pattern, the total relationship of the dancers to one another, as well as a full view of each individual dancer. Agnes said she did not want any "arty shot" of an eyebrow or a disembodied hand; that this was not dance; that the entire movement had to be seen. She felt that cutting from shot to shot or zooming in for extreme close-ups often gave unwanted and unnecessary accents which departed from the intent of the choreographer.[24]

In the pursuit of making dance more interesting to the home viewer, some technical tricks were tried. A dance solo in *The Art of Ballet* by Mary Ellen Moylen featured a full shot of the dancer, with a close-up of her feet superimposed in a corner. But for the most part, respectful long shots were the order of the day, particularly in *Les Sylphides* where not a single close-up was employed. The excerpt from *Rodeo* in *The Art of Choreography* was particularly impressive, with camerawork that served the sweep and velocity of the dancing. The use of an elevated camera, placed on a flexible, moving crane that looked slightly down on the proceedings, provided a graceful perspective (de Mille's "center balcony" view) from which to see the ballet's spirited ensemble numbers.

One other *Omnibus* program from this period is worth noting. Eager to set the record straight and prove that male ballet dancers are as physically adept and as "masculine" as their counterparts in professional athletics, Gene Kelly assembled a famous 1958 show called *Dancing: A Man's Game*. The program, broadcast live like most *Omnibus* features, opened in a large gymnasium, where boxers, gymnasts, fencers, tennis players, baseball players, and male dancers were all warming up for their various activities. Walking through the ensemble, Gene Kelly began his defense. "All of these people possess physical movement in rhythm," he cheerily stated, and for the next hour, he argued, with indefatigable charm, for an understanding of the mutual gracefulness and prowess male athletes and dancers share. To demonstrate the inherent choreography of athletics, Kelly asked Mickey Mantle, Sugar Ray Robinson, Bob Cousey, Vic Seixus, Johnny Unitas, and Vic Gnezzi to go through the basic moves of their sports, which he then transposed into a short dance. Other links between the two realms followed. After explaining the evolution of ballet positions from fencing, Kelly next showed gymnasts and fencers practicing their skills accompanied by ballet music. Shots of Dick Button skating were intercut with Edward Villella dancing. With the smiling confidence that he'd proven his case, Kelly concluded with an informative history of the influences which helped to shape American popular dance. The entire program, like the earlier lecture/demonstrations of Agnes de Mille, moved with a Broadway dancer's sense of pacing and joy in performance.

TV Problems

Yet, despite the advances of programs like *Omnibus*, critics and choreographers were still mixed on what television could do for dance. The advantages of making ballet and modern dance available to millions who would never have come to the theater were frequently outweighed by the restrictions and compromises TV performances entailed. Many agreed with *New York Times* dance critic John Martin's 1954 assessment of televised dance:

> Television in its present form is utterly incapable technologically of presenting a ballet on the average small screen. The figures of the dancers are scarcely distinguishable from each other and the scenery; little gray splotches an inch or two high, they have heavily shadowed faces of miniature witches, their bodies are uninvitingly distorted and their movements rendered largely unintelligible by overhead photography and poor lighting.[25]

Martin objected strongly to the very qualities Agnes de Mille singled out as television's hallmark—its ability to underline the drama in dance movement. For Martin, the medium's "story" emphasis was achieved at the expense of choreographic considerations of form and line; the *Omnibus* production of Loring's *Billy the Kid* failed to capture the ballet's dance qualities because, "everything possible was done to focus on the plot, as if it were a Hollywood western."[26]

Television's technological limitations and its small, flat screen posed particular problems in capturing the three-dimensional vitality of dance.

Even with the gradual introduction of color broadcasting in the mid–1950s, the medium's tonal range and clarity of detail were extremely narrow. Ensemble numbers featuring anything more than a half-dozen members of the corps de ballet were next to impossible. Relying on the close-up camera was not a practical or an aesthetic solution either, primarily because it robbed the dance of its shape and enacted a cruel electronic surgery on the performers by cutting their forms in halves and quarters. As Jack Gould observed in a 1957 article in the *New York Times*, "Doing ballet on TV is not easy. There are the twin difficulties of either being so far away from the stage that the dancing figures seem only an inch or two high or being so close that a spectator cannot embrace the whole."[27]

George Balanchine, who had felt particularly upset at the production standards of CBS during his 1958 *Nutcracker* telecast, presented the case against television even more vigorously:

> Always, before one of my ballets are put on television, I find myself wanting to make a little speech to the audience. I want to say, "Listen, people, what you're going to see is really going to be pretty awful. It's not going to be at all what ballet can be. The ballerina that you'll be seeing is very beautiful, really. She has very long legs, and she's very young. She has the most beautiful costumes of the most wonderful colors. But you're not going to see anything like that on your screen. What you'll see is a short-legged, oldish-looking woman with an elongated nose (for some reason, the nose in particular always comes out misshapen). . . . And—oh, yes—this ballerina is supposed to dance very, very beautifully. But you'll have to imagine it, because you won't really be able to see that either in the image appearing on your screen."[28]

There were other complications associated with dance telecasting. While TV studio space had enlarged considerably since the cramped quarters of the 1930s, it was hardly an environment hospitable to dancers. Solid concrete floors and a fundamental lack of spaciousness made it difficult to reproduce the springy bounce and freedom of movement afforded by most proscenium stages. Live broadcasting, which was the norm through the mid–1950s until videotape became more widely used, posed considerable challenges as well. Though the live nature of television was often exciting, TV performances still called for precise coordination between dancers and a technical staff frequently unschooled in the nuances of choreographic design. Even in the best of circumstances, the pressures and demands of commercial television inevitably affected the final product. Once again, George Balanchine provides a vivid example:

> In my experience with television productions what happens is something like this—you do some rehearsals, and then the television crew—all very nice and intelligent people, usually—come over to see how things are going and to work out the technical details of presentation. We discuss this and that—camera angles, exits

and entrances, lighting and so on—and they take notes and they're very agreeable. But when the work is produced, it doesn't come out quite the way it's been contemplated. As the production hour approaches a kind of panic sets in. *Something* takes over—a fear of responsibility perhaps, a fear that they're all going to be thrown out of their jobs if the result does not emerge as standard television.[29]

Most of the solutions to the problems of televised dance were usually impractical or economically unfeasible. Paul Feigay idealistically proposed "a permanent, flexible dance company rehearsing continuously and building a repertoire which would range from the classics to musical comedy."[30] In the same spirit, choreographer Valerie Bettis urged the networks to "regard dance in the way they approach music, and create and support a dance company as they would orchestras and opera companies."[31] Jack Gould hoped for the development of "a new school of choreography, one that can harmonize and integrate movement on stage and movement by cameras."[32]

As these quotations reveal, the medium's technical restrictions and the increasingly rigid demands of commercial broadcasting proved frustrating to dancers, choreographers, and critics alike. By the middle of the 1950s, dance on television had settled into three distinct categories, each with its own specific limitations and programming rules. Scheduled the least frequently, but furnishing the most rewards in terms of network publicity and prestige, were the ballet "specials." Programs such as *Sleeping Beauty*, *Cinderella*, and seasonal broadcasts of *The Nutcracker* were designed to show off the networks' resources, both economic and technical, and to fend off public criticism concerning the low standards of prime-time fare. Viewers eager for more regularly programmed dance fare were forced to seek out time slots that were not as commercially valuable, such as Sunday mornings and afternoons, which had traditionally, since the early days of network radio, been reserved for high-minded "sustaining programs" incapable of attracting a sponsor. It was here that shows like the innovative *Camera Three*, *Lamp Unto My Feet* (a religious program often featuring original choreography), and *Omnibus* could be found by their selective audiences.

Variety Shows

The final network forum for dance had little interest in the experimental approach of the Sunday "high culture" shows but did provide an abundance of classical ballet in the guise of short, five- or six-minute excerpts and pas de deux. These were the prime time variety programs, which since their beginnings in the late 1940s had customarily included brief ballet selections in the midst of more crowd-pleasing entertainment. The long-running *Ed Sullivan Show* made it a point to highlight dance performers from all over the world, as long as they were of certified star quality. With his love for the spectacular, Sullivan presented the first American TV appearance of the Sadlers Wells Ballet Company in 1954 for a program that included *Les Patineurs* and Margot Fonteyn and Michael Somes dancing a pas de deux from Ashton's *Homage to the Queen*. In 1956, he featured the Royal Danish Ballet in a selection from their famous production of August Bournonville's *Napoli*. In 1958, the program expanded its international focus. Within a three-month period, Sullivan offered the London Festival Ballet, Ruth Page's Chicago Opera Ballet, Roland Petit's Ballets de Paris, and the Moiseyev dancers from Russia, who, because of their large numbers, were photographed in an extended long shot that took in the full stage of the Metropolitan Opera where the telecast originated.

The appearance of Jerome Robbin's dance company Ballet: U.S.A. in 1960 on *The Ed Sullivan Show* deserves special mention. After his celebrated, breezy choreography for *The Ford Fiftieth Anniversary Special* in 1953, Robbins had, for the most part, stayed away from television as he continued with his Broadway and ballet projects. His dissatisfactions with the medium, like most stage choreographers, stemmed from what it made dance look like. Stating the case against TV dance, he argued, "but television is a two-dimensional medium. And you never sense in television the limitations of space. You cannot sense, either, the kinetic energy of the dancer nor his dangers, feats, and pleasures."[33]

Nevertheless, Robbins was granted special privileges for letting his company appear on the Sullivan show that made working on television a bit more enticing. Unlike most of the performers on the program who simply went on the stage and did their act, Robbins was permitted an extraordinary amount of creative control. Ballet: U.S.A. was granted an unprecedented two days of camera rehearsals, which Robbins closely supervised. Instead of three cameras, seven were used. And instead of having to deal with the hectic atmosphere of live broadcasting, Ballet U.S.A. appeared on videotape, in a presentation that spread over two programs.

In addition to *The Ed Sullivan Show*, most of the variety shows originating from New York in the 1950s included dance excerpts on an occasional basis. Some of these programs, like *The Tonight Show* or *The Kate Smith Show* brought on ballet stars for their celebrity value or to add a note of "refinement," but there were two programs that tried to provide a more inviting atmosphere for dancers to perform. One was *The Voice of Firestone*, which had a long broadcast history of programming devoted to the arts. The dancers who appeared on the show were certainly not new to TV—they included such veterans as Andre Eglevsky and Maria Tallchief—but this time they were surrounded by opera singers and classical musicians rather than jugglers and nightclub comedians.

The other regularly scheduled, prime-time variety program with a cultural orientation was *The Bell Telephone Hour*. Premiering in 1959, the show offered a showcase for classical dance, as long as it stuck to a ten-minute time limit. Among its many highlights were the frequent appearances of the New York City Ballet. Several Balanchine works, or at least excerpts from Balanchine works, received their only American broadcast during the program's ten-year run. Included were selections from *Scotch Symphony*, danced by Eglevsky and Tallchief; *Square Dance*, with Patricia Wilde and Nicholas Magallanes; *Apollo*, with Jacques D'Amboise and Melissa Hayden; *Harlequinade*, with Patricia McBride and Edward Villella; *Concerto Barocco*, with Suzanne Farrell, Colleen Neary and Conrad Ludlow; and *Allegro Brillante*, danced by Maria Tallchief and Nicholas Magallanes.

With its limited time and resources, *The Bell Telephone Hour*, like every variety show, was forced to rely on the most ubiquitous of dance programming staples—the pas de deux. At one time or another, most of the standard ballet duets, performed by most of the celebrated ballet stars of the period, were telecast by the series. Many of the dances, and the dancers, appeared over and over again. For example, *The Nutcracker* pas de deux was danced by Violette Verdy and Edward Villella in 1961 and by Melissa Hayden and Jacques D'Amboise in 1965; the Black Swan pas de deux from the third act of *Swan Lake* was danced by Lupe Serrano and Jacques D'Amboise in 1960, Sonia Arova and Erik Bruhn in 1963, and later in the same year by Svetlana Beriosova and Rudolf Nureyev.

The Non-Commercial Alternative

The networks' three principal dance categories—occasional specials, Sunday culture programs, and short excerpts and pas de deux on prime-time variety shows—posed serious limitations for choreographers, dancers, and audiences alike. Pressures from advertisers and the networks' never-ending concern with ratings made it difficult to venture out of very narrow definitions of acceptable dance programming. Thus, it was with some degree of enthusiasm that advocates of TV dance greeted the prospect of educational televison, with its strictly non-commercial orientation.

Dance had been one of the earliest offerings of the National Educational Television and Radio Center, which provided several hours a week of shows produced by member stations. The programs were, like everything associated with educational television, put together under severe budgetary restrictions, but they still reflected an interest in presenting dance in a way commercial networks would rarely consider.

WQED in Pittsburgh produced two of the first dance shows distributed nationwide. Both focused on Martha Graham, who had not appeared on commercial television since 1939, and both proved to be influential in setting the pattern for what future non-commercial dance programs would be like. The first, *A Dancer's World*, released in 1957, was a film documentary examining Graham's trailblazing career and dance philosophy. The second, released a year later, was a performance of her *Appalachian Spring* that, interestingly, used many of the techniques of three-camera dance telecasting, even though it was shot with one camera on film. Director Peter Glushanok, who also photographed the production in what appears to be a typical-size TV studio, employed his camera in much the same way a dance sensitive TV director would. Like the ballets broadcast on *Omnibus*, this *Appalachian Spring* avoided a strict center row, proscenium stage viewpoint. While the camera did not penetrate the performing area of the dancers, as it had in *Billy the Kid*, it did offer a variety of different vantage points that changed, sometimes dramatically, the ballet's perspective.

What's surprising about WQED's production of *Appalachian Spring* is how well Graham's lyrical ballet of pioneer life functions within the confines of the small screen. As Agnes de Mille discovered, television seems to naturally favor dances with a strong narrative line. Obviously, a TV version of *Appalachian Spring* could not reproduce the ballet's expansiveness, but what television did capture was its taut emotionalism and eloquence. The strength of this production rested on a combination of factors. First, there was Isamu Noguchi's elegantly stark set which, while never completely visible in any single shot, provided a poetic series of outlines and boundaries for the dancers to be framed by. Second, there was director Peter Glushanok's graceful sense of camera movement that frequently mirrored the expressive qualities of the choreography. But chiefly, there was *Appalachian Spring*'s superb cast. This TV version featured a still-vibrant Martha Graham as the wife (she was 64 at the time), Stuart Hodes as the husband, and a thrilling performance by Bertram Ross as the preacher.

In 1960, the Center (which later changed its name to NET) distributed a nine-part dance series that would have been difficult to imagine on commercial television. The programs, hosted by an assistant professor at Smith College Martha Myers and produced by WGBH in Boston, were called *A Time to Dance* and focused on a different issue each week, using interviews and demonstrations to prove their point. Though it was put together with very limited resources, the series featured some of the dance world's top talent. Producer Jac Venza believed that the untainted atmosphere of educational television served as the chief lure.

> When asked to participate in filming these programs for television, the best performers and choreographers agreed enthusiastically, despite the limitations of budget and space. For the first time they found the same artistic standards and integrity of purpose that they applied to themselves.[34]

A Time to Dance covered a large amount of material. Individual episodes looked at new trends in ballet with Antony Tudor (with appearances by

Nora Kaye and Hugh Laing dancing three pas de deux from Tudor works); ethnic dance with Geoffrey Holdern; dance as a reflection of modern times, with Herbert Ross choreographing artists from the American Ballet Theatre; great ballet stars of the past and the present; and the language of dance featuring Jose Limon and his company in a performance of his *There Is a Time*.

As the 1960s progressed and the Ford Foundation increased its financial support, NET started to produce its own programs. In 1964, it presented one of the first dance shows filmed "on location" outdoors—John Butler's *Carmina Burana*, performed by the Netherlands Dance Theater at Doornberry Castle in Holland. A year later, it embarked on its largest commitment to dance so far—an ambitious six-part series called *USA: Dance*. The programs were, in the words of producer Jac Venza, designed to emphasize "significant American qualities of dance in each of its forms."[35] Like *A Time to Dance*, the shows surveyed a wide territory, but their technique was a bit more sophisticated. Rather than employing a single host or format, *USA: Dance* let the subject matter dictate each program's approach. The series' tone mixed education and accessibility. Skillfully photographed dance performances usually alternated with documentary-style material on the choreographers and the dancers.

A typical example of this method was the program on the Robert Joffrey Ballet Company. After an offscreen announcer certified the troupe's credentials ("their versatility and range of repertory mark them as American"), the company was seen in brief excerpts from their modern repertoire (Joffrey's *Gamelon*, Gerald Arpino's *Incubus* and *Viva Vivaldi*, Anna Sokolow's *Opus 65*). In between the selections, the dancers happily re-created the patterns and movements of a ballet class while in a brightly lit TV studio.

In contrast, a program on the New York City Ballet transformed a TV studio into a dark, intimate chamber where George Balanchine and his dancers observed the rigorous demands of their art. The show opened with a stone-faced Balanchine, surrounded by his prize performers, as they intently watched a tape of the pas de deux from his ballet *Agon*. With a camera circling around them, the dancers were heard, in simple, quiet comments, discussing choreography and the joys of dancing for "Mr. Balanchine." After a razor-sharp performance by Suzanne Farrell and Arthur Mitchell of the *Agon* duet, the program returned to more views of Balanchine and his ensemble, casually poised around a TV monitor. These were followed by some brief rehearsal scenes, three more Balanchine pas de deux (*Tarantella* danced by Edward Villella and Patricia McBride, *Meditation* danced by Suzanne Farrell and Jacques D'Amboise, and *Grand Pas de Deux* with D'Amboise and Melissa Hayden), and some intriguing off-camera conversational snippets. One memorable interchange involved Balanchine and D'Amboise discussing *Meditation*. To D'Amboise's belief that "I think there's a pleasure in the [ballet's] sorrow," Balanchine snappily answered, "no, it's not a pleasure at all." The program was quite successful in making the audience feel like they were getting an insider's view of City Ballet performance style and group dynamics.

NET's other dance programs during the 1960s followed the basic patterns of *USA: Dance*. In 1967 they presented a special show called *Five Ballets of the Five Senses*, with five different works choreographed by John Butler, unified by the drawings of Ben Shahn. In the same year, they also produced an elaborate *Ballet Gala*, which gathered together soloists from the Bolshoi, Royal Ballet, Royal Danish Ballet, and Paris Ballet companies in a program of pas de deux. Dance was also covered in formats mixing interviews, documentaries, and performances. A new series, called *The Creative Person*, featured programs on choreographer Benjamin Harkarvy and on the Robert Joffrey Ballet. There were documentaries covering the past—Anna Pavlova—and the present—the life and philosophy of choreographer Maurice Béjart. Other programs looked at the Jacob's Pillow Dance Festival, the career of Jose Limon (with performances of *The Moor's Pavanne* and *Missa Brevis*), and the world premiere of Merce Cunningham's *Raindance* at the Second Buffalo Arts Festival.

NET's increase in dance programming was also accompanied by an increasing reliance on overseas productions. Always strapped for funds, the network recognized the value of imported programs in providing high quality content at a greatly reduced cost. Some of the imported dance programs NET distributed in the 1960s included a 75–minute version of Ashton's *Cinderella*, danced by the Royal Ballet and produced by Granada Television in England; a Canadian documentary on Igor Stravinsky's life; a performance of *L'Histoire du Soldat* with choreography by Robert Helpmann from England; and Birgit Cullberg's *The Evil Queen* from Sweden. In the late 1960s, when the Public Broadcasting Service took over many of NET's distribution functions, its series *International Performances* offered many ballets originally produced by French television, including a *Firebird* choreographed by Georges Slabine, the Paris Ballet in *La Sylphide*, and Maurice Béjart's *Salome*.

Dance on the Commercial Networks During the 1960s

Treatment of dance on the commercial networks in the 1960s was similar to the previous decade, except for a general reduction in the number of dance specials, especially American-produced dance specials. Perhaps because there were fewer of them, those dance events which were televised received tremendous promotion and attention, with CBS's June 1962 broadcast of Stravinsky's *Noah and the Flood* serving as the most notorious example.

Work on the program began in 1960, when the network commissioned

Stravinsky to compose an original composition for television, to be accompanied by special choreography by George Balanchine. Stravinsky finally completed *Noah and the Flood* two years later, but one major problem remained. The piece was only 22 1/2 minutes long, which was considerably less than the one-hour special both CBS and the sponsor, Breck Shampoo, had been promised by the show's producer. The obvious solution—to cut the program to fit the actual length of the work—was, in TV terms, out of the question. Too much money had already been spent; an enormous publicity machine heralding the show's "significance" was already in operation; and, more importantly, the time and the advertising dollars had already been allocated.

What emerged instead was a new version of *Noah and the Flood*, fashioned around Stravinsky and Balanchine's original core. Thirty-five minutes of extraneous "padding" was added that, for the most part, left viewers floating at sea in bewilderment. A tuxedoed Laurence Harvey introduced the program on a note of silly, high-mindedness which typified the entire proceedings. In his sternest voice, he offered a rambling discourse on, among other things, the meaning of man, the importance of anthropology and tribal sculptures, and the relevance of the Flood to our time. After a 90–second address by Stravinsky and shots of him conducting the orchestral prelude, abstract designs and primitive masks flooded the screen. Sebastian Cabot read from the Bible. Satan's fall was depicted using artsy special effects. Finally, after 30 minutes, *Noah and the Flood* actually began.

The work was, as Balanchine insisted, "*not* a ballet,"[36] and its dancers, including Jacques D'Amboise, Jillana, and Edward Villella were basically organized into processional movements or theatrical poses. The only strictly dance sequence, entitled "The Building of the Ark," and performed by members of the City Ballet's corps, appeared, like most of the production, to be overwhelmed by the ponderousness of Rouben Ter-Arutunian's set design and costumes. Balanchine admits he was dissatisfied with the results:

> I wanted to make choreography that was not too obtrusive—which did not interfere with the music. But the choreography that was seen was really just a rough draft—my first sketchy thoughts. I intended to make changes and improvement—but we got into the studio, the panic took over, and then suddenly it became impossible to do what needed to be done.[37]

Even if Balanchine had had more time, it is doubtful if *Noah and the Flood* could have emerged unscathed from the trappings that surrounded it. As Allen Hughes noted, "The false fanciness of the entire production ran counter to the tasteful simplicity he [Balanchine] sought throughout his entire career."[38] The program's only successful section occurred near its end when, for a few privileged minutes, viewers were able to watch Balanchine choreograph his dancers (still mercifully free of their costumes) in a City Ballet rehearsal studio.

Critical reaction to the program was unusually severe. The *New York Times* decried *Noah and the Flood* as "an indigestible concoction."[39] The *Saturday Review*, with a bit more restraint, noted that "the result was not satisfactory."[40] *Dancemagazine*'s TV critic Ann Barzel found the telecast "a quite baffling experience that didn't quite come off. Judging from the letters to the daily press, the general public reacted with vulgar merriment. And some have seriously felt it was a Stravinsky-Balanchine hoax."[41]

Perhaps the best explanation of why *Noah and the Flood* failed came from Arthur Todd, who felt the problem lay entirely in prevailing network attitudes to "cultural" specials. "Either CBS or Sextant, Inc. [the show's producers], or both, made the cardinal mistake," he wrote, "of underestimating its audience. When you play down and try to be all things to all people, you alienate everyone."[42]

Other dance specials on the commercial networks during the 1960s were neither as controversial nor as initially ambitious. Though there were a few interesting efforts, such as CBS's 1964 live broadcast of the opening of the New York State Theater with the New York City Ballet in excerpts from *Stars and Stripes* or a 1968 *Bell Telephone Hour* documentary looking at the dancing, and assorted muscle ailments, of Edward Villella, the decade was also typified by an ominous new trend—the use of imported program material to cut down on costs. CBS's 1964 Christmas season broadcast, *England's Royal Ballet*, was originally made for English television. The network's 1965 Christmas telecast of *The Nutcracker* was a West German production (with Patricia MacBride and Edward Villella) which, in a concession to American taste, included homespun narration added by actor Eddie Albert. ABC's two-part *Best of the Bolshoi* was another example of reduced programming expenditures—the program was purchased from a pay-TV company which had been responsible for the original production expenses.

While the commercial networks did reduce the number of American-made, prime-time dance specials during the 1960s, the popularity of ballet excerpts on variety shows still remained strong. If anything, ballet filled the airwaves in short doses more than ever before, largely because of the allure of one man—Rudolf Nureyev. The publicity surrounding Nureyev's defection to the West in 1961 had quickly turned him into an international celebrity. By the time of his first American TV appearance in January 1962 (a surprise substitution for the injured Erik Bruhn on *The Bell Telephone Hour*), he had brought more excitement to the usually rarefied world of ballet than any performer in years. His vibrant stage presence and his extraordinary feats of elevation captured the public's attention, and by the end of the decade he had become a virtual TV regular, making at least a score of appearances on every type of variety program. His most frequent outlet was *The Bell Telephone Hour*, where he performed five times in three years. But perhaps his most celebrated, and certainly his most watched, appearance was with Dame Margot Fonteyn on *The Ed Sullivan Show*; Sullivan was so thrilled by their work that he invited them back again on his next program and then replayed both broadcasts a few months later. Nureyev also turned up on shows ranging from *The Hollywood Palace* to *The Jimmy Durante Show*, *The London Palladium*, and *The Dean Martin Show*. Until the defection of Mikhail Baryshnikov a few years later, no classical dancer had ever been received with greater enthusiasm on commercial television.

Still, Nureyev was not the only ballet dancer to visit the popular variety shows. Edward Villella and Patricia McBride were an almost ubiquitous duo on programs like *The Ed Sullivan Show*, *The Bell Telephone Hour*, and *The Dick Cavett Show*. Other New York City Ballet soloists would also make occasional television appearances. Suzanne Farrell and Arthur Mitchell, for example, turned up one night on *The Tonight Show* in 1969, performing a selection from *Slaughter on Tenth Avenue* and, surprisingly, an excerpt from Balanchine's sharply modern ballet, *Agon*. Dancers from the Harkness Ballet and the Joffrey Ballet were guests on *The Joey Bishop Show* in the same year. Unlike the decade that would follow, the 1960s was still filled with variety shows that, no matter how devoutly mainstream in orientation, were not averse to an infrequent visit from a dancing representative of the higher arts. A short pas de deux or ballet solo may have been an odd sight amid the lavish trappings of *The Perry Como Show* or *The Dean Martin Show*, but the broad mandate of the variety format had not yet been replaced by the more precise, demographically targeted entertainment specials that began to take over in the 1970s.

Dance on Sunday Mornings

Throughout the 1960s, the commercial networks continued to reserve Sunday mornings and afternoons for unsponsored programs devoted to the arts and religion. CBS's *Camera Three* was the most distinguished example of the "low rent" approach to cultural programming that typified these essentially unrated time slots. With a minimum of funds, little network interference, and a small but committed staff, *Camera Three* produced at least a couple of dance programs every season, usually with an eye for the provocative or the instructive.

More than anything else, *Camera Three*'s focus resembled that of educational television, and its dance programs were created with the same kind of low budget/high purpose attitude that characterized NET shows like *A Time To Dance* and *USA: Dance*. Discussion and demonstration served, by necessity, as one of the principal formats. Dance critic Walter Terry hosted many of *Camera Three*'s conversation/performance shows, with guests such as Ruth St. Denis and Ted Shawn (on the occasion of their 50th wedding anniversary) in 1964 and Maria Tallchief in 1966. In its search for the non-traditional, the program also featured several episodes examining the traditions of foreign dance, including those from Ceylon, India, and Spain.

Camera Three's straight performance dance programs aimed for works that would never be considered for the crowd-pleasing realms of commercial prime time. Modern dance found an especially welcome haven. A 1960 show looked at the choreography of Yuriko. The Alvin Ailey Dance Theater was featured on a 1962 program. A 1965 episode offered an abridged version of Valerie Bettis's *As I Lay Dying*; an excerpt from Jean Erdman's theater/dance piece, *The Coach with Six Insides*, was telecast the same year. In 1968 both Katherine Litz and Norman Walker and his dancers made appearances as well.

CBS's Sunday commitment to the innovative and the offbeat (and the inexpensive) was also evident in the series *Repertoire Workshop*, produced by the network's five owned and operated stations. Like *Camera Three*, dance was one of the program's prominent elements. In fact, its premiere on January 2, 1963, was devoted to an original dance work by Norman Walker called *Reflections*, set to Norman Dello Joio's *Variations*. Over the next few years, *Repertoire Workshop* presented shows on the Dance Theatre of Alwin Nikolais, Murray Louis, and the choreography of Ruth Page, whose pieces were seen on four different occasions.

A noteworthy highlight of the series was its telecast of Alwin Nikolais's *Limbo* in 1968. The program, produced and directed by Ray Abel, was an unusual merger of dance and television gimmickry, all moving to a hypnotic electronic score created by the choreographer. Nikolais explored practically every tool in the medium's technological arsenal to see what would happen when it was mixed with dance. Chroma keying (which electronically inserts images at precise points on the screen), superimpositions, and fancy split screens were used, in the words of Anna Kisselgoff, "to achieve the quality of real abstraction."[43] Dancers with rainbow-silhouetted bodies pranced across the screen on three identical horizontal rows. Sometimes their forms would be occupied by images of swarming ants or swirling lines; other times their outlines would be splashed against oscillating geometrical backgrounds. During one sequence, a fully visible dancer was accompanied by a corps of disembodied arms. Later, principal male soloist Murray Louis danced with two women whose bodies were magically ablaze with fire. The program helped confirm television's potential to create a type of dance impossible to perform on stage.

The experimentation characteristic of the Sunday arts shows was, interestingly enough, also reflected on many of the religious programs that all three commercial networks felt a duty to provide. CBS, once again, was in the forefront in allowing its producers the freedom to operate pretty much as they pleased, as long as it didn't cost too much. In Pamela Illott, who produced the network's religious shows *Lamp Unto My Feet* and *Look*

Up and Live, the cause of modern dance on television found a rare champion. Illott, who had been at CBS since 1954, believed strongly in the direct, expressive possibilities of modern dance and defended her frequent use of the form in appropriately spiritual terms. "There's an urgency and poignancy in modern dance for people who've never seen it and indeed, they soon forget that this *is* modern dance," she said. "Instead, they're watching human souls reaching out for hope, struggling for meaning, rising up out of the intricacies of contemporary living into something they can't put into words but which lifts them from inside."[44]

Unlike her counterparts in prime-time programming whose idea of serious dance was restricted solely to ballet, Pamela Illott made a decisive effort to break the barriers separating new types of choreography from the TV audience. As she remarked, "We have not used classical ballet on these religious programs because this dance forum is usually identified with theater and entertainment and, as such, it has a quality that removes it from the daily experience of most people."[45]

Twenty-five percent of the episodes on *Look Up and Live* and *Lamp Unto My Feet* used dance in one form or another, and many choreographers received commissions to produce original works for television based on broad, religious themes. John Butler created almost a dozen new "Bible" ballets for the programs, with titles such as *Ballet of the Nativity*, *David and Bathsheba*, *Esther*, and *Saul and the Witch of Endor*. A piece he choreographed for the 15th anniversary of *Lamp Unto My Feet* in 1963 offers a typical example of the style of these religious dance presentations. Called *The Mark of Cain*, the ballet was prefaced by a dramatic reading from the Book of Genesis by Mercedes McCambridge. Then, in a darkly lit studio with sparse, bleak settings, two dancers, representing Adam and Eve, begin a pas de deux. The camera, mounted on a pedestal, glided around them, as they danced back and away from the lens. Their forms dissolved to a painted image of the sun and then to a true overhead view of two male dancers, lying on the floor, inside the sun's outline. They performed a dance on their backs, photographed from above in Busby Berkely fashion. The ballet continued, dramatizing the story of Cain, with choreography that was moderately interesting and with moderately interesting direction by Jerome Schnur. Like most of John Butler's Sunday morning ballets, the piece included the spirited dancing of Carmen de Lavallade.

CBS's religious series also presented dance pieces by Anna Sokolow, Pearl Lang, Grover Dale, and, in one memorable instance, Alvin Ailey, whose *Revelations* received its TV debut on *Lamp Unto My Feet* in 1962, just a few years after its stage premiere. This first TV production of Ailey's powerful ballet (there would be three others in the years to follow) captured the work in its early, chamberlike incarnation, before it had become more populated and more explosively theatrical.

Public Broadcasting's Growth in the 1970s

While the orientation of the Sunday morning religious and culture shows remained fairly much the same during the 1970s, practically every other aspect of TV dance went through a dramatic transformation. The primary arena of activity was educational television, which now operated under the title of the Public Broadcasting Service. With increased funding from government and corporate sources, PBS was able to expand its dance programming steadily throughout the period and, in the process, help institute challenging new standards and directions for dance telecasting.

PBS's initial dance programs in the 1970s continued the patterns of the previous decade. There were numerous imported telecasts of ballet classics—a *Swan Lake* and a *Sleeping Beauty* from the National Ballet of Canada; a BBC presentation of Frederick Ashton's *The Dream* danced by the Royal Ballet; a program of the Paris Ballet in *Les Sylphides*. But there were also several non-traditional foreign broadcasts as well. Other than a co-production with the BBC of Alwin Nikolais's experimental dance piece *Relay*, perhaps the most interesting was a documentary on Swedish choreographer Birgit Cullberg. Cullberg, with the financial support of the Swedish broadcasting system, had worked for many years creating a striking alternative to the standard approaches of TV dance. Her original ballets for television were designed to exploit the medium's technical possibilities, while emphasizing its perceptual differences. To realize her goal of using "the whole screen, entirely out to the edges" and to test the limits of dance "bound to this little camera eye," all camera movement was eliminated.[46] Instead, movement was accomplished through the precise positioning of her dancers and the mobility of the superimposed paintings she often employed as her backgrounds.

The selections from her Swedish TV ballets featured in PBS's documentary demonstrated the colorful variety, and the sometimes gimmicky restrictions, of Cullberg's style. A prime example was *Red Wine in Green Glasses*, a 15-minute pas de deux that celebrated the cultivated sensuousness of seventeenth-century France. The work's two dancers, attired in noble peasant costumes, pursue a fabulously dreamy courtship, surrounded by paintings from the era of Antoine Watteau. Thanks to superb special effects, these radiant landscapes served as more than backdrops—the dancers literally moved through them, above them, behind them, and below them. In one sequence, the male swims through a superimposed forest and then hangs on to the foot of the ballerina as she appears to fly through pale blue skies. At another time, they both seem to fall from the heavens, with white clouds zooming around them. The effects were often striking, but like many video ballets, the basic choreography often seemed overwhelmed against the swirl of technology which enveloped it. (In 1974, Cullberg brought her TV explorations to America, where she created two half-hour ballets for WHA-TV, the PBS affiliate in Madison, Wisconsin. While they were visually impressive, both *The School for Wives* [inspired by Moliere's comedy] and *The Dreamer* [inspired by Eugene O'Neill's *A Touch of the Poet*] suffered from the same qualities of gimmickry that marred her choreography for Swedish television.)

PBS's domestic productions in the early 1970s continued to follow through on the modestly innovative, and modestly budgeted, guidelines of the past. A new series called *Vibrations* presented shows on Lar Lubovich and a performance of Nikolais's *The Tent*. Another program, *Rhythmetron*, was a documentary on Arthur Mitchell, with excerpts from his *Fête Noire*, *Boistera*, and *Rhythmetron*.

An important breakthrough occurred, however, with an August 1973 production, *American Ballet Theatre: A Close-Up in Time*. Though similar in some respects to past performance/documentaries, the program showcased its product with a new and beguiling combination of sophistication and glossiness. During the course of 90 minutes, American Ballet Theatre was surveyed from every conceivable angle, from backstage views of rehearsals to interviews with choreographers, and glimpses of ABT's varied repertoire.

A Close-Up in Time's chief distinction was its beautifully photographed selections of the ABT in action, performing highlights from many of its signature works. Director Jerome Schnur took a different approach to each piece, possibly as a way to approximate the diverse styles the works embody. The Waltz from *Les Sylphides*, for example, was filmed from the traditional vantage point of the proscenium stage, using mostly long shots to capture the entire ensemble. While there were no close-ups, there were frequent views off to the sides revealing the stage lighting and scenery ropes. In contrast, the opening two scenes from Agnes de Mille's *Rodeo* were shot in a studio, with the cameras taking a far more participatory role. When they were not craning above the dancers to emphasize their diagonal lines or gliding down into the exciting fray of the cowboy's strutting dance, the three cameras were constantly being repositioned to locate the dramatic center of each moment. Like Agnes de Mille's earlier *Omnibus* presentation of the ballet, the TV cameras were used here to accent and underline; they were not simply passive recorders. The melodrama at the heart of this excerpt from *Rodeo*—the rejection of the cowgirl by the cowboys—was emotionally underscored by the slow camera movement backing away from her at the end of scene one and the more vividly langorous leap up and away the camera makes from her fallen figure at the conclusion of scene two.

A Close-Up in Time's centerpiece was its complete presentation of Antony Tudor's psychological ballet, *Pillar of Fire*, with Sallie Wilson in a fierce performance as Hagar. Tudor helped rechoreograph portions of the ballet for television, primarily in the final moments where the dancers, instead of moving across the rear of the stage and disappearing behind scrims, now move directly towards the camera and then turn around and retreat, as the camera shifts to a first balcony, medium long shot. But even without these changes, the ballet's force was eloquently rendered on the small screen, particularly as a result of Jerome Schnur's handling of the close-up camera, which brings us in greater intimacy with Hagar's panic and despair in a way no orchestra seat could provide. As dance critic John Mueller has pointed out, Schnur also made interesting use of the resources of the wide-angle lens to emphasize Hagar's isolation from the other characters by exaggerating her distance from them.[47]

A Close-Up in Time was a landmark in tastefully packaging the accomplishments of an American dance company. Its smooth assemblage of elements, its colorful displays of performance styles, and its well-rounded survey of ABT's activities and personalities would prove highly influential in setting the tone for future PBS dance profiles. The program would also prove important in setting new standards for the treatment of dancers themselves. Wooden floors were placed over the punishing concrete; there was ample rehearsal time; and the choreographers had a chance to work with the dancers in adapting to the new conditions of a TV studio.

Meanwhile, PBS continued to explore other types of dance presentations. In 1974, the network began a series of live broadcasts from the Wolf Trap Park for the Performing Arts in Virginia, with several programs devoted to modern dance and ballet. The dance works featured on *In Performance at Wolf Trap* were hampered in some ways by the park's huge stage and semi-open air conditions, but the telecasts compensated for their lack of ideal production control by their ability to mirror the genial spirit and flavor of Wolf Trap events. Dancers appearing on the series included the Eliot Feld Company; Galina and Valery Panov, in a concert of great classical pas de deux; the 1976 American debut of Mikhail Baryshnikov in a performance with American Ballet Theatre dancers Gelsey Kirkland, Marianna Tcherkasky, and Martine van Hamel; and the Martha Graham Dance Company.

As part of its *Soul* series in 1974, PBS broadcast a vivid dance profile of the Alvin Ailey Dance Company. Like *A Close-Up in Time*, *Alvin Ailey: Memories and Visions* offered a well-photographed, diverse sampling of the company's repertory works, but this time with only a few minutes of background material, consisting primarily of Ailey's personal discussions of choreographic philosophy. In keeping with the strong flavor of work such as *Blues Suite* and *The Lark Ascending*, the dancers performed in dramatically lit stage areas bathed in darkness or suitably expressive color contrasts. Director Stan Lathan heightened several of the solo numbers by electronically combining close-ups, side views, and long shots together in one frame.

By its mission and its bursts of enterprise, educational television had gradually become the chief forum and the chief hope for classical and modern dance on American television. Choreographers and critics looked to PBS as a refuge from the pressures and compromises of commercial television, and as a creative environment willing to treat all types of dance with seriousness, ingenuity, and intelligence. Yet the hard reality of tight production schedules and even tighter financing had, through the years, done its part to temper these dreams. PBS's increasing reliance on imported dance programs during the early 1970s (eight of its eleven dance shows from 1970–74 originated overseas) had become a matter of survival and simple economics. The high technical standards and sophisticated veneer domestic productions now demanded were just too expensive to provide on any kind of regular basis. *American Ballet Theatre: A Close-Up in Time* ended up costing $250,000; the final tally for *Alvin Ailey: Memories and Visions* was $300,000.

Dancers and choreographers pondering PBS's difficulties during this period were also reassessing television's ability in general to reproduce dance movement and design. A 1974 National Conference on Dance and Television held at WGBH's New Television Workshop in Watertown, Massachusetts, was typical of the type of informed discussion raging at that time over what the medium could do and should do for dance. The choreographers, filmmakers, directors, and technicians gathered at the conference shared a belief that ballet and modern dance needed to be tackled with new sensitivity and care when adapted or created for television. Eliot Feld voiced a common complaint of many choreographers when he observed that "certain forceful elements don't read on television the way they do on stage. There's no sense of gravity; there's little use of energy."[48]

Other members of the conference noted that since television inevitably distorted traditional stage choreography, maybe it was time to move away from the medium's principal use as a recorder of performances and pursue the unique electronic opportunities of TV-inspired dance. Birgit Cullberg argued for special effects, such as chroma keys and superimpositions, because they afford "the dance fantastic opportunities for getting away from the floor, which otherwise gives such dull weight to ballet in television."[49]

A few years earlier, John O'Connor of the *New York Times* assembled an equally forceful case against the present state of TV dance, pointing out the inherent production limitations of American television—inadequate time, inadequate facilities, and inadequately prepared producers—and stressing the need for a new sense of purpose and vision. Choreographers should no longer simply let their work be photographed for television, with the risk that "in long shots, the dancers are going to be two inches tall."[50] Instead, O'Connor called for a greater understanding of television's technical nature and an awareness that dance must be completely rethought before it is televised. "As a medium of communication, television has its own rules and regulations, and if dance is to be effective on the small screen, choreographers will have to translate their works into the terms of that medium."[51]

Dance in America

John O'Connor's belief in the value of translation would be borne out during the next few years, primarily in PBS's ambitious new series *Dance in America*. Funded by a $1.5 million grant in 1975 from the National Endowment for the Arts (NEA), the Corporation for Public Broadcasting, and Exxon, *Dance in America* was designed to "celebrate American achievement in dance."[52] The series' basic thrust, as defined by the NEA in its original offering letter, was "to take existing choreographic works and translate them into television."[53] This process would be the principal task of producers Jac Venza, Merrill Brockway, and Emile Ardolino.

Translation on *Dance in America*, however, involved much more than simply documenting repertory work. It was approached as a collaboration between choreographer and TV director, with the goal of reaching a television re-creation as true to the spirit of the dance work as possible. Unlike the annoyingly gimmicky West German films of Balanchine ballets that aired on PBS in 1975, the producers of *Dance in America* hoped to mirror dance design, not obscure it. The choreographers and artistic directors of each company featured in the series were made active participants right from the start. Every production began, as Jac Venza recalls, with the question, "How do you see an opportunity to work with television in relation to your work?"[54]

The series placed special emphasis on the idea of choreographers "working with television." Previously choreographers were often at the mercy of TV directors and technicians too busy with the complex problems of their own craft to treat TV dance with care or sensitivity. The results usually ended up as flat, simple reproductions of stage repertory. Emile Ardolino and Merrill Brockway sought a different approach that "aimed not merely to reproduce, but to interpret dances for a new medium."[55] This process involved a close relationship between the people responsible for what was in front of the camera and the people responsible for what was behind the camera. As Emile Ardolino explained to *Dancemagazine*:

> The unique thing about the Dance in America series was that companies and choreographers were going to have a great deal to say about how their work was translated onto the screen and what the content of the show was going to be.... These decisions, of course, are made by mutual agreement, because sometimes the choreographers might not really know what will translate well to television. We have to explain this or that will not work for us, and we explain the reasons why.[56]

Merrill Brockway, in another interview, underscored the nature of this collaborative process further by stressing that "it's essential that the director know the dancers well enough to perform them himself, and it's essential that both sides be willing to make compromises."[57]

For its premiere season *Dance in America* broadcast four shows that revealed its commitment to intelligent, wide-ranging explorations of American dance. The first and last programs were company profiles very much in the mold of PBS's 1973 telecast, *American Ballet Theatre: A Close-Up in Time*. The City Center Joffrey Ballet was seen in a kaleidoscopic, hour-long portrait that managed to include everything from rehearsal footage, brief discussions of company philosophy and history, interviews with choreographers, and five selections from the repertory. Jerome Schnur, who also directed *A Close-Up in Time*, brought the same attentive style to his taping of the Joffrey as he did with ABT; but this time, in keeping with *Dance in America*'s concern with "translation," company choreographers played an even more active role in deciding how their work should be presented. Authenticity became a hallmark. Kurt Jooss was brought over from Germany to help adapt the first two sections of his anti-war ballet, *The Green Table*. Leonide Massine was flown from Italy to supervise a section from *Parade*. While the changes made in *The Green Table* and *Parade* were primarily in terms of the arrangement of dancers and selected camera movements, Robert Joffrey chose to embrace TV technology more directly by using slow motion at the beginning and end of the excerpt from his *Remembrances*. Carefully determined special effects were integrated into the performance of Gerald Arpino's *Trinity*, where, as Wallace White notes, "the effect of vitality and rapid change is achieved by a series of fleeting superimpositions."[58]

The program on the Pennsylvania Ballet followed a similar format. Repertory highlights, company interviews, and semi-candid rehearsal moments alternated with historical material on the evolution of dance in Philadelphia and the shaky growth of the company during the last 15 years. There were, however, differences between this last episode of the season and the first (on the Joffrey). The most noticeable was in directorial style. While there were moments in the Joffrey program where the editing patterns seemed a bit rushed or the selection of camera angles a bit awkward, Merrill Brockway's direction of the Pennsylvania Ballet was marked by a feeling of utter smoothness and clarity. Rather than cut sharply from one position to another, Brockway preferred to use dissolves, which he varied in tempo, as a way to minimize the harshness of editing and to enhance the fluid patterns of the dance.[59]

Through the skillful coordination of a sweeping crane-mounted camera and continually shifting floor-level cameras, Brockway was also able to impart an extraordinary feeling of depth to a medium that needs all the three dimensionality it can get. His partiality towards diagonals was another tool to give TV dance a sense of spaciousness. Anna Kisselgoff singled out this feature when she commented on the program's excerpt from Balanchine's *Concerto Barocco*. "Anyone who has seen the ballet on stage knows that its patterns are usually seen from the front, not the side. Yet there are frequent diagonals in the ballet, and this spirit of the work is transmitted in the new diagonal created by the camera."[60]

Brockway's directorial vocabulary on this program also included some special effects, employed primarily during adagio passages. For example, during the second movement of *Concerto Barocco* a close-up view of the lead couple was slowly superimposed over a medium long shot of the group of women who accompanied them. At the end of an excerpt from Hans Van Manen's *Adagio Hammerklavier*, a similar feeling of lyric stillness was achieved by a few moments of slightly slowed down motion.

In contrast to the legato temperament of this episode on the Pennsylvania Ballet, Brockway's work on an earlier *Dance in America* program on Twyla Tharp emphasized the freewheeling quirkiness and light-headed speed that had made Tharp such a dance phenomenon in the 1970s. The two had collaborated once before on a 1971 *Camera Three* broadcast of *The Bix Pieces*, and their styles seemed to mesh. Through alert camera movement and a rhythmic sense of editing, Brockway had found a perfect way to capture the darting wit of *The Bix Pieces*' mixture of choreography and lecture as well as the casual brashness of Tharp's dance troupe. For their *Dance in America* program, Tharp and Brockway took a rather unusual approach, combining a performance of her 1930s inspired ballet *Sue's Leg* with a half-hour documentary, written by *New Yorker* dance critic Arlene Croce, on fads and trends in popular dance during the Depression years. The two sections were meant to play off of one another—brief shots of Tharp's dancers striking suitably apt poses were intercut throughout the documentary, and *Sue's Leg* used both the music and the styles featured in some of the 1930s footage—but the results were not completely successful. Though the giddy bounce and ease of Tharp's ballet was liltingly captured, the biggest problem was that Tharp's choreographic homage seemed oddly out of joint when so closely compared with the original dances seen in the documentary. As Anna Kisselgoff observed, "Unfortunately, the minute Bill "Bojangles" Robinson was seen stepping out of a car to do a tap dance on the roadway, Tharp was dead. The real thing was so much better that the so-called distillation turned out to be a trivialization of the significant."[61]

Dance in America's other presentation during its first season was a 90–minute program on the Martha Graham Dance Company. This too took a somewhat different format than the mixtures of history, documentary, and performance that typified the shows on the Joffrey and Pennsylvania Ballets or the innovative juxtapositions involved in the episode on Twyla Tharp. Instead, the program concentrated almost exclusively on the careful mounting of five of Graham's works, without including too much in the way of supplementary material, other than brief but utterly arresting introductions delivered by a regally poised Martha Graham herself.

The novel feature of this first *Dance in America* show devoted to Martha Graham (there would be a second three years later) was the decision by the producers to help finance one of the pieces. Graham was not only given money to buy a new set for *Adorations* but was also provided with a few weeks of extra rehearsal time to rechoreograph the work for the camera. The commission allowed her to eventually move the piece to Broadway. Despite an initial reluctance to come to terms with the medium's principles (at a preproduction meeting she began by stating "I don't like cameras; I've never liked cameras; I don't watch television!"[62]), Graham mastered TV technique, according to Merrill Brockway, "faster than anybody I have ever seen. She got it like *that*—what it was about, what the difference was—and she began adjusting."[63] The changes she made in *Adorations* were designed to improve the work's TV legibility by using the camera as an expressive tool rather than a simple documentary device. As she explained in an interview in the *Cultural Post*:

> Most things I'd done for a camera before had been just straight head on. This time we were endeavoring to use the camera creatively not just to record, but to convey the emotion of the dance. The TV screen tends to dehumanize, because of its size. You want to see the whole human body—that marvelous instrument—on the screen, and instead you see some ants crawling across. So we had to use close-ups, and special angles, to try to humanize the images.[64]

The other works on the program went through a similar process of camera adjustment and change. Particularly interesting was the treatment of the three solo pieces. *Frontier* was shot using mostly long shots, or extra long shots, to convey the fullness of the outdoors space surrounding Janet Eilber. *Lamentations*, on the other hand, was interrupted by frequent close-ups of Peggy Lyman's face that had the unfortunate effect of breaking the work's concentrated spell. Close-ups in *Medea's Dance of Vengeance* from *Cave of the Heart*, however, didn't detract from the piece's slow building fury. If anything, their selective use helped to intensify the power of Takako Asakawa's electrifying performance.

The program opened with the second television appearance of *Appalachian Spring*—the first was 19 years before on an early NET broadcast. The 1976 version had some obvious differences with its black-and-white, filmed predecessor. For one thing, color videotape technology provided a significant advance in terms of registered detail and clarity. The dance now seemed to sparkle rather than being bathed in gloomy shadows. Merrill Brockway's fluid, three-camera direction also eliminated some of the choppiness associated with the one-camera film technique of Peter Glushanok.

But the changes in the telecasts of *Appalachian Spring* were more than simply technical. In a provocative article examining the 1957 versus the 1976 versions, John Mueller observed that there had been substantial alterations in emphasis and characterization in the piece over the course of 19 years. "In general, the 1976 version is more athletically flamboyant, more decorative, more effusively and ingratiatingly theatrical," he wrote. "What gets lost is some of the directness, simplicity, and careful, unhurried articulation that can make this dance masterpiece so deeply moving."[65]

Dance in America's first season represented the largest single commitment to dance made by any network. The four programs helped establish new standards for intelligent, responsive "translations" of ballet and modern dance to television. They also had another important effect: they helped to increase exposure and attendance. Nearly five million people saw the series debut episode on the Joffrey Ballet (a figure which equalled almost half the number of paid attendances at dance concerts for all of 1975), and many viewers were obviously pleased by what they saw. In a survey conducted by the National Research Center of the Arts, 59 percent of the audience attending a Joffrey Ballet concert for the first time, seven weeks after the telecast, said the program had convinced them it might be interesting to see the company live. A similar effect was reported in England, where box office sales for Martha Graham zoomed the day after the BBC broadcast the episode featuring her company.

Diversity characterized the five shows of *Dance in America*'s second season as well. The first featured American Ballet Theatre. Since the company's history and philosophy had already been profiled on *A Close-Up in Time* four years earlier, this new program shifted its focus to complete performances of two of ABT's most popular works, *Billy the Kid* and *Les Patineurs*. Both ballets were intelligently directed by Merrill Brockway and photographed with extraordinary care. The sets, in particular, were unusually handsome and colorful. Like its previous TV incarnation on *Omnibus* in 1953, *Dance in America*'s *Billy the Kid* included short passages of narration, this time delivered by an offscreen Paul Newman. And like its TV predecessor, this 1976 version came under similar criticism for its efforts to explain and heighten the ballet's dramatic impulses. Marcia Siegel observed about the new rendition:

> At every point where Loring had originally worked with the proscenium stage and the ballet medium to create a nonliteral image, TV substituted narration, camera techniques, and cinematic editing to draw attention to the story, sacrificing most of the dance innovation that had distinguished the piece.[66]

Similar comments had been voiced by John Martin 25 years earlier when he accused *Omnibus* of turning the ballet into a Hollywood western. Though it's true that *Billy the Kid*'s more flavorful western themes are underscored somewhat excessively in both TV versions, it's also true, as Agnes de Mille once observed, that television, by its very nature, seems to emphasize the drama in dance movement to begin with.

The season's second episode was devoted to the mercurial, modern dance genius of Merce Cunningham and his dance company. The program was directed, once again, by Merrill Brockway, who had worked with Cunningham three years earlier for a special two-part installment of *Camera Three*. Given the somewhat broader mandate of *Dance in America*, it's not surprising that Cunningham's efforts for *Camera Three* were a bit more experimental in their scope and purpose. The 1974 program, entitled *A Video Event with Merce Cunningham*, offered a suggestive sampler of Cunningham's attempts to employ video technology in the structuring of his pieces. *TV Rerun* was shown using four screens simultaneously. Three screens were monitor images of what the three different studio cameras saw as they photographed the dancers, while the fourth screen featured a playback of Cunningham rehearsing his company in the same piece, taped in black and white at his studio at Westbeth. *Changing Steps* also used a four screen setup to emphasize the variety of coexisting perspectives by which dance could be seen.

For his *Dance in America* program, Cunningham arranged his selections with a greater sense of polish and flow. As Arlene Croce noted, "Cunningham understood television spectacle not only as environment but also as changing environment; his show was organized as if by channel selector, with a master's hand at the switch."[67] The excerpts from *Antic Meet*, *Scramble*, *Rainforest*, *Sounddance*, and *Video Triangle* were seamlessly woven together, with alternating cuts from one ballet to the next to the next and then back again. Original costumes and sets were also used, including Andy Warhol's famous silver inflated pillows for *Rainforest*, which made the fluid back and forth editing even more striking and colorful. In rearranging his choreography for television, Cunningham was particularly alert to the nuances of camera vision. As he told an interviewer, "What further appealed to me, was the idea that this [television] was another way of looking, like the stage is a way of looking at something, so is the camera a way—a poetic way of looking at something."[68] With its gentle, philosophical narrations by Cunningham and its shifting leaps from ballet to ballet, without the use of any fancy special effects, the program emerged as one of the most interesting hours *Dance in America* would ever produce.

The second season also included two well-crafted, profile shows on two strikingly different companies—the Dance Theatre of Harlem and the Pilobolus Dance Theater—and a new type of dance documentary that represented a departure from the series' mission of performance "translation." *Trailblazers of Modern Dance* combined interestingly assembled historical material on the careers of Isadora Duncan, Ruth St. Denis, and Ted Shawn with modern performances of their work (or pieces in the style of their work). Documentary footage examining Isadora Duncan's vivid dance life concluded with Sir Frederick Ashton's *Five Brahms Waltzes in the Manner of Isadora Duncan*, danced by Lynn Seymour. The section which focused on the impact of the Denishawn school and dancers ended with Ruth St. Denis-Doris Humphrey group dance *Soaring* and Ted Shawn's *Polonaise*, as reconstructed by Norman Walker.

From 1977 through 1979, during its third and fourth seasons, *Dance in America* presented a four-part series devoted to the choreography of George Balanchine. Through the years, Balanchine had had many unhappy experiences with American television, from CBS's broadcasts of *The Nutcracker* in the 1950s (which he attacked for the producers inability "to *want* to take the trouble or spend the time and money" to recreate the ballet's magic and enchantment[69]) to his disastrous experiences with *Noah and the Flood* in 1962. Beginning in the early 1960s, Canadian television offered Balanchine and the New York City Ballet an artistic refuge on their series, *L'Heure du Concert*. As Balanchine told Bernard Taper, the orientation of television north of the border was dramatically different:

> But we've found the whole approach in Canada freer and more workmanlike and more responsible than in America. It's noncommercial. There's a sense of responsibility. There's very little of that production panic I was talking about. . . . More time goes into preparing a program there. We all work together slowly, with thought. . . . I don't say that the final result in Canada is ideal or perfection, because the lens still effects some distortion in the dancers' lines; but there's no doubt it's better there.[70]

After one episode of *U.S.A.: Dance* in the mid–1960s, Balanchine stayed away from American commercial television for more than a decade. Finally, after more than a year and a half of negotiations, the staff of *Dance in America* was able to persuade him to work with the series by assuring him, according to Merrill Brockway, of "our willingness to trust the dancing without having all the glitz and fast sequences of shots."[71]

The four shows of the Balanchine series are, in many ways, an embodiment of *Dance in America*'s ability to responsively and lucidly capture dance spirit on television. The Balanchine works surveyed on the programs range from the melodramatic (*Tzigane*) to the classical (an excerpt from *Divertimento #15*), from the charming (*The Steadfast Tin Soldier*) to the ethereal (*Chaconne*), from the wittily expressionistic (*The Four Temperaments*) to the cooly modern (*Stravinsky Violin Concerto*); but all reflect a vivid determination to make stage dance legible and eloquent within the limits of the small screen. Typical of his choreographic process, Balanchine was flexibly alert to altering his ballets for new circumstances. As producer Emile Ardolino observed: "Great choreographers do not like to have their work fossilized. He changed things in *The Four Temperaments* and

"Emeralds" section of *Jewels* that he'd wanted to change for years. Many were just changes in detail. And some changes haven't been kept in the repertory."[72]

The alterations in the TV versions of Balanchine's work proved particularly stimulating to *New York Times* dance critic Anna Kisselgoff, who began an article examining the third program in the series by asking, "Can television make us see something that we cannot see onstage? The question is whether television can offer new insights into a familiar dance work and even modify our view of that work?"[73] In a stimulating analysis, she argued that the TV adaptations of both *The Prodigal Son* and *Chaconne* afforded intriguing new ways to view two of Balanchine's greatest works. In the case of the former, television's reduction of the ballet "to a series of pictures" prompted her to see how the medium's "pictorial emphasis" actually brought the work closer to its source in Alexander Pushkin's story "The Station Master."[74] For Kisselgoff, the TV version of *Chaconne* also provided a new perspective. This fourth reworking of the ballet was different than Balanchine's usual revisions. As she points out: "Mr. Balanchine has frequently revised his ballets. The direction has been to streamline them. In this case, the style of a Baroque court ballet has given way to a romantic reverie. Television has allowed us to see the subtext of the Balanchine Chaconne."[75]

This transformation was poetically heightened by the lyric quality of Merrill Brockway's direction which, through its dreamy dissolves between painted clouds and statuesque views of Suzanne Farrell and Peter Martins, made Balanchine's two premier dancers seem like poignant gods.

Dance in America's other productions during its third and fourth seasons included a nicely produced program profiling the Paul Taylor Dance Company, a full-length presentation by the San Francisco Ballet of Michael Smuin's *Romeo and Juliet*, a sprightly survey of the Feld Ballet, and a 90-minute, rechoreographed-for-TV version of Martha Graham's *Clytemnestra*, danced by the Graham Company. The latter ballet had to be cut almost in half, with the express purpose, as Graham put it, "not to deny the old but for the eye of the camera. I wanted this to be alive and vibrant for people. I felt I'd sacrifice 'choreographic' design for meaning, because I only use choreography to express meaning."[76]

The result was a program far more expressively dramatic than most *Dance in America* episodes. Beginning with Christopher Plummer's portentous retelling of the Clytemnestra legend, the production resembled a mythological landscape, with Ralph Holmes's heavy lighting effects, the powerful set designs of Isamu Noguchi, and Halston's shimmering costumes. Working in close collaboration with Martha Graham, Merrill Brockway departed from his customary use of smoothly flowing full-view shots of the dancers to a tighter, emphatic style, which relied on more close-ups, superimpositions, and cutting from different areas of the stage—all for the purpose of highlighting the ballet's strong narrative line.

Live from Lincoln Center and Videodance

The triumph of *Dance in America* was not PBS's only dance achievement during the latter half of the 1970s. There was also *Live from Lincoln Center*, a series that played an important role in establishing new standards for live dance telecasting. Ballet, specifically ballet performed by Lincoln Center's two principal dance tenants—American Ballet Theatre and the New York City Ballet— was featured at least once every season on the program's broadcasts through the end of the decade.

The series' hallmark was its ability to televise the happenings on Lincoln Center's various stages with a minimum of interference to the attending audience and with a sizeable degree of fidelity to the audience watching at home. New technologies, such as low-light cameras and special lenses, no longer made it necessary to overintensify and exaggerate stage lighting. Viewers could now see TV broadcasts which, at their best, approximated the conditions and the excitement of actually being at an event live. The dance programs on *Live from Lincoln Center* showed off the advantages of these new techniques superbly.

The foremost quality *Live from Lincoln Center* brought to dance telecasting was a sense of energy. From its first dance broadcast in June 1976 of *Swan Lake* with American Ballet Theatre, the series captured the sweep and thrill of live ballet in a way few TV programs ever had. This was partially due to the general pageantry of the ABT production and to Natalia Makarova's stunning Odette-Odille, but it was also the result of the carefully unobtrusive directorial style of Kirk Browning. Unlike most previous, live-dance TV directors, Browning avoided fancy angles and frantic cutting, preferring to use his four or five cameras (stationed in the New York State Theater's upper balcony, the middle of the first balcony, to the right of the stage, and at the center of the orchestra) primarily for the benefit of performance clarity.

Swan Lake, like most large cast ballets, posed a special challenge for a medium with limited depth and focus. How can the small screen reproduce the expansiveness of the stage and the dynamic shape of ensemble numbers? One approach would be to rely on long shots as a way of making sure that the full range of dance activity could at least be seen. The problem with this was that while the broad choreographic contours would be visible, nothing else would have any definition. Balcony views tend to reduce humans to the dimensions of inky gnats. Kirk Browning's solution was to use distant long shots only to convey the opening outline of a new scene or a broad dance piece and then to skillfully combine various mid-shots as a way to suggest the sweep of movement on the stage. Though not always successful (there are still times when it's difficult to figure out exactly what the choreographic shape of a number is), the technique is still an improvement over the generally haphazard style of most live dance telecasts of the past.

Where Browning clearly excelled was in his selective use of the close-up camera. His wide background in directing cultural programming on the commercial networks had obviously provided him with the ability to see arts performances in dramatically human terms. As his work on *Swan Lake* and subsequent *Live from Lincoln Center* broadcasts revealed, he knew how to make a stage ballet unfold with the speed and directness of a TV play. Kirk Browning's attachment to emphasizing story values, however, did not often fall prey to the perils of severe dance distortion. If anything, his highlighting of the key performers at a given moment more than likely mirrored the way an audience in the theater would probably be watching the ballet as well. Browning took special care with solo numbers or pas de deux, making certain to preserve an essential element of stage space around the dancers by usually relying on one, medium shot camera, positioned in the orchestra, that gracefully tracked the artists as they moved.

Still, there were limits to the types of dance best suited to this TV style. As Arlene Croce pointed out, "The trouble with broadcasting dance live is that only the nineteenth-century ballets, with their discursive mime scenes, which move the plot and allow for closeups, work in camera terms."[77] *Live from Lincoln Center* stuck fairly closely to the crowd-pleasing, three-act, grand ballet formula. *Swan Lake* was followed a year later by American Ballet Theatre's *Giselle*, then by *Coppelia* with the New York City Ballet, *Sleeping Beauty* with ABT, and then *La Bayadere* with the same company. Even its departure into an evening of shorter selections in 1978 stayed firmly within the boundaries of the nineteenth-century classical tradition (*Les Sylphides*, the Grand Pas de Deux from *Don Quixote*), and the pictorially grand twentieth-century classical tradition (Mikhail Fokine's *The Firebird* and Balanchine's *Theme and Variations*). Like the arts complex from which it broadcast, *Live from Lincoln Center* was aware of its audience's attachment to the more ordered glories of the past. Storybook ballets, with American Ballet Theatre's big name stars, were ideally suited to the medium's inherently dramatic eye and to PBS's refined appeal to its public.

Meanwhile, another form of TV dance was the subject of growing interest and experimentation. The form was called videodance; and it represented an intriguing merger between a new group of video artists, working mostly with small-scale equipment, and dancers and choreographers eager to see how television could alter and enhance dance. Videodance tapes were often shown in conjunction with live dance performances or as part of intermedia events, but because of their innovative, modernistic approach and their sometimes poor technical quality, they were rarely aired on broadcast television. The one prominent exception was the PBS affiliate in Boston, WGBH, which actively encouraged videodance production and telecasting. As part of its New Television Workshop, the station had set up a special Dance Project in 1974 to "explore ways of breaking down the barriers between the worlds of dance and video" and, in the words of current project director Susan Dowling, "to commission artists to create new works for video—and in the process, to create new video art forms."[78]

Though produced with extremely low budgets, many of the pieces which emerged from the WGBH Dance Project offered exciting approaches to what video technology can do for dance. For example, Rudy Perez's *District 1*, directed and produced by Fred Barzyk, used a variety of sophisticated editing techniques to help shape the rhythmic qualities of Perez's cheerfully inventive choreography. To the sound of a teletype, dancers, shot on location at Boston's Government Center, were initially seen in frozen postures, only to then be shown leaping back and forth against concrete walls. A sequence involving a merry-go-round featured still frames at the end of each dance phrase, accompanied by clanging bells, gongs, and electronic sound effects.

Yet perhaps because of their experimental attitudes and non-traditional subject matter, PBS has generally been reluctant to broadcast many examples of videodance. Only three of the WGBH pieces were aired on the network nationally. (*District 1* and Dan Wagoner's *George's House* were seen as part of a 1976 mini-series *Dance for Camera*; the other, *Tzaddik* was a stage work by Eliot Feld translated for television by producer/director Rick Hauser.) A type of videodance which did, however, fit the network's format a bit more comfortably was Twyla Tharp's 1978 program *Making TV Dance*. Unlike the conceptually ambitious, somewhat distanced video efforts of Merce Cunningham, Tharp's sprightly personality and choreographic wit helped make her venture in technology and dance seem both charming and accessible. Co-produced by WNET in New York, *Making TV Dance* was a survey of Tharp's year-long experiment at the station's Television Laboratory, where she was given free reign to try any approaches that suited her fancy. Alternating black-and-white rehearsal scenes with color sequences of her videodances, the program provided an appealing introduction to the many ways technology could help create a new type of choreography. In a series of four pieces, taped at four different dance studios, she compiled a virtual catalog of videodance techniques. *Etude on Focus* employed double images; *Etude on Speed* relied on multiple images at varying speeds; *Etude on Repetition* used repeated sequences; *Etude on Retrograde* experimented with passages run in reverse. Other parts of the program included a fascinating but essentially extraneous scene of Tharp and Mikhail Baryshnikov rehearsing her ballet *Sinatra Songs*, as well as presentations of *The Event* (which consisted of a square dance sequence taped in Nashville with multiple images and keying effects added later in the studio) and *Borderline* (a solo number which displayed only Tharp's video-enhanced outline).

The Commercial Networks During the 1970s

While PBS can be criticized for its relative indifference to the growing avant-garde interest in videodance, the overall achievements of the network in terms of dance programming during the 1970s were undeniably spectacular. Never before had so much intelligently produced dance been seen so regularly on television by so many. *Dance in America*'s impact even went beyond the medium: it helped boost the live concert attendance of every company it profiled.

The commercial networks, meanwhile, were devoting less time to dance than ever before. With the demise of the broadly oriented, variety format in the early 1970s (the giant of the breed, *The Ed Sullivan Show*, went off the air in 1971, after 23 years), there was very little space left for classical, or even popular, dance in prime time. Still, as the ballet world's chief emissary, Rudolf Nureyev managed to appear every so often on various types of entertainment specials. In 1971, for example, he performed an excerpt from Paul Taylor's *Big Bertha* with Bettie de John on a Burt Bacharach special. Two years later, he was seen on ABC's *Wide World of Entertainment* in a selection from Balanchine's *The Prodigal Son*. In 1974, he was interviewed on *60 Minutes*.

But with the exception of Nureyev, classical dance on commercial television was now largely relegated to the status of an extraordinary special event, at the very time that interest in serious dance was growing throughout the country. One area, however, where ballet and modern dance could still be occasionally seen was in children's programming, especially on CBS. Following the lead of its landmark *Young People's Concerts* series, the network instituted *Festival of the Lively Arts for Young People*, which presented numerous dance events. Two installments featured the choreography and dancing of Edward Villella. The first, broadcast in 1974, was an original ballet entitled *Harlequin*, with Rebecca Wright and the National Ballet of Canada. Villella followed this two years later with a program called *Dance of the Athletes*, which, like the famous Gene Kelly *Omnibus* episode *A Man Who Dances*, set out to demonstrate the correspondences between athletics and dancing, using such sports figures as Tom Seaver, Bob Griese, Virginia Wade, and Muriel Grossfield. CBS also commissioned Alvin Ailey to create a series of six dances to the music of Duke Ellington for another *Festival of the Lively Arts for Young People* program, this one telecast in 1974 and introduced by pop singer Gladys Knight.

Recognizing that ballet programs needed some type of commercial sparkle if they were to be going to be even mildly competitive in the ratings, both CBS and NBC made it a point to use celebrities from outside the world of dance to introduce their special cultural events. The tradition was not a new one. David Wayne spent the first ten minutes of NBC's 1956 broadcast of Ashton's *Sleeping Beauty* telling the story to a group of children; June Lockhart narrated Balanchine's *The Nutcracker* on CBS in 1959; and Eddie Albert performed the same task for a West German version of the ballet which CBS imported in 1965. In keeping with the fiercer Nielsen climate, the mid–1970s version of the system made star status a bit more important. CBS's 1976 broadcast of the Bolshoi Ballet's *Romeo and Juliet* featured one of the network's most popular personalities, Mary Tyler Moore, as a rather ill-at-ease mistress of ceremonies and interviewer. Not to be outdone, NBC employed former First Lady Betty Ford to host their Bolshoi presentation of *The Nutcracker* in 1977. NBC also featured two more programs devoted to Russian ballet during the late 1970s—a special on the Moiseyev dancers hosted by Orson Welles in 1977 and a 1979 performance of *Giselle* with the Bolshoi Ballet, hosted by Edward Villella—as part of a general boosting of Russian culture prior to their planned, but ultimately ill-fated, broadcasting of the 1980 Moscow Olympics.

Ever eager for star talent and promotable personalities, the three commercial networks increased their enthusiasm for classical dance somewhat with the defection of Mikhail Baryshnikov in 1974. Like Nureyev before him, Baryshnikov captivated the public not only because of the romance of his flight to the West but also because of his dazzling feats of elevation. It took a while for Baryshnikov to become popular (As Arlene Croce remarked in January 1975 a few months after his defection, "If Ed Sullivan and the 'Bell Telephone Hour' were still in business, Mikhail Baryshnikov would be known to millions more Americans than know him today."[79]), but gradually he began to be seen on a variety of different programs.

By the end of 1977, Baryshnikov had appeared on CBS's *Camera Three*, an *ABC News Closeup*, twice on PBS, and in a special Christmas season telecast of his new American Ballet Theatre version of *The Nutcracker* on CBS. The latter program was not just one of the network's first non-imported ballet presentations in many years, but also one of the most handsome commercial dance broadcasts ever offered, mirroring the kind of transparent approach to dance pioneered by PBS. Baryshnikov's darker version of the familiar ballet, emphasizing Clara's "psychology" and containing no child performers, was nicely directed by Tony Charmoli, who captured the dancing's charm, without overusing the far easier enchantments of special effects. The program set a precedent in its use of a hand-held minicam camera as a way to literally walk into the dance action. Though Charmoli employed the technique selectively, it seemed to work best only when it followed the sweep and movement of Baryshnikov's daring leaps. As a tool for offering new dance "angles," such as tipping the camera on its side, minicam technology quickly proved itself to be as capable of misuse as any other electronic device.

As a measure of how far Baryshnikov's star continued to rise, it's only necessary to note the range and number of his TV performances during the next few years. In 1978 he appeared five different times: in an ABT sampler on *Live from Lincoln Center*, as a partner for Twyla Tharp on her PBS program *Making TV Dance*, twice on *Dance in America*, and in a special telecast of *Sleeping Beauty*, with the Royal Ballet, transmitted from London by satellite and broadcast in the United States by Metromedia. In 1979, he turned up on practically every network. He was interviewed on CBS's *60 Minutes*, a guest on NBC's *Bob Hope in China*, and taped in a performance at the White House on PBS. A year later, ABC would use his talents in the kind of popular TV breakthrough ballet dancers of the past could only dream of—as the star of a slick, prime-time special with Liza Minelli celebrating *Baryshnikov on Broadway*. CBS featured him in west coast surroundings on *Baryshnikov in Hollywood* in 1982.

Baryshnikov's American TV debut in 1975 took place on one of the few commercial network programs where dance still had a featured place—CBS's *Camera Three*. Throughout the 1970s, the always unsponsored *Camera Three* devoted at least several shows a year to dance in all its forms. Executive producer Merrill Brockway, who remained with the program until 1975 when he left for *Dance in America*, continued to use *Camera Three* as a forum for international dance (featured companies included the Goddess Dancers of Cambodia, the National Dance Company of Morocco, the Sierra Leone National Dance Company, and the Darpana Dance Company of India), as well as encouraging close collaborations with choreographers eager to explore the medium. Two of *Camera Three*'s most celebrated productions were Brockway-directed programs that highlighted the special properties television could bring to dance. The first was a 1973 show with Twyla Tharp and her company in a performance of her *Bix Pieces*. The work's mixture of dancing and confessional lecture (delivered by actress Marion Haley)/demonstration (delivered by Tharp) provided an arresting combination on the small screen. Merce Cunningham's two-part show a year later, *A Video Event with Merce Cunningham*, appeared equally in tune with the medium's demands, though from an entirely different perspective. Rather than stress television's affinity for the personal and the emotionally dramatic, Cunningham employed its technological arsenal to explore his more distanced choreographic views. By electronically combining four screens showing the same dance event, but from varying angles, Cunningham was able to create a unique way of seeing unavilable to anyone in a theater. Television permitted him the chance to experiment with new approaches to simultaneity and juxtaposition and, as *A Video Event* reveals, to lead viewers on a fascinating journey through a dance time and space reconstructed by technology.

During the 1970s, *Camera Three* also presented programs on Maurice Béjart, the Pennsylvania Ballet, the Metropolitan Opera Ballet Ensemble, a discussion program on the filming of the ballet sequences in *The Turning Point*, and an ambitious staging of Anna Sokolow's Holocaust-inspired ballet *Dreams*, directed by Roger Englander in an old warehouse building in New York. After the series was cancelled on CBS in 1979, it moved to PBS for a few seasons, where two other dance programs were produced: one on Paul Draper and tap dancing, and one in which three ballroom dance teams teach the basics of their style to members of the American Dance Machine.

TV Dance in the 1980s—PBS

As *Dance in America* moved into its fifth season at the start of 1980, the series' focus and style underwent a modification. The major American dance company profiles and repertory "translations" that had been the program's signature began to be supplemented by an expanded definition of mission and approach. An example of this was an April 1980 show entitled *Divine Drumbeats: Katherine Dunham and Her People*. After a panel of experts in 1979 recommended to the National Endowment of the Arts that *Dance in America* should no longer be solely an archivist, the NEA, one of the series' three primary funders, in turn suggested a program on black dance. Noted dancer, choreographer, and longtime champion of black dance Katherine Dunham was selected to be the show's focus. The hour-long episode offered a whirlwind tour not only of Dunham's varied career, including excerpts from her Hollywood films, but also of the history of Haiti and its native dancing. In an unusual move for the series, a camera crew actually accompanied Dunham to Haiti to visit a village whose dances she had studied in the early 1930s and to provide background for the ballet that was the program's centerpiece—*Rites de Passage*.

Dance in America's first show of the fifth season was also a departure of sorts. *Two Duets* was not a company profile or historical documentary but a close study of Jerome Robbins rehearsing Natalia Makarova and Mikhail Baryshnikov in his *Other Dances*, followed by a performance of the piece and of Peter Martins's *Calcium Light Night*. This was Robbins's first *Dance in America* participation and, as a result of his previous TV experience and his frequently voiced dislike of TV dance, he demanded several things that would make his segment less subject to electronic distortion and studio interference. In direct contrast to previous programs, *Other Dances* was to be shot on film and performed live in a theater before an audience. Robbins insisted on film for a specific reason. As director

Emile Ardolino explained, Robbins wanted the ballet "to have the softer, romantic qualities of film, and the sense film gives that you're watching something that happened a while ago, as opposed to the immediacy of videotape."[80] *Calcium Light Night*, on the other hand, was done in the traditional *Dance in America* method—on tape, in a studio, with precisely controlled conditions. Though there is a sharp contrast between the production techniques of the two dances, it's nevertheless appropriate for their respective styles. The lyrical sweep of Robbins's ballet seems best expressed in the muted shadings of film, while the brittle wit and design of Martins's duet is ideally suited for videotape's sharp clarity.

For its third production of the 1980 season, *Dance in America* finally devoted an entire program to the previously neglected contributions of contemporary avant-garde dancers. *Beyond the Mainstream* presented selections from the choreography of Steve Paxton, Laura Dean, Kei Takei, Yvonne Rainer, Trisha Brown, and David Gordon, with brief documentary excerpts and interviews to help orient viewers new to the style of post-modern dance. Taped in what appeared to be the auditorium of an old New York City public school, the program deliberately veered away from the sometimes overly slick veneer of former *Dance in America* profiles. Instead, the emphasis was on the "process" situations of these works and the new types of meanings and approaches these pieces attempt to produce. Director Merrill Brockway, fearful that the repetitive elements of their dances would bore the TV audience, was insistent that the show's choreographers edit their work down for television. Laura Dean, for example, cut her *Dance* from its original length of 35 minutes to six. Similar excisions were practiced on the show's other pieces, with the result that no single work was seen in its entirety. While this potpourri approach annoyed some critics (David Vaughan in *Ballet News* felt that by deliberately catering to the attention span of the so-called average viewer "something fundamental to the aesthetics of post-modern dance gets lost in the shuffle."[81]), it probably was the right decision. Given the traditional kinds of dance and the elegant presentations which have been typical of *Dance in America* and other PBS offerings, it is doubtful if any but the most enthusiastic dance partisans would have tolerated full length, unedited avant-garde performances. Whatever sacrifices *Beyond the Mainstream* may have made in authenticity and completeness, it tried to offset with an accessible survey of a far too infrequently seen dancing style.

The variety characteristic of *Dance in America*'s fifth season continued during the series' sixth year in 1981. The season opened with Rudolf Nureyev and the Joffrey Ballet in a colorful tribute to Vaslav Nijinsky. Three of the ballets most closely associated with the dancer (*Petrouchka*, *La Spectre de la Rose*, and *L'Apres-midi d'un Faune*) were performed by an energetic Nureyev, here only slightly past his prime. The program featured settings close to the original Ballet Russe designs and was vividly directed by Emile Ardolino. Ardolino also directed the season's three other installments: a live broadcast of Michael Smuin's *The Tempest*, with the San Francisco Ballet; a concert appearance of American Ballet Theatre in nineteenth-century classical ballet standards; and *Dance in America*'s first made-for-television work, Balanchine's *L'Enfant et les Sortilèges*. Balanchine had previously created three stage versions of the Maurice Ravel opera, including its premiere in 1925, but had always been disappointed by the results. Television represented a new, challenging arena for his ideas. *Dance in America*'s executive producer, Jac Venza, remarked that Balanchine's "explanation for wanting to do the piece was that we could use other techniques—we could use scale differently, we could use puppets, things that never worked in the theater."[82]

Working with collaborator Kermit Love, designer of *The Muppets*, Balanchine used the medium to weave a spell of intimate fantasy. His choreography even went so far as to take occasional cues from the latest tricks of video technology. Teapots and cups magically dissolved into dancers; two-dimensional drawings of shepherds and shepherdesses plumped themselves out into human form, after being lifted dreamily from a sheet of torn wallpaper.

Balanchine also made other changes in his TV version of *L'Enfant* to express, in a way the stage couldn't, the opera's childlike sense of reality and wonder. Not only was the work now performed for the first time in English, but the lead was actually played and sung by a ten-year-old boy, instead of the customary soprano. As Balanchine noted: "It's an easier thing to make *L'Enfant* for television than it is to adapt ballets made for our enormous stage. People can listen to the words. The clock can walk. . . . And we rearrange things so that it looks nearer—the squirrels are closer, the frog is there talking."[83]

Yet despite the alterations and additions and Kermit Love's marvelously inventive costumes, the production was a bit stilted. The special effects, while interesting to observe, rarely appeared to serve the choreography and ended up, like most choreographic video effects, as bordering on the intrusive. Even the small portions of the program devoted to dancing (Balanchine made it clear that this was not a ballet but a remounting of an opera) seldom rose into the kind of spirited enchantment the production so obviously was hoping to achieve. Only at the end, in a final, simple processional of brilliantly costumed frogs, dragonflies and other wildlife did this TV version quietly leap into another realm. Director Emile Ardolino observed that neither he "nor Balanchine was totally satisfied with the result,"[84] a condition which he blames primarily on budget and production problems. "Even though we had eleven days in the studio," Ardolino remarked, "it was not enough time. He [Balanchine] couldn't really choreograph until we got into the studio, until he saw the effects."[85] Ambitious in scope, *L'Enfant et les Sortilèges* emerged as a project more interesting for what it revealed of Balanchine's method of TV creation than for its durability and resonance as an original work for the medium.

In 1982, *Dance in America*'s two senior producers, Merrill Brockway and Emile Ardolino, left the series, and Edward Villella was named as their replacement for a season. His only project as director and co-producer was *Bournonville Dances*, an hour show featuring rehearsal footage and excerpts from the New York City Ballet's *Bournonville Divertissements*, staged by Stanley Williams.

Dance in America's eighth season during 1982–83 reflected the series' continuing evolution. By this point, it had profiled most of the major American dance companies and documented the principal American dance movements. Its programs now began to focus more on full-length performances drawn from the repertories of groups they had worked with in the past. In December 1982, the Joffrey Ballet made their third appearance in a complete version of Kurt Jooss's ballet *The Green Table*. Jooss had been flown in especially to help coach the company for the excerpts they had performed on their 1976 program. With his death in 1979, his daughter Anna Markard took over the task, not only working with the dancers to insure the work's original shape and vision but also helping to produce the show as well. The resulting program was strikingly effective, primarily because this most dramatic of ballets was ideally suited for television. Its powerful but easily grasped storyline and its gripping expressionistic form came across vividly on even the smallest of screens. As John Gruen observed, "Unlike more elaborate works, 'The Green Table' profited from the confinements of the cameras because Jooss's particular spareness of choreographic design could be captured without loss or fuzziness of detail."[86] After the ballet's performance, the program concluded with a well-produced, 18–minute documentary, written by critic Tobi Tobias, on Jooss's dance career.

The 1982–83 season also included two shows devoted to new choreography. Twyla Tharp's *The Catherine Wheel* had received its premiere on Broadway the year before. The TV version, which was done on film and co-produced with the BBC, was a curiously disorienting amalgam of special effects, jumpy editing techniques, and a nearly impossible-to-follow storyline involving, among other things, a bizarrely cartoonish "American" family and a masked chorus with Sara Rudner as its leader. The addition of a computerized, whirling, circlelike figure, which appeared throughout Rudner's dances during the first part of the hour, only complicated matters further. *The Catherine Wheel* calmed down a bit during its final third, when it offered an extended sequence of gimmick-free dancing, but on the whole the program was among *Dance in America*'s least successful efforts. In contrast, the series' next installment, Peter Martins's *The Magic Flute*, had an entirely different problem. It seemed far too simple and uncomplicated a ballet to merit full-length presentation. Even the work's small charms tended to get lost in the taped-in-performance approach the program adopted. The vast spaces of the New York State Theater's stage had to be made legible for the TV cameras, which meant, in this case, an unfortunate reliance on the part of director Merrill Brockway to employ frequent close-ups and rapid cutting to keep the action moving. While this helped clarify *The Magic Flute*'s storyline, it also inevitably minimized some of the ballet's gentle sense of scale and movement.

The difficulties of "in theater" dance telecasting were also encountered by director Emile Ardolino in two *Live from Lincoln Center* programs taped during the New York City Ballet's Stravinsky Festival held in May 1982. The challenge of the occasion was particularly formidable. How could the small screen possibly capture the intricacy, daring, and sweep of Balanchine works performed in a theater? A ballet like *Agon*, which spreads across the stage and sometimes employs over a dozen dancers in endlessly changing, arresting configurations, would be rendered virtually meaningless on television. Rather than pursue intimacy through close-ups, the customary route of most live telecasting, Ardolino wisely chose to preserve as much of Balanchine's choreographic design as possible, even at the expense of total picture clarity and detail. Works with a smaller scale or a tauter narrative line, such as *Apollo* and *Orpheus*, managed to survive the transition fairly well, despite some occasionally erratic editing decisions. Larger enterprises were notably less successful. The oratorio/ballet *Persephone* emerged as even more bloated than it had been on stage, and the glorious structural beauty of *Agon* was, for the most part, lost, largely as a result of the medium's inability to make a long shot of a group of dancers look like anything more than a collection of tiny specks.

A New York City Ballet program taped a year later proved, however, that it is possible to broadcast large ensemble dance pieces from a proscenium stage without invariably sacrificing all sense of scope. Entitled *A Lincoln Center Special: New York City Ballet Tribute to George Balanchine* and directed once again by Emile Ardolino, the show featured two of Balanchine's most populous ballets, the sensuously elegant *Vienna Waltzes* and the effervescent *Who Cares*, as well as his luminous chamber work, *Mozartiana*. All three pieces presented special problems of space and design. *Vienna Waltzes* lyrically sweeps across the entire stage and concludes with a glittering array of nearly 100 waltzing dancers. The frequent ensemble numbers of *Who Cares* are choreographed in such a way that it becomes very difficult to fracture the dance line with any type of close camera perspectives. And in *Mozartiana* the corps of supporting dancers, while not large, must never be lost sight of due to their importance in suggesting the work's almost spiritual structure. Emile Ardolino's solutions depended on maintaining a beautiful feeling of balance between longer views from cameras in the balconies, delicately employed medium shots, and just a few close-up shots from the orchestra. A sumptuous ballet like *Vienna*

Waltzes, which would seem by its very nature to defy the squeezing down demanded by the small screen, made the transition to television in surprisingly fine form. The cameras may not have been able to reproduce the work's expansiveness, but they were able to capture its romance and flavor. Even its final section, with its dozens of magnificently attired dancers, waltzing across a mirrored, chandelier-lit stage, looked dazzling, thanks to a skillful blending of various types of full-view long shots, subtly caught reflections from the rear mirrors, and the vivid contrast of the black tuxedos of the men with the bejeweled white gowns worn by the women. The smaller scale glories of *Mozartiana* were also preserved through an approach which sensitively stressed the ballet's spatial integrity. Close-ups were generally resisted in favor of wider views revealing the significant formal relationships linking the dancers with one another.

An interesting, though not very successful, contrast to this gracefully nuanced treatment was provided by the opening program of *Dance in America*'s 1983–84 season. Michael Smuin's homage to the pride and desperation of American Indians, *A Song for Dead Warriors*, was without question the most explicitly dramatic ballet the series had ever run. Certainly no other dance show in TV history was preceded by a warning that it contained material unsuitable for children. The challenge for director Merrill Brockway was not only to capture the work's raw power (a task he met largely by emphasizing its scenes of beatings, rape, and murders with harsh close-ups) but also to find a suitable TV method for integrating the old and new photographs which are projected on a scrim in front of the dancers during stage performances. The latter task was accomplished by shooting the ballet in a studio resembling a large black box, so that the pictures could be overlayed on this neutral background. The results were often impressive, especially as the dancers moved through translucent images of clouds or forests or, in one instance, around a herd of buffalo. Nevertheless, while the production's technological wizardry and its extraordinary lighting effects enhanced the ballet's flavor, they also underscored its melodramatic excesses and choreographic gimmickry. Despite being framed by an earnest documentary on American Indian history and a heartfelt explanation by Michael Smuin on how he came to create the piece, *A Song for Dead Warriors* came across as gaudy and slickly superficial.

The series returned to its customary lean elegance with a February 1984 program focusing on Peter Martins's Stravinsky piano ballets. Subtitled *A Choreographer's Notebook*, the episode offered a rare glimpse into the variety of forces which prompt dance creation. In the case of Peter Martins, these forces often depended on circumstances. The New York City Ballet needed a new piece for a Stravinsky festival, and Martins's mentor, George Balanchine, urged him to create one. Scenes of Martins explaining the origins of a particular ballet were followed by a few minutes of rehearsal footage and finally with a performance of the work itself filmed in front of a pastel blue backdrop from the stage of the New York State Theater. The four ballets featured on the program were directed by Merrill Brockway from a proscenium perspective. There were no side shots taken from the stage, but because the majority of the pieces were small in scale, there was a pleasant feeling of intimacy and forthrightness that made the dances seem like they were shot in the more controlled atmosphere of a studio.

Dance in America's 1984 season also included a festive concert performance by American Ballet Theatre of *Don Quixote*, taped at the Metropolitan Opera House and directed, with an alert sense of the drama of the diagonal line, by Brian Large. Appropriately, the year concluded with a stirring tribute to the century's greatest choreographer, the late George Balanchine, reminding viewers not only of the extraordinary scope of his achievements but also how well some of his ballets had been brought to TV life by *Dance in America*'s sensitively attuned approach.

With *Baryshnikov by Tharp*, the series' tenth season began on a flashy, glimmering note. While it often resembled a slick and rather cutesy commercial network special, the program nonetheless provided Mikhail Baryshnikov with possibly his best TV forum. The ballets choreographed for him by Twyla Tharp exploited the range and daring of his talent, from graceful courtier in *The Little Ballet* to frisky toughguy and elegiac night wanderer of *The Sinatra Suite* and the frenetically elastic clown of *Push Comes to Shove*. The three works were imaginatively staged, using bold lighting effects and dramatic camera placements to underscore Tharp's choreographic tension and wit. Particularly noteworthy was the taping of *Push Comes to Shove*, which employed all the resources of a disciplined studio environment (fluid and mobile camerawork and intricate spotlighting patterns) even though it was performed in front of a live audience.

The series' tenth season also featured another American Ballet Theatre concert, taped at the Metropolitan Opera. Director Brian Large faced the challenge of filming the large corps de ballet in works like *Les Sylphides* and *Paquita* by steadfastly using long shots from the balcony, with very little cutting. Though the dancers sometimes resembled white blurs, the choreographic line of each ballet was still carefully preserved.

PBS's other dance programs during the period came in a diversity of formats. A 1982 *Kennedy Center Tonight* featuring the Dance Theatre of Harlem combined a stirring documentary on the company rehearsing John Taras's *The Firebird* with an actual taped-in-concert performance of the work. In contrast, a 1983 telecast of Ruth Page's *The Merry Widow* was filmed entirely in the studio. Unfortunately, the ballet's undistinguished choreography and director Dick Carter's overly dramatic close-ups and clumsy efforts at soft focus lyricism made it painfully clear that not every dance program could aspire to the high standards of *Dance in America*. The network also aired Agnes de Mille's 1978 lecture/demonstration, *Conversations about the Dance*, which resembled the style of her famous *Om-*

nibus programs but, because of a recent stroke, left a still forceful de Mille to present her material seated in a chair.

In 1985, *Great Performances*, the umbrella series that contained *Dance in America* as one of its elements, broadcast Chris Hegedus and D.A. Pennebaker's lively concert documentary, *Dance Black America*. A record of a festival celebrating old and new black dance held over the course of four nights at the Brooklyn Academy of Music, the program intermixed backstage views, warmup scenes, and historic footage with performances by a variety of dance companies (the Charles Moore Dance Theatre, the Chuck Davis Dance Company, Garth Fagan's The Bucket Dance Company, the Alvin Ailey Dance Theater) along with virtuoso displays of tapdancing by Chuck Green, breakdancing by the Magnificent Force, and choreographic jump-roping by the Jazzy Jumpers. In contrast to the sometimes overly bright and glossy, videotape veneer of many *Dance in America* presentations, *Dance Black America* was shot on film, often with hand-held cameras—an effect which made the show, with its deliberate moments of informality, appear much warmer and inviting.

Beginning in 1980, PBS also showed itself to be an adept repackager of the old time variety format. Its annual *Gala of Stars* was essentially an all-cultural *Ed Sullivan Show*, and, like the latter, it invariably contained a brief classical dance number. In 1981 Gelsey Kirkland performed the standby of many a *Bell Telephone Hour*: *The Dying Swan*. In 1982, Bart Cook and Merrill Ashley danced the pas de deux from Balanchine's *Stars and Stripes*. Suzanne Farrell and Sean Lavery were seen on the program's 1983 edition in a sparkling performance of the pas de deux from Balanchine's *Chaconne*. A larger dance extravaganza took place in May 1984 with the telecast of *In Concert at the Met*, a three-and-a-half-hour salute to the non-operatic events performed at both the old and new Metropolitan Opera House. Dancers and former dancers flew in from around the world to be part of the event, including Nureyev, Carla Fracci, Natalia Makarova, Margot Fonteyn, Lynn Seymour, and Frederick Ashton. Among the many highlights was a thrilling Act II pas de deux from *Giselle*, performed by Alicia Alonso and Jorge Esquivel, a brief waltz danced by Alexandra Danilova and Frederick Franklin from *Gaite Parisienne*, and a fairy-tale version of *La Spectre de la Rose* with Patrick Dupond and actress Lillian Gish.

PBS also continued to import many foreign dance programs, including Margot Fonteyn's lackluster documentary series, *The Magic of Dance*, as well as venturing into an area best left to its commercial competitors—the murky waters of celebrity profiles. Its 1983 show, *Godunov: The World To Dance In*, not only tried to make the shaky case that Alexander Godunov was one of the world's great dancers but supported its arguments with far too few dance excerpts and far too much "candid" footage of Godunov shopping and being surrounded by beautiful women.

Dance on the Commercial Networks in the 1980s

As PBS generally continued to refine its techniques and expand the scope of its dance presentations during the 1980s, the commercial networks, for the most part, abandoned their interest in dance, except on extremely rare occasions when prestige concerns overruled more hard-edged programming judgements. One such instance was NBC's short-lived arts showcase, *Live from Studio 8H*. In July 1980, the series devoted 90 minutes to the work of Jerome Robbins, a choreographer who has always voiced his strong objections to television's treatment of dance. Certainly the results of the show would have done little to change his opinion. As directed by Rodney Greenberg, the program was a peculiarly listless affair that seemed to miss the flavor of every Robbins piece that was broadcast. In contrast to the reverential attitudes towards "translation" characteristic of *Dance in America*, *Live from Studio 8H* tended to discolor and overdramatize its Robbins sampler. *Fancy Free*'s athleticism was highlighted, with little sense of its charm. Selections from *Dances at a Gathering* were performed in a "rehearsal" setting, complete with stage ladders, bright lighting, and dancers suddenly walking into and out of their parts, that, in the words of John Gruen, "played havoc with continuity, intimacy, and structure."[87] In the most grievous instance, the evocative tenseness and mystery of *Afternoon of a Faun* was transformed into a merely pretty, earthbound vehicle. The televised version not only mistakenly reached for literalism by giving the dancers an actual mirror to look into but also displayed a rather dewy-eyed romanticism through continual soft focus and hazy lighting that was entirely inappropriate.

ABC fared a little better, though with an enterprise of much smaller range, in a short dance segment by Twyla Tharp included on its brief revival of *Omnibus* in June 1980. Tharp's choreography for a trio consisting of herself, Peter Martins, and Pittsburgh Steeler Lynn Swann was a fast-paced, sassy piece based on movements drawn from football. While not very substantial, the work at least had the virtues of cleverness, which made it stand out from the solemnly self-inflated offerings that surrounded it. ABC's one other dance presentation during the early 1980s was more representative of the network's customary disinterest in original dance programming throughout the past 25 years—a repeat of the Royal Ballet's *Sleeping Beauty*, which had been seen on the Metromedia stations the previous New Year's Eve.

Meanwhile, both NBC and CBS began occasional broadcasts of a new type of high-style variety show—salutes to new presidents or distinguished national arts figures originating from the Kennedy Center in Washington, D.C. Dance was usually featured as one of the key program elements. NBC's *The Stars Salute the President*, telecast in March 1981, included performances by Natalia Makarova and Gelsey Kirkland. CBS's *Kennedy Center Honors: A Celebration of the Performing Arts* was an annual special event that generally highlighted the achievements of a prominent choreographer among its five honorees. George Balanchine was celebrated on the program's first broadcast in 1978; Martha Graham, on its second in 1979; Agnes de Mille, on its third in 1980; Jerome Robbins, in 1981; and Katherine Dunham, in 1983.

The only other commercial network dance events during the period were, characteristically, broadcast in the afternoons, far removed from the prime-time ratings fray, and targeted to children. In November 1980 CBS aired another installment of its *Festival of the Lively Arts for Young People*, this one entitled *Julie Andrews' Invitation to the Dance*, taped at a concert the previous summer at the Merriweather Post Pavillion in Columbia, Maryland. Andrews proved a genial hostess for a show that attempted to glide over the main events in dance history, with demonstrations of folk dancing, classical ballet with Rudolf Nureyev, Martha Graham's technique with Peggy Lyman, and Broadway-style hoofing. In October 1983, NBC broadcast a lively documentary about Jacques D'Amboise's remarkable National Dance Institute, a project which takes D'Amboise and other professional dancers out to the New York City public schools to choreograph dozens of eager schoolchildren for an annual dance extravaganza at Madison Square Garden. *He Makes Me Feel Like Dancin'* was originally scheduled for prime-time airing as part of NBC's *Project Peacock*, but, according to director Emile Ardolino, the network, fearful that no one would be interested in a dance program for kids, decided to push it back to the afternoon.[88] The reviews for the program were so favorable, however, that the network was forced to concede that yes, maybe there might be an audience for such happy fare, and eventually the show was rebroadcast at an early prime-time hour. The show later went on to win both the Emmy and the Oscar for best documentary.

The Cable Networks and Dance

While the commercial networks were taking less and less interest in dance and PBS was encountering increased budgetary difficulties, there was one place in the early 1980s which promised to be a mecca for all types of arts-related television—the newly formed, and widely heralded, cultural cable networks. These cable networks offered a small flood of culturally oriented programming, with dozens of classical and modern dance shows among the more prominent attractions. CBS Cable, which began operations in October 1981, was typical in its commitment to dance as one of the most active components of its schedule. Hired from *Dance in America* to head the network's arts programming, Merrill Brockway featured a wide variety of dance shows during CBS Cable's sadly abbreviated lifespan (the network was on the air for only 11 months). Intelligently produced classical dance programs from overseas alternated with several intriguing original efforts. Perhaps the most notable was Brockway's elegantly directed version of Balanchine's *Robert Schumann's Davidsbundlertanze*. This haunting, ambiguous chamber ballet for four couples lent itself especially well to television, by virtue of both its small ensemble and its curiously dark emotional intimacy. Balanchine himself suggested that the work might be suitable for television, because, according to Merrill Brockway, "he saw places where you can use close-ups."[89] The piece was photographed from a frontal view, with just one shot done from the side, but the effect did not feel like a boxed-in, proscenium stage telecast. Instead, thanks to Brockway's lilting camerawork and sensuous dissolves from angle to angle, the ballet appeared quite open and spacious. More importantly, the camera's intense gaze provided the ballet with a greater sense of personal poignancy. As Brockway observed, "The characterizations—or the implications of characterizations—seem to be more defined on television than they are on stage."[90]

CBS Cable also presented two other noteworthy original productions: Twyla Tharp's *Confessions of a Cornermaker* and *May O'Donnell's Dance Energies*. In a rare move for an American choreographer, Tharp directed *Confessions of a Cornermaker* herself and in the process completely revamped her stage piece *Short Stories* for television. The program also included two shorter works, *Bach Duet* and *Baker's Dozen*, as well as Tharp's personal commentaries about the meaning of her ballets, melodramatically delivered from a forlorn seashore. In contrast to the performance focus of Tharp's show, *May O'Donnell's Dance Energies*, was done more in the manner of a *Dance in America* profile, offering an introductory survey of O'Donnell's achievements as a choreographer and teacher. The program covered a great deal of ground, ranging from excerpts of O'Donnell's past and present dances to classroom scenes, demonstrations by O'Donnell of her technique, and testimonials from former students such as Gerald Arpino, Norman Walker, and Robert Joffrey.

Like CBS Cable, Hearst/ABC's ARTS network broadcast a diverse assortment of dance programming, combining a mixture of inexpensively purchased imported shows, with more costly and ambitious original productions. Foreign presentations included Kenneth MacMillan's *Manon*, a *Cinderella* featuring Lesley Collier and Anthony Dowell, Hugo Romero's *Firebird*, a study of Frederick Ashton's choreographic method, and a close-up of the Kirov Ballet. While the network's new dance shows came in a variety of different formats, some of its most interesting and unusual programs attempted to bring new perspectives to the documentary. In *A Portrait of Giselle*, host Anton Dolin, prompted by a rehearsal session of the ballet with Patricia MacBride and Helgi Tomasson, pursued the question of how *Giselle* has been danced over the years by conducting interviews with eight important dancers associated with the role. Discussions with

Alicia Markova, Yvette Chauvire, Carla Fracci, Olga Spessivtzeva, Galina Ulanova, Tamara Karsavina, Natalia Makarova, and Alicia Alonso were mixed with fascinating, and often rare, historical footage of their performances (the Spessivtzeva film was from 1932). As David Vaughan remarked, the program provided "a real sense of the continuity of tradition" as ballerinas from one generation talked about what they had learned from watching the dancers of the generation that had preceded them.[91]

While not as successful or as calmly measured, another ARTS documentary, *To Dance for Gold*, made a dramatic stab at breaking the traditional mold of dance coverage. Using the flashy manner and electronic techniques pioneered by ABC's *Wide World of Sports*, the program treated the second International Ballet Competition held at Jackson, Mississippi, as if it were the Olympics. Dancers were followed around like athletes and often asked to comment on how they thought they had done immediately after a performance; viewers were treated to backstage views to underscore the competitiveness of the events; and figure skater Dick Button and dancers Jacques D'Amboise and Marge Champion were brought in to provide appropriate color commentary. Far too slick and self-consciously theatrical, *To Dance for Gold* nonetheless did capture the excitement and tension of the sometimes thrilling dancing which took place at Jackson and, if nothing else, proved that Jacques D'Amboise might have a new career ahead of him as a cultural sportscaster.

Many of ARTS's performance-oriented productions were also cast in a different mold. *Swan Lake, Minnesota* was a playfully surrealistic piece which took only one element from Peter Tchaikovsky's classic ballet—the swans—and transposed them to a midwestern farm community, where they appeared in various odd poses all over town. The unconventional choreography was by Loyce Houlton and the program was one of several produced for the network by Joseph Papp. Another show, *Moses Pendleton Presents Moses Pendleton* sought to combine dance movement with autobiographical essay. The Pilobolus Dance Theater's *Artist and Athlete: The Pursuit of Perfection* showed the group in conjunction with the athletes of the 1980 Winter Olympics. A few years later, Twyla Tharp, adding another notch to her record of being the most televised modern dance choreographer of the decade, contributed the *Twyla Tharp Scrapbook 1965–1982*, a beguilingly casual assemblage of snippets from over a dozen of her video dances.

In addition to its more offbeat projects, ARTS also aired several more traditional dance programs. *Ailey Dances* was a record of a City Center concert danced by the Ailey Company in 1980. *The Romantic Era* was a program of four romantic pas de deux, danced by Alicia Alonso with Jorge Equivel, Eva Evdokimova with Peter Schaufuss, Carla Fracci with James Urbain, and Ghislaine Thesmar with Michael Denard, taped in performance at the 1980 Cervantes Festival in Guanajuato, Mexico. The network also broadcast documentaries on the making of Jiri Kylian's *The Overgrown Path* and on Doris Jones and Claire Haywood, the two founders of the Capitol Ballet in Washington, D.C.

Bravo, the other cultural cable network of the 1980s and the only one charging its subscribers a monthly fee, was not as devoted to dance programming as its competitors. The extremely high cost of production has limited the service to just a few original dance programs. These included a performance by Ballet West of John Butler's *Carmina Burana* and Bruce Mark's *Pipe Dreams*, taped in Salt Lake City; shows on the Joyce Trisler Dance Company and Pilobolus; and short profiles of the Boston Ballet and the Houston Ballet. Bravo's remaining dance presentations were imported, with programs featuring the Bolshoi, Ballet Folklorico, and several evenings with the Royal Ballet.

CONCLUSIONS

Television dance has progressed tremendously since the day 50 years ago when Maria Gambarelli stepped in front of a camera to perform a brief number. Her small, primitive "stage," with its brutal lighting, harsh concrete floors and rigid technical conditions, would, by the 1980s, be replaced by studio environments sensitively attuned to the needs of choreographers and dancers, complete with wooden floors, computerized consoles to control and modulate every aspect of the production, and directors and producers fully schooled in the nuances of dance movement. The audience for dance, which may have numbered in the dozens when Miss Gambarelli made her premiere, would grow into the millions and, in the process, spill over into dramatic boosts in live concert attendance of those companies fortunate enough to have been featured on television.

However, despite these great advances, televised dance continues to be a controversial subject, in much the same way it has been since the 1930s. While the medium's technical standards have improved—from poorly detailed, live black-and-white transmissions to vibrantly colored, somewhat better detailed, videotaped productions—the basic physical limitations of television still remain as formidable stumbling blocks. Screen size may have grown from five inches to over two feet, but choreography involving more than six people invariably reduces the televised dancers to the size of flying insects. The TV camera itself enacts a fundamental alteration in ballet shape. No matter where it is positioned, the camera changes a work's three-dimensional space and form. The switching from one perspective to another through editing also imposes an inevitable deformation of dance design originally created for the expanse and openness of the proscenium stage.

Attempts to answer these problems have varied through the years. Some choreographers have simply stayed away or retreated from television, finding its compromises too high a price to pay. Others have tried to work imaginatively within the medium's confines by coming to terms with the full range of its possibilities. In the 1940s, dancers like Pauline Koner and Kitty Doner began to experiment with television's special electronic effects as a vital element of their light, popular ballets. Agnes de Mille's efforts in the 1950s to understand how the TV camera actually saw dance led to a variety of interesting programs on *Omnibus* that emphasized television's affinity for the inherently dramatic and intimate. By the 1970s, several new approaches to dance telecasting had emerged. PBS programs such as *A Close-up in Time* and the series *Dance in America* fostered a smooth, clear-eyed style of "translation," which depended on full cooperation with the choreographer in deciding what a three-dimensional stage piece should look like when transformed into two-dimensional space. Artists and technicians working in the field of videodance pioneered an alternative method. Rather than document existing works, they created dances expressly for television, taking advantage of every resource—portability, technological enhancements, editing interpolations—the medium could provide.

Though the products of videodance were often crude or non-dramatic in comparison with the conventionally "elegant" TV dance terms of PBS, they were able to solve, or at least dispose of, the types of difficulties that have often plagued dance telecasting since its beginnings. Instead of worrying about television's lack of "plasticity" or its inability to accurately mirror the structure of a work designed for the breadth of the proscenium stage, videodance choreographers like Merce Cunningham, and even Twyla Tharp, chose to exploit the medium's inherent advantages: its ease and fluidity in creating new feelings of time and space.

Nevertheless, mainstream TV dance has largely stayed away from these and other types of experiments and focused on forms more suitable to majority demographic interests. It is important to remember that the history of broadcast dance in this country has been shaped far more by economic forces than it has by the battle to conquer television's visual limitations. Until the 1960s, televised dance was carefully restricted by the commercial networks' concern for what sponsors and audiences would tolerate. While there was an abundance of popular dance on live variety shows and some extraordinary specials with Fred Astaire, ballet was generally confined to the narrow range of the romantic pas de deux or to the storytelling grandeur of a nineteenth-century epic when a network decided to present an occasional "prestige" event. Modern dance, when it occurred, was relegated to the non-rated, Sunday morning and afternoon "culture" slots. Dancers and choreographers who worked on television during this period found it difficult to deal with the unfamiliar pressures of severely limited rehearsal time, cramped, unaccommodating studios, and a technical staff frequently insensitive to dance design.

Matters improved considerably with the development of National Educational Television in the late 1950s. Programs such as *A Time to Dance* and *USA: Dance* proved that it was possible to mount intelligent productions, featuring the country's best dancers, with only a shoestring budget and a great deal of dedication. As NET grew and evolved into PBS, televised dance entered a new era. Landmark shows like *ABT: A Close-up in Time* and *Alvin Ailey: Memories and Visions* revealed the rich possibilities television could bring to all types of dance when the right combination of talent and funding was made available. A few years later, PBS created *Dance in America*, probably the most influential and impressive dance series in TV history. Audiences for *Dance in America* were introduced to the achievements and repertoire of the country's leading dance companies and choreographers in tasteful, imaginative ways. The series' cultivated polish and sheen helped make even previously inaccessible areas of modern dance seem inviting and non-threatening.

An unfortunate byproduct of PBS's growth has been a corresponding reduction on the part of the commercial networks to use their much larger resources and greater audience reach for dance-related programming. The number of dance specials and appearances by ballet performers on ABC, CBS, and NBC has dropped off significantly during the past decade and a half, and, given the increasingly ferocious ratings climate, there is little reason to believe the future will yield anything but further dance cutbacks. At the same time, the bright promise of the cultural cable networks has also largely faded away—the result of economic pressures and lack of advertising support.

PBS remains the greatest champion and supporter TV dance has ever known. Thanks to the creative efforts of directors and producers such as Merrill Brockway, Emile Ardolino, Jac Venza, and Charles Dubin, the network has been able to develop an approach which, even if it does not completely solve all of the problems associated with televising dance, at least has given TV versions of ballet and modern dance a significant new clarity. Choreographers no longer have to feel that television is their natural enemy and that their stage works would end up in shambles once they were exposed to the eye of the electronic camera.

The transformations in TV dance during the past five decades have been remarkable. What was formerly just a crude instrument for conveying a fuzzy, upper body view of a lone dancer's swaying movements has emerged into a sophisticated tool that can register, with surprising richness, a wide range of choreographic design and nuance. Though the medium is far from perfect in its abilities to accurately capture the formal beauty, power, and tension of dance created for an audience seated in a theater, its compensations—to transport dance into millions of living rooms—have, in the long run, more than made up for its shortcomings.

NOTES

1. Sara Revell Estill, "Dance in Television," Master's thesis, New York University, 1945, p. 24.

2. Nelson D. Neal, "Early Television Dance," *Dancescope*, Winter 1979, p. 52.

3. Andrew N. McLellan, "The Challenge of Television," *Dancemagazine*, January 1947, p. 16.

4. Worthington Miner, "A Producer's View of Television," *Theatre Arts*, October 1944, p. 587.

5. Atholie Bays, "The Seeker Finds," *American Dancer*, October 1939, p. 10.

6. Maurice Stoller, "Terpsichore Among the Megacycles," *Dancemagazine*, May 1946, p. 10.

7. Bays, "Seeker Finds," p. 10.

8. Bays, "Seeker Finds," p. 32.

9. Stoller, "Terpsichore," p. 10.

10. McLellan, "Challenge," p. 16.

11. Pauline Koner, and Kitty Doner, "The Techniques of Dance in Television," *Telescreen*, Winter 1945/46, p. 2.

12. Koner and Doner, "Techniques," p. 5.

13. McLellan, "Challenge," p. 18.

14. Arthur Todd, "Dolly In on Television Dance," *Theatre Arts*, September 1951, p. 58.

15. James Starbuck, "The Dance: A New Field—TV," *New York Times*, 8 July 1951, Section II, p. 4.

16. Doris Hering, "Conversation with Max Liebman," *Dancemagazine*, March 1955, p. 28.

17. Hering, "Conversation," p. 28.

18. Lillian Moore, "Thirty Million Viewers," *Dancing Times*, February 1956, p. 298; and Jack Gould, "Dancing on the Air," *New York Times*, 18 December 1955, Section II, p. 13.

19. "Cinderella," *Newsweek*, 6 May 1957, p. 68.

20. Paul Feigay, "The Dance of *Omnibus*," *Dancemagazine*, March 1955, p. 25.

21. Feigay, "Dance of *Omnibus*," p. 25.

22. Feigay, "Dance of *Omnibus*," pp. 24–25.

23. Ann Barzel, "Looking at TV," *Dancemagazine*, December 1953, p. 7.

24. Janet Mason, "Dance Seen Through The 'Eyes' of a Television Camera," *Impulse*, 1960, p. 39.

25. John Martin, "TV Ballet," *New York Times*, 10 January 1954, Section II, p. 7.

26. Martin, "TV Ballet," p. 7.

27. Jack Gould, "Tedious Fairy Tale," *New York Times*, 5 May, 1957, Section II, p. 11.

28. George Balanchine and Bernard Taper, "Television and Ballet," in *The Eighth Art* (New York: Holt, Rinehart, & Winston, 1962), p. 118.

29. Balanchine and Taper, "Television," p. 119.

30. Feigay, "Dance of *Omnibus*," p. 83.

31. Valerie Bettis, Ralph Beaumont and John Butler, "Dance on Television," in *The Creative Experience*, edited by A. William Bluehm (New York: Hastings House, 1967), p. 292.

32. Jack Gould, "Tedious Fairy Tale," p. 11.

33. John P. Shanley, "Ballet on Television," *New York Times*, 10 January 1960, Section II, p. 13.

34. Jac Venza, "Educational TV Loves Dance," *Dancemagazine*, September 1965, p. 44.

35. Venza, "Educational TV," p. 87.

36. Arthur Todd, "What Went Wrong," *Dancemagazine*, August 1962, p. 39.

37. Balanchine and Taper, "Television," pp. 120–121.

38. Allen Hughes, "The Dance and Video," *New York Times*, 24 June 1962, Section II, p. 13.

39. Hughes, "Dance and Video," p. 13.

40. Robert Lewis Shayon, " 'The Flood'—Before and After," *Saturday Review*, 30 June 1962, p. 32.

41. Ann Barzel, "Looking at TV," *Dancemagazine*, August 1962, p. 19.

42. Arthur Todd, "What Went Wrong," p. 61.

43. Anna Kisselgoff, "Dance: How to Treat It on Television," *New York Times*, 10 July 1968, p. 22.

44. Arthur Todd, "For the Wonders of God's Universe," *Dancemagazine*, December 1962, p. 40.

45. Todd, "Wonders," p. 40.

46. Birgit Cullberg, "The Influence of Television Techniques on the Creation of Ballet," *Dancing Times*, November 1965, p. 76; and John O'Connor, "Moira Shearer, Some of Us Will Love You Forever," *New York Times*, 20 June 1971, Section II, p. 19.

47. John Mueller, "Twyla Tharp and the Wide-Angle Lens," *Dancemagazine*, September 1977, p. 99.

48. Nancy S. Mason, ed. *Dance and Television* (Boston: WGBH, 1976), p. 9.

49. Mason, *Dance*, p. 21.

50. John O'Connor, "Who'd Give Up Marcus Welby For a Two Inch Dancer?," *New York Times*, 6 June 1971, Section II, p. 15.

51. O'Connor, "Who'd Give Up," p. 15.

52. Anna Kisselgoff, "How Dance Conquered The TV Screen," *New York Times*, 30 May 1976, Section II, p. 1.

53. Herbert M. Simpson, "WNET TV's Dance in America," *Dancemagazine*, January 1977, p. 45.

54. Simpson, "WNET," p. 45.

55. Jennifer Dunning, "Dance in America," New York City Ballet *Stagebill*, December 1978, p. 20.

56. Simpson, "WNET," p. 50.

57. Alex Ward, "Dance in America," *The Cultural Post*, no. 5, 1976, p. 1.

58. Wallace White, "Videodance—It May Be a Whole New Art Form," *New York Times*, 18 January 1976, Section II, p. 10.

59. Nevertheless, his fondness for the device was not without its dissenters. John Mueller, writing in *Dancemagazine*, presented a strong case that dissolves should be used sparingly and only as a certain type of dramatic special effect.

A dissolve, particularly when it occurs between scenes or between sections of a work, implies a passage or disorientation of time—it may even have a kind of dream-like effect. It is not just a pretty way to cut from one camera to another and I don't think it should be used unless there is some kind of special point to be made.

John Mueller, "The Close-up, the Dissolve, and Martha Graham," *Dancemagazine*, January 1978, p. 95.

60. Kisselgoff, "How Dance Conquered," p. 8.

61. Kisselgoff, "How Dance Conquered," p. 8.

62. Simpson, "WNET," p. 46.

63. Simpson, "WNET," p. 46.

64. Ward, "Dance in America," p. 1.

65. John Mueller, "Martha Graham Then and Now," *Dancemagazine*, December 1977, p. 107.

66. Marcia Siegel, *The Shapes of Change* (New York: Avon Books, 1979), p. 119.

67. Arlene Croce, " 'Locale'—The Motion Picture," *New Yorker*, 25 February 1980, p. 118.

68. Peter Z. Grossman, "Talking with Merce Cunningham about Video," *Dance Scope*, Winter/Spring 1979, p. 57.

69. Balanchine and Taper, "Television," p. 117.

70. Balanchine and Taper, "Television," p. 121.

71. Tullia Bohen, "The Man Behind the TV Dancing," *Soho Weekly News*, 17 May 1979, p. 35.

72. Jennifer Dunning, "Dance in America," pp. 22–23.

73. Anna Kisselgoff, "Dance on TV—A New Phase," *New York Times*, 10 December 1978, Section II, p. 19.

74. Kisselgoff, "Dance on TV," p. 19.

75. Kisselgoff, "Dance on TV," p. 20.

76. Jennifer Dunning, "Martha Graham Remakes Her 'Clytemnestra' for TV," *New York Times*, 27 May 1979, Section II, p. 14.

77. Croce, " 'Locale'—The Motion Picture," p. 118.

78. Burt Supree, "Nothing Looks Like Live," *Village Voice*, 18 October 1983, p. 111.

79. Arlene Croce, *Afterimages* (New York: Alfred A. Knopf, 1977), p. 113.

80. Tullia Bohen, "Making Television Dance," *Ballet News*, May 1980, p. 27.

81. David Vaughan, "TV," *Ballet News*, August 1980, p. 43.

82. Jac Venza, personal interview, 29 November 1983.

83. Holly Brubach, "TV Dance for May," *Ballet News*, May 1981, p. 21.

84. Panel discussion, "Television and Dance," Museum of Broadcasting, New York City, 13 December 1983.

85. Panel discussion, 13 December 1983.

86. John Gruen, "dancevision," *Dancemagazine*, April 1983, p. 112.

87. John Gruen, "dancevision," *Dancemagazine*, September 1980, p. 110.

88. Panel discussion, 13 December 1983.

89. Arlene Croce, " 'Davidsbundlertanzen' on Television—Merrill Brockway talks to Arlene Croce," New York City Ballet *Stagebill*, Fall 1981, p. 6.

90. Croce, "Davidsbundlertanze," p. 6.

91. David Vaughan, "TV," *Ballet News*, July 1982, p. 38.

REFERENCES

There is a great deal of material available regarding the history of TV dance in the United States. A good place to start is Nelson D. Neal's "Early Television Dance," which provides a thorough portrait of what the first dance telecasts were like and what kinds of aesthetic problems the medium posed for dancers during the early 1930s. Sara Revell Estill's 1945 Master's thesis, "Dance in Television," follows the story of TV dance through World War II, focusing on the efforts of early experimenters like Bud Gamble. For an interesting contrast, there is Janet Rowson Davis's "Ballet on British TV—1933–39," which examines the BBC's dozens of original dance programs, featuring the country's leading choreographers, at the very time American TV dance was in its primitive infancy.

Despite its lack of sophistication and technical expertise, televised dance in the United States was greeted, almost from its beginnings, with an enthusiasm bordering on visionary fervor. Contemporary articles such as Atholie Bays's "The Seeker Finds," Virginia Kelley's "Television: A New World for Dancers," and Maurice Stoller's "Terpsichore Among the Megacycles" are lively paeans to the idealistic spirit that often characterized TV dance in its first decade. More sober views, with some practical advice on the best ways to put dance in front of the camera, can be found in Andrew N. McLellan's "The Challenge of Television," Worthington Miner's "A Producer's View of Television," and Pauline Koner and Kitty Doner's "The Techniques of Dance in Television."

As dance became an increasingly active part of the broadcast schedule during the late 1940s and early 1950s, magazines and newspapers began to increase their coverage as well. Always an interested observer of dance on television, *Dancemagazine* in 1953 started a monthly column, "Looking at TV," written by Ann Barzel, that has remained the most complete and informative chronicle of TV dance activities for more than three decades. (Miss Barzel was succeeded by Norma McLain Stoop in 1971; John Gruen took over the column in 1979.) *Dancemagazine* also continued to publish many special features and articles on TV dance. Its 1954 book, *25 Years of American Dance*, contained an interesting historical survey by Judy Dupuy entitled "Television: A Reality with Problems," and its March 1955 issue featured several pieces looking at both popular and serious TV dance, including Doris Hering's "Conversation with Max Liebman" and Paul Feigay's "The Dance of 'Omnibus.' "

During the 1950s, both the TV and dance critics of the *New York Times* wrote about the nature and problems of televising dance. Jack Gould and John Martin were particularly harsh in their objections to broadcast ballet techniques. Two articles provide a fairly good summary of their respective views: Jack Gould's "Tedious Fairy Tale," written after a telecast of the Royal Ballet's *Cinderella*, and John Martin's "TV Ballet," which attacks the medium's partiality to story ballets.

The triumphs of TV dance in the 1950s seemed to take place primarily on one program—*Omnibus*—and there are several works discussing the show's achievements. In addition to the previously mentioned article by Paul Feigay, there is Janet Mason's "Dance Seen Through the 'Eyes' of a Television Camera" and John T. Barrett's dissertation, "A Descriptive Study of Selected Uses of Dance on Television 1948–58," which contains a detailed section examining Agnes de Mille's contributions to the program.

The 1960s were a time of transition and disillusionment with TV dance. Commercial television was proving to be an environment less and less hospitable to dance specials and features, and the few choreographers able to find work in the medium were increasingly frustrated. This growing mood of discontent was vividly captured in a couple of interviews published during the period. Bernard Taper's conversations with George Balanchine, recorded in the article "Television and Ballet," provides a spirited account of Balanchine's run-ins with American TV technicians and his thoughts on the enormous difficulties inherent in any form of televised dance. Three choreographers who worked extensively in television, Valerie Bettis, Ralph Beaumont, and John Butler, voice similar concerns in an interview conducted a few years later, entitled "Dance on Television."

The promising alternative of educational television was a phenomenon which received considerable attention. Martha Myers's "Dance Series for National Educational Television" documents her pioneering efforts to mount NET's first dance series, *A Time to Dance*, in the late 1950s. Jac Venza's 1965 article, "Educational TV Loves Dance," offers a wide-ranging view of NET's accomplishments. As NET evolved into PBS and its commitment to dance continued to grow, the network became the principal subject of most writing concerned with the issues of TV dance. John J. O'Connor and Anna Kisselgoff, who covered television and dance respectively for the *New York Times* throughout the 1970s, focused frequently on the full range of PBS's dance activities. O'Connor's "Dance Companies Contemplate TV's Potential" and Kisselgoff's "How Dance Conquered the TV Screen" are useful introductions to the network's dance approach in the mid–1970s.

The launching of PBS's *Dance in America* in 1976 produced a flurry of articles in practically every major newspaper and magazine. Among the best assessments are Wallace White's "Videodance—It May be a Whole New Art Form," Herbert M. Simpson's "WNET-TV's Dance in America," John Mueller's "Twyla Tharp and the Wide-Angle Lens," and Richard Lorber's " 'Dance in America' on TV in America." Lincoln Kirstein's vituperative comments on PBS's companion series, "Live from Lincoln Center," in his book, *Thirty Years/The New York City Ballet*, provide an alternative view. Statistics on how the series increased dance concert attendance can be found in the National Research Center of the Arts' pamphlet, *The Joffrey Ballet Audience—A Survey of the Spring 1976 Season at City Center* and in Richard Lorber's previously mentioned article.

Dance in America continued to provoke spirited critical response in the years that followed, including Anna Kisselgoff's "Dance on TV—A New Phase," John Mueller's "Martha Graham then and now," Jennifer Dunning's "Martha Graham Remakes Her 'Clytemnestra' for TV" and "Dance in America," and Tullia Bohen's historical overview, "Making Television Dance." The columns on TV dance by David Vaughan in *Ballet News* and John Gruen in *Dancemagazine* also offered consistently discerning commentary on *Dance in America*'s varied programs. For a closer look at the problems of directing the series' ambitious dance productions and directing TV dance in general, four articles discussing Merrill Brockway are well worth reading. They are "The Man Behind the TV Dancing" by Tullia Bohen, "Merrill Brockway" by John Gruen, Brockway's own essay "Capturing Dance on Camera," and Arlene Croce's " 'Davidsbundlertanzen' on Television—Merrill Brockway talks with Arlene Croce," which examines Brockway's later work with CBS Cable. In addition, there is Emile Ardolino's "Balanchine and Television: Trust the Dancers," which provides a first-rate analysis of Balanchine's TV aesthetic, as seen by a producer/director who worked closely with him on both *Dance in America* and *Live from Lincoln Center*.

The 1970s also saw the rise of alternatives to conventional TV dance presentations. A transcription of the proceedings of the 1976 "Dance and Television" conference held at WGBH in Boston, edited by Nancy S. Mason, offers a collection of fascinating remarks about new perspectives to televised choreography by Birgit Cullberg, David Loxton, Charles Dubin, and Elliot Feld, among others. WGBH's efforts to encourage the collaboration of artists and technicians in the creation of videodance are well documented in Burt Supree's article, "Nothing Looks Like Live." As the extent of videodance activity increased, the movement has been the subject of numerous essays examining the form's theory and practices. These include Peter Grossman's "Video and Dance" and "Talking with Merce Cunningham about Video," Richard Lorber's "Towards an Aesthetic of Videodance" and "Experiments in Videodance," and Ronn Smith's "The Pioneers."

There are a few other sources for those interested in general historical appraisals of American TV dance. Herbert M. Simpson's "American Dance on Television" is a brief overview of the form's principal landmarks up to 1976. Phyllis A. Penny's dissertation "Ballet and Modern Dance on Television in the Decade of the 1970s" is also recommended for its more detailed discussion of the past three decades of TV dance and for its comprehensive listing of every single dance program broadcast on all four networks during the 1970s.

Equally valuable are the proceedings of two lively and fascinating seminars conducted at the Museum of Broadcasting and available on audio tape at the Museum's research facilities in New York City. The first, concerning the problems and triumphs of televised dance, was recorded on December 13, 1983; the second, examining Balanchine's work in the medium, was recorded on September 21, 1984.

Books

Croce, Arlene. *Afterimages*. New York: Alfred A. Knopf, 1977. *Dance and Television*. Watertown, Mass.: WGBH, 1974.

Kirstein, Lincoln. *Thirty Years/The New York City Ballet*. New York: Alfred A. Knopf, 1973.

Mason, Nancy, ed. *Dance and Television*. Watertown, Mass.: WGBH, 1974.

Siegel, Marcia. *The Shapes of Change*. New York: Avon Books, 1979.

Articles

Ardolino, Emile. "Balanchine and Television: Trust the Dancers." In *A Celebration of Balanchine: The Television Work*. New York: The Museum of Broadcasting, 1984, pp. 9–18.

Balanchine, George, and Bernard Taper. "Television and Ballet." In *The Eighth Art*. New York: Holt, Rinehart, & Winston, 1962, pp. 117–123.

Barzel, Ann. "Looking at TV." *Dancemagazine*, March 1953–1971.

Bays, Atholie. "The Seeker Finds." *American Dancer*, October 1939, p. 10.

Bettis, Valerie, Ralph Beaumont, and John Butler. "Dance on Television." In *The*

Creative Experience, ed. A. William Bluehm. New York: Hastings House, 1967, pp. 290–295.

Bohen, Tullia. "Making Television Dance." *Ballet News*, May 1980, p. 27.

———. "The Man Behind the TV Dancing." *Soho Weekly News*, 17 May, 1979, p. 35.

Brockway, Merrill and Glenn Berenbeim. "Capturing Dance on Camera." In *Promise and Performance: ACT's Guide to TV Programming for Children*. ed. Maureen Harmonay. Cambridge: Ballinger Publishers, 1979, pp. 54–59.

Bush, Jeffrey and Peter Z. Grossman. "Videodance." *Dance Scope*, Spring/Summer 1975, pp. 11–17.

"Cinderella." *Newsweek*, 6 May 1957, p. 68.

Croce, Arlene. " 'Davidsbundlertanzen' on Television—Merrill Brockway talks to Arlene Croce." New York City Ballet *Stagebill*, Fall 1981, p. 6.

———. " 'Locale'—The Motion Picture." *New Yorker*, 25 February 1980, p. 118.

Cullberg, Birgit. "The Influence of Television Techniques on the Creation of Ballet." *Dancing Times*, November 1965, pp. 76–79.

Davis, Janet Rowson. "Ballet on British TV—1933–39." *Dance Chronicle*, Winter 1982–83, pp. 244–305.

Dunning, Jennifer. "Dance in America." New York City Ballet *Stagebill*, December 1978, pp. 20–22.

———. "Martha Graham Remakes Her 'Clytemnestra' for TV." *New York Times*, 27 May 1979, Section II, p. 14.

Dupuy, Judy. "Television: A Reality with Problems." In *25 Years of American Dance*. ed. Doris Hering. New York: R. Orthwine, 1954, p. 188.

Feigay, Paul. "The Dance of *Omnibus*." *Dancemagazine*, March 1955, pp. 24–25.

Frost, Barbara. "Television . . . friend or fiend?" *Dancemagazine*, May 1952, pp. 18–19.

Gould, Jack. "Dancing on the Air." *New York Times*, 18 December 1955, Section II, p. 13.

———. "Tedious Fairy Tale." *New York Times*, 5 May 1957, Section II, p. 11.

Grossman, Peter Z. "Talking with Merce Cunningham about Video." *Dance Scope*, Winter/Spring 1979, p. 57–63.

———. "Video and Dance." *Videography*, September 1977, pp. 16–19.

Gruen, John. "dancevision," *Dancemagazine*, 1979–.

———. "Merrill Brockway." *Dancemagazine*, August 1981, pp. 50–53.

Hering, Doris. "Conversation with Max Liebman." *Dancemagazine*, March 1955, p. 28.

Hughes, Allen. "The Dance and Video." *New York Times*, 24 June 1962, Section II, p. 13.

Kelley, Virginia. "Television: A New World for Dancers." *Dancemagazine*, December 1944, p. 4.

Kisselgoff, Anna. "Dance: How to Treat It on Television." *New York Times*, 10 July 1968, p. 22.

———. "Dance on TV—A New Phase." *New York Times*, 10 December 1978, Section II, p. 19.

———. "How Dance Conquered The TV Screen." *New York Times*, 30 May 1976, Section II, p. 1.

———. "A TV Tribute Upsets Balanchine Stereotypes." *New York Times*, 23 September 1984, Section II, p. 6.

Koner, Pauline, and Kitty Doner. "The Techniques of Dance in Television." *Telescreen*, Winter 1945/46, p. 2.

Lorber, Richard. " 'Dance in America' on TV in America." *Dance Scope*, Spring 1976, pp. 21–28.

———. "Experiments in Videodance." *Dancescope*, Fall 1977, pp. 7–14.

———. "Towards an Aesthetic of Videodance." *Arts and Society*, Summer 1976.

McLellan, Andrew N. "The Challenge of Television." *Dancemagazine*, January 1947, pp. 16–19.

Martin, John. "TV Ballet." *New York Times*, 10 January 1954, Section II, p. 7.

Mason, Janet. "Dance Seen Through The 'Eyes' of a Television Camera." *Impulse*, 1960, pp. 39–41.

Miner, Worthington. "A Producer's View of Television." *Theatre Arts*, October 1944, p. 587.

Moore, Lillian. "Thirty Million Viewers." *Dancing Times*, February 1956, p. 298.

Mueller, John. "The close-up, the dissolve, and Martha Graham." *Dancemagazine*, January 1978, pp. 94–95.

———. "Martha Graham then and now." *Dancemagazine*, December 1977, p. 107.

———. "Twyla Tharp and the Wide-Angle Lens." *Dancemagazine*, September 1977, p. 99.

Myers, Martha. "Dance Series for National Educational Television." *Impulse*, 1960, pp. 33–38.

Neal, Nelson D. "Early Television Dance." *Dancescope*, Winter 1979, pp. 51–59.

O'Connor, John J. "Dance Companies Contemplate TV's Potential." *New York Times*, 27 October 1974, Section II, p. 31.

———. "Moira Shearer, Some of Us Will Love You Forever." *New York Times*, 20 June 1971, Section II, p. 19.

———. "Who'd Give Up Marcus Welby For a Two-Inch Dancer?" *New York Times*, 6 June 1971, Section II, p. 15.

Shanley, John P. "Ballet on Television." *New York Times*, 10 January 1960, Section II, p. 13.

Shayon, Robert Lewis. " 'The Flood'—Before and After." *Saturday Review*, 30 June 1962, p. 32.

Simpson, Herbert M. "American Dance on Television." *Dancemagazine*, January 1977, pp. 41–45.

———. "WNET TV's Dance in America." *Dancemagazine*, January 1977, pp. 45–50.

Smith, Ronn. "The Pioneers." *theatre crafts*, October 1983, p. 22.

Stoller, Maurice. "Terpsichore Among the Megacycles." *Dancemagazine*, May 1946, pp. 10–11.

Supree, Bert. "Nothing Looks Like Live." *Village Voice*, 18 October 1983, pp. 111–113.

Terry, Walter. "On TV: America's Dances and Dancers." *Saturday Review*, 25 June 1977, pp. 38–40.

Todd, Arthur. "Dolly In on Television Dance." *Theatre Arts*, September 1951, p. 58.

———. "For the Wonders of God's Universe." *Dancemagazine*, December 1962, p. 40.

———. "What Went Wrong." *Dancemagazine*, August 1962, p. 39.

Vaughan, David. "TV." *Ballet News*, 1980–.

Venza, Jac. "Educational TV Loves Dance." *Dancemagazine*, September 1965, p. 44.

Ward, Alex. "Dance in America." *The Cultural Post*, No. 5, 1976, p. 1.

White, Wallace. "Videodance—It May Be a Whole New Art Form." *New York Times*, 18 January 1976, Section II, p. 1.

Dissertations and Theses

Barrett, John T. "A Descriptive Study of Selected Uses of Dance on Television, 1948–58." Ph.D. diss., University of Michigan, 1968.

Estill, Sara Revell. "Dance on Television." Master's thesis, New York University, 1945.

Penney, Phyliss A. "Ballet and Modern Dance on Television in the Decade of the 1970s." Ph.D. diss., University of North Carolina-Greensboro, 1980.

Pamphlets

National Research Center of the Arts. *The Joffrey Ballet Audience—A Survey of the Spring 1976 Season at City Center*. Washington, D.C.: National Research Center of the Arts, 1976.

VIDEOGRAPHY

Program: *Omnibus*
Network: CBS
Date: November 8, 1953
Ballet(s): *Billy the Kid*
Choreographer(s): Eugene Loring
Performers: John Kriza, Scott Douglas
Producer: Robert Saudek

Program: *Omnibus*
Network: CBS
Date: February 26, 1956
Ballet(s): lecture/demonstration by Agnes de Mille on "The Art of Ballet," with excerpts from *Swan Lake*, *Oklahoma*, and *Paint Your Wagon*
Choreographer(s): Lev Ivanov and Marius Petipa, Agnes de Mille
Performers: Agnes de Mille, Diana Adams, Andre Eglevsky, James Mitchell
Director: Charles Dubin
Producer: Robert Saudek

Program: *Omnibus*
Network: ABC
Date: December 30, 1956

Ballet(s): lecture demonstration by Agnes de Mille on "The Art of Choreography," with excerpts from *Serenade*, *Les Sylphides*, *Rodeo*, and *Fall River Legend*
Choreographer(s): George Balanchine, Michel Fokine, and Agnes de Mille
Performers: Frederick Franklin, Diana Adams, Sonia Arova, James Mitchell, Jenny Workman
Director: Charles Dubin
Producer: Robert Saudek

Program: *Producer's Showcase*
Network: NBC
Date: April 29, 1957
Ballet(s): *Cinderella*
Choreographer(s): Frederick Ashton
Performers: Margot Fonteyn, Michael Somes, Frederick Ashton, Kenneth MacMillan
Director: Mort Abrahams
Producer: Clark Jones

Program: *Appalachian Spring*
Network: NET
Date: 1957
Ballet(s): *Appalachian Spring*
Choreographer(s): Martha Graham
Performers: Martha Graham, Stuart Hodes, Bertram Ross
Director: Peter Glushanok
Producer: Nathan Kroll

Program: *Omnibus*
Network: ABC
Date: December 21, 1958
Ballet(s): lecture/demonstration by Gene Kelly on "Dancing—A Man's Game"
Choreographer(s): Gene Kelly
Performers: Gene Kelly, Edward Villella
Director: Gene Kelly and William A. Graham
Producer: Robert Saudek

Program: *Playhouse 90*
Network: CBS
Date: December 25, 1958
Ballet: *The Nutcracker*
Choreographer: George Balanchine
Performers: Diana Adams, George Balanchine, Arthur Mitchell, Allegra Kent
Director: Ralph Nelson

Program: *A Time to Dance*
Network: NET
Date: 1960
Ballet(s): the six programs in the series included a variety of short ballets and excerpts, including *There is a Time*, *Sylvia Pas de Deux*, *Pillar of Fire*

Choreographer(s): Jose Limon, George Balanchine, Antony Tudor
Performers: a variety of dancers from the Jose Limon Dance Company, the John Butler Dance Company, as well as Nora Kaye and Hugh Laing
Director: Greg Harney
Producer: Jac Venza

Program: *Noah and the Flood*
Network: CBS
Date: June 14, 1962
Ballet(s): *Noah and the Flood*
Choreographer(s): George Balanchine
Performers: Jacques D'Amboise, Edward Villella, Jillana
Director: Kirk Browning
Producer: Robert de Graff

Program: *USA: Dance—New York City Ballet*
Network: NET
Date: 1966
Ballet(s): pas de deux from *Agon*, *Tarantella*, *Meditation*, *Grand Pas De Deux*
Choreographer(s): George Balanchine
Performers: Suzanne Farrell, Arthur Mitchell, Patricia MacBride, Edward Villella, Jacques D'Amboise, Mellissa Hayden
Director: Charles Dubin
Producer: Jac Venza

Program: *ABT: A Close-up in Time*
Network: PBS
Date: August 13, 1973
Ballet(s): waltz from *Les Sylphides*; excerpts from *Rodeo*, *The River*, and *Etudes*; Black Swan pas de deux from *Swan Lake*; *Pillar of Fire*
Choreographer(s): Michel Fokine, Agnes de Mille, Alvin Ailey, Harald Lander, Lev Ivanov and Marius Petipa, Antony Tudor
Performers: Christine Terry, Terry Orr, Marcos Paredes, Sallie Wilson, Ellen Everett, Gayle Young, Cynthia Gregory, Eleanor D'Antudio, Ivan Nagy
Director: Jerome Schnur
Producer: Jac Venza

Program: *Camera Three—Bix Pieces*
Network: CBS
Date: October 7, 1973
Ballet(s): *Bix Pieces*
Choreographer(s): Twyla Tharp
Performers: Twyla Tharp, Sara Rudner, Isabel Garcia-Lorca, Kenneth Rinker
Director: Merrill Brockway
Producer: Merrill Brockway

Program: *Camera Three—Merce Cunningham: A Video Event*
Network: CBS
Date: October 27, 1974; November 3, 1974
Ballet(s): excerpts from *Winterbranch*, *Sounddance*, *Changing Steps*,

Landrover, *Signals*, *TV Rerun*, *Second Hand*
Choreographer(s): Merce Cunningham
Performers: members of the Cunningham Dance Company, including Ellen Cornfield, Meg Harper, Susan Heman-Chaffey, Cathy Herr, Buyner Mehl, Charles Moulton, Julie Roess-Smith, Valda Satterfield, Merce Cunningham
Director: Merrill Brockway
Producer: Merrill Brockway

Program: *Dance in America—City Center Joffrey Ballet*
Network: PBS
Date: January 21, 1976
Ballet(s): excerpts from *Parade*, *The Green Table*, and *Remembrances*; *Trinity*
Choreographer(s): Leonide Massine, Robert Joffrey, Gerald Arpino
Performers: Gary Chryst, Francesca Corkle, Christian Holder
Director: Jerome Schnur
Producer: Jac Venza

Program: *Live from Lincoln Center—American Ballet Theatre: Swan Lake*
Network: PBS
Date: June 30, 1976
Ballet(s): *Swan Lake*
Choreographer(s): Lev Ivanov and Marius Petipa
Performers: Natalia Makarova, Ivan Nagy
Director: Kirk Browning
Producer: John Goberman

Program: *Dance in America—Merce Cunningham and Dance Company*
Network: PBS
Date: January 5, 1977
Ballet(s): *Minutiae*, *Solo*, *Westbeth*, *Septet*, *Antic Meet*, *Scramble*, *Rainforest*, *Sounddance*, and *Video Triangle*
Choreographer(s): Merce Cunningham
Performers: Merce Cunningham, Catherine Kerr and Cunningham Company
Director: Merrill Brockway
Producer: Jac Venza

Program: *Dance in America—Choreography by Balanchine, Parts I-IV*
Network: PBS
Date: December 14, 1977; December 21, 1977; November 29, 1978; and March 7, 1979
Ballet(s): *Tzigane*, *Divertimento No.5*, *The Four Temperaments*(I); excerpts from *Jewels* and *Stravinsky Violin Concerto* (II); *Prodigal Son* and *Chaconne* (III); *Ballo della Regina*, *The Steadfast Tin Soldier*, *Elegie*, *Tchaikovsky Pas de Deux*, and *Allegro Brilliante* (IV)
Choreographer(s): George Balanchine
Performers: Merrill Ashley, Bart Cook, Adam Luders, Heather Watts, Kain von Aroldingen, Daniel Duell, Suzanne Farrell, Sean Lavery, Peter Martins, Kay Mazzo, Patricia MacBride, Robert Weiss, Mikhail Baryshnikov
Director: Merrill Brockway
Producer: Jac Venza

Program: *Making TV Dance*
Network: PBS
Date: October 4, 1977
Ballet(s): *Speed*, *Repetition*, *Fugue*, *Retrograde*, and *The Event*
Choreographer(s): Twyla Tharp
Performers: Shelley Washington, Tom Rowe, Jeniffer Way, Christine Uchida, Mikhail Baryshnikov, Twyla Tharp
Director: Don Mischer
Producer: Twyla Tharp

Program: *Live from Studio 8H*
Network: NBC
Date: July 2, 1980
Ballet(s): excerpts from *Fancy Free*, *The Concert*, and *Dances at a Gathering*; *The Cage* and *Afternoon of a Faun*
Choreographer(s): Jerome Robbins
Performers: Heather Watts, Ib Andersen, Patricia MacBride, Bart Cook, Jean-Pierre Frohlich, Christopher D'Amboise, Lourdes Lopez, Stephanie Saland, Sean Lavery, Sarah Leland
Director: Rodney Greenberg
Producer: Alvin Cooperman and Judith de Paul

Program: *Davidsbundlertanze*
Network: CBS Cable
Date: October 1981
Ballet(s): *Robert Schumann's Davidsbundlertanze*
Choreographer(s): George Balanchine
Performers: Suzanne Farrell, Jacques D'Amboise, Karin von Aroldingen, Peter Martins, Adam Luders, Sarah Leland, Heather Watts, Ib Andersen
Director: Merrill Brockway
Producer: Catherine Tatge

3

Classical Music on Television

In contrast to the golden days of network radio in the 1930s and 1940s when classical music could be heard on as many as 20 different shows per season, television has generally proved to be an uncomfortable environment for symphonic concerts or chamber recitals. Despite many noble efforts, the medium seems to function least successfully with instrumental music than with any of the other performing arts.

Television's problems with music stem, in large part, from the fundamental differences between listening and watching. Attending a concert or playing a record is clearly not the same thing as viewing a musical event at home with the aid of powerful camera close-ups. As Samuel Lipman observes:

> Music, after all is sound; it is meant to be heard, and when it is clearly heard, it is, in principle, fully experienced. The visual aspect, welcome and even vital as it is to many, is felt by most experienced and trained listeners to be often a distraction and sometimes even an adulteration.[1]

Even when it attempted to serve music with understanding and sensitivity, television's appetite for the visually interesting posed difficulties in terms of covering the fixed and static nature of most concerts. Unlike opera or ballet, an orchestra provided little opportunity for colorful movement, strong conflict, or unexpected novelty. The 100 or so formally dressed, seated musicians could hardly compete with singers or dancers as dramatic performers. Playing a string, wind, or brass instrument is an activity which, no matter how unusual, appears to lose its TV appeal after the third or fourth exposure. To compensate, many telecasts chose to focus almost exclusively on the conductor—a figure who it was hoped would offer viewers a compelling symbol of musical excitement and energy. When the conductor was Arturo Toscanini or Leonard Bernstein, the results could be magical, but with less charismatic maestros what emerged was a program which did indeed make television's visual emphasis seem like an unwelcome distraction.

The inherent problems of simply putting the cameras in the concert hall led to many experiments in alternative methods of musical presentation. Some of these, such as the attempts to accompany selections with paintings, photographs, or abstract images, turned out, like Walt Disney's *Fantasia*, to be more intriguing for their ambition than for their final execution. Others, such as programs exploring the inner workings of a particular piece of music or the psychology of a performing ensemble, were imaginative efforts to use television's close-up scale for new types of musical documentaries.

But despite these endeavors at branching out, the majority of programming featuring classical music on television has been of the "concert style" variety, in part because of tradition and the simple fact that no other technique allows instrumental performance to come across with greater vividness. Telecasts with Vladimir Horowitz, Itzhak Perlman, Artur Rubinstein, and of course Toscanini and Bernstein have demonstrated the medium's ability to capture the intensity and occasional ecstasy of a live event without compromising musical values. On rare occasions like these, the camera served not only as a documentarian but also as a source of aesthetic revelation.

In general, however, the limitations of the "in concert" method—the predictability of approach, the lack of narrative interest—have helped make televised classical music a somewhat weary format whose principal excitement rests on the attractions of a few superstar performers rather than any innovative matching of TV resources with musical means. Nearly four decades of music telecasting have yielded only a few tentative answers to the form's sizeable difficulties in coming to life on the small screen.

HISTORICAL DEVELOPMENT

From Radio to TV—Toscanini and the NBC Symphony

Classical music found a welcome haven on American radio almost from the start of the commercial networks. In its first season of operation, NBC featured performances by no less than eight orchestras, including the Boston Symphony Orchestra and the National Symphony. A year later, the New York Philharmonic, with conductor Arturo Toscanini, made its radio premiere. For the next two decades, both NBC and CBS, as Christopher Sterling and John Kittross note, "always scheduled at least 20 such programs, usually sponsored by prestigious firms," who were attracted by the surprisingly large audiences and the chance to associate their products with quality fare.[2] While concert formats predominated, classical music could also be heard on educational shows such as NBC's popular *Music Appre-*

ciation Hour, hosted by Walter Damrosch, which aired conveniently during school hours.

The success of weekly radio series like those with the New York Philharmonic and the NBC Symphony Orchestra prompted the networks to experiment with serious music programming during the early days of commercial television. In 1944, NBC televised a film made by the Office of War Information of Toscanini conducting Verdi's *Hymn of the Nations*. However, efforts to broadcast musical events planned specifically for the medium were halted until March 18, 1948, when American Federation of Musicians' President James C. Petrillo lifted his ban prohibiting live music telecasting. Two days later, both CBS and NBC battled it out to see which would be the first to air a video concert. CBS won by 90 minutes with its late Saturday afternoon Philadelphia Orchestra broadcast, which, like a good many TV shows at this time, was also heard simultaneously on radio. Cameras for this premiere network event, according to critic Howard Taubman, "ranged over the various sections of the orchestra, emphasizing shots of the women musicians" and catching, in one close-up moment, an obviously unaware Eugene Ormandy popping some mysterious chewy object into his mouth.[3]

At 6:30 P.M. that same day, NBC transmitted the first telecast of a series that had been one of its crown jewels on radio for more than a decade—the weekly concerts of the NBC Symphony Orchestra with Arturo Toscanini. A sense of history and occasion marked the program from its opening minutes. After a formal invitation welcomed viewers and announcer Ben Grauer asked the studio audience to think of the enjoyment of millions of listeners and withold their coughing, RCA Chairman David Sarnoff appeared. This broadcast, he said, "represents the realization of a dream, a dream we have dreamed for 25 years or more" whereby the "magic of science combines with the glory of the arts to bring to countless people in their homes on the wings of the radio waves all of this great production with this great music." With typical energy and determination, maestro Toscanini then walked on the stage of Studio 8H and began what was to be a stirring, all-Wagner concert.

Even in this first, somewhat technically clumsy telecast, it was apparent that television had found one of its great subjects with Toscanini. The cameras, which were positioned around the front and sides of the orchestra, rarely stayed away from his magnetic presence, veering only occasionally to broad, sectional views of the musicians, with very few close-ups of individual instrumentalists. Shots of the 81-year-old maestro were held for minutes at a time, his commanding manner capturing viewers in the same firm grip with which he controlled the NBC Symphony.

A second TV concert a few weeks later offered further proof of the rare power Toscanini could bring to televised music and of the growing advances the medium was bringing to bear on symphonic broadcasts. As *Newsweek*'s critic remarked:

Here was music screened the way perfectionists had dreamed it might be—no woman in the audience to be fascinated, no man in the audience to be bored. As directed by Hal Keith, with the advice of Samuel Chotzinoff, NBC's serious music director, the three cameramen concentrated on 1). Toscanini, 2). on the orchestra, and 3). on the first desk men. . . . It was a revelation.[4]

In this performance of Beethoven's Ninth Symphony, the excitement and drama of Toscanini's conducting style came across once again with startling vividness to home viewers. Seeing Toscanini at close range on these telecasts was an experience best described by Howard Taubman of the *New York Times*:

His face was vital and intense. . . . The music welled out of him with a force that he seemingly could not brook, and one could see him humming, chanting, almost roaring. It was as though every instrument were singing within him. Watching him via television gave you the illusion that a new dimension had been found for your comprehension of music.[5]

The natural eloquence of Toscanini's TV image seemed to increase even more once the NBC telecasts moved from the boxy studio quarters at Rockefeller Center to the spaciousness of Carnegie Hall. In the darkened concert auditorium, with the audience no longer visible, Toscanini's expressively alert face and hands stood out like softly glowing beacons. A few broadcasts later, after he took to wearing a ruffled white collar, he resembled nothing so much as a late Rembrandt masterpiece suddenly brought to life.

The Carnegie Hall programs marked an evolution in the manner with which symphonic music was televised. More cameras were added, as well as more camera movement. In the case of the Toscanini series, however, the additions did not necessarily make for improvements. A November 1951 telecast prompted harsh comments from several critics who attacked the new roving camera style. Jack Gould of the *New York Times* noted that

frequently throughout the hour, the director of the TV pick-up was infuriatingly restless and kept moving the cameras around every few minutes. This visual activity was very distracting and made it difficult to pay proper attention to the music. Time after time the score called out for more close-ups of Toscanini, but off the cameras would go to meaningless "shots" of the orchestra or over-all distance scenes from the back of Carnegie Hall.[6]

Quaintance Eaton of *Musical America* voiced similar objections to camerawork that "was so restless, so arbitary, and aimless that one might have thought televising orchestras was in its dawn,"[7] and offered this prescription for future programs:

> Some lessons should have been learned from earlier experiments, and one of these surely is that the close-up is the only valuable shot after a locale has been established. Another, in this particular case, is that close-ups of Toscanini were the only really interesting shots at all.[8]

These suggestions eventually became common practice, especially once Kirk Browning became director of the broadcasts. Browning, who had been working as an assistant director of the series, received his promotion after an unfortunate telecast where the sports director who handled all of NBC's remote work decided, in a moment of creativity, to superimpose a picture of a girl, combing her hair next to a lily pond, over the face of Toscanini during a performance of Claude Debussy's "The Girl with the Flaxen Hair." NBC music chief Samuel Chotzinoff was furious and gave Browning the direction of the series with the admonition, "I don't care how you do them as long as everything is on Toscanini and nothing else. There is never to be any element on these programs except Toscanini. Nothing is ever to take precedence over Toscanini."[9]

The NBC Symphony telecasts now took on a new and impressive stateliness as a result of Kirk Browning's long, concentrated shots of Toscanini (some lasting several minutes) and the general absence of fussy camera movements and distracting changes in viewpoints. To achieve his effects, Browning rearranged the camera positions in Carnegie Hall, so that all three units were now behind the orchestra. As he recalled in a recent interview:

> In those days, you didn't have zoom lenses, so the only way I could get various pictures of the maestro, without his back, was to move everything around. That really started the whole technique of shooting the reverse angle. . . . I recently saw the first show I ever did with Toscanini—it's at the Museum of Broadcasting. I wouldn't change it today. The miracle of the whole thing is that the constraints of the medium of that time were just right for Toscanini. You couldn't move the camera, and you had to have enormously long takes. . . . But the maestro was one of those extraordinary people. The more you stayed on him, the better the picture.[10]

The ten TV concerts Toscanini made with the NBC Symphony from 1948 to 1952 still remain among the most compelling music programs ever made, but even at the time of their original broadcasts there was some concern that the medium was not completely suited to the aesthetic demands of the musical experience. Could television's dramatic focus properly serve pieces which required intense listener concentration? Is the very act of visualizing an inevitable distraction? As Howard Taubman observed:

Does seeing musicians scrape and blow or pound and pluck the instruments of their craft help the listener to hear the music any better? Does a close-up of a conductor's gyrations and facial expressions make music more expressive? In short, should conductors be seen?[11]

Taubman continued by pointing out television's essential problem with instrumental performance—its need for novelty. "Once you have seen a conductor, his act so to speak, remains essentially the same. So does that of his players. Can television give enough visual variety to these performances to make each concert a fresh adventure?"[12]

The Toscanini TV concerts certainly proved that, at least in some special cases, all that was needed to make music appear magical was a conductor of genius and a few cameras to keep him constantly in view. Visual variety itself seemed like a distraction when the medium confronted someone with Toscanini's dynamic qualities. Unfortunately, however, personalities with this kind of power were far too rare; and with the maestro's retirement in 1954, television was left, in a sense, back at the beginning. In the absence of a superstar conductor, what were the best ways to present classical music for the home viewer? Could instrumental performance be imaginatively televised? The 1950s would be a time of great experimentation in the effort to answer these questions.

A Decade of Different Approaches

The unembellished style that typified the Toscanini programs proved to be one of the most popular and influential methods of presenting music on television. This "purist" approach, where it is felt, in the words of Bert Briller, "that musicians by themselves make engrossing pictures"[13] could be seen on numerous shows of the period. NBC employed this technique not only for the NBC Symphony broadcasts but also for its short-run summer series, *NBC Concert Hall*, in 1948 and two interesting live music programs in the early 1950s. The first, *TV Recital Hall*, sought to re-create the ambience of an intimate concert auditorium. Each week, during the show's intermittent four-year run from 1951 to 1955, a lesser-known musician would perform for 30 minutes before a small studio audience "in a recital-hall type setting."[14] Kirk Browning's direction focused attentively on the soloist, with no isolating close-ups of the hands and with slow panning camera movements that sometimes remained stationary for minutes at a time. *Heritage*, NBC's other music series premiering in 1951, was telecast live from the National Gallery of Art in Washington, D.C., and offered an unusual mixture of performance and lecture. Viewings of paintings on current exhibition and interviews with one of the evening's featured composers were displayed in between selections by the National Gallery

Orchestra. Hosted by Frank Blair, the program aired for a month during summer prime time.

One of broadcasting's most famous music series, *The Voice of Firestone*, also pursued an "in concert" approach, while managing to include a few modest examples of "production values." Like the Toscanini programs, *The Voice of Firestone* began originally on radio and made the move to television in the late 1940s; simultaneous transmissions on both media continued for many years. In a sense, the traditional styles of radio performance helped set the somewhat stodgy pattern the show adopted during its early years on television. Formally attired classical singers and instrumentalists simply stepped out in front of the Firestone Concert Orchestra onto a rather barren stage. They sang or played without much fussiness and were photographed in a generally straightforward manner. Recognizing that television required a more lively approach, the producers attempted to add fancier sets and costumes, but with little success. As contemporary critic Marks Levine reported, "In spite of all the effort, the program is still visually static."[15] Eventually, *The Voice of Firestone*'s stiff qualities and sober manner prompted NBC to cancel the show in 1954 for dragging down its Monday night ratings. To enhance its appeal after moving to ABC, the program decided to expand its format a few years later by adding both a narrator (John Daly) and a broader selection of popular artists, but even with these changes, the show rarely strayed from the "purity" and the confines of the concert-style method.

Interestingly, the networks were not alone in providing classical music programs. Enterprising TV stations throughout the country broadcast concerts of their local symphony orchestras, just as their radio counterparts had done during the 1930s and 1940s. Orchestras receiving TV exposure included the Indianapolis Symphony, the Baltimore Symphony, the Chicago Symphony, the Charlotte Symphony, the Kansas City Symphony, and the Little Symphony of San Francisco.

An unusual experiment in local music programming occurred in 1952 with a 13–week TV version of the long-running radio series *The Standard Hour*, sponsored by the Standard Oil Company of California. The company was eager to explore the possibilities of the new medium to see how television might enhance *The Standard Hour*'s traditional format, which mixed opera highlights, ballet interludes, and short orchestra pieces performed by the San Francisco Symphony. Imaginative visual treatment was a high priority. Vocal and dance sequences were staged in appropriate settings, and camera positions and editing patterns were matched to reflect the mood of the instrumental music. Careful preparations at rehearsal insured that musicians would be seen in close-up during solos and other key passages and that viewers would receive a varied perspective on the orchestra's activities. All 13 orchestra sequences were kinescoped (shot on film from a TV screen) at the same time and then later distributed as individual programs from station to station on the west coast.

Another interesting experiment in local music programming took place in 1953, with a series of 14 telecasts by the Minnesota Symphony, airing under the title *A Great Symphony Orchestra and the Region It Serves.* In addition to their goodwill mission to explain the orchestra's relationship to the community during intermission features, the concerts broke new ground for television in its mixture of music with imagery that flashed on the screen during appropriate passages. Manuel de Falla's *The Three Cornered Hat* was accompanied by a few abstract shapes; Johann Strauss's *Tales from the Vienna Woods* was illustrated by superimposed cutouts documenting Viennese life; *Till Eulenspiegel's Merry Pranks* featured narrative drawings by the Minnesota Symphony's conductor Antal Dorati. In the absence of supporting visuals, the series strove for camerawork that would highlight and underscore musical structure and meaning. Not only were the orchestra players seen in close-up during their solos, but superimpositions brought together musicians from different sections at the same time on the screen to reveal instrumental harmonies and relationships. These techniques were then combined with dramatic camera movements, dictated by the rhythm of the piece, to heighten the effect of musical climaxes.

As concert performance telecasts continued on both network and local stations in the early 1950s, questions persisted about the most effective method of presentation. While few would still subscribe to Olin Downes's belief in 1948 that TV transmission of orchestra programs "is best witnessed from dead center in front of the screen, rather than from either side,"[16] the issues of just where to place the camera and what to show remained troublesome. In a generally enthusiastic discussion of serious music's potential on television, conductor Andre Kostelanetz argued against the use of severe close-ups and fancy camera movements in symphonic broadcasts. "They distract and rob the audience of a certain magic and illusion which should be a part of a good musical performance," he wrote. "In showing an orchestra on the screen, we should remember that when we attend a live performance, we never lose sight of the entire orchestra, although our eye may move for a moment to a particular section."[17] While he also disliked the practice of overly-elaborate televised concerts, where "the pictures draw attention to themselves, rather than to the music," Robert Cantrick felt strongly that the camera should "reveal aspects of the performance inaccessible to the eyes alone."[18] Rather than being stuck with simply documenting an experience, Cantrick encouraged directors to experiment with

> subjective-camera techniques, with choreography, and with abstract imagery. Then the television medium will be exploiting the great advantage it possesses over

radio—not to take the place of a person present at a performance but, on the contrary, to witness in its own unique way.[19]

The Innovations of *Omnibus* and Leonard Bernstein

The time and the freedom to test suggestions like those of Robert Cantrick were becoming more difficult to find, especially given the increasing pressures of network television and the understandable reluctance of advertisers to sponsor music programs that lacked broad popular appeal. One commercial series, however, did offer an outlet for experimentation of all varieties—*Omnibus*, created in 1952 by the TV/Radio Workshop of the Ford Foundation. The program's approach to music was characteristically fresh and unusual. An early telecast featuring selections from Modest Mussorgsky's *Pictures at an Exhibition* provides an example. Instead of a traditional, concert-style performance, the program enlisted the talents of the music world's great showman/maestro, Leopold Stokowski, to explain the story behind the work's composition. Viewers were led on a guided tour through a mock art gallery, as Stokowski pointed to and talked about the pictures inspiring each musical section. Excerpts from the piece were played between the various stops along the way. This "Classics Illustrated" method upset a few critics. As Howard Taubman noted, "If the television audience must be led by the hand, it should get its verbal guidance at the beginning and the end, but once the composer has the floor he should be allowed to hold it."[20] Yet it demonstrated *Omnibus*'s pursuit of new ways to make the arts come alive on television.

The series' most striking music program was a November 1954 broadcast with Leonard Bernstein, discussing the structure of Beethoven's Fifth Symphony. Its opening moments set the stage for Bernstein's dramatic TV approach, as the then 35-year-old conductor stood on a huge studio floor painted with the score of the first movement and pointed to the first four notes with his shoe. During the half hour that followed, Bernstein took viewers on an intense and fascinating exploration of the process of musical creation. Moving over to the piano, he talked about the difficulties Beethoven encountered in composing the work—the themes developed but never used; the sketchbooks filled with passage-after-discarded-passage in the struggle to fuse each section into an organic whole. To make this more meaningful and vivid, Bernstein laced his lecture with demonstrations at the piano and with imaginative sequences featuring members of the Symphony of the Air. Using the giant score on the floor as a backdrop and with the camera looking down from a high angle, the orchestra members were arranged in the position which corresponded precisely with their instrument's notation in the score—the oboist was seated above the oboe's musical part, the clarinetist above his part, and so on. As they played a few selected variations, viewers needed no further words of explanation to grasp the way instruments blend and balance in an orchestral grouping.

This first TV appearance by Leonard Bernstein opened up an exciting era in music telecasting. The dashing young conductor brought to the medium more than just his boundless enthusiasm and his natural gifts as a combination teacher, performer, and priest. He also knew how to convey the intellectual and emotional passion of the musical experience in a way that was both accessible and stimulating to all types of viewers. More than any musician before, or since, Bernstein understood television's potential to unlock the mysteries of music and make the home audience care as deeply as he did about the glories of its expressive language.

An *Omnibus* appearance a year later confirmed Bernstein's status as one of the medium's "great communicators." In a segment entitled "The World of Jazz," he applied the same skill in explaining the intricacies of "The St. Louis Blues" as he had previously done with Beethoven. With slides, piano demonstrations, and a jazz quintet to support his points, Bernstein once again revealed his knack for making fairly serious musical discussions vivid and fun. Even if viewers failed to completely grasp all of his examples of harmony and minor scale development, it was hard not to be carried along by Bernstein's telegenic charm and infectious enthusiasm for the music.

A little more than a year after his third and final *Omnibus* program (devoted to a lively exploration of musical comedy), CBS decided to feature Bernstein's talents on a more regular basis by televising the New York Philharmonic's Young People's concerts. The concerts, which had been a long-time Philharmonic tradition, provided the conductor with a perfect forum to showcase his flair for instruction and inspiration. But the question remained of how to transform these live music events from Carnegie Hall into interesting television. The format devised by producer and director Roger Englander for the first broadcast on January 18, 1958, recognized that while few people could match Bernstein's attention-holding powers, it was also important to use some of the medium's special resources to enhance and underscore the concert's primary themes. Not only was camerawork carefully planned in advance to coordinate with the music being played but special visual material was also inserted to illustrate key points. Pictures of composers appeared at the mention of their names. So did views of rocket ships when they were needed to demonstrate the propulsion of a Gioacchino Rossini overture. In this way, the Young People's telecast combined the best features of a live concert program—the excitement of musicians performing before a large audience—with the technical feats more commonly found in studio productions.

Bernstein's magic rapport with the crowd at Carnegie Hall and his fervor in discussing the concert's topic of "What Does Music Mean" came across with such effectiveness that two more Young People's broadcasts aired in the months that followed. In November 1958, he returned to the more adult-oriented format he pioneered with *Omnibus*. On a late Sunday afternoon, in the slot usually reserved for *Ted Mack's Amateur Hour*, Bernstein, along with the New York Philharmonic, offered another of his ebullient lecture/demonstrations, this time on the final movement of Beethoven's Ninth Symphony. Seated in what appeared to be his office, the conductor opened the program with typical buoyancy. Grabbing the score in front of him and looking directly into the eye of the camera, he proclaimed, "What a phenomenal work; there's so much in this work," and then launched into an enthusiastic introductory discussion. At the piano a few minutes later he once again uncovered the wonders of musical structure in a way that helped even inexperienced listeners come to terms with Beethoven's formal power. As Howard Taubman of the *New York Times* observed:

> [Bernstein] has the gift of making music fascinating. His talks are knowledgeable, witty, serious and ingeniously threaded with musical illustration. . . . As an intelligent musician he never loses sight of the fundamental nature of the art he is analyzing. As a performer who rejoices in the pleasure that flows from a responsive audience, he has mastered the knack of throwing light on the processes of music in an exciting way. He knows the uses of legitimate showmanship; he can illuminate his subject without patronizing or demeaning it.[21]

After a performance of the "Ode to Joy," with the Westminster Choir and soloists Leontyne Price and Maureen Forrester, the program concluded with the same kind of beguiling display of personality with which it began. Back in his office, Bernstein was seen calmly smoking a cigarette, the toll of conducting apparent in his sloped shoulders and more relaxed manner. Like the host at the end of a long party, he graciously, and somewhat wearily, thanked the home audience for watching and invited them to tune in to his next program two months later. The intimacy of television made a small moment like this seem irresistibly glamorous.

While Bernstein would appear in several more "adult" telecasts (covering topics as varied as jazz in serious music and the meaning of rhythm), he also continued his *Young People's Concerts*, which were scheduled three or four times a season. Under producer/director Roger Englander, the series had become a landmark example of how to adapt television to the fixed demands of the concert situation. Englander's approach stressed preparation, imagination, and musical sensitivity. Working closely with Bernstein's script and the orchestra score, each camera shot was planned in advance. The task was made somewhat easier by the conductor's instructional mission. As Englander notes, "Much as any good teacher does, Bernstein tells you what he is going to say, and he says it, then he tells you again what he said. So there are clues as to what the camera director should point out, just to strengthen and reinforce what Bernstein has asked us to look for."[22]

With his musical training, Englander was unusually responsive to a work's shape and drama. As one of the first American TV directors who could read a score, he was able to plot precisely where his eight cameras should be, what they should focus on, and when they should move or be shifted. The *Young People*'s telecasts, as a result, were characterized by their clarity. The visual design was so carefully matched to musical activity that viewers could easily follow both the development of key themes and the complicated dynamics of orchestral performance.

In his nearly 15 years with the series, Bernstein covered an enormous range of topics, including tributes to composers from every period (with a heavy emphasis on the twentieth century), examinations of musical forms, as well as yearly salutes to young performers. Given their sophisticated style, it's not surprising that the telecasts reached an audience much older than their title would indicate. A 1964 survey revealed that 83 percent of Bernstein's viewers were adults, with women outnumbering men by a few percentage points; 5 percent were teenagers; and 11 percent were tots.[23] These figures and the program's euphoric critical acclaim made it less difficult to understand why CBS decided, in the wake of FCC Chairman Newton Minow's attack against commercial television's "vast wasteland," to move the series, for a few years at least, from the ghetto of weekend afternoons to the main street of weekday prime time.

Other Network Approaches to Music

Leonard Bernstein brought televised classical music more attention and prestige than anyone since Toscanini. His programs, however, were special events, which while widely promoted, interrupted the regular TV schedule only sporadically, often during the less frantic holiday viewing periods. Shows attempting to present serious music on a more frequent basis were not treated as kindly. *The Voice of Firestone* was the most notorious example of the difficulties involved in non-popular music telecasting. Despite efforts to expand its base and include a broader range of performing talent, ABC (which took the show over after it was cancelled on NBC), decided in 1959 that *The Voice of Firestone*'s semi-elite orientation was disrupting its prime-time schedule. The program was given a new slot at 10:00 P.M. "so as not to hurt the shows that followed it."[24] When the Firestone Tire Company, who underwrote the program for $1 million a year, refused to go along, the program was cancelled once again.

The resulting outcry from critics and members of Congress prompted ABC to air a low-budget replacement series from the same producers, *Music for a Summer Night*, that lasted for two seasons. When the network changed management, *The Voice of Firestone* returned in 1962 to critical cheers, a 10:00 P.M. time slot, and a loyal, but still far too "small" audience of two and a half million viewers. At the end of the next season, it received its third, and final, cancellation.

Classical music fared somewhat better on *The Bell Telephone Hour* on NBC, which like *The Voice of Firestone*, began originally on network radio as a semi-serious musical variety show. The program's relative success on television came from its lighter touch and smoother finish. In contrast to *Firestone*'s stiff concert manner, *The Telephone Hour* presented its performers in a tasteful, gracious environment that didn't make viewers feel like they needed to be formally dressed to watch. During its ten years on the air, the show featured an impressive range of musical talent, including Gregor Piatagorsky, Clifford Curzon, John Browning, the Casadesus family, and Jose Iturbi, who were usually mixed in with appearances from popular singers and musicians.

The idea of combining artists from the classical and popular worlds was, of course, developed and popularized on the network variety programs. Most of the big name variety series during the 1950s and 1960s would, on occasion, bring on concert performers to add a dash of class and style to the proceedings. The chief outlet for short doses of serious music was *The Ed Sullivan Show*, which throughout its 23 years on the air presented an extraordinary number of the country's top musicians, usually in five- or six-minute segments designed to display their virtuosity. *The Tonight Show* was also willing to book classical artists, as long as they were well known, suddenly newsworthy, or possessed of the kind of colorful personalities the show's host, whether it be Steve Allen, Jack Paar, or later, Johnny Carson, would find particularly amusing.

Other than the variety series and the occasional specials, viewers interested in serious music on the commercial networks were left to search out the little-watched and unrated programs scheduled on Sunday mornings and afternoons. There they would find unsponsored, low-budget, cultural and religious shows like *Camera Three*, *Look Up and Live*, *Lamp Unto My Feet*, and *Directions*, which often featured music too adventurous for prime time. Premiering in 1955, *Camera Three* was willing to tackle any aspect of the arts, so long as the topic could be explored with minimum expense in the studio. Its musical investigations during its first decade looked at everything from the art of frontier ballads to demonstrations of electronic music; from performances of Bach's *The Goldberg Variations* with pianist Glenn Gould and harpsichorist Wanda Landowska to modern American composer David Amram's *Dirge and Variations* with the Marlboro Trio. Under producer Pamela Illott, CBS's religious programs *Look Up and Live* and *Lamp Unto My Feet* also opened its door to all forms of musical expression. Not only were there classical recitals by artists like E. Power Biggs and Rosalyn Tureck, but new works were commissioned on a regular basis. George Antheil and Robert Ward were among the many composers who benefited from this largesse.

Music Specials in the 1960s

If classical music was encountering difficulties as a regular prime-time offering, the success and prestige of attractions like the Leonard Bernstein telecasts seemed to encourage the networks to schedule at least one or two music specials each season. With its reputation as the Tiffany of the networks and as the home of *The Young People's Concerts* series, CBS led the way against its competitors in terms of stylish, big-league classical events, helped in no small part by the talented producers and directors the network maintained in its stable. An example of this was a pair of specials directed by Roger Englander which the network aired in 1960. Grouped under the title *Spring Festival of Music* and produced by Robert Herridge, they included a responsively paced, live broadcast from the Academy of Music by the Philadelphia Orchestra and a striking program that showcased "American Soloists," with Alfredo Antonini conducting the Symphony of the Air.

The highlight of the latter telecast was a virtuoso performance, both musically and visually, of the third movement of Sergei Rachmaninoff's Second Piano Concerto. In contrast to the traditional concert hall ambience of previous studio music telecasts, Englander rearranged everything to accommodate the demands of the TV cameras. The orchestra members, rather than being bunched in a bulky half circle, were spread out so that they could be seen in a more horizontal sweep. John Browning's piano, instead of opening towards an unseen audience, was turned around to place him closer to the conductor for more interesting shot possibilities. Even the studio was transformed, its technological function now fully visible, with a decor composed of tall microphone stands serving as elegant accents against the white background.

To capture the music's romantic verve, Englander relied extensively on a crane-mounted camera, which he directed with choreographic precision. During one of Browning's solos, the camera swept down from above, circled around him, and ended up with a view of the pianist and the conductor at the exact moment the orchestra launched into a stirring accompanying section. Another solo began with the camera gracefully arcing around the keyboard and then holding on a view of Browning for two minutes as he played the main theme. At the grand conclusion which followed, a quick cut to Antonini hitting the dramatic downbeat was instantly replaced by a full, sweeping shot of the orchestra, closing at the finale with a high-angled view of the studio that finished on a close-up of Browning's hands. Concert music has rarely been televised with such brio.

CBS's other prime-time specials throughout the decade focused on either the activities of Leonard Bernstein, special musical events, or the packaged presentations of impressario Sol Hurok. Hurok had previously put together a series of programs for NBC entitled *Festival of Music* that provided a tasteful and expensively produced showcase for the major artists he represented. His four specials for CBS followed a similar pattern. Taped in a studio, they featured elegantly photographed, brief performances by the superstars of the Hurok roster, including Isaac Stern, Andres Segovia, Van Cliburn, David Oistrakh, Artur Rubinstein, Emil Gilels, and Mstislav Rostropovich.

During the 1960s, Leonard Bernstein continued to remain the most widely seen classical musician on television (a distinction still true today), especially once CBS moved his *Young People's* broadcasts to a 7:30 P.M. weekday starting time beginning in 1961. In addition to these children's concerts, Bernstein maintained his series of adult programs that varied from lecture/demonstrations on the role of rhythm in music or jazz in the concert hall to a documentary on the New York Philharmonic's trip to Japan. The conductor also played a major role in CBS's live telecast of the opening night festivities at Lincoln Center in 1962, where he appeared leading the Philharmonic in a performance of Gustav Mahler's Eighth Symphony.

Lincoln Center activities would be covered extensively on CBS, including the opening of the New York State Theater, the rededication of the Juilliard School of Music, as well as a few "survey" programs highlighting the performing arts groups which make up the Center. However, the decade's most impressive TV music event did not take place at the multi-million dollar arts complex but at the venerable Carnegie Hall less than a mile away. There in February 1968, pianist Vladimir Horowitz overcame a long-standing personal bias against concert telecasting and performed an historic one-hour recital, expressly for television.

The broadcast had been planned for many months, after Horowitz finally agreed to the entreaties of *New York Times* critic Howard Taubman (who would serve as the show's executive producer) to allow TV cameras to capture a concert for posterity. Both CBS and the pianist agreed to certain ground rules. Horowitz demanded the familiar environment of Carnegie Hall rather than the sterility of a studio. The network insisted that no piece last more than ten minutes. As the date of the taping approached, Horowitz grew concerned about the method of presentation. He was particularly eager to avoid the pitfalls plaguing most music telecasts. "Everything I've seen on music has been a flop," he told a reporter from *TIME*. "There are too many things that distract the eye at the expense of the ear."[25] In order to calm his fears, a dry run through was arranged a few days before, so that the camera crew could rehearse their moves (to prevent creaks on stage, they were required to wear velvet slippers and to apply talcum powder between the boards) and the pianist could play back the tape to see how he came across.

Horowitz need not have worried. Under the direction of Roger Englander, the program was an extraordinary example of how television can reflect and respond to the formal beauties of the musical experience. The broadcast's distinguishing feature was its simplicity. There were no interruptions, no announcements (only five words, "Ladies and gentlemen, Vladimir Horowitz," were spoken), and no attention-grabbing techniques. Rather than concentrate on extreme close-up views of Horowitz's performance rigors or the lightning speed of the pianist's fingers, Englander employed his five cameras to mirror each work's structure and mood. The sectional divisions inherent in Robert Schumann's *Arabesque* were underscored by relatively fixed camera shots that changed only when a new segment began. A similar process was used during Alessandro Scarlatti's Sonata in G Major. The first movement, filmed with just one camera, featured a slow tracking shot that craned down and gently zoomed in on the pianist. The second movement shifted to another solo camera, a bit more restrained in its visual focus, for its entire duration.

Englander's disciplined, quiet, musically responsive techniques resulted in a telecast that captured the intensity and artistry of a Horowitz recital. By placing the emphasis on both the pianist and the music, viewers were able to watch Horowitz framed by camerawork and editing approximating the underlying architecture of each selection. Though the program was enthusiastically acclaimed by most critics, its somewhat rarefied approach did have its detractors. Jack Gould of the *New York Times* objected to the program's lack of contrast and especially to the personal distance it kept from the pianist. His argument centered on the role of any musician on television:

> In the concert hall, perhaps, it is contrary to tradition for a soloist to speak from the stage. But in the intimacy of TV, it can be of enormous assistance to hear an individual speak in his own voice, inject his own choice of emphasis, humor or disdain, to discuss even for a sentence or two a work he's about to play. On television, it is almost the only way to establish a bond among humans about to start a common pleasure.[26]

While Gould may be right about the medium's attachment to the immediately personal, his suggestion that Horowitz introduce the selections or speak directly to the home audience would have run counter to everything the pianist believed about performance style. Even if such an idea was considered an essential accommodation for the telecast, it is doubtful, given Horowitz's high-strung nerves and intensely private manner, if anyone would have seriously proposed it.

Hoping to maximize the prestige value of this expensively produced recital (total costs came to a bit more than a quarter of a million dollars) while minimizing the inevitable drop-off in viewership, CBS chose an interesting strategy. The show was delayed seven months after its taping in order to make its premiere a glittering occasion at the start of the new TV season. CBS's public relations department orchestrated an enormous press buildup. The network's programmers, meanwhile, found the perfect spot on the schedule where the telecast's limited audience appeal would do the least amount of ratings damage. Recognizing that nothing could effectively compete against the season premiere of television's then number-one show, NBC's *Bonanza* or the first network showing of *Zorba the Greek* on ABC, Vladimir Horowitz seemed as good a choice as any.

This strategic thinking was pursued by necessity for most classical music programs, which inevitably posed a disruption to commercial television's dominant mission to reach as many viewers as possible at all times. The increasingly infrequent music broadcasts of the 1960s were usually scheduled in either out-of-the-way places, such as non-rated holiday periods or low-viewing months of the summer, or pushed into conventional prime time by the presence of a celebrity narrator or the clout of a prestige sponsor. An example of the latter was *The Bell Telephone Hour*, a program still given fairly respectable time periods even after it switched formats in 1966 from light, concert-style presentations to serious music documentaries. The series now covered topics as varied as Gian-Carlo Menotti at the Spoletto Festival, the opening of the Metropolitan Opera's production of Samuel Barber's *Antony and Cleopatra*, a remembrance of Toscanini, Pablo Casals at the Marlboro Music Festival, and George Plimpton conducting the New York Philharmonic. Yet, as *The Voice of Firestone* demonstrated, powerful sponsors were sometimes not enough to keep a show alive in the face of network imperatives. Two seasons after its less than crowd-pleasing documentary format premiered, *The Bell Telephone Hour* was itself cancelled, ending an NBC run that started on radio 26 years before.

Non-Commercial Television and Music

From its beginnings in the mid–1950s, educational television provided classical music with the kind of regular forum it was unable to find on the commercial networks. Though production budgets were at times barely adequate, publicly funded stations were eager for any type of alternative programming. Music shows, both instructional and performance oriented, proved to be among the most popular material these stations broadcast.

In contrast to ABC, CBS, and NBC's concentration on scattered specials, the majority of the music programs distributed by NET to educational stations around the country were in series form. Produced either by station affiliates, independent producers, NET, or imported from foreign sources, these shows fell into a number of different categories. Some featured straight performances by ensembles ranging from small chamber groups to major orchestras, such as the Vienna Philharmonic or the Boston Symphony. Others offered various forms of instruction. On a series like the *Fine Arts*

Quartet Plays Beethoven, a selection was first discussed, illustrated, and then played without interruption. *Music and the Renaissance* followed a matching course with demonstrations of ancient instruments concluding with a concert performance. Howard Hanson's *Music as a Language* was, as its title indicates, more formal in nature. Like similarly named programs, such as *Music in Focus*, *Music in the Life of Man*, and *Passing Notes on Music*, its purpose was to explore musical meaning, often in a lecture format.

The most illuminating of NET's instruction programs was its series of master classes, featuring world-famous musicians tutoring small groups of students in the subtleties of their art. The success of its first such endeavor with cellist Pablo Casals led to other productions showcasing the professorial and musical talents of Andres Segovia, Jascha Heifetz, Yehudi Menuhin, and Lotte Lehmann.

Gradually, however, the educational tone of the network's music presentations began to change. As Richard Dasher observed, by the start of the 1960s, "the number of didactic series acquired rapidly declined, while the number of series whose function was informative entertainment rose."[27] Lecturers were replaced by programs with a greater personality orientation. Series like *The Creative Person*, *Heritage*, and *Creativity* let viewers visit with musicians and composers without a sense of formal barrier.

Beginning in 1962, NET embarked on an ambitious series of orchestral programs, grouped under the title *NET Symphony*. Some of the shows were acquired from outside producers, such as a group of concerts by the Cleveland Orchestra, originally broadcast on the Group W commercial station in Cleveland, but many were produced by NET and its affiliated educational stations. Often, these in-house efforts took the form of two separate, one-hour shows, mixing documentary and rehearsal footage with filmed performances. Profiled orchestras included the Chicago Symphony with conductor Jean Martinon, the Houston Symphony with John Barbirolli, the American Symphony Orchestra with Leopold Stokowski, and the Cincinnati Symphony led by Max Rudolph.

As the network began to shift towards more performance programming, it also started to distribute more music special events, as opposed to multipart series. There were profiles of Jean Sibelius, Igor Stravinsky, and Bela Bartok; the television premiere of the Juilliard String Quartet; individual concerts by the California Chamber Symphony and the Pittsburgh Symphony on tour in Warsaw; a celebration of Lincoln Center on its anniversary; and annual broadcasts of the United Nations Day Concert. Even the series which were broadcast often seemed to be characterized more by diversity than by any single unifying theme. *ARTS: U.S.A.* jumped from explorations of electronic music and the avant-garde to discussions with composers Elliot Carter and Leon Kirchner to a documentary on life as a student at the Eastman School of Music. *The Sounds of Summer*, an 18–

part series telecast in 1969, included concerts from all over the Western hemisphere, opening with a performance by Yehudi Menuhin from the Festival Casals at San Juan, moving to Tanglewood for Erich Leinsdorf's final night with the Boston Symphony Orchestra, and stopping along the way to feature dance and popular music events. *Music on Television* in 1970 was a short-lived conversation series with an equally varied agenda. One week Alexis Weissenberg and TV director Jordan Whitelaw discussed the piano; another week composer Jack Beeson talked with William Saroyan about how he converted the latter's play, *My Heart's In the Highlands*, into an opera. Rudolf Bing also appeared to reminisce about his career at the Metropolitan Opera.

Great Performances

By the early 1970s, music programming on educational television, now renamed PBS, was beginning a new phase. Generous funding from Exxon and the Corporation for Public Broadcasting made it possible to launch *Great Performances*, an umbrella arts series designed initially to showcase American theater and elegant (and inexpensive) music productions from abroad. The program's first music presentation in April 1974 was a performance of Bach's B Minor Mass, with Karl Richter and the Munich Bach Choir and Orchestra. Though rather traditional in approach, the telecast was beautifully filmed at Klosterkirche, Diessen am Ammersee, a setting that only enhanced the music's spiritual power. The imported concerts offered by *Great Performances* in the years that followed were just as aesthetically pleasing and tasteful. American viewers were now able to regularly sample the kind of attractively packaged music programs widely available on European broadcasting systems. In addition to a continuing cycle of Bach choral works with Karl Richter, the series showcased performances by Artur Rubinstein, the Concertgebouw Orchestra of Amsterdam with Bernard Haitink, Mstislav Rostropovich, Karl Bohm, and, especially, Herbert von Karajan. Von Karajan's commanding presence made him a natural TV star. He seemed to embody the very image of the formidable continental conductor, driven by the mysterious forces of the music in front of him. On *Great Performances*, he could be seen, often twice a season, conducting symphonies, the Verdi Requiem, and operas from La Scala. Only one musical personality would appear more frequently: against the power and TV charisma of Leonard Bernstein even von Karajan appeared outclassed.

Bernstein's association with *Great Performances* began with a 1974 concert taped at Tanglewood with the Boston Symphony Orchestra, but by and large his appearances would be with foreign orchestras, including the Israeli Philharmonic, the London Symphony Orchestra, and, most prominently, the Vienna Philharmonic. His filmed performances, usually directed with great sensitivity by Humphrey Burton, were, in a sense, continuations of the Bernstein TV tradition pioneered by his earlier work with *Omnibus* and *The Young People's Concerts*. The conductor—his hair flying, his face engulfed by the moods of the music, his body springing like a dancer's—was invariably the center of attention. While there were integrated shots of the musicians, keyed to appropriate passages in the score, Bernstein served as the pivot point—the chief source of energy, the magnet to which the camera always returned for dynamic expression and feeling. A Bernstein TV performance depended on seeing Bernstein. No conductor in the electronic age, other than Toscanini, has been a more potent emblem of the glories of musical performance. His appearances on *Great Performances* and on such PBS programs as his 1976 series of Norton Lectures and his 60th birthday salute from Wolf Trap only confirmed his TV status as the preeminent classical musician of the last three decades.

Leonard Bernstein was not the only American conductor to be showcased on *Great Performances*. There were also several concerts featuring Eugene Ormandy and the Philadelphia Orchestra, as well as programs highlighting American orchestras (and their international music directors), including the Los Angeles Philharmonic with Zubin Mehta, the Cleveland Symphony with Lorin Maazel, and the Chicago Symphony with Sir Georg Solti. These domestic symphonic telecasts normally followed a predictable, if somewhat dull, pattern. The five or six cameras placed in the auditoriums gave the impression of constant motion, panning the musicians, closing-in on a performer, or mostly switching to various views of the conductor. Editing was, by now, largely determined in response to musical demands. Cuts were made according to the rhythmic pattern of a work and the seeming imperative to spotlight any orchestra player at the start of a solo. The essential problem with the majority of these intelligently directed programs, however, was a certain lack of excitement. As many commentators have observed, the mechanics of instrumental performance rarely make for compelling television. A straining oboist or furiously bowing cellist simply fail to hold one's interest after a while, no matter how judiciously they've been assembled into the overall visual conception. The answer was either to find a totally new stylistic strategy or to offer viewers a more forceful sense of drama. The latter approach proved to be the key to *Great Performances*' most successful series-within-a-series, *Live from Lincoln Center*.

Premiering in January 1976 with a concert by the New York Philharmonic, *Live from Lincoln Center* was the outgrowth of years of experimentation to develop an acceptable method of live concert telecasting. New technologies played an important role. Cameras with greater light sensitivity and sharper long-focus lenses made it possible to broadcast auditorium events without disturbing patrons. FM stereo simulcasts made it possible to hear full audio dynamics without having music squeezed almost beyond recognition through a tinny TV speaker. But the most significant factor, according to John Goberman, the head of Lincoln Center's TV department, wasn't just the equipment; it was learning the best way to employ it.[28] Goberman's emphasis centered on reproducing the experience of live performance. "The whole theory behind *Live from Lincoln Center*," he remarked in an interview, "is that it's event television. . . . The goal is to capture as much as possible the 'event' quality—the vitality, the excitement, the thrust."[29] Every aspect of the telecast, from the special cameras to the direction, was designed to enhance the inherent drama of live concert presentation. The use of the telling close-up, a specialty of the series' director, Kirk Browning, and the privileged camera positions helped home viewers feel that they were sharing in the intimate rapport and immediacy previously reserved for only the wealthiest ticketholders. Performers on stage also seemed to sense the thrill of electronically communicating with vast new audiences. As John Goberman has noted, response to the cameras often provided an "extra edge," generally resulting in "a better performance for people in the hall of the live telecast" as well.[30]

Live from Lincoln Center's music programs were characterized by their close-range perspective. Broadcasts of New York Philharmonic concerts or recitals from Avery Fisher Hall stressed Goberman's "commitment to the very notion of live performance"[31] through camerawork that frequently seemed to sit in the lap of the absorbed musicians. Director Kirk Browning was a strong believer that televised concerts demanded an intimate, personal approach rather than majestic sweep. "In this medium," he once observed, "you absolutely owe your audience detail that will make them care about and respond to what they see."[32] This often took the form of extremely tight close-ups and a reliance on expressive images to dramatize the nature of a given passage. As he explained to the *New York Times*:

> What we are trying to do today in these concerts is to represent the *character* of the music. If there is a fortissimo in the orchestra and everyone's playing, you have a certain aural energy. You can't represent that energy by shooting 110 people. By the time you get to a small screen, there's no energy left. So you get the *essence*—one timpani roll or one strong string accent—anything that represents the energy of the music.[33]

Live from Lincoln Center's greatest asset—its "liveness"—gave its music broadcasts a vitality rarely found in any pretaped or studio produced concert. Knowing that the event was being televised as it happened seemed to make every musical experience a bit more exciting, a fact the series capitalized on by offering viewers the chance to see the music world's star personalities as they faced the demands of live performance. Showcased artists included Van Cliburn, Emil Gilels, Isaac Stern, Itzhak Perlman,

James Galway, Rudolf Serkin, and Zubin Mehta, who was seen at least twice a season in his role as conductor of the New York Philharmonic.

New Approaches and New Music Series on PBS

Even with its success in capturing the thrill of the concert hall, *Live from Lincoln Center* was not able to solve all of the problems associated with classical music telecasting. The series was still locked into the standard formula of displaying, at appropriate musical moments, close-up views of instrumentalists and conductors as they worked their way through the score in front of them. Despite the "event" quality of each broadcast, after a while only the most charismatic of performers proved capable of elevating the program into the realm of the truly special.

Efforts to break the rigidity of the serious music format on television had been attempted since the 1950s. However, other than the lecture/example techniques practiced by Leonard Bernstein on his CBS specials, no promising avenues emerged until the appearance of an intriguing PBS program in 1973. Entitled *The Bolero* and created by Allan Miller, an associate conductor of the Denver Symphony, the show was an unusual exploration of Maurice Ravel's orchestral tone poem *Bolero*. Rather than present a sober lecture on the work's style and meaning, the half-hour program allowed members of the Los Angeles Philharmonic to discuss their thoughts about the piece, intercut with an actual performance, strikingly filmed by William Fertik. The result was an interesting and celebrated example (the program went on to win an Oscar—an unusual feat for a TV show) of how to present classical music without feeling trapped by strict fidelity to the dictates of the score.

Two years later, Allan Miller went on to create, produce, and direct a six-part series for PBS called *The Music Project Presents . . .*, that, in his words, hoped "to show that every piece of music can become its own television program."[34] Several of the episodes continued *The Bolero*'s investigations into the process of music-making. *The Secret Life of an Orchestra* mixed candid observations by members of the Denver Symphony with a rehearsal and performance of Richard Wagner's overture to *Die Meistersinger*. *Romeo and Juliet in Kansas City* switched gears and examined the audience, in this case a group of young people, listening to the Kansas City Philharmonic. In addition to a program using animation to illustrate the characteristics of specific instruments, the series also ventured into the realm of video art accompaniment, combining Fred Barzyk's electronically created imagery to suggest a visual approximation of Karel Husa's *Music for Prague, 1968*. The results were particularly impressive to critic Alan Kriegsman of the *Washington Post*, who observed that "the visual component of this program is no longer an accessory; it has become an equal partner in the generation of a securely integrated esthetic whole.

And it shows how a plethora of video techniques can be made to serve a practical artistic end."[35]

Yet, intriguing as the final outcome might be, the time, cost, and effort involved in such video experimentation made it difficult to employ these advanced practices as anything more than occasional novelties. The only place which seemed to be willing to try even the most rudimentary of techniques was, curiously enough, one of the oldest music series on educational television—the concerts of the Boston Symphony Orchestra. When the orchestra launched its national PBS series *Evening at Symphony* in 1973 (its concerts had been televised locally since the mid–1950s to viewers in Boston), producer Jordan Whitelaw used devices like divided screens and superimpositions to help emphasize the architecture of the score. Even though his primary objective was always to see "that the show compliments the music, without getting in the way,"[36] he recognized the value of certain of the medium's technological enhancements. As he told an interviewer, television

> is a visual medium, and I am not afraid to use visual effects. If I've got a duet between a violin and a basson, why shouldn't I use a split screen to show the duet?
>
> I'm told by a lot of people that the split screen is gimmicky. Well, of course it's a gimmick. It's a device. But there it is in the music, so if you can attractively demonstrate it, why not?[37]

Jordan Whitelaw's use of gimmicks, however, wasn't as much for a sudden jolt of splashiness as it was part of his general effort to disclose the structure and operations of a work of music in pictorial terms. In contrast to the intimate, energetic approach of Kirk Browning, Whitelaw was more concerned with musical revelation. The Boston Symphony telecasts contained no extreme shots of the performers or lingering portraits of dramatic maestros. What was featured instead were camera views that followed, in a restrained and stately fashion, the process by which music unfolds. Whitelaw offered this vivid example of his methods:

> Let's assume you have a big fortissimo, followed by a lovely decrescendo, and finally, a bassoon solo. There you have three situations. What I would do, rather than take three shots, is have a wide shot of the orchestra for the fortissimo. Then I would take my sweet time while the music is pooping out, gradually zooming in on the bassoon. Its gives you some legitimate motion, you only use one shot, and it gives the thing some *elegance*.[38]

Yet regardless of Jordan Whitelaw's techniques, the strict performance aspect of the Boston Symphony telecasts did have its limitations. Other than a brief introduction by announcer William Pierce, very little context was provided for the experience which was to follow. As Whitelaw noted in an interview, "I broadcast these programs to anyone who is interested in serious music,"[39] a policy that often seemed, in its austere practice, to limit the programs to viewers already familiar with the classical repertoire. Subsequent PBS concert series attempted to be more inviting. Premiering in 1977, *Previn and the Pittsburgh* mixed performances with both documentary footage of orchestra rehearsals and discussions with Andre Previn and guest artists, resembling, in some ways, a looser version of the Leonard Bernstein/New York Philharmonic broadcasts of the late 1950s. *The Guilini Concerts*, *The Fabulous Philadelphians*, and a complete cycle of the Beethoven symphonies with Antal Dorati and the Detroit Symphony Orchestra, all observed a similar pattern.

In addition to these expanded format presentations, PBS also offered several special concert events series, modeled on *Live from Lincoln Center*. *In Performance at Wolf Trap* featured a wide variety of artists, including Mstislav Rostropovitch, Yehudi Menuhin, Leonard Bernstein, and the New Orleans Preservation Jazz Hall Band. *The Kennedy Center Tonight* was equally broad in scope. There were tributes to Aaron Copland and opera singer George London, a Christmas concert with Leontyne Price, a production of Leonard Bernstein's *Mass*, as well as programs spotlighting Sarah Vaughan and vibraphonist Lionel Hampton. A more intimate atmosphere characterized *In Performance at the White House*. Among the recitalists and chamber ensembles who appeared before the president and a small gathering of distinguished guests in the East Room were Vladimir Horowitz, Mstislav Rostropovitch, Leontyne Price, Rudolf Serkin, the Juilliard String Quartet, and Itzhak Perlman, accompanied by 20-year-old pianist Ken Noda. Mention should also be made of one of PBS's most durable series, *Evening at the Pops*, which through the years has presented a virtual smorgasbord of light musical fare, with guest artists ranging from Itzhak Perlman and Marilyn Horne to Joel Grey, Tony Bennett, and Ben Vereen, all festively accompanied by the Boston Pops.

Music Programming on the Commercial Networks—1970s and Beyond

The cancellation of *The Bell Telephone Hour* in 1968 and *The Ed Sullivan Show* in 1971 signalled the end, for all intents and purposes, of regular presentations of classical music in commercial prime time. Serious music on ABC, CBS, and NBC would now be relegated to the less frequently viewed, and less frequently sponsored, slots of Sunday mornings and afternoons. Occasionally, however, the networks would offer a prime-time special devoted to a major music personality. Following the lead of CBS's 1968 Horowitz concert, NBC broadcast a 90–minute documentary on pianist Artur Rubinstein in 1969 that combined some previously shot French TV footage with at-home glimpses and concert excerpts. A program on

Jascha Heifetz two years later employed roughly the same balance between conversations and performance.

The sorry state of classical music programming at the start of the 1970s can best be gauged by CBS's handling of a special Beethoven bicentennial tribute with Leonard Bernstein. Originally designed to be shown in December 1970 to coincide with the composer's 200th birthday, the show featured a typically rhapsodic Bernstein touring Beethoven's Vienna, discussing Beethoven's genius, rehearsing excerpts from *Fidelio*, and leading a concert performance of *The Ode to Joy* with the Vienna Philharmonic. CBS, however, for reasons never explained, delayed broadcasting the program for over a year, finally scheduling it on Christmas Eve 1971, when viewership was traditionally low (and unrated) and when the timeliness of its "tribute" message would be effectively blunted. The special marked one of Bernstein's last prime-time appearances for the network whose prestige he had enhanced so much. After retiring as conductor of *The Young People's Concerts* in 1973, the majority of his TV activities would now take place on PBS.

If classical music was a commodity fast approaching extinction on commercial prime time, it still could be found in scattered scheduling pockets where high ratings were not as important. As it had in the past, CBS used its off-hours on Sundays to present a wide range of musical programming. Even without Bernstein's participation, *The Young People's Concerts* continued, led for several years by the conductor many observers viewed as the charismatic maestro's heir apparent, Michael Tilson Thomas. Sunday mornings the network's religious programs *Lamp Unto My Feet* and *Look Up and Live* and its arts showcase *Camera Three* often presented concerts and music documentaries. Under producers such as Merrill Brockway and Roger Englander, the low-budgeted but consistently innovative *Camera Three* seemed particularly eager to explore topics outside of the traditional classical repertory. There were musical essays on Edgar Varese, with Pierre Boulez, and on Carl Ruggles, with Michael Tilson Thomas; examinations of black composers; performances of Dmitri Shostakovich's score for the film *New Babylon* and of George Crumb's *Ancient Voices of Children*; a collaborative concert with the Modern Jazz Quartet and the Juilliard String Quartet; documentaries on Pierre Boulez and on Mahler's career in New York; and dramatizations of the life of Maurice Gottschalk and the final days of Stephen Foster.

Sunday morning cultural shows like *Camera Three* were not alone in seeking an alternative approach towards musical programming. In the 1970s, several other commercial network products also tried to expand their focus, though their efforts were usually limited to more obvious integrations of classical music with contemporary trends and styles. An *NBC Experiment in Television* in February 1970 offered a survey of music in Britain, hosted by Alistair Cooke, that included performers ranging from Yehudi Menuhin to the Beatles. A month later, the same network broadcast *The Switched On Symphony*, an uneasy attempt to find a common ground between classicism and rock and roll. Among the program's dubious examples was a performance by Zubin Mehta and the Los Angeles Philharmonic of excerpts from Richard Strauss's *Also Sprach Zarathustra* (announced in its more familiar guise as the theme from *2001*), accompanied by, of all things, the Dancing Waters of Vienna. The English group Jethro Tull also appeared to do their version of a Bach Bouree. A 1977 episode of *The Young People's Concerts* on CBS, entitled "Making Pictures with Music," was an effort once again to discover appropriate visual correlatives for the musical experience, in this case by combining modern animation techniques with colorful symphonic selections. (A similar experiment occurred at the conclusion of one of Leonard Bernstein's 1976 Norton Lectures on PBS, when Wagner's Prelude and Liebestod from *Tristan and Isolde* was "visualized" with striking computer-generated animation by Ron Hays.)

At the beginning of the 1980s, NBC attempted to bring back the classical concert hall style to commercial television with a highly publicized series of prime-time specials, *Live from Studio 8H*. The first program, fittingly enough, was a tribute to Arturo Toscanini, who conducted so many of his broadcasts with the NBC Symphony from the very same studio in Rockefeller Center. To accommodate the expanded forces of Zubin Mehta and the New York Philharmonic, the studio stage was rearranged, though it was still far from ideal as a facility for TV concerts. As John J. O'Connor noted, the auditorium "leaves the performers disconcertingly in a sort of pit," and its "overall design suggested one of those giant pavillions at the New York World's Fair."[40] But despite its architectural limitations, the special proved as tasteful, given its commercial interruptions, and as aesthetically resourceful as a typical broadcast on *Great Performances*. The camerawork was musically sensitive; the performances of Mehta and the Philharmonic, along with guest artists Leontyne Price and Itzhak Perlman, came across with great vividness; and the FM stereo simulcast was a model of clarity. Unfortunately, the program turned out to be little more than a noble experiment. Only three other installments were ever aired in the series.

With the abandonment of *Live from Studio 8H*, the cancellation of *Camera Three* a few years before, and the increasingly infrequent scheduling of *The Young People's Concerts* (and its offshoot, *The Festival of Lively Arts for Young People*), classical music on commercial television by the mid–1980s was essentially a curiosity, something to be featured only in connection with a news event (such as a report on the Tchaikovsky Piano Competitions) or on programs showcasing personality interviews (*The Today Show*) or personality documentaries (CBS's *Sunday Morning* and *60 Minutes*). Full-length programs devoted to serious music would now be the exclusive province of PBS and the cultural cable networks.

Music Programming on the Cable Networks

The widely heralded cultural cable networks which began in the early 1980s—CBS Cable, ARTS, and Bravo—offered many hours of concert programming, most of which was imported from overseas. Like PBS's *Great Performances*, these services recognized that original, high-quality, domestic productions were extraordinarily expensive. English, French, German, and Italian music telecasts presented a much better opportunity. Not only were they far cheaper to purchase but their artistic standards were also usually superb. American viewers would be able to see Europe's best musicians, in sumptuous productions almost impossible, given ever rising costs, to duplicate on these shores.

The ill-fated CBS Cable, which lasted a little less than a year, offered one of the most impressive music series of recent times, *Bernstein Conducts Beethoven*, featuring performances of all nine Beethoven Symphonies with the Vienna Philharmonic. Instead of the usual custom of videotaping, the programs were filmed at the lavish Musik zur Einsald, a process which, in the hands of director Humphrey Burton, yielded extraordinarily handsome results. Like many of CBS Cable's series, all nine Beethoven shows later aired on PBS.

While the majority of music programming on ARTS (renamed The Arts and Entertainment Network in 1984) consisted of imported concert telecasts and documentaries, Bravo, a cultural pay cable service owned by Cablevision, initially offered viewers a wide variety of original, domestic productions, ranging from symphonic programs to piano competitions to jazz quartets. In contrast to the New York City and major metropolitan emphasis of PBS, Bravo telecasts were often taped in less frequently portrayed locations, where expenses were not quite so high. Telecasts originated from Aspen (the Aspen Chamber Symphony and the Aspen Festival Orchestra), Baltimore (the Baltimore Symphony), Houston (the Houston Symphony), and St. Louis (the St. Louis Symphony). Spiraling costs, however, eventually forced Bravo to sharply cut back the scale of its original efforts. By the mid–1980s, the network's music programming was limited to a series of low budget interview/performance shows, entitled *Counterpoint*, and, inevitably, the same type of imported material which characterized the schedules of its few cultural TV competitors.

CONCLUSIONS

The problems associated with classical music telecasting have changed little since the first symphonic programs in the late 1940s. William J. Hoffmann's observations, made more than 30 years ago, are still true today: "First of all, it is essential to understand that music, in general, is and will continue to be a difficult subject to treat successfully on television. Of course, the basic reason for this condition is the fact that music appeals to the ear rather than the eye."[41]

The varying approaches adopted by producers and directors to televising classical music have all been plagued by the challenges of making a fundamentally auditory experience come to life on the small screen. The most common technique has been to simply broadcast a concert performance as a straight event, counting on the dynamics of the conductor to supply any excitement. When charismatic maestros like Arturo Toscanini or Leonard Bernstein were at the podium, this method often proved enthralling. With lesser figures, however, the results were frequently static and dull.

Attempts to focus visual interest in the orchestra itself have largely been unsuccessful because of the basic physical nature of music making. Oboists or trumpeters or violinists don't dance around the stage or share their thoughts with the audience. They sit in a chair and blow or pluck their instruments. Despite the frantic efforts of some TV directors, the orchestral experience offers very little variety. As Samuel Lipman points out,

> The instruments of one orchestra look, after all, very much like those of another, and they are all played in much the same way; oddly enough, one emoting, gesticulating, coiffured conductor also begins to look like all the others. Not only is the resultant effect one of boredom; paradoxically the repetitive screen images serve to concentrate attention not on the music, but on the activity of music-making, and on the peculiar and funny-looking ways that some people behave. Even the merest hint of such a reaction on the part of a viewer can distract attention from the music and eventually come to discredit the entire musical enterprise.[42]

Donal Henahan of the *New York Times* makes a similar point when he attacked

> the television set's need to take apart a musical performance while it is in progress, even when the whole aim of the musicians is, or should be, to keep it glued together. Orchestral performance in particular is an exercise in unity against all the odds, a struggle to transcend individual differences in the interests of a common goal. But my televison set wants nothing so much as to dissect the performance. Nothing is too trivial to escape its restless eye. It is forever zooming in for tight shots of the concertmaster's bow tie, moving on to examine the flutist's moist embouchure, panning over the hard-working tuba section.[43]

The practice of carefully selecting camera shots and movements to follow the musical score has helped to make some concert telecasts more involving and pleasurable. The Boston Symphony Orchestra programs produced by the late Jordan Whitelaw or the varied music shows directed by Roger Englander have made it easier for viewers to understand the formal values of a composition by matching visual sequences and musical structure. As Englander's remarkable direction of Vladimir Horowitz's concert in 1968 demonstrated, the process can be just as effective with solo recitals as with large ensembles.

Yet whether the approach is modulated and structural or more action oriented, like Kirk Browning's dashing techniques on *Live from Lincoln Center*, televised concerts are still a problematic area, increasingly producing a sense of ennui not only in the audience (which has dropped off sizably in the last few years) but also among its practitioners. Roger Englander now reports that he's "bored by concert TV,"[44]—a sentiment shared by Kirk Browning, who remarked in an interview of his increasing frustration as "I go into each new season wondering what can you do that hasn't been done."[45] Curtis Davis, former head of arts programming for NET and currently a vice-president of the Arts and Entertainment Network, speculated at a 1983 panel that "the nature of television is in some respects antithetical to music."[46]

Whether this is true or not, it is clear that straight concert telecasting needs to be supplemented by more ambitious programming experiments if classical music on television is to survive as anything other than a somewhat moribund arena for superstar performances. Leonard Bernstein's adult lecture shows on CBS and a series such as *The Music Project Presents* . . . prove that television can offer imaginative ways to explore the musical experience. It would be a shame if the medium remained simply a documentor instead of a powerful instrument of enhancement in its own right.

NOTES

1. Samuel Lipman, "On the Air," *Commentary*, April 1980, p. 76.
2. Christopher Sterling and John Kittross, *Stay Tuned* (Belmont, Calif: Wadsworth Publishing Co., 1978), p. 118.
3. Howard Taubman, "Toscanini Concert Is Telecast by NBC," *New York Times*, 21 March 1948, Section II, p. 64.
4. "Toscanini by Television," *Newsweek*, 29 March 1948, p. 79.
5. Howard Taubman, "Should Conductors Be Seen or Just Heard?," *New York Times*, 25 April 1948, Section VI, p. 28.
6. Jack Gould, "Radio and Television," *New York Times*, 5 November 1951, p. 39.
7. Quaintance Eaton, "Arturo Toscanini Returns for Fifteenth NBC Season," *Musical America*, 1 December 1951, p. 19.
8. Eaton, "Arturo Toscanini," p. 19.
9. Kirk Browning, personal interview, 9 August 1983.
10. Jack Kuney, "Calling the Shots at the Metropolitan Opera," *Television Quarterly*, no. IV, Winter 1984, p. 77.
11. Taubman, "Should Conductors," p. 17.
12. Taubman, "Should Conductors," p. 17.
13. Bert Briller, "Music for the Ear and for the Eye," *House and Garden*, December 1951, p. 160.

14. Tim Brooks, and Earle Marsh, *The Complete Directory to Prime Time Network TV Shows, 1946–Present* (New York: Ballantine Books, 1981), p. 735.

15. Marks Levine, "Television: Trend or Variable?," *Musical America*, February 1951, p. 104.

16. Olin Downes, "Seeing and Hearing," *New York Times*, 11 April 1948, Section II, p. 7.

17. Andre Kostelanetz, "Music's Potentialities in Television," *Variety*, 2 January, 1952, p. 224.

18. Robert Cantrick, "Music, Television, and Aesthetics," *The Quarterly of Film, Radio, and Television*, IX, Fall 1954, p. 61.

19. Cantrick, "Music," p. 62.

20. Howard Taubman, "TV Deaf to Good Music," *New York Times*, 11 January 1953, Section II, p. 7.

21. Howard Taubman, "Clipped Wings," *New York Times*, 22 March 1959, Section II, p. 11.

22. Roger Englander, "Music on TV—What Works, What Doesn't," *High Fidelity/musical america*, October 1969, p. 10.

23. Val Adams, "Young People's Concerts are Young at Heart," *New York Times*, 30 August 1964, Section II, p. 15.

24. Brooks and Marsh, p. 799.

25. "All Out for Project X," *TIME*, 20 September 1968, p. 80.

26. Jack Gould, "The Pedestal Was High, The Rating Was Low," *New York Times*, 6 October 1968, Section II, p. 25.

27. Richard T. Dasher, "The Musical Programming of National Educational Television," Ph.D. diss., University of Michigan, 1968, p. 59.

28. John Goberman, personal interview, 22 February 1984.

29. Goberman, personal interview.

30. Goberman, personal interview.

31. John Rockwell, " 'Live From Lincoln Center' Rated a Plus," *New York Times*, 29 February 1984, Section III, p. 22.

32. Lucy Kraus, "He Calls the Shots on Those 'Live From' Programs," *New York Times*, 29 April, 1979, Section II, p. 34.

33. Kraus, p. 34.

34. Alan M. Kriegsman, "Innovative Television: Making Music for the Eyes," *Washington Post*, 1 June 1975, Section K, p. 7.

35. Kriegsman, p. 7.

36. Allan Kozinin, "He Turns Orchestras Into TV Stars," *New York Times*, 2 October 1977, Section II, p. 19.

37. Kozinin, p. 19.

38. Kozinin, p. 34.

39. Brien R. Williams, and Cheryl Fulton, "A Study of Visual Style and Creativity in Television," *Journal of Film and Video*, Winter 1984, p. 31.

40. John J. O'Connor, "TV: '8H' Salutes Toscanini," *New York Times*, 11 January 1980, Section III, p. 23.

41. William J. Hoffmann, Jr., "Opera on Television," *Opera News*, 10 October 1952, p. 24.

42. Samuel Lipman, p. 79.

43. Donal Henahan, "Music and TV Just Don't Mix," *New York Times*, 5 February 1984, Section III, p. 19.

44. Roger Englander, personal interview, 1 October 1983.

45. Browning, personal interview.

46. Remarks by Curtis Davis, panel discussion, "Music on Television," Museum of Broadcasting, New York City, 25 October 1983.

REFERENCES

One of the best places to obtain an overview of classical music and broadcasting is Samuel Lipman's essay, "On the Air." Lipman discusses concert music from its earliest days on radio up to the current offerings of *Live from Lincoln Center* and provides a shrewd analysis of why classical music failed to be as popular on commercial television as it had on network radio.

Information on the popularity of concert broadcasting on radio can be found in Christopher Sterling and John Kittross's concise history, *Stay Tuned*. George Willey's 1956 dissertation, "The Visualization of Music on Television, with Emphasis on The Standard Hour," examines concert broadcasting on television during the late 1940s and 1950s. Willey's thesis reviews the philosophy and the problems of transposing music to a visual medium, as well as the difficulties of finding advertisers willing to sponsor classical music programs. There is also useful material on the numerous concert experiments, such as *The Standard Hour*, which local TV stations conducted at a time when commercial pressures were not so forceful. Burton Paulu looks at one of the most interesting efforts in his article, "Televising the Minneapolis Symphony Orchestra."

The key musical figure in early television was clearly Arturo Toscanini, and his NBC Symphony broadcasts were the subject of considerable attention. Contemporary accounts by Howard Taubman ("Toscanini Concert Is Telecast by NBC") and Quaintance Eaton ("Arturo Toscanini Returns for Fifteenth NBC Season") are highly recommended for their ability to capture the excitement these extraordinary concerts produced. Tim Page offers a thoughtful retrospective on the Toscanini television legacy in his more recent article, "Toscanini Lives on in Some Rare Video."

The popularity and enthusiasm generated by the Toscanini programs also led to frequent critical discussions of the challenges of transforming the concert experience to television. *New York Times* music critic Olin Downes looked at the problems involved in music telecasts in his article "Seeing and Hearing"; so did his colleague Howard Taubman in a 1948 essay entitled "Should Conductors Be Seen or Just Heard?" and in subsequent pieces such as "TV Deaf to Good Music," "Truman, the Critic," and "Clipped Wings." Other articles examining the issue of serious music and television include Quaintance Eaton's "Tschaikovsky's Pique Dame Has NBC-TV Production," William J. Hoffmann, Jr.'s, "Opera on Television," Bert Briller's "Music for the Ear and for the Eye," Marks Levine's "Television: Trend or Variable?," Andre Kostelanetz's "Music's Potentialities in Television," and, from a more academic perspective, Robert B. Cantrick's "Music, Television, and Aesthetics."

Probably more than any other figure, Leonard Bernstein revolutionized the presentation and the status of classical music on American television. Howard Taubman's "Clipped Wings" provides a good assessment of Bernstein's strengths and weaknesses. An interesting look at the methods used in Bernstein's *Young People's Concerts* can be found in an article by the series' producer and director, Roger Englander, entitled "Music on TV—What Works, What Doesn't."

At the same time he was working on *The Young People's Concerts*, Englander also directed Vladimir Horowitz's historic 1968 recital on CBS. *TIME* magazine's "All Out for Project X" offers fascinating information on the difficulties involved in getting the show produced. Jack Gould's "The Pedestal Was High, The Rating Was Low" is a provocative postmortem.

Non-commercial television's alternative efforts in the 1950s and 1960s are thoroughly charted in Richard Dasher's 1968 dissertation, "The Musical Programming of National Educational Television." During the 1970s and 1980s, numerous articles appeared examining the ambitious music telecasts of NET's successor, PBS. Among the best are John Rockwell's " 'Live From Lincoln Center' Rated a Plus," John J. O'Connor's "TV: Lincoln Center Proving PBS Asset," and Alan M. Kriegsman's "Innovative Television: Making Music for the Eyes." Attention was also focused on PBS's music producers and directors. George Movshon's "Serious Music's Ambassador to the Home Screen" discusses the career of David Griffiths of *Great Performances*. Lucy Kraus's "He Calls the Shots on Those 'Live From' Programs" and Jack Kuney's "Calling the Shots at the Metropolitan Opera" examine the techniques and practices of *Live from Lincoln Center* and *Live from the Met*'s Kirk Browning. Allan Kozinin's "He Turns Orchestras Into TV Stars" looks at Jordan Whitelaw of *Evening at Symphony*. Brien R. Williams and Cheryl Fulton's "A Study of Visual Style and Creativity in Television" is a detailed analysis contrasting Browning and Whitelaw's tele-musical approach.

Recently several articles have questioned whether the medium can really offer anything to the concert experience. Critic Donal Henahan of the *New York Times* has been the most vocal antagonist of current broadcast approaches towards music. The titles of his articles—"When Music Plays Second Fiddle," "Music and TV Just Don't Mix," and "Must Symphony Concerts and Television Be Incompatible?"—provide a fairly accurate summary of his position. Jack Hiemenz in his review "Orchestra Shows: Are Producers Running Scared?" raises equally strong objections. While *New York Times* TV critic John J. O'Connor has voiced just as many doubts concerning music telecasting practices, his comments usually tend to be a bit more balanced, as indicated by an essay such as "Can Serious Music Be 'Visualized'?"

Books

Brooks, Tim, and Earle Marsh. *The Complete Directory to Prime Time Network TV Shows 1946–Present*. Rev. ed. New York: Ballantine Books, 1981.

Sterling, Christopher, and John Kittross. *Stay Tuned*. Belmont, Calif.: Wadsworth Publishing Company, 1978.

Articles

"All Out for Project X." *TIME*, 20 September 1968, p. 80.

Briller, Bert. "Music for the Ear and for the Eye." *House and Garden*, December 1951, p. 160.

Cantrick, Robert. "Music, Television, and Aesthetics." *The Quarterly of Film, Radio, and Television*, IX, Fall 1954, p. 61.

Downes, Olin. "Seeing and Hearing." *New York Times*, 11 April 1948, Section II, p. 7.

Eaton, Quaintance. "Arturo Toscanini Returns for Fifteenth NBC Season." *Musical America*, 1 December 1951, p. 19.

———. "Tschaikovsky's Pique Dame Has NBC-TV Production." *Musical America*, 15 January 1952, p. 17.

Englander, Roger. "Music on TV—What Works, What Doesn't." *High Fidelity/musical america*, October 1969, p. 10.

Gould, Jack. "The Pedestal Was High, The Rating Was Low." *New York Times*, 6 October 1968, Section II, p. 25.

Hiemenz, Jack. "Orchestra Shows: Are Producers Running Scared?" *High Fidelity*, December 1980, pp. 13–14.

Henahan, Donal. "Music and TV Just Don't Mix." *New York Times*, 5 February 1984, Section III, p. 19.

———. "Must Symphony Concerts and Television Be Incompatible?" *New York Times*, 20 February 1983, Section II, p. 21.

———. "When Music Plays Second Fiddle." *New York Times*, 9 July 1978, Section II, p. 1.

Hoffmann, William J., Jr. "Opera on Television." *Opera News*, 10 October 1952, p. 24.

Kostelanetz, Andre. "Music's Potentialities in Television." *Variety*, 2 January 1952, p. 224.

Kozinin, Allan. "He Turns Orchestras Into TV Stars." *New York Times*, 2 October 1977, Section II, pp. 19, 34.

Kraus, Lucy. "He Calls the Shots on Those 'Live From' Programs." *New York Times*, 29 April 1979, Section II, p. 34.

Kriegsman, Alan M. "Innovative Television: Making Music for the Eyes." *Washington Post*, 1 June 1975, Section K, p. 7.

Kuney, Jack. "Calling the Shots at the Metropolitan Opera." *Television Quarterly*, No. IV, Winter 1984, p. 77.

Levine, Marks. "Television: Trend or Variable?" *Musical America*, February 1951, p. 104.

Lipman, Samuel. "On the Air." *Commentary*, April 1980, pp. 76–81.

Movshon, George. "Serious Music's Ambassador To the Home Screen." *New York Times*, 5 December 1976. Section II, p. 29.

O'Connor, John J. "Can Serious Music Be 'Visualized'?" *New York Times*, 18 January 1976, Section III, p. 27.

———. "Music Is Becoming a Big Item On the Small Screen." *New York Times*, 11 July 1982, Section II, p. 27.

———. "TV: Lincoln Center Proving PBS Asset." *New York Times*, 10 November 1977, Section III, p. 22.

Page, Tim. "Toscanini Lives on in Some Rare Video." *New York Times*, 23 October, 1983, Section II, p. 33.

Paulu, Burton. "Televising the Minneapolis Symphony Orchestra." *The Quarterly of Film, Radio and Television*, VIII, No. 2, Winter, 1953, pp. 157–171.

Rockwell, John. " 'Live From Lincoln Center' Rated a Plus." *New York Times*, 29 February 1984, Section III, p. 22.

Taubman, Howard. "Clipped Wings." *New York Times*, 22 March 1959, Section II, p. 11.

———."Should Conductors Be Seen or Just Heard?" *New York Times*, 25 April 1948, Section VI, p. 28.

———. "Toscanini Concert Is Telecast by NBC." *New York Times*, 21 March 1948, p. 64.

———. "TV Deaf to Good Music." *New York Times*, 11 January 1953, Section II, p. 7.

Williams, Brien R. and Cheryl Fulton. "A Study of Visual Style and Creativity in Television." *Journal of Film and Video*, Winter 1984, pp. 23–32.

Dissertations

Dasher, Richard T. "The Musical Programming of National Educational Television." Ph.D. diss., University of Michigan, 1968.

Willey, George A. "The Visualization of Music on Television, with Emphasis on The Standard Hour." Ph.D. diss., Stanford University, 1956.

VIDEOGRAPHY

Series: *NBC Symphony Orchestra Conducted by Arturo Toscanini*
Network: NBC
Date: Premiere—March 20, 1948
Occasional specials, running through 1952
Directors: various, including Kirk Browning
Producer: Samuel Chotzinoff

Series: *Voice of Firestone*
Network: NBC (1949–1954), ABC (1954–1963)
Date: Premiere—September 5, 1949
Last broadcast—June 16, 1963
Directors: various
Producers: various

Series: *TV Recital Hall*
Network: NBC
Date: Premiere—July 1, 1951
Last broadcast—September 6, 1954
Director: Kirk Browning
Producer: Charles Polachek

Program: *Omnibus*—Leonard Bernstein discusses Beethoven's Fifth Symphony
Network: CBS
Date: November 14, 1954
Director: Andrew McCullough
Producer: Robert Saudek

Series: *Young People's Concerts*
Network: CBS
Date: Premiere—January 18, 1958
Still Running, but retitled *Young People's Festival of the Lively Arts*
Director: Roger Englander (through 1976)
Producer: Roger Englander (through 1976)

Series: *Bernstein and the New York Philharmonic*
Network: CBS
Date: Premiere: November 30, 1958
Occasional series of specials running through the early 1960s
Director: William A. Graham
Producer: Robert Saudek

Series: *The Bell Telephone Hour*
Network: NBC
Date: Premiere—October 9, 1959
Last broadcast—April 26, 1968
Directors: various
Producers: various

Series: *Music for a Summer Night*
Network: CBS
Date: Premiere: May 26, 1960
Occasional series of 1960 summer music specials
Director: Roger Englander
Producer: Robert Herridge

Series: *Sol Hurok Presents*
Network: CBS
Date: Premiere: December 6, 1966
Annual specials running through 1970
Director: Roger Englander
Producer: Sol Hurok

Program: *Horowitz at Carnegie Hall*
Network: CBS
Date: September 22, 1968
Director: Roger Englander
Producer: Howard Taubman

Program: *Beethoven's Birthday: Celebration in Vienna*
Network: CBS
Date: December 24, 1971
Director: Humphrey Burton
Producer: Schuyler Chapin

Program: *The Bolero*
Network: PBS
Date: February 17, 1973
Director: Allan Miller, with William Fertik, filmmaker
Producer: Allan Miller

Series: *Evening at Symphony*
Network: PBS
Date: Premiere—September 1973
Still running, but as infrequently scheduled specials
Directors: various
Producer: Jordan Whitelaw (who also served as chief visual designer) until 1982

Series: *The Music Project Presents . . .*
Network: PBS
Date: Six specials, broadcast occasionally through 1975
Director: Allan Miller
Producer: Allan Miller

Series: *Live from Lincoln Center*
Network: PBS
Date: Premiere—January 30, 1976
Still Running
Director: Kirk Browning
Producer: John Goberman

4

Opera on Television

The sheer musical and dramatic expansiveness of opera has provided television with one of its greatest challenges. How can a small screen capture the sweep of *Aida* or the rousing passion of *Tristan and Isolde*? How can the soaring emotional currents of *Otello* or *Die Walküre* be felt when they are reduced visually and sonically? The grandeur of a huge opera stage, the thrill of singers heard live, the dynamic surge of a large accompanying orchestra—all of these vital ingredients of the opera experience would seem to be beyond television's reach.

In tackling opera, the electronic medium's very puniness is its chief liability, since no theatrical form demands a broader sense of scale. Not only is operatic action larger than life but also its musical vitality is meant to be felt in the combined charge of vocalists and instrumentalists filling up the space of the auditorium that encloses them. Television's diminished visual and auditory field poses an essential conflict for operatic style, which frequently depends on the expression of feelings and dramatic impulses far grander than the home screen can contain. While television may be a perfect place to sing quietly of love and heartache, louder, more passionate music making, especially when voiced in ensemble, loses its vital intensity and scope. Opera's climactic spectacles and bursts of rapturous emotion are not easily transportable to a miniaturizing environment.

Yet, despite these formidable obstacles, TV producers and directors have continually tried, and often succeeded surprisingly well, to bring opera's sizable pleasures to home viewers. Their efforts have ranged from simple studio projects, with just a few singers and a few selected scenes, to elaborate remountings, complete with strong vocalist/actors, intricate sets and costumes, and a full chorus and orchestra. Opera on television has included everything from originally commissioned works to live presentations from the great stages of the world.

The productions that have worked best in the more than 40 years of opera telecasting have recognized television's affinity for the intimate and comfortably realistic, finding ways to retailor operatic theater style for the small screen. Overblown operas with posturing heroes and hysterical heroines do not seem to play as well as works with direct characters and direct emotions. Bloated acting techniques and bloated physiques, when seen in close-up, make it very hard to accept the love story of carefree Bohemians.

However, the many similarities between opera and television have helped ease some of the inevitable compromises in transplanting. Both forms share a fondness for melodramatic action, strong characterization, and the heightened pathos of romance. By highlighting these qualities, opera telecasts have often imparted a convincing approximation of the musical and dramatic energy possible on the stage.

Televised opera will never capture live opera's spaciousness or the thrill of its passion and power—not at least until three-dimensional holographic television becomes a common living room reality. Still, the medium has often brought grand opera into the living room in imaginative and occasionally exciting ways. A study of four decades of opera telecasting offers an interesting chapter in American television's efforts to reshape a venerable art form for millions of new viewers.

HISTORICAL DEVELOPMENT

The Early Years

Opera was one of the earliest commodities broadcast on American airwaves. In 1910, listeners throughout the New York area and on a few ships in the Atlantic were able to hear Enrico Caruso, direct from the Metropolitan Opera House, thanks to an experimental transmission by radio pioneer Lee de Forest. Twenty-one years later the Met was once again the site of experimentation. NBC performed a special closed circuit test to convince Met manager Giulio Gatti-Casazza that live broadcasts from the Opera House could be done. Impressed with the results, and needing the money, Gatti-Casazza approved the idea of a series of one-hour programs. On Christmas Day, 1931, the Metropolitan went on the air for the first time coast to coast, with a broadcast of the conveniently short *Hansel and Gretel* transmitted over NBC's 190 stations. The first season proved such a success that broadcasts were expanded the next year to include complete performances regardless of length.

The Metropolitan also played a role in one of the first operatic telecasts (although the very first took place over NBC's experimental station W2XBS in November 1939, when the Miniature Opera Company, consisting of a twelve-year-old soprano and a nine-year-old coloratura, presented scenes from *Carmen*). On March 10, 1940, several singers from the Met travelled uptown from the company's location at 39th and Broadway to NBC's TV studio at Radio City to perform the first act of *I Pagliacci*. Thirty-two musicians from the NBC Symphony Orchestra, conducted by Frank St. Leger, provided the accompaniment. Three cameras filmed the proceedings, which took place on a small stage decorated by plants and Japanese lanterns. The program was introduced by the Met's general manager, Edward Johnson, and also included a potpourri of famous arias.

TV opera experimentation continued during the war. General Electric's innovative station in Schenectady, WRGB, broadcast several operas in different formats. Some were sung in English by students at a Hartford, Connecticut, music school (including the first complete opera telecast in the country, a December 1942 studio production of *Hansel and Gretel*), while performances of Peter Tchaikovsky's *Pique Dame* and *Eugene Onegin* were given in Russian by Pauline Achmatova's Opera Company, with plot summaries provided by an announcer during scene changes.

In the summer of 1944, NBC hired Herbert Graf, a stage director at the Metropolitan, as "Director of Operatic Production," and he helped to establish a number of precedents. Graf was one of the first to recognize that opera on television is a drastically different creature from opera in an auditorium. As he relates in his book, *Opera for the People*, the problems he encountered in his first TV assignment, staging the meeting of Rodolfo and Mimi in Act I of *La Bohème*, underscored the realistic demands of the new medium. Recitative, especially Italian recitative, seemed to bring the scene to a dead halt. Graf ordered the singers to switch to English and the conductor to eliminate the accompanying music, but still "the mood simply was not there."[1] Finally, the conductor suggested playing the music softly underneath, in the manner of Hollywood background music, until the aria begins—a procedure which preserved the appropriate romantic spell without making Rodolfo and Mimi seem too stylized.

Graf also experimented with novel stagings and techniques. Figaro's aria from *The Barber of Seville* was performed both inside and outside his barbershop; a condensed English version of *Carmen* used the imprisoned Don Jose to tell the opera's story in three flashback episodes. The production of a shortened English adaptation of *I Pagliacci* was the first to use attractive young singers, who lip-synched the recorded voices of others, as a way to improve video opera's appearance (and, in this case, to satisfy James Petrillo, president of the American Federation of Musicians, who had recently banned live music on television). Graf's year at NBC taught him the value of extensive rehearsals (he was given the luxury of one-hour rehearsal time for each minute of program time), as well as the importance of naturalistic acting, English translations, and camerawork attuned to opera's poetic style.[2]

Televised opera remained a low priority during the immediate postwar years, as the networks marshalled all their resources into the push to establish the medium's economic viability. The next live studio opera production did not take place until November 1948, when NBC's Philadelphia station broadcast Gian-Carlo Menotti's one-hour work, *The Medium*. A month later, the same opera turned up on CBS, as part of the network's *Studio One* series. The CBS version featured the current City Center cast, including Marie Powers, who originated the role two years before. Like many live telecasts of the period, the program suffered from some occasional moments of technical clumsiness, but by and large, the hour came across as credible and absorbing. Menotti's operatic sensibility—with its attraction to mildly offbeat characters and sudden bursts of pathos—was ideally suited to television, as *Amahl and the Night Visitors* would conclusively prove a few years later. Despite its murky dramatics, *The Medium*'s intimate scale proved to be a considerable asset in this TV adaptation. Director Paul Nickell, who also directed the NBC version, kept the cameras in fluid movement to suggest the opera's shifting relationships and its stifling sense of space. Dark, shadowed lighting added to the general atmosphere of sadness and doom.

Opening Nights at the Met

In November 1948, TV opera moved out of the studio to the grand stage of the Metropolitan Opera House. The occasion was the opening night performance of *Otello*, presented live over ABC and sponsored (a rare occurrence for opera telecasts) by Texaco, the Met's longtime radio patron. Coverage of the event matched its musical and social significance. Eight cameras were deployed to capture the full sweep of the spectacle: two were stationed in the lounge for celebrity interviews and shots of the crowd, one was backstage, one (which never functioned) was outside to photograph arriving socialites, and four were placed in various parts of the theater to catch the performance (from the left and center balconies, the rear center, and 25 feet closer to the right-center of the auditorium floor).

The broadcast was announced only a few days before, after ABC's engineers, during the course of two dress rehearsals, finally decided that the program's enormous technical problems could be overcome. Even then, the actual program was marred by difficulties. The opera's moody lighting was often too dim for the insensitive cameras of the day, despite the use of special infrared gelatines in the footlights to boost intensity (a feature that did not affect spectators in the theater). Camera locations, dictated by the Met's desire not to interfere with patron's sightlines, also posed a challenge. The balcony cameras were too far back, often making stage activities virtually impossible to decipher, and one of the floor cameras was improperly positioned—a fact noted by critic Quaintance Eaton when she observed that "one camera, like the trick mirrors in a carnival sideshow, distorted all figures into squinty dwarves—the result of shooting from too low an angle, according to one technician."[3]

The biggest criticism was leveled at the inexperienced direction of Burke Crotty, who committed numerous dramatic and musical sins. His cameras often lagged behind the singers as they moved, and his decisions to cut from one camera to another seemed to have little to do with the action on stage. The critic from *Opera News* complained that:

> Many times we had one actor thrust at us in a close-up when, because of the action, we were longing to see another. At other times, so absorbed in a close-up that we felt as if the actors were only a few feet away in the same room, we were suddenly yanked out by a long shot that reduced them to pinpricks on the screen, and shattered the illusion just at the climax.[4]

Crotty was also attacked for his overreliance on long shots and the length of time he held them. *New York Times* TV critic Jack Gould wrote, "Time after time . . . a distant shot wherein the Metropolitan stage resembled a puppeteer's platform was held almost beyond endurance, with the figures so small as to defy identification."[5]

Even at this early stage of opera telecasting, critics recognized a fundamental requirement for successful TV opera production—the integration of camerawork with musical and dramatic ideas. The failures of the Met broadcast underlined this necessity. As Jack Gould noted, "One lesson clearly learned from the Otello performance was that the television director must be intimately acquainted with both the plot and score if video is not to miss a great deal."[6]

Regardless of its sizable shortcomings, this first live commercial telecast from the Met was greeted as a landmark by observers contemplating the future of opera on television. *Opera News* hailed the program as a "brilliant debut, not only because it coincided with the opening night but because it combined a high technical achievement on the part of video with the implication of new and far-reaching possibilities in regard to opera itself."[7] Jack Gould of the *New York Times* was even more sanguine. "In taking its cameras onto the lyric stage, television now promises to do for opera what radio did for the concert hall. What the acquisition of a mass following may mean for opera almost exceeds the bounds of the imagination in its challenging and provocative implications."[8]

Opera's mass following for this broadcast was estimated at a respectable half a million homes (in New York City, the Hooper rating was 42.3—higher than all the other TV stations in the area combined), leading ABC and Texaco to embark on another opening night program the following season.

The November 1949 telecast of *Der Rosenkavalier* represented a determined improvement in practically every department. This time all eight cameras functioned properly; more sophisticated lenses made it easier to see darkened areas of the stage, without the need of special infrared lighting; the four cameras in the auditorium were placed in better positions; and the direction, once again by Burke Crotty, was smoother and less marred by a reliance on indistinct long shots. As Jack Gould remarked:

The most noticeable progress came in resolving to surprising degree what twelve months ago appeared to be a major problem: satisfying television's need for the intimate approach yet doing it without disturbing a production that had been planned for the spacious stage of the Met.[9]

In addition to the broadcast's enhanced technical considerations (which were also acknowledged by the Met cast, who applied special video makeup for the event), ABC did everything possible to reduce the interference its transmission caused patrons attending the performance. Not only were camera operators required to wear dinner jackets, but their cameras were redesigned for Opera House use. The dry ice used to cool the machines a year earlier was replaced by camera blowers equipped with mufflers; the bright red tally light near the top of the lens mounting was disconnected; and the intercom was shut off. The telecast's production costs came to $40,000, including $5,000 in network line fees. The show was available to viewers in six cities.

A year later, when ABC televised its third opening night at the Met, a performance of Giuseppe Verdi's *Don Carlo*, the number of cities increased to nine, with an estimated four million homes tuning in. The number of cameras covering the event also increased from eight to twelve, with a camera now placed in the orchestra pit for the first time. The new cameras were accompanied by better stage illumination as well. Responding to repeated criticisms of muddy picture quality during previous programs, ABC installed special TV lighting, which, as Quaintance Eaton reported, "made a scene more clearly visible on the screen than in the house."[10] These additions let the director choose from a greater variety of camera shots and angles without worrying about the loss of stage detail due to shadow and darkness.

Don Carlo was the Metropolitan's last opening night broadcast on commercial television. ABC's expenses were high; its programming mission was broadening; and the Met itself was thinking of new avenues for marketing its product. Two years later, it embarked on an ambitious experiment in closed circuit telecasting. Thirty-one theaters in 27 cities were equipped for a live, black-and-white transmission of *Carmen*. While attendance was fairly strong, audiences were distracted by the many technical problems. The difficulties ABC had faced in its broadcasts were now magnified when a televised image was projected on a large screen. Even with special enhancements, lighting was still too dark, and details dropped out when shots were taken from the balcony, making it hard to see what was going on on stage. Nevertheless, the Met persisted, and in 1954, it transmitted its opening night festivities to 32 theaters, earning a profit of $62,000. Network opera broadcasts would rarely be so fortunate.

Studio Telecasts 1949–1950

CBS's Opera Television Theater

ABC's live programs from the Metropolitan Opera House were, like any remote telecast, an expensive proposition with numerous built-in technical obstacles. Transmissions from a studio represented a much easier and economical way to get a show on the air with far more control and skill. With opera production in a studio, television's special resources could also be used to enhance a work's believability. Close-range cameras and flexible staging could bring viewers nearer to the performers than the best seats of any house, intensifying the emotional experience. But this very power also posed problems to a theatrical form burdened by grand excesses. If opera was to succeed on a medium which valued small-scale realism, its methods would have to be rethought. Broad acting would have to be replaced by naturalism; stale sets would have to make way for modern scenery. The dramatic license possible on the stage of the Metropolitan needed to be drastically pared down when transferred to the confines of the studio.

One solution to these problems was to eliminate the action all together—a procedure NBC tried in 1949 and 1950 with its concert presentations of *Aida* and *Falstaff*, conducted by Arturo Toscanini. Obviously, however, this static treatment would never succeed without a maestro of Toscanini's extraordinary appeal and aura. A more lively approach was clearly needed, and by the late 1940s, both CBS and NBC attempted to meet the challenges of studio opera by setting up special in-house opera production organizations. CBS's *Opera Television Theater* was headed by one of the Met's leading singers, Lawrence Tibbett, and by producer Henry Souvaine. In announcing the theatre's broadcast plans in December 1949, Tibbett was adamant about the importance of shaping opera to television's demands. Singers were to be cast in roles where they looked the part. Facial over-extending was to be avoided. Plus, operas were to be performed in English as frequently as possible and streamlined for the home screen.

The first fruit of this policy was a 5:00 P.M., unsponsored Sunday broadcast on New Year's Day, 1950, of *Carmen*. The sense of occasion was emphasized by the program's unusual prologue. As the opening credits were revealed in the style of a formal invitation and an announcer proclaimed, "*Carmen*—of all the operas ever heard—the most perfect opera," the program began with a shot of well-dressed people chatting in a studio. Whispering in solemn tones, the off-screen announcer clued the home audience in—the people on the screen are critics, producers, and directors who've "accepted our invitation to come to this television performance of this opera because surely they all will participate in your future entertainment." The camera settled on Lawrence Tibbett, seen talking with CBS president Frank Stanton. Tibbett then stepped forward to introduce the show. Reminding us that *Carmen* is "a lusty, middle-aged opera masterpiece," he explained the work's meaning and the program's method. Since the broadcast was coming from a TV studio there would be no proscenium and no audience. Tibbett concluded with this philosophical affirmation. "We believe that is inevitable that studio produced opera . . . must have its own important place in television as pure television." In another studio, Boris Goldovsky then mounted the podium to conduct the orchestra.

The opera opened imaginatively, with cast credits introduced as posters on the wall glanced at by a passing resident of Seville. As he walked away, the village square of Act I came into view, and clusters of singers moved through the surprisingly spacious set. These beginning moments were typical of the production as a whole—they were directed with a feeling of fluidity and a nice attention to detail. The costumes were handsome, the singing ranged from fair to good (contrary to Tibbett's pledge, the program was done in French), but the acting was a bit stiff. Even though Carmen's seduction of Don Jose later in the act lacked the necessary fire, Gladys Swarthout's and Robert Rounseville's performances were respectable. When the scene changed to Lillas Pastias's tavern in Act II, the program's spirits picked up, aided by some peppy dancing and the appearance of Robert Merrill's dashing Escamillo. The opera concluded with an effective TV moment—Carmen's dead body lay spread on the ground in front of Don Jose, who sang his final aria clutching her to him in close-up.

Despite the difficulties of an all-French performance and some occasionally shaky moments, this first attempt to transform a complete opera for network television came off rather well. The histrionics so characteristic of the opera auditorium were largely stripped away, and the majority of the performers recognized that television demanded a more natural way of singing and moving. What was especially impressive about this TV *Carmen* was its sense of scale—the dextrous use of six full sets and three half sets gave the production a feeling of sweep that made the action seem less confined by a small screen. Boris Goldovsky's staging and Byron Paul's direction capitalized on the comparatively large space at their disposal by keeping actors and cameras in pleasantly constant movement. The judicious cutting, which kept performance time down to 75 minutes, also helped in this case to improve the program's pace and impact, especially considering the fact that few people in the audience could understand what was being sung.

Three months later, the *Opera Television Theater* was back on the air with a 95–minute production, this time in English, of *La Traviata*. The program, staged by Herbert Graf, was even more elaborate than the *Television Theater*'s first outing, with more sets and a richer sense of atmosphere. Considerable effort was made to bring the opera to life for television, including the use of material not in the original libretto. The preludes to

Act I and Act III both featured interpolated scenes designed to set the stage emotionally for what was to come—Act I opened with a brief moment set a year before the curtain rises, as a somewhat shaky Violetta enters a flowershop and asks for water, while an interested Alfredo watches her from outside; Act III offered a panoramic view of Violetta's desolate room, with the camera finally coming to rest on a bowl of camellias. Purists might object, but these scenes, and similar, small dramatic flourishes, helped give the program an affecting quality appropriate to *La Traviata*'s tearful passion.

Performing the work in English proved to be a great asset. For the first time, American TV viewers were able to follow most of the dialogue and plot of one of the classic grand operas. Practically every word sung by the production's lead singers—Elaine Malbin, Brooks McCormack, and Lawrence Tibbett—could be clearly understood, and what was lost in diction was more than made up for in expressive acting. The translation was stilted, however, and awkward phrasings and stiff conversations made it hard to enter *La Traviata*'s spell. As future English opera telecasts would reveal, music and natural sounding language needed to be carefully matched in order to bring the TV audience closer to the form's dramatic heart.

While both *Opera Television Theater* broadcasts were well received, they were also unsponsored. Despite efforts by Tibbett and Souvaine to line up advertisers, there were no takers, and *La Traviata* was CBS's last effort to produce opera on a sustaining basis. The many challenges of studio opera would now be faced exclusively, for the next decade, by the *NBC Opera Theatre*.

The Beginnings of the NBC Opera Theatre

In 1949, the Czech-born conductor Peter Herman Adler paid a visit to NBC's director of music, Samuel Chotzinoff, who had already played an important role in the network's cultural programming. In 1937, while still a music critic for the *New York Post*, he was enlisted by NBC president David Sarnoff to visit Arturo Toscanini in Italy and convince him to return to America, where he would be given his own orchestra, comprised of the country's best musicians and paid for by NBC. The maestro agreed, and his yearly series of radio broadcasts became one of the network's most celebrated achievements.

Adler was to bring opera to the radio audience in a way that would emphasize its accessibility and reinterpret it for listeners at home. Chotzinoff shared Adler's enthusiasm for a "young American opera company,"[11] but David Sarnoff had to be convinced that the network should invest its money in such an ambitious experiment. They arranged a special dinner for Sarnoff and a few guests, concluding it with a surprise living room performance of the finale from *La Bohème*, sung in English by a cast including two soon-to-be famous "unknowns"—George London and Mario Lanza. Adler recalls the evening:

The young cast performed brilliantly, and the impression was all we had hoped for. I will never forget the face of Sarnoff, who at first didn't want his digestion disturbed by Puccini but ended up sitting there with tears streaming over his face. "Can that be on television?" he asked me. "What is television?" I asked.[12]

Adler was soon to find out, as Sarnoff approved the idea of an NBC *Opera Theatre* for his still struggling TV network. The Theatre's initial offerings in 1949 were strictly on an experimental basis and consisted of four short programs of excerpts from *The Barber of Seville*, *The Bartered Bride*, *The Old Maid and the Thief*, and *La Bohème*. All were performed in English and produced under extraordinary economic restrictions. "Budget? It didn't exist," remarked Samuel Chotzinoff, who would serve as the Theatre's producer until his death in 1964. "We were lucky to get fifteen-minute spots once a week for our bold venture."[13]

The limitations the series faced during this period were obvious from its debut broadcast on February 2, 1949, which re-created the after-dinner offering that had so moved Sarnoff—the last act of *La Bohème*—but this time without Lanza or London. The set was drab; the lighting was harsh; camerawork was awkward at best; and the editing was unusually jarring. The half-hour program seemed to move in fits and starts, without smoothness or sustained musical feeling.

Nevertheless, there were glimmers in this first NBC telecast of what studio opera in English could be like. With a little more practice and control, the performers might have been able to make Rodolfo and Mimi come to life. With a little more money, the production might have come across with greater flavor and less clunkiness. The production staff of the *NBC Opera Theatre* were clearly aware of the uphill battle which faced them, but they approached their task with a sense of mission. As they proclaimed in an announcement at the beginning of the show, "Opera in America has never enjoyed the wide popularity of other forms of entertainment, but we have the hope that television permits the possibility of such popularity."

After three additional experimental broadcasts, the *NBC Opera Theatre* officially premiered on January 14, 1950, with a production of Kurt Weill's *Down in the Valley*. The half-hour program aired on a Saturday night at 10:00 P.M. and was seen only on NBC's east coast affiliates. (The entire country would not be linked by coaxial cable until 1951.) Weill's "folk" opera seemed an ideal opening work because of its very lack of theatrically distancing conventions. The singers did not sing operatically; the setting was familiar Americana; and the plot was simple and vivid. To establish its rural locale, the production employed numerous film inserts for atmosphere. Shots of activity in the valley and of a train hurtling through the night served as an introduction; at the close, there were views of fields and clouds alternating with an in-studio close-up of the heroine's silhouette.

This final mixed effect prompted critic Quaintance Eaton to observe that "perhaps this smacked a little too much of a hackneyed movie device, but it showed a way for television opera to open its sights, and create new vistas."[14]

The artistic success of the program, which Eaton felt "swept through the musico-entertainment world like a fresh breeze,"[15] encouraged NBC to expand the series' time length. Beginning with its next telecast three weeks later of *Madame Butterfly*, the *Opera Theatre* was given a full hour. Although a short time, it permitted a work's major highlights to be adequately represented. The additional 30 minutes helped enlarge the program's dramatic resources and its critical reputation. *Newsweek* hailed *Madame Butterfly* with the announcement that grand opera had "ceased to be a video novelty and become material for straight television entertainment. . . . Opera can be adapted to the pleasures of the mass American television audience."[16]

The *Opera Theatre* presented four more hour-length productions that year, usually preceding the program with the title card "Scenes from. . . ." The works included *The Bat* [*Die Fledermaus*], *Tales of Hoffmann*, *Carmen*, and a Christmas Day performance of *Hansel and Gretel*. The December 17th broadcast of *Carmen* serves as an example of how the series tried to overcome its time limitations by rearranging for narrative coherence. The program opens with a new scene that would have occurred after *Carmen* was over—Don Jose is seen in prison, awaiting his execution. In a frantic state, he begins to tell his story (and the opera's) to the silent priest standing next to him. His brief narration sets the stage for the three flashback scenes to follow—his meeting with Carmen in Act I, the tavern scene from Act II, and finally the moments leading up to Carmen's death in Act IV.

In contrast to the CBS production almost a year earlier (which ran for an extra 15 minutes), there was very little sense of "Spanish" atmosphere or elaborate stagecraft to this NBC *Carmen*. The singing was not as accomplished. Nor was the camerawork or direction as sophisticated, particularly in the crowd scenes of Act I and the dancing interlude in Act II. But what the *NBC Opera Theatre* lacked in technical skill, it made up for in its efforts to reach viewers with immediacy and directness. The series' shoestring budget was, in some ways, an advantage, since it forced the production staff to rethink operatic convention in terms of TV effectiveness. Thus, there was little hesitancy to alter a libretto if the results yielded a clearer, more forceful program. Its rearranged *Carmen* was just an indication of the new methods the *Opera Theatre* would bring to the task of proving, in the words of Samuel Chotzinoff, that "television is the only hope of opera in America."[17]

The 1950–51 season concluded with Giacomo Puccini's *Gianni Schicchi*, a work ideally suited to the program's format because it only lasts about 50 minutes and could therefore be performed in its entirety. The production established a new emphasis on simplicity of effect. The detailed scenery originally planned for the telecast was replaced right before air time by just a few pieces of furniture and a dark curtain. Chotzinoff made the decision after realizing "how much more effective to leave the view of 'beloved Florence' to the imagination."[18] The result, wrote Quaintance Eaton, was the series' "first milestone."[19]

NBC Opera Theatre's Triumphant Third and Fourth Seasons

With a dozen productions to its credit, the *NBC Opera Theatre* had gradually evolved into a lively and ambitious organization. The "team" of musical and artistic director Peter Herman Adler, producer Samuel Chotzinoff, associate producer Charles Polachek, and director Kirk Browning (who had previously worked on the Arturo Toscanini telecasts) consistently tried to approach opera on television from a fresh vantage point. As Adler observed, "Television . . . is too young and unformed a medium to have developed the motion pictures' frozen conventions and resistance to experimentation."[20] Together all four men shared a belief that opera could be brought to home viewers without fussiness or fulsomeness.

The *NBC Opera Theatre* philosophy centered on accessibility. Foreign conventions and foreign languages were outlawed. "English is the only language used," remarked Samuel Chotzinoff a few years later, "and judging from the enormous mail response, the people watching the television operas appear to be delighted at the good fortune in having the language barrier removed."[21] Translations, however, had to be thoughtfully retailored "to avoid the ridiculous locutions of the standard, printed English translations of opera librettos and . . . to approximate the vowel sounds of the original."[22] Stagecraft was also modified to fit the limits of the small screen. Broad, auditorium gestures and movements were ruthlessly excised. To encourage a more natural acting and singing style, new talent was actively sought out, with special attention paid to TV "appearance." Commenting on their casting requirements, Samuel Chotzinoff notes: "A performer, in addition to having a good voice, must also be photogenic. We're also looking for young people who aren't set in their ways. We keep away from big names and dyed-in-the-wool opera singers."[23]

Recognizing that television changed some of the fundamental aspects of the operatic experience, the *Opera Theatre*'s production staff focused on works which lent themselves to the medium's distinctive requirements. "The essential feature of television is closeness," Adler observed. "It cannot at present handle successfully large, panoramic ensembles, and perhaps it will never be able to."[24] Small-scale operas, with few characters and intimate settings, yielded better TV results than attempts to squeeze epic musical dramas into the camera's limited range. Ultimately, the *Opera Theatre* needed to fully test its potential. That dream finally came to life in 1951, during its third season, with the historic Christmas Eve broadcast of *Amahl and the Night Visitors*.

Gian-Carlo Menotti, who had been commissioned by NBC in 1939 to compose the first opera for radio (*The Old Maid and the Thief*), was hired once again in 1949, this time to compose the first opera for television. After almost a year and a half of delay, Menotti got to work, rushing so much at the end that the orchestration for *Amahl and the Night Visitors* was not completed until five days before the broadcast. Menotti's feverish pace was matched by that of the production staff, which continued to alter lighting and costumes right up to air time. The results, however, more than compensated for the last minute flurry. The broadcast was an instant sensation, with a front-page *New York Times* review by music critic Olin Downes lauding its achievement. Downes, who had been skeptical of opera on television, was now an enthusiastic convert.

> Mr. Menotti with rare art has produced a work that few indeed could have seen and heard last night save thru blurred eyes and with emotions that were not easy to conceal.
>
> It may be said at once that if nothing else has been accomplished by this work, television, operatically speaking, has come of age.[25]

The opera's great charm lay not only in its touching story of a handicapped boy who is visited by the Three Wise Men enroute to Bethlehem but also in the graceful way its musical and dramatic effects were wedded to the medium's size and limitations. Television enhanced *Amahl*'s virtues—its characters, action, and simple lyricism belong far more to an environment of natural intimacy than the broader confines of the stage. The production was itself a triumphant affirmation of the *Opera Theatre*'s methods. Its superb cast, headed by Chet Allen as Amahl and Rosemary Kuhlman as his mother (who would repeat her role many times in future telecasts), was completely without operatic ostentation. The entire program was characterized by an air of ease and innocence, thanks in part to its rustically naive sets and costumes and to Kirk Browning's smooth, unforced TV direction. The resultant acclaim (*Newsweek* called the broadcast "the best production of opera yet seen on TV,"[26]—an opinion seconded by most critics) underscored the basic lessons Peter Herman Adler had begun to discover about producing musical drama for this new medium. "*Amahl*," he observed, "represents the style of opera most effective on television—not too long, and with strong emotional appeal."[27]

Amahl also represented a turning point in the *NBC Opera Theatre*'s history. For the first time, one of its broadcasts received commercial sponsorship (from Hallmark Cards). Though the practice, unfortunately, did not carry over into other productions, *Amahl* never went unsponsored during its numerous repeat telecasts (which, as a result of public demand, began the following Easter and continued every year at Christmas time). Since the *Opera Theatre*, like most studio television during the period, was performed live, these repeat airings were actually new programs, with the title character periodically replaced as an actor matured into adolescence.

The success of *Amahl* encouraged the series' producers to search for works which, regardless of their current opera house popularity, could be effectively reshaped for television. Thus, the next broadcast, 11 days later, was of Tchaikovsky's rarely performed opera, *The Queen of Spades*, with a new libretto that restructured the story in flashback form to eliminate some of the work's dramatic staginess. The remainder of the season contained two short operas by Puccini (*Il Tabarro* and *Gianni Schicchi* once again) and a lively, one-hour version of *The Barber of Seville*.

For its fourth season, the *Opera Theatre* was granted a new time period. Instead of being scheduled at 11 o'clock at night, as it had been through most of the 1951–52 season, the program was given the more hospitable slot of Sunday afternoons at 3 P.M. To celebrate the move, *Theatre* was granted an extra 30 minutes for a production that was to be one of their most famous—the American premiere of Benjamin Britten's *Billy Budd*.

Peter Herman Adler had gone to London to ask Britten for permission to broadcast the work as soon as he read the score. (The opera had received its debut in Covent Garden less than a year earlier.) Britten was initially reluctant when he discovered that the American TV version would require numerous cuts. However, he finally gave in, persuaded of the series' high standards after viewing a kinescope of *Gianni Schicchi*, which the producer had conveniently brought with him.

Paring *Billy Budd* down by almost 90 minutes proved to be extremely difficult. Several scenes had to be completely excised. Adler felt particularly sad about losing one 12-minute aria by the villain Claggart because "it is so revealing of his character,"[28] but Samuel Chotzinoff came up with a solution— "it was discovered . . . that we could compensate for the aria by showing Claggart in some evil visual action . . . that did in one minute what it would have taken ten minutes of music to do."[29] While this decision aroused the ire of many critics (notably B.H. Haggin of the *Nation*[30]), Chotzinoff pointed to both its limitations, and its possibilities.

> Of course, in the case of a great piece of music, like the Credo from Verdi's *Otello*, no close-up could substitute for the imagination and power of that inspired composition. Yet it seems probably that the composers of the future, writing especially for television, will find no necessity for explanatory and illuminating solo arias, once they realized the revealing potentialities of the television cameras.[31]

Regardless of the questionable cuts, the resulting production of *Billy Budd* was a compelling broadcast whose power came from its concentrated effect. Once again, right before air time, Chotzinoff eliminated scenery he felt was too realistic,[32] favoring instead a setting that contained just a few shipboard props and a background of darkness. The opera's moody currents were expressively rendered by the high contrast lighting, which accented the characters in pools of white against the imaginary sea's surrounding blackness. Television proved to be a perfect medium to focus on *Billy Budd*'s interior battles of conscience and guilt—the moral agony of Captain Vere looms large when viewed in unremitting close-up. The opera's tortured intimacy was well served by the performances of Andrew McKinley as Vere, Leon Lishner as Claggart, and Theodor Uppmann, who created the role of Billy a year before in London.

Critical reaction to *Billy Budd*'s rescaling was uniformly enthusiastic. Leading the cheers was Olin Downes of the *New York Times*, who was astonished by "the fact that the television production of the opera is so much better than the opera itself in its original form."[33] Downes had disliked *Billy Budd* at its stage premiere the year before, but the NBC version struck him as "a marvel of streamlined drama of an intense and gripping power that could hardly be expected of a work condensed from Britten's score."[34] *Billy Budd* was "by far the most successful televising of an opera performance that the writer has seen," as well as "a triumph for all concerned in the presentation."[35]—echoing the sentiment virtually word for word by Ronald Eyer in *Musical America*, who acclaimed the production as "a milestone."[36] Irving Kolodin in the *Saturday Review* noted that "the results were light years ahead of the old primitive qualities considered acceptable in bygone Pagliaccis and Carmens."[37] Perhaps the highest praise came from TV viewers. As Peter Herman Adler recalls, the program produced "one of our strongest public reactions. Was it from an opera audience or a television audience? Mostly the latter, for NBC estimated the public at close to ten million."[38]

A month later, the *NBC Opera Theatre* charted another ambitious course with its production of Leonard Bernstein's *Trouble in Tahiti*. Even though it had originally been created for the stage, *Trouble in Tahiti* seemed designed with television in mind, since so much of its flavor derives from TV's commercialism and pop energy. Bernstein's satiric jabs at suburban consumption and ennui are couched in the vivid terms of TV advertising, and the program emphasized the connection by presenting the work as a playfully stylized version of prime-time entertainment.

What gave the NBC production of *Trouble in Tahiti* its freshness was the inventive way it matched Bernstein's musical and dramatic tone with TV techniques. Director Kirk Browning employed an ever changing arsenal of camera positions and movements to complement the opera's shifts from cartoonish barbs to a growing sense of poignancy. In the opening scene, the work's two characters, Sam and Diana, were photographed like rigid commercial models, locked in the stereotyped poses of domestic suburban life, as the camera restlessly drew towards them. Later, at Sam's office, the camera assumed a witty, first person viewpoint, when it literally became two different people—Sam's friend Bill and his secretary Miss Brown. With Bill's entrance, we saw the confident, glad-handing Sam, treating the camera to a warm but aggressively manipulative walk around the office. Miss Brown's appearance was a different matter. The camera's movements were more demure and funny, as Sam looked down into its eye, asked if he's ever made improper advances to her, and quickly tried to recover his poise when it/she nodded back at him. Camera perspective became even more suggestive during the next two scenes, with both Sam and Diana singing arias directly to the lens, finding its impassive gaze more comforting than similar conversations with one another. By the opera's conclusion, the tone deepened to a surprising feeling of bleakness and melancholy, underscored by Sam and Diana's near frozen forms and the camera's intense concentration on their emotional immobility.

The contrasting grey sets and the use of line drawings were among the program's most distinctive features, contributing to its sly lampoon of prevailing commercial styles. Yet, like so many *Opera Theatre* productions, this design was a last minute decision. Originally, Saul Steinberg, the noted *New Yorker* artist, had executed a series of cartoon renderings for the background, but right before air time, Samuel Chotzinoff ruled that they were a "lousy idea" and told his staff to get rid of them. They quickly painted the walls with a pale grey hue and sketched in just a few items to set the locale. While it's sad that Steinberg's set met such a cruel fate, the drawings might not have yielded the same spirited, pop transparency of the "cleaned-up" broadcast.

With two triumphs in a row, the *NBC Opera Theatre* continued its fourth season with its first Christmas rebroadcast of *Amahl*, and in February 1953, another world premiere—a commissioned opera by Bronuslav Martinu entitled *The Marriage*, based on the play by Nikolai V. Gogol. Though the program was well received, the opera itself was generally felt to be rather slight. *The Marriage* was followed by Puccini's one-act opera, *Sister Angelica*, and finally by the company's biggest production yet—a two-part, three-hour presentation of *Der Rosenkavalier*.

For the first time, the *Opera Theatre* had been given the chance to tackle a large-scale work without severe editing, and the opportunity clearly inspired everyone concerned. Elaborate sets were constructed for the special program, which was offered in two 90–minute installments, airing on successive Sundays. Great care was taken with the staging to capture the opera's lilting mood and frequent moments of delicacy. A new English translation was prepared by one of TV opera's greatest champions, John Gutman. The cast, headed by Wilma Spence and Ralph Herbert, was dramatically skillful and picture perfect for the roles they were to play. Yet, ultimately *Der Rosenkavalier*'s shimmering atmosphere never really came to life on the small screen. The camera reduced the players and the settings surrounding them to a prosaic level which made it hard to accept the work's rococo conceits and Viennese aristocratic flavor. Though this was, as *Musical America* notes, in many ways the *Opera Theatre*'s "most ambitious presentation,"[39] it was also somewhat leaden and uninvolving. Irving Kolodin's harsh assessment ("For this viewer, the *Opera Theatre* bit off more of a tough nut than it can chew with television techniques that have barely cut their eye teeth."[40]) must, however, be tempered with the recognition that the series' greatest successes have generally been with operas intimate in scope and naturalistic in range, not with works as rich in theatrical artifice as *Der Rosenkavalier*.

Opera on *Omnibus*

After the demise of the CBS *Opera Television Theater* in 1950, NBC was the only network regularly experimenting with the largely unsponsored realm of opera. Beginning in 1952, however, CBS, with its Sunday afternoon series *Omnibus*, once again returned to occasional operatic ventures. Produced by the TV-Radio Workshop of the Ford Foundation, *Omnibus* was dedicated to spirited explorations of creativity and cultural diversity. It achieved an impressive coup when it turned its sights towards opera—the first studio appearances by the Metropolitan Opera Company.

Omnibus had previously presented a few brief operatic moments, mostly of the lighter variety, including a couple of scenes from *The Mikado* with Martyn Green, a production of *The Merry Widow* with Patrice Munsel and Theodore Uppmann, and Menotti's half-hour chamber work, *The Telephone*. The appearance of the Met in February 1953 was of a different caliber altogether. The 65–minute English adaptation of *Die Fledermaus* employed the resources of more than 300 people and was staged with great finesse and style. The sets were lavish; the costumes were elegant; the direction by Bob Banner was smooth and assured, which was quite a feat considering the complicated logistics involved with a large cast and playing area; and the performances were, for the most part, sprightly and musically lilting.

Yet the *Omnibus* version of *Die Fledermaus* did more than simply transfer a Met performance to a TV studio. It represented a clever rethinking of Johann Strauss's operetta in TV terms. The camera was not used as just a passive recorder of stage activities but as an energetic element in its own right. Sometimes characters addressed it directly, as they would a friendly confidante. Other times it served as a brisk guide through the whirlwind of personalities and plotlines cluttering the set. In its most dramatic moments, it offered the drunken perspective of the prison warden Frank, tilting and going out of focus as he stumbled back from Count Orlovsky's party to return to work. Later, while Frank sat at his desk, dreamily singing a few bars of the "Champagne Chorus," the objects of his reflections, Olga and Ida, suddenly appeared in superimposed cameos above his head.

As staged by Herbert Graf, this TV production of *Die Fledermaus* made every effort to invite the home audience to share the festivities. There was a feeling of intimate celebration from its opening moments. After Eugene Ormandy took a brief bow to the camera before beginning the overture, a member of the Met's production staff introduced the performers in their dressing rooms, and the character of Dr. Falke cheerfully stepped forward to acquaint viewers with what was about to take place. The engaging camerawork, the lively translation by Garson Kanin (with lyrics by Howard Dietz), and the gentle comic turns of Brenda Lewis, Jude Thompson, and Charles Kullman all contributed to a sense that in the right hands, opera (or at least operetta) could make a sparkling transition to the small screen.

Three weeks later, the Met reappeared on *Omnibus* with a 65–minute version of *La Bohème*, which, like *Die Fledermaus*, was adapted directly from the company's current repertoire. Once again, the show's producers faced the challenge of rescaling a presentation originally designed for the Met's broad auditorium. Practically every element needed to be modified for television's restricted scope. The sets and costumes transported from the Opera House to the studio required alterations and some color changes. Joseph L. Mankiewicz's new staging, which had just premiered that season, had to be rethought for the camera's many eyes. Scenes and arias had to be trimmed to fit the rigid time limit. The transformations, however, worked well. Howard Taubman of the *New York Times*, who decried the rapid pacing of the Met's previous TV production, saluted this program for its "honesty. . . . It has been proved before, and this TV 'Boheme' was further proof that opera, done straight and with no apology for the ineluctable fact that it is opera, is a natural for television."[41]

Though this was the Met's last studio appearance, *Omnibus* continued its own operatic explorations, usually with works that, in keeping with the show's spirit, were adventurous or offbeat. A month after *La Bohème*, it offered the premiere of a "lost" George Gershwin piece written when the composer was 22. *135th Street*, which lasted only 20 minutes, was a distinctly minor effort, whose chief value lay in its hints of what was to come later in *Porgy and Bess*. Still, the opera's tale of Harlem street life was staged with some flourish, thanks to Valerie Bettis's jazzy choreography. Nine months later, *Omnibus* tackled another comparatively unknown work—Ottorino Respighi's *Sleeping Beauty in the Woods*, a fairy-tale opera that proved to be more enchanting visually (there were several imaginatively used effects) than musically. The next two operatic presentations stuck more closely to American themes—a 1955 program featuring the premiere of William Schuman's *The Mighty Casey* and a 1957 show offering a very abridged version of Douglas Moore's little seen *The Ballad of Baby Doe*.

NBC Opera Theatre During the 1950s

While *Omnibus* pursued its distinctively erratic course, the *NBC Opera Theatre* maintained its carefully selected restagings of repertory opera, with assorted premieres and commissions. By the start of its fifth season in 1953, the validity of its approach was no longer in question. Notable programs such as *Amahl and the Night Visitors*, *Billy Budd*, and *Trouble in Tahiti* proved Herbert Graf's belief that "television can be the most decisive medium for forcing opera to take off its top hat and enter the American home."[42] The series' producers were willing to boldly experiment (sometimes trampling on cherished conventions) in their goal of making opera accessible, immediate, and popular. As Samuel Chotzinoff told the *New York Times*, "Opera should be entertainment. . . . Opera has more color than a football game, finer drama than all but the best of the motion pictures, and music and song far superior to anything heard on Broadway."[43]

Despite Chotzinoff's carnival-barker tone, the *NBC Opera Theatre* succeeded in turning most music critics from skeptics to often ardent converts to their methods. Under the sophisticated artistic direction of Peter Herman Adler, the series skirted a wise course around the pitfalls Howard Taubman noted about TV opera in 1949:

> The basic artistic problem is the broadcaster's attitude towards opera. Will he approach it as if he were tiptoeing into a cathedral with head bared? Or will he give it the palsy-walsy treatment? Both attitudes, too familiar on the radio, are obnoxious. The one leads to sanctimonious pomposity, the other to irritating condescension.[44]

The techniques of the *NBC Opera Theatre* involved a respect for both opera and television's power and a fundamental recognition that only certain kinds of musical and dramatic expressions could be transposed from one form to another. Experience had proved the virtue of selecting operas with simple effects and a feeling for naturalism. The "enormous advances" Lincoln Kirstein noted in the *Opera Theatre*'s development were the result of its movement "towards intimacy and away from spectacle, towards the immediate head-on collision with the image in the familiarity of one's fireside, rather than from the baroque picture-frame proscenium of a Grand Opera."[45] After 26 productions, the key to the program's success was its passionate belief that television could offer opera not just a new environment but a new voice.

In pursuing this voice, the *Opera Theatre* continued to expand its methods. Its technique of placing the orchestra in a separate studio from the singers and stage, which originated when the unit moved to a smaller broadcast facility and could no longer squeeze everyone together, proved, in the long run, to be a tremendous asset. Though there were still complications involved in electronically connecting the cast with the conductor and orchestra elsewhere in the building (music was piped in on speakers above the singers' heads with the conductor's cues relayed by TV monitors placed around the set), the system permitted far greater technical control. The orchestra could now be carefully balanced by sound engineers for maximum musical effect. More importantly, by isolating the instrumental ensemble, the singers and production staff were freed from the power of the proscenium. No longer did everything need to be designed to face an imaginary theatrical front. Instead cameras, sets, and performers could operate in a "wall-less" universe. Action could take place from the sides, the back, and the rear with a sense of mobility that standard stage arrangements rarely permitted.

The *Opera Theatre* also experimented with other technical aspects of the medium. *Carmen*, the opening program of its 1953–54 season, took full advantage of NBC's recently introduced system of color broadcasting. According to Jack Gould of the *New York Times*, "The use of color in the Carmen production . . . was often truly inspired. The soft pastel shadings in some scenes were startling in their restrained beauty. The color screen had a warmth and visual excitement that simply did not exist on a black and white set."[46]

In addition to the atmospheric enhancement of color, the *Carmen* telecast also employed new audio techniques. Rather than worry about losing the voices of the chorus as singers moved about the stage (and wandered out of specific microphone ranges), the producers hired actors to mouth the words while their parts were sung off-camera. This process of "lip-synching" opera (which had last been used at NBC by Herbert Graf during the days of the Petrillo live music ban of the 1940s) would be adopted many more times, especially in parts that demanded physical dexterity or particular aesthetic appearances.

The rest of the fifth season was characterized by similar experiments with approaches and production methods. A November 1953 performance of *Macbeth* eliminated most of the subsidiary characters to concentrate on the opera's two leads. In February 1954, the *Opera Theatre* offered its first uncut grand opera, presenting Wolfgang Mozart's *The Marriage of Figaro* in two, 90–minute parts on successive Sundays. A month later, the company launched into the modern American opera repertoire once again, this time with a full-blown production of Vittorio Giannini's *The Taming of the Shrew*, which had previously been performed only by small regional groups. There was also an ambitious broadcast of Claude Debussy's *Pelleas and Melisande* and, to conclude the season, what Howard Taubman regarded as the *Opera Theatre*'s "most daring venture"[47]—a virtually complete performance of Richard Strauss's *Salome*.

The program was unusually dramatic, with physical casting playing an important role. Both John Cassavetes and Sal Mineo were hired primarily for their looks and bearing; their voices were supplied by off-screen singers. Another substitution took place during the dance of the seven veils, when dancer Carmen Guitterez deftly stepped into the title role, replacing Elaine Malbin only for the choreographic sequence. The producers considered this attention to realistic atmosphere essential if opera was not to appear ludicrous in close-up.

The company's range during its sixth season was characteristically fresh and provocative. A color telecast of Mozart's *Abduction from the Seraglio*, designed by Rouben Ter-Arutunian, was followed by revivals of Puccini's *Sister Angelica* and *Amahl and the Night Visitors*. There was also an intriguing attempt to re-create the original production of Richard Strauss's *Ariadne auf Naxos* by featuring shortened versions of both the opera and the Moliere play, *The Would-Be Gentleman*, that first accompanied it. Menotti's *The Saint of Bleeker Street* was also presented, in a well-regarded production, just a few months after its stage premiere in New York. Perhaps the season's most notable achievement was its January 1955 broadcast of *Tosca*, starring Leontyne Price in her first full-length opera performance anywhere. Though opportunities for black opera singers at that time were still limited, this did not deter the series' producers, whose chief concern in selecting talent was dramatic and musical believability. The warm reviews Price received confirmed the accuracy of their judgment. *Musical America* praised her "eminently convincing Tosca" and her "sharply focused and warmly communicative portrayal."[48] Olin Downes of the *New York Times* applauded her "vivid performance."[49] Despite the acclaim, Miss Price's debut was marred by a note of ugly controversy, when many of NBC's southern affiliates refused to air the program because it featured a black performer. Nevertheless, the show helped establish her career as a major opera singer and would be the first of many equally demanding *Opera Theatre* appearances in the years that followed.

If diversity characterized the *Opera Theatre*'s 1955–56 season, ambition distinguished the season that followed. For its seventh year, the company launched two world premieres, offered a bold new translation of *The Magic Flute* by W.H. Auden and Chester Kallmann, and announced plans to start a touring ensemble. The season opened with Lukas Foss's *Griffelkin*, a whimsical children's opera commissioned by NBC. While not particularly memorable as a musical experience, the work was often playful and charming, and its production was ingenious. Designer Rouben Ter-Arutunian captured *Griffelkin*'s fantasy aura (the piece concerns a young devil who eventually comes to live on earth) with an imaginative array of costumes, masks, and scenic backdrops that made both hell and the city above it seem delightfully spirited. A cast of over 40 people, many of them actors and dancers whose voices were provided by off-screen singers, were deployed with great skill by director Kirk Browning and by choreographer

Robert Joffrey, who created some frisky dances for characters ranging from an assortment of demons to a mailbox.

The season's second premiere was Norman Dello Joio's retelling of the legend of Joan of Arc, *The Trial of Rouen*, featuring the *Opera Theatre*'s chief dramatic soprano, Elaine Malbin, in another highly praised performance. The premiere which received the most attention, however, wasn't a new musical work but a new translation. Commissioned by NBC, W.H. Auden and Chester Kallman created a new English version of Mozart's *The Magic Flute*, for a production staged by George Balanchine. Introduced in a January 1956 telecast, their collaborative effort received sharply mixed reviews. While Howard Taubman felt the Auden/Kallman translation was "a decided asset" possessed of "grace and wit,"[50] Robert Sabin of *Musical America* attacked the two writers for "manhandling of the opera. . . . The result," he argued, "was a product so mediocre that I suspect that Mr. Kallman wrote most of it and so wrong in its approach and treatment that I could only decide, more in sadness than in anger, that their love of Mozart was musically blind."[51] B.H. Haggin of the *Nation*, who was a harsh opponent of the *Opera Theatre*'s editing tactics, took a middle ground towards the new English version, noting that though

> a great deal that is obscure in the opera house—the large philosophical ideas, the enmity of the Queen and Sarastro—remained obscure in this performance . . . what was clear in the spoken dialogue—the love of Pamina and Tamino, his submitting himself to the trials, the less high-minded preoccupations of Papageno—was made distinguished and at times delightful by Auden and Kallman's words.[52]

Questions of translation aside, the production remains one of the *Opera Theatre*'s most affecting accomplishments, due in part to Balanchine's gracefully pageantlike staging and to the youthful sweetness of Leontyne Price's Pamina and John Reardon's Papageno. Rouben Ter-Arutunian's set designs and costumes combined fancifulness (Tamino is dressed in an outfit that looks like a Buck Rogers's castoff) with an appropriate sense of fairy-tale mystery and splendor. The opera's simplicity of spirit was also reflected in Kirk Browning's direction. The cameras moved with a fluidity to match the pace of Balanchine's measured groupings; there were no rapid editing shifts or tricky expressive techniques (other than a playful point-of-view shot of Tamino, as seen from on-high by the dragon in Act I).

The seventh season was also marked by the creation of the NBC Opera touring companies. Announcing the new organization during a December 1955 performance of *Madame Butterfly*, RCA chairman David Sarnoff said the company would make appearances throughout the country, "presenting opera in English produced with realism and imagination."[53] The company's repertory would include *The Marriage of Figaro* and *Madame Butterfly*; its members and production staff would be drawn from the *Opera Theatre*;

and its costs would be underwritten by RCA and NBC. A natural extension of Adler and Chotzinoff's belief in fresh and immediate approaches to opera, this innovative plan demonstrated Sarnoff's belief in artistic patronage. His support was directly responsible for the *Opera Theatre*'s continued existence, keeping it afloat in the face of rising expenses (its productions were now running in the $30,000 to $40,000 range), no commercial sponsorship (other than for its Christmas telecast of *Amahl*), and, in terms of mass television, comparatively small audiences (five to ten million). Also without a financial guarantee, the NBC Opera Touring Company, which lasted only two seasons, reflected Sarnoff's commitment and the commitment of his son Robert, then president of NBC, to the *Opera Theatre*'s work and methods.

This commitment was impressively underscored in January 1957, when the network financed the American premiere of Sergey Prokofiev's *War and Peace*, at a cost of $160,000. The production was the *Opera Theatre*'s largest in every way—the cast included more than 90 singers; the orchestra was enlarged to 63 pieces; 246 uniforms and formal gowns were ordered; and to accommodate the opera's epic size, the time period was expanded to two-and-a-half hours. Other productions during the *Opera Theatre*'s eighth season were on a much smaller scale. In addition to two classics (*La Bohème* and *La Traviata*) and the traditional Christmas revival of *Amahl*, it also presented the world premiere of Stanley Hollingsworth's *La Grande Breteche*, based on a short story by Honore de Balzac. The work, like *Amahl*, was especially tailored to television's techniques, but it was greeted with little enthusiasm.

For the opening of its ninth season in December 1957, the company selected an opera perfectly suited to its intimate, concentrated approach. Francis Poulenc's *The Dialogue of the Carmelites* was similar to *Billy Budd* in its moody exploration of moral dilemmas and spiritual meaning. The opera's intense psychological landscape seemed to be composed for the close-up camera. The cast of characters was small, the environment (a French convent during the time of the Revolution) was largely self-contained, and the drama of faith and martyrdom was expressed in grippingly personal and immediate terms. More than any of the *Opera Theatre*'s previous efforts, *The Dialogue of the Carmelites* focused on the faces of its performers, letting their feelings fill the screen. The simple costumes and settings, as well as the direction, which often featured a singer in tight close-up for minutes at a time, served as eloquent accompaniments to the opera's religious themes. The production was a triumphant example of how, with deliberately minimal resources, television could create a powerful operatic experience.

The *Opera Theatre*'s next few years included two programs drawn from the standard repertory (*Rigoletto* and *Cosi Fan Tutte*), a highly praised production of Ludwig von Beethoven's *Fidelio* (Irving Kolodin singled out "the excellent camera work" which "permitted Kirk Browning some illusions of space and grandeur not possible in the opera house"[54]) and a performance of Menotti's *Maria Golovin*. Although the work was Menotti's third commission from NBC, the company decided not to premiere it on television but to launch it in the far grander surroundings of the 1958 Brussels International Exposition. Later that fall, the company funded the work for a Broadway run, which lasted only five performances. Finally, in March 1959, *Maria Golovin* came to television, complete with its original cast and staged, according to Howard Taubman, so that its "dramatic elements . . . emerged with power."[55]

Perhaps because of NBC's financial and artistic commitments to that opera, *Maria Golovin* was the only new production of the 1958–59 season. It was also the first program in the series to be videotaped prior to airing, introducing a procedure that would be followed in all future telecasts. Taping presented enormous advantages, especially to a company which had always frantically scrambled to get a show ready for live telecasting. Greater control could be exercised over practically every area. Quick scene changes didn't need to be executed so quickly; mistakes could be eliminated; the pressures and tensions of live performance could be greatly reduced. In addition, videotaping also permitted programs to be repeated, a factor which would play an important role in the company's production schedule during the 1960s.

The Commercial Networks and Opera During the 1950s

Opera was not limited to *Omnibus* and the *NBC Opera Theatre*. Packed in short doses, operatic excerpts were often featured on variety shows. The Met's star performers could handsomely supplement their income by singing an aria or two on *The Perry Como Show* or *The Ed Sullivan Show*. A few even participated in comic skits poking fun at stuffy operatic decorum and traditions, as when the famed tenor Lauritz Melchior allowed himself to be decked with a whipped-cream pie on *The Milton Berle Show*.

While opera would never really be a central attraction on most variety shows, it did find a comfortable niche, especially during the early part of the 1950s, when programming practices were a bit more flexible. Producer Max Liebman indulged his passion for grand opera by scheduling notable Met performers on his NBC spectaculars and on *Your Show of Shows*. Met personalities also performed on such New York-based programs as *The Tonight Show* and Kate Smith's afternoon NBC show.

The nation's premier variety program, *The Ed Sullivan Show*, featured sporadic bursts of opera, most notably on a November 1953 program broadcast live from the stage of the Metropolitan Opera House. The show was the first to be aired from the Met since ABC had stopped televising the company's opening night performances in 1950. The occasion called for something special. Not only did some of the Metropolitan's leading stars, such as Robert Merrill, Roberta Peters, and Cesare Siepi, take to the stage for brief selections but the program also climaxed with an excerpt from the current production of *Carmen*, performed by Rise Stevens and Richard Tucker.

Sullivan allied with the Met again in 1956, after charges that his show was devoting too much attention to rock 'n roll. To prove his sense of cultural "mission," he signed the company to appear on five different programs for the then enormous sum of $100,000. The first was deliberately designed as a blockbuster. Maria Callas, then at the height of her fame, would be making her American television debut in an 18–minute excerpt from *Tosca*. Unfortunately, an attraction which might lure opera fans from around the world did not hold much drawing power for Sullivan's traditional Sunday night audience. His ratings went down six points during the course of her rendition. The Met's second appearance—a scene from *Madame Butterfly* starring Mario Del Monaco and Dorothy Kirsten—fared even worse. The situation demanded immediate attention, and Sullivan rushed to the Metropolitan's general manager Rudolf Bing, suggesting changes both in the method of presentation (from full production excerpts to simple concert staging) and the number of future performances (from three to two). Bing testily agreed to the latter. However, by the time of the company's third appearance, which lasted for a mere eight minutes, he made his grievances public, describing Sullivan to *Newsweek* as "the worst musical illiterate in the world."[56] The Met's final *Ed Sullivan Show* performance took place a month later on March 10, 1957. Richard Tucker and Renata Tebaldi sang a duet from *La Bohème*, which lasted just four minutes.

Opera found a more hospitable harbor with *The Voice of Firestone*, a program that had since its TV premiere in 1949 regularly showcased classical singers and instrumentalists. Unlike the more ratings-conscious *Ed Sullivan Show*, *The Voice of Firestone* offered Metropolitan stars like Rise Stevens, Robert Merrill, and Jerome Hines a less frantic performing atmosphere. The program resembled a sedate recital hall rather than a vaudeville arena. After a brief introduction, the formally attired singers simply stepped in front of the orchestra and launched into their arias, with the assurance that they were not going to be upstaged a few minutes later by a ventriloquist or trapeze artist. While the results were often thrilling musically, they left much to be desired in terms of television. Opera in these circumstances invariably came across as a stiff and sober experience, with little sense that it could be emotionally or theatrically engaging.

For his second *Festival of Music* special on NBC in 1956, producer Sol Hurok tried a different approach. Instead of presenting singers in the traditional concert-style setting, he chose to mount an elaborate staging of the opening scene from *La Traviata*, with Victoria de Los Angeles as Violetta. The 15–minute excerpt looked as handsome as most *NBC Opera*

Theatre productions, with an imaginatively conceived multi-level ballroom, elegant costumes, and the typically resourceful TV direction of Kirk Browning. The entire enterprise proved an ideal vehicle for Miss de Los Angeles, as well as a lively (and expensive) demonstration of how short operatic selections could be successfully adapted for television.

There were other experiments with opera telecasting during the 1950s. One of the most curious was a short-lived series entitled *Opera Vs. Jazz*, that aired on ABC for a few months in 1953. Despite its title, the program was not a contest but more like a *Hit Parade* of popular songs and arias. Each week a different pair of guest performers would appear (one from "jazz," one from opera) and to the accompaniment of the ABC Piano Quartet alternately belt out examples from their respective musical worlds. Robert Merrill and Jan Peerce were among those chosen to stand up for opera.

A more serious effort began on an independent New York City station, WPIX-TV, in 1950. *Opera Cameos* offered condensed versions of well-known works, broadcast in their original language and introduced by Giovanni Martinelli, who helped set the scene before each aria. While production expenses were minimal, the casts were often comprised of leading performers, such as Regina Resnik and Brenda Lewis, as well as younger singers, including Beverly Sills, who was just getting started. In 1954, the program moved to the flagship station of the always shaky Dumont Network, WABD in New York, where it was sent out to the network's other affiliates for close to a year. *Opera Cameo*'s format may not have pleased serious music lovers, especially since every aria was followed by a jarring commercial, but it was an unusual effort to present opera directly, without apology or fussiness. (Later *The Voice of Firestone* would try something similar, when it devoted its entire half hour to the best-known arias from one opera, complete with appropriate sets and costumes, a cast of two or three singers, and a narrator to tie the plot together.)

CBS's innovative and unsponsored Sunday morning program, *Camera Three*, also tackled various types of operatic presentations. A 30–minute version of Mozart's *Cosi Fan Tutte* was telecast in 1956, and two years later, Lotte Lenya appeared to sing songs of Kurt Weill. The series' severely limited budget forced it to search for projects which needed little in the way of production values—hence the favored format of performers sitting on a stool in a bare studio—but in later years *Camera Three* would venture into more enterprising opera telecasts, including commissions and rare revivals.

Opera on Television in the 1960s

The commercial networks saw little need to expand the range or the volume of their opera programming. The 1950s had proved that the TV opera audience was not a large one. Nor was it particularly attractive to advertisers. Of the *NBC Opera Theatre* telecasts, only *Amahl and the Night Visitors* was sponsored each year, and that was because its appeal was seen as broad enough to transcend opera's narrow cultural ghetto. The Met's unhappy experiences on *The Ed Sullivan Show* provided further confirmation of the form's inability to hold many viewers for longer than a few minutes. Only variety shows controlled directly by well-meaning sponsors, such as *The Voice of Firestone* and *The Bell Telephone Hour*, risked featuring opera performers on a regular basis. By the early 1960s, both *The Voice of Firestone* and *Omnibus* were gone, victims of network programming policies that left little room for shows with less than crowd-pleasing potential.

The Bell Telephone Hour, which premiered at the end of 1959, did endure throughout most of the decade, offering an agreeable mixture of popular and classical music. Famous opera stars of the period were a frequent attraction, and the show could boast among its many operatic highlights the American debut of Joan Sutherland in 1961 and several thrilling appearances by Birgit Nilsson. In contrast to the sometimes too somber *Voice of Firestone*, *The Bell Telephone Hour* presented its performers with a greater sense of style and confidence. The sets appeared more open, and the camerawork far more fluid. Even when singers launched into an aria simply standing in front of the Bell Telephone Orchestra, they were photographed in a way that de-emphasized the stiff, recital-like aspects.

As they had been throughout most of the 1950s, larger scale opera productions were the almost exclusive province of the *NBC Opera Theatre*. There were, however, a few alternative efforts. On its short-lived replacement for *The Voice of Firestone*, entitled *Music for a Summer Night*, ABC broadcast three standard repertory works—*Madame Butterfly*, *La Traviata*, and *Tosca*—the latter in an unusual production set in Fascist Rome. In 1960, the *Hallmark Hall of Fame* presented a new opera which obviously hoped to tap into the Christmas "naivete" genre pioneered by *Amahl*. Composer Philip Bezanson and librettist Paul Engle's *The Golden Child* was an updating of the nativity story, this time set during the period of the California Gold Rush. The opera, however, received dismal reviews, and unlike Menotti's treasure, it was never repeated. In 1962, CBS offered a "Leonard Bernstein Spectacular" devoted to "The Drama of *Carmen*." Employing a cast of 34, Bernstein demonstrated the musical and theatrical vitality of Georges Bizet's work, with two Carmens to make his points clear—singer Jane Rhodes for the arias and actress Zohra Lampert for the spoken parts. The only other major network endeavor during the decade was a 1965 Sunday afternoon presentation of *Martin's Lie*, Gian-Carlo Menotti's fourth TV opera commission (and his first from CBS). Produced, staged, and narrated by the composer, the 52–minute work, designed for amateur church groups, met with tepid critical response.

Without the ratings pressure and strict commercial mentality of the rest of the broadcast schedule, Sunday morning television proved to be a fertile ground for opera, as long as expenses were kept to a minimum. Even with low budgets, programs such as *Directions*, *Lamp Unto My Feet*, and *Look Up and Live* were able to commission operas with religious themes. ABC's *Directions '61* offered *Break of Day*, an original Easter opera by Leo Brady and George Thaddeus Jones; a bit later, after the program changed its name to *Directions '62*, Abraham Ellstein's *Thief and the Hangman* and Earl Wild's oratorio, *Revelation*, were presented. David Amram's original Passover opera, *The Final Ingredient*, was broadcast in 1965. In 1967 CBS commissioned composer Erza Laderman to write an opera based on the life of "Galileo," which was broadcast on *Look Up and Live*.

During the 1960s, *Camera Three* also continued its operatic explorations, opening the decade with a performance of excerpts from Baldesarri Galuppi's rarely seen *Filosofo di Campagne*, followed a year later by *The Accused*, an originally commissioned operatic monologue about the Salem witch trials by composer John Strauss and librettist Sheppard Kerman, starring Patricia Neway. The program also broadcast an abridged production of Mozart's *The Impressario*, as well as documentaries on Jennie Tourel and Beverly Sills and a special salute to Jan Peerce's 25th year as an opera star in 1967.

The Last Years of the *NBC Opera Theatre*

The *NBC Opera Theatre* began the decade on an auspicious note. Its January 1960 telecast of *Cavalleria Rusticana* was the series' first regular, non-*Amahl* production to receive commercial sponsorship. Finally, after more than a decade of operating primarily on a sustaining basis, the *Opera Theatre* was able to find in the Florist's Telegraph Delivery Association an advertiser who recognized that its small but loyal Sunday afternoon audience represented a clientele worth reaching. Initially, critical reaction to the idea was gracious, but with the sponsored broadcast of *Don Giovanni* three months later, critics began to view commercials as a harsh intrusion of commerce amidst the trappings of high culture. Writing in the *New Yorker*, Winthrop Sargeant felt the presence of advertising damaged the *Opera Theatre*'s artistic spirit. "Rather than listen to *Don Giovanni* on these terms, I would prefer not to hear it at all. If I had not heard some really good unsponsored produced by the NBC Opera, I would have concluded that opera on the air, under present broadcasting circumstances was a menace to culture."[57] Although he recognized the necessity of commercials, Ronald Eyer of *Musical America* lamented the kind of trappings modern TV advertising demanded.

> We realize that opera needs a sponsor if its continued existence is to be assured. But, as ever, the plaint must be that the commercials were too long and too frequent.

Wouldn't a short, tasteful announcement at the beginning and at the end serve just as well?[58]

These and similar attacks appeared to have a rather drastic effect. According to an interview with producer Samuel Chotzinoff conducted by Richard Burke, the Florist's Association (and other advertisers), faced with the outcry their generally well-meaning efforts provoked, decided to stay away from future *Opera Theatre* telecasts. The series lost a valuable source of outside funding and support at a time when it could ill afford to survive solely on NBC's largesse.

Even with its budgetary uncertainties, however, the company still offered exciting and frequently challenging operatic productions. Despite the swirl of controversy surrounding its use of commercials, the *Don Giovanni* broadcast was largely greeted with cheers for its musical verve and wonderful casting, which featured a dashing Cesare Siepi in the title role (the first time the program had used a famous Metropolitan Opera performer). For its 1960–61 season, the *Opera Theatre* presented another commissioned world premiere—this time of Leonard Kastle's romantic opera about Brigham Young, *Deseret*—as well as a large-scale staging of *Boris Godunov*. Even more than its earlier telecast of *War and Peace*, this 1961 *Boris Godunov* deserved the title "epic," with its surging crowd scenes, expansive sets, and ornate costumes. The program seemed populated with hundreds of peasants and noblemen—the small screen sometimes appeared ready to burst at the seams—but Kirk Browning's direction provided everything with an appropriate choreographic sweep. The care and attention which went into every aspect of the production, especially its striking use of color (from the rich reds of the court to the heightened blues and blacks of the night scenes), supported Irving Kolodin's belief that "televised opera in this country reached a high point of excellence with the NBC-TV Opera Theatre's latest and most ambitious venture."[59]

The next few years demonstrated a similar willingness by the company to expand the boundaries of TV opera, but the *Opera Theatre* was increasingly hampered by growing scheduling and financial obstacles. *Deseret* and *Boris Godunov* were the only new productions of the 1961–62 season. During 1962–63, only one new program surfaced; a staging of Italo Montemezzi's rarely seen *The Love of Three Kings* was placed among three episodes of repeats. When asked by *Newsweek* about the decrease in the number of original programs, Samuel Chotzinoff took a suitably reflective stance.

I have been fortunate with this company in that the brass upstairs trusts me completely. They don't ask me any questions, and let me do the things I want. They just tell me whether I can do eight operas, five operas, or two a year. . . . I believe that as long as General Sarnoff and Bobby are around we will have opera, symphony, Bach Masses or something equivalent. We had Toscanini for seventeen years. The opera company seems to be the successor, although it's in another field. I believe the Sarnoffs think so too.[60]

Chotzinoff's optimism was partially vindicated by the 1962–63 season, when the *Opera Theatre* scheduled two original productions (and two repeats). The first of these new programs was Gian-Carlo Menotti's fourth commission for NBC since 1939. Unlike *Maria Golovin*, his last *Opera Theatre* effort which played in theaters before its TV premiere, *Labyrinth* was designed specifically for television. The 45–minute work employed numerous special effects and examples of trick photography to tell its jumbled space-age allegory. While the technological enhancements were apparently intriguing, the opera itself proved far less successful. Even Menotti's introductory admonition to view *Labyrinth* as "an operatic riddle, and perhaps it is more a riddle than an opera" did little to disguise the work's frantic lack of substance. As Harold Schonberg noted in the *New York Times*, "On the whole, 'Labyrinth' is one of the thinnest musical concoctions Menotti has ever put together."[61]

The final program of the 1962–63 season was an unusual departure—a complete presentation of Johann Sebastian Bach's *St. Matthew Passion*, offered in two parts over Easter weekend. Since the piece was clearly not an opera, some way had to be found to dramatize it for television. The solution was in keeping with the solemnity and grandeur of Bach's music. Rather than have actors "play" the parts, scenes from religious paintings and sculptures were intercut at appropriate moments during an actual choral performance. The actions leading up to and including the crucifixion, however, were not "visualized"; instead director Kirk Browning focused on more abstract Christian symbols.

The *Opera Theatre*'s 1963–64 season, its 15th, was to be its last. The problems of mounting expensive and unsponsored programs ultimately proved to be more than even NBC's generosity could support. The only new presentation was a January 1964 telecast of Gaetano Donizetti's *Lucia di Lammermoor*. Its production statistics reveal the reason for the declining number of original *Opera Theatre* episodes over the years. Costing $140,000, the program required three-and-a-half weeks of rehearsal, as well as three full days for videotaping. Expenses had been rising steadily ever since the company's first season—a 1950 program ran $15,000; *Billy Budd* in 1952 came in at $40,000; and *War and Peace* in 1957 hit the record books at a whopping $160,000. Moreover, the funds spent on *Lucia* came directly out of the network's pockets, with no realistic expectation that they would ever be offset by advertising revenue. Thus in 1964 with the death of Samuel Chotzinoff, who had been the *Opera Theatre*'s driving force, NBC lost interest in its much acclaimed musical philanthropy, and the program never returned. With its cancellations, the challenges of creating opera shaped for the TV studio would rarely be attempted on the commercial networks again.

Non-Commercial Television and Opera

If opera could no longer find a hospitable environment on ABC, CBS, or NBC, it would eventually discover, like most of the minority arts, a much warmer welcome on educational television. Certainly, the small number of stations devoted to non-commercial programming in the 1950s were not in the competitive position to do battle with *Omnibus* or the *NBC Opera Theatre*. They barely had enough funds to stay on the air for a few hours a day, but they were able to offer a couple of opera shows more in keeping with their instructional (and limited financial) perspective. Among the first was *Spotlight on Opera*, a 1955 collection of introductory appreciation lectures by Jan Popper of UCLA. Total cost for the 16–part series was a little more than $25,000. In 1956 WQED in Pittsburgh presented six lecture programs with Boris Goldovsky entitled *Opera for Today*, which were also budgeted at the equally low rate of about $1250 per episode. A sequel, *Opera for Tomorrow*, consisting of ten shows, was prepared a year later.

As National Educational Television (NET), the production/distribution collective of educational television, stations grew, so did the nature and expense of its operatic efforts. While there were still a few instructional series—in 1960, NET, in conjunction with the Metropolitan Opera Guild, assembled an expensive, three-part series called *This Is Opera*—the production of full-length works began to be more common. WGBH in Boston collaborated with musicians from the New England Conservatory of Music and from Boston University to produce several programs drawn from the more obscure realms of the operatic repertory. The first was a 1957 telecast of Mozart's *La Finta Giardiniera*, whose total budget came to $3100. Three years later, costs were still at the same level for Maurice Ravel's *L'Heure Espangol*. By 1961, however, they had doubled for Henry Purcell's *Dido and Aenaeas* (to $7130) and zoomed to more than $62,000 for a 90–minute presentation of Luigi Nono's *Intolleranza* in 1965. In addition to importing 11 operas from European broadcasters, NET also produced a one-hour version of Bela Bartok's *Bluebeard's Castle* in 1964. In 1967 they offered a coup of sorts by presenting a telecast of Jack Beeson's *Lizzie Borden*, just a few months after its world premiere at the New York State Theater.

Educational television's most ambitious opera efforts began a couple of years later when NET and the Ford Foundation hired Peter Herman Adler to draw up a blueprint for the best ways to present opera and other serious music on non-commercial television. He offered a preliminary report in February 1969, and two months later the Ford Foundation made $500,000 available to start an NET opera company. This new project was clearly modeled on the valuable lessons Adler had acquired from 15 seasons as the musical head of the *NBC Opera Theatre*. Works would be sung in English; clear diction would be stressed; and grand-scale productions would be avoided in favor of television's attachment to intimate realism. More importantly, there would be no hesitancy to reshape opera for the electronic medium. "If you hope, as we do," Adler wrote, "that TV has the potential to make friends of people who have never had a chance to see a live performance of opera, the need to cut and adapt to television seems unquestionable."[62] Editing was essential, in Adler's view, because of television's perceptual demands. As he stated in an outline of his beliefs in the *New York Times*:

> First, an opera of approximately one hour's length can, on TV, be a perfectly satisfactory experience; even more, an hour and a half in front of the home screen corresponds easily to a full evening at the opera house. The extraordinary concentration which the little screen both requests and provides is the difference.[63]

The NET Opera Company would also resemble the *NBC Opera Theatre* in its extraordinary attention to production standards. In contrast to many European TV operas, where the soundtrack was prerecorded and the singers lip-synched their roles during filming, Adler insisted on the value of actual performance.

> At the NET Opera, and before at the NBC Opera, we tape *live*, thus catching the singer's actual emotion while singing. And to liberate him further from being closed in, we have developed over the years, the technique of utilizing two studios simultaneously—one for the orchestra, the other for the singers. Through modern technology (sound being piped from one studio to the other, closed-circuit-television monitors, etc.) conductor and singers have as much contact with each other as if they were working in the opera house. Using separate studios for singers and orchestra also frees the technicians for more imaginative lighting and camera angles and gives the singers more space for moving.[64]

To insure that the NET Opera Company's productions would be conceived for television with freshness and originality, Adler hired director Kirk Browning, who had helped pioneer most of the major techniques of opera telecasting since the early days of the *NBC Opera Theatre*.

The *NET Opera Theater*'s first program in October 1969 was a perfect example of Adler's approach. Instead of a repertory with some degree of built-in audience appeal, the company opened with an adventurous work rarely heard outside of Europe, Leos Janacek's *From the House of the Dead*, based on the Fyodor Dostoyevski novel. Adler's emphasis was, as always, on reconceiving opera for television. He boldly cut and reshaped to make the production understandable for home viewers. Narrated flashbacks were added to provide a more dramatic structure, and scenes were pared down to shorten the work's running time. Adler also took great care in assembling "a very strong group of singing actors,"[65] characterized by an intimate performing style and clear English diction. Resembling in scope and intentions the best of the *NBC Opera*'s efforts, the program marked an auspicious beginning for this new series.

Reaffirming his belief that television could provide a viable and vital alternative to auditorium opera, Adler's next project for the *NET Opera Theater* was the world premiere of Jack Beeson's *My Heart's in the Highlands*. Based on a William Saroyan story, the opera suited television's reduced scale, with a cast of only seven players and a small chorus of 12. Critics found the piece a minor work at best but praised its evocation of Saroyan's gentle vision.

In addition to its first premiere, this second *NET Opera* program was noteworthy for another aspect because it answered many years of complaints about the terrible audio qualities of TV opera, or at least the terrible way opera sounded on tinny TV speakers. NET organized links with FM stations throughout the country to broadcast the stereo soundtrack of *My Heart's in the Highlands* simultaneously with the telecast. By turning off the volume of their televisions and turning on their stereos, home viewers could now have the chance to hear opera with extraordinary fidelity and range. The technique would become an important adjunct of non-commercial television's music programming from that point onward.

Generous as the Ford Foundation's $500,000 grant was, it could not cover the complete cost of three domestic opera productions. Some type of partnership was essential, and fortunately NET was able to enter a consortium with two major foreign broadcasters (the CBC and the BBC) to help share expenses and programming. The first of these mutual international efforts was a highly acclaimed BBC telecast of Britten's *Peter Grimes*, which concluded the *Opera Theater*'s opening season. Imported TV opera made up a much larger portion of the schedule during the following year. In addition to airing two co-productions—a CBC *Hansel and Gretel* and a BBC presentation of Britten's written-for-TV opera *Owen Wingrave* (which received its world premiere on the same day in England, Canada, and America)—the *NET Opera Theater* also began to show noteworthy (and inexpensive) programs drawn from other overseas sources. An interesting example was a February 1971 telecast, offering two different productions of the Orpheus legend—Claudio Monteverdi's *Orfeo* from Italian television and Yasushi Akutagawa's *Orpheus in Hiroshima* from NHK in Japan.

The Ford Foundation increased funding for the second season to $580,000, allowing the company to not only import more material but also to put on two more domestic productions. The first was a 90–minute version of Mozart's *Abduction from the Seraglio*, which was praised by Raymond Ericson for its imaginative visual atmosphere. "Richly patterned backdrops against which solid-color flat props were positioned, carried out the abstract, two-dimensional nature of Persian paintings. The effect was simple, brilliant, often delightfully childlike and playful."[66]

NET Opera's second original program, Tchaikovsky's *Queen of Spades*, was, like *Abduction from the Seraglio*, a return for Adler to a work he had mounted once before at *NBC Opera Theatre*. His 1971 staging closely followed his reconstruction of the opera in 1952, where the libretto written by Tchaikovsky's brother was eliminated in favor of a new version based more closely on Alexander Pushkin's novel. Though it was cut for television to a little more than half its length (provoking Donal Henahan of the *New York Times* to headline his review " 'Queen of Spades' in Miniature,"[67]), this new production was generally admired, especially for the radiant performance of Jennie Tourel.

Despite the successes of its first two seasons, the *NET Opera* ran into funding difficulty during its third year of operations when the Ford Foundation, preparing to leave public broadcasting entirely by 1972–73, declined to renew its grant and PBS was left to cover the majority of expenses. Nevertheless, artistic director Peter Herman Adler remained confident of the company's future and about the relevance of its mission to reach new audiences. As he told the *New York Times*' TV critic John O'Connor in 1971, his principal concern was not pleasing opera purists but attracting the average TV viewer, who he felt was "perhaps less knowledgeable but more open to new cultural experiences."[68]

NET Opera's great promise lay in its ability to expand opera's horizons by commissioning works designed expressly for the creative possibilities of the small screen. One such example was an opera the series premiered in February 1972, Thomas Pasatieri's *The Trial of Mary Lincoln*, with a libretto written by Anne Howard Bailey. Following through flashbacks the story of Lincoln's wife from courtship to widowhood (with her 1875 Chicago trial serving as a framework), Pasatieri and Bailey fashioned an opera that seemed comfortably at home in television's restricted range. The dramatic emphasis centered firmly on the title character's psychological impressions, and, as Irving Kolodin observed, "Thanks to the strikingly suggestive portrait of Mrs. Lincoln by Elaine Bonzanni . . . the viewer was held in constant anticipation of the next turn in her troubled life."[69]

The Trial of Mary Lincoln was just the first of what Peter Herman Adler hoped would be a long line of original, made-for-TV operas created for the series. To underscore its commitment to new directions, *NET Opera* during its third season went ahead with plans to commission two unusually ambitious projects—a Brechtian-style "vaudeville" by avant-garde German composer Hans Werner Henze and an "opera comique" from Duke Ellington. Unfortunately, the Ellington work was never produced because the composer died before its completion, but Henze's *Rachel, La Cubana* finally did make it to the air in 1974, at the then extravagant cost of

$505,000. With a libretto by Hans Magnus Enzenberger, *Rachel, La Cubana* took a deliberately distanced approach to its subject matter, the reminiscences of a once-famous Cuban nightclub singer told on the eve of the revolution in Havana. The opera resembled a mixture of various Brecht-Weill collaborations, with its cabaret trappings, title announcements at the beginning of each act, and boldly drawn political caricatures; but unlike *The Three Penny Opera* or *Mahagonny*, there were few moments of musical or emotional power. *Rachel, La Cubana*, however, was extraordinarily impressive as a visual experience, thanks to Rouben Ter-Arutunian's colorfully inventive (and expensive) set designs and costumes. Kirk Browning's direction also gave the program an appropriately expressive sheen, and his efforts were matched by a strong cast, including Lee Venora, Alan Titus, and Robert Rounseville, who did their best to dramatize the brittle qualities of Henze's twelve-tone score.

Rachel, La Cubana's problems—its high budget and generally inacessible atmosphere—signalled the end of the *NET Opera Theater*'s era of original productions. Despite some critical enthusiasm, affiliates, by and large, hated Henze's two-years-in-the-making TV opera; and with other decidedly more popular projects vying for their funding dollars, PBS stations severely cut back their support. For the next few years, *NET Opera*'s schedule resembled its fourth season, when the series' name served primarily as a forum for inexpensively purchased imported material, such as the Japanese TV opera *The Death Goddess*, by Shin-Ichiro Ikebe, or domestic acquisitions, such as an Indiana University production of John Eaton's *Myshkin*. Among the many overseas programs aired under the *Opera Theater* title in the mid–1970s were an outstanding British version of Leonard Bernstein's *Trouble in Tahiti*, a haunting psychological treatment of Wagner's *The Flying Dutchman* directed by Brian Large, and BBC productions of Verdi's *Falstaff* and William Gilbert and Arthur S. Sullivan's *The Mikado* and *The Gondoliers*. By 1978, *NET Opera Theater* had ceased even this minor importing function—its role having been taken over by the much larger resources of PBS's umbrella series, *Great Performances*.

Television Rediscovers Live Opera: PBS's *Live from Lincoln Center* and *Live from the Met*

Complete, live opera telecasts, broadcast directly from the stage of an opera house, had not been part of American television for more than 20 years. The enormous technical difficulties of remote auditorium broadcasts—the lack of proper lighting, the inflexibility of the cameras—had driven TV opera into the studio, where conditions could be more tightly controlled. However, by the mid–1970s new developments in camera sensitivity made it possible to present works live from the concert stage with remarkable clarity and with very little disruption to those attending the performance.

The first fruits of this breakthrough (outside of a few experiments on cable television) occurred on PBS's *Live from Lincoln Center*. After successfully premiering its techniques in a January 1976 concert from Avery Fisher Hall with the New York Philharmonic, the series shifted its attention four months later to the fraught-with-hazards realm of live opera broadcasting. Unlike a symphonic telecast where the music itself could often carry the proceedings, opera on television demanded tremendous clarity and legibility. Viewers watching the experience at home must not only be able to see the performance but follow it, grasping the meanings of a production intended for the expansiveness of the large stage. Great skill would be needed to creatively transmit the opera in terms of the medium's smaller boundaries and to make certain that the camera was always focused at the center of every musical and dramatic moment. Luckily, the direction of this first *Live from Lincoln Center* opera telecast was in the able hands of Kirk Browning, who knew more about the perils and possibilities of opera on television than anyone else in the country. Browning brought to the broadcast of Douglas Moore's *The Ballad of Baby Doe*, performed by the New York City Opera, the same attention to detail and story line which distinguished his work at both NBC and NET. Though the program was far from perfect technically (the lighting was still a bit too dark), this experiment in bringing network television back to the opera stage was a valuable step forward in reacquainting viewers with the pleasures of live operatic performance.

New York City Opera broadcasts became a regular part of *Live from Lincoln Center*'s schedule in the years that followed, but the excitement surrounding these events would be largely overshadowed once the Metropolitan Opera decided to return to live television in March 1977. The Met had been experimenting with the possibility of telecasts from their new home at Lincoln Center since 1968, when a crew from NHK in Japan videotaped a performance of *The Barber of Seville*. Picture and sound quality were considered inadequate, however, and the program was never aired in America. With the setting up of the Lincoln Center media development department in 1972, the Met and the Center's other constituents embarked on an ambitious program, headed by John Goberman, testing how far television could go in accurately capturing their varied activities. After several years of experimentation, trial tapings of *The Tales of Hoffmann* and *I Pagliacci* offered the Met a convincing demonstration of television's new power. Plans were made to broadcast an *Aida* in 1976, but when labor negotiations made this impossible, a production of *La Bohème* was selected for the following year.

Texaco, the Metropolitan Opera's longtime radio sponsor, underwrote the considerable costs of this first *Live from the Met* telecast on PBS. Basic production expenses (salaries, equipment, crew) were $200,000; another $25,000 was spent on FM simulcasting hookups; and $50,000 on advertising. The results, however, amply rewarded Texaco's generous financial support. The program attracted one of PBS's largest audiences (including a million and a half viewers in New York alone), and helped earn the always hard-pressed network a whopping $1 million in its fundraising efforts.

Artistically, the Met's *La Bohème* broadcast was a triumph as well, with a wonderful, though not especially youthful looking, cast of Luciano Pavarotti, Renata Scotto, and Ingvar Wixell, and the spirited conducting of James Levine. Pavarotti, who was just starting his meteoric rise on the American opera scene (a rise that would be propelled by TV events like this one), was in marvelous voice, and his great charm and eager enthusiasm proved to be a natural TV asset.

The program's only problems were in small technical areas. Long shots, taken from the top balcony, were, because of occasionally dim lighting and the sheer vastness of the auditorium, often difficult to "read." As a result, the home audience was occasionally deprived of a sense of stage space and of the ways characters fit together with the broad sets around them. To compensate, director Kirk Browning stayed primarily with a variety of close-up cameras (situated throughout the orchestra and first balcony), which gave the opera a directness and intensity entirely in keeping with Puccini's fervent emotionalism. Reaction to the telecast was uniformly enthusiastic, with Harold Schonberg of the *New York Times* flatly declaring:

> this was television that really evoked the opera. It was by far the best production of its kind that this opera-goer has ever come across, with everything accurately worked out (the crew had made a trial run at the previous Saturday's "Bohème" and had prepared themselves for all contingencies). The cameras invariably were where they should have been; there was no nervous hopping from stage to orchestra, for instance. The idea was to give the television audience a real opera; and [producer John] Goberman and his crew did just that.[70]

Live from the Met's three programs during the following season were drawn from the company's mainstream repertoire (*Rigoletto*, *Don Giovanni*, and the inevitable pairing of *Cavalleria Rusticana* with *I Pagliacci*), but more adventurous fare began to be presented with the 1978–79 season. In addition to an opening night telecast of *Otello*, with Jon Vickers in the title role, and a *Tosca* starring Shirley Verrett and Pavarotti, the series also offered two rarely performed works which the company had recently revived—Bedrich Smetana's *The Bartered Bride* and Verdi's *Luisa Miller*. A highlight of the next season was a broadcast of the Met's celebrated new production of Kurt Weill's *Rise and Fall of the City of Mahagonny*, an opera that lent itself especially well to television. British director Brian Large, who had established an outstanding reputation in Europe for his innovative handling of TV operas, capitalized on the Met's bold staging by repeatedly emphasizing group tableau rather than individual close-ups. A musicologist as well as a gifted technician, Large knew precisely how long to hold shots and when to shift camera perspectives for maximum musical and dramatic impact. His measured approach to direction, combined with Gil Wechsler's super-vivid lighting, Jocelyn Herbert's arresting production design and an extraordinary cast featuring Teresa Stratas, Richard Cassily, and Cornell MacNeil made this one of PBS's most compelling live telecasts.

In addition to *Mahagonny* and another opening night presentation of *Otello* (this time with Placido Domingo in the title role), the Met's 1979–80 TV season was also marked by the introduction of programs taped live and then rebroadcast at a later date. Transmissions of both *Don Carlo* and Donizetti's *Don Pasquale* (starring Beverly Sills) were examples of this delayed technique—the former having been recorded two months before, the latter a document of a performance which took place almost a year-and-a-half earlier. Though *Live from the Met* would still occasionally offer a "live simulcast," the majority of its future programs would be previously taped presentations (in decided contrast to *Live from Lincoln Center*, which always honored the technical meaning of the first word in its title).

In the years that followed, *Live from the Met* steered a course between operas with a guaranteed popular appeal (the series was, after all, the Met's most visible enterprise) and new mountings of less frequently performed works. A typical TV season would usually feature two or three crowd-pleasing attractions (starring either Pavarotti or Domingo) and an acclaimed revival such as Alban Berg's *Lulu* or Hector Berlioz's *Les Troyens*. By its fourth year, the series had attained a remarkable level of production sophistication. Home viewers could look forward to outstanding camerawork (offering perspectives better than any seat in the house), English subtitling, superb audio (through FM stereo simulcasts), and lighting that appeared warm and natural. Unfortunately, the comfortable pleasures of watching a telecast were often purchased at the expense of the audience actually attending the event live. Opera house patrons were forced to endure numerous inconveniences to accommodate TV technology, including brightened lighting, rearranged visual effects (no scrims in front of the stage or slide projections), changes in makeup and costumes, and singers who scaled down their vocal performances, tempted, as John Rockwell described it, "into singing for the microphone even when there is a paying public beyond the footlights."[71]

But regardless of the disadvantages live opera telecasts posed to full-price ticketholders, there was little question of their considerable power as a document of the Met's stage glories, a power made all the more impressive by the skill that directors Kirk Browning and Brian Large brought to the task of making a large production come to life on the small screen.

Their efforts proved that capturing a performance on television is not the same thing as simply photographing it. Opera telecasting demands the ability to shape stage pictures into understandable TV pictures, while trying to preserve as much theatrical sweep and musical vitality as possible.

In their quest to re-create the richness of the operatic experience for distant viewers, both Browning and Large stressed the value of accurate and sensitive reportage, but each went about this goal from a slightly different perspective. The contrasts between a 1980 *Don Carlo*, which Browning directed, and Large's version of the same production four years later offer an interesting example of their varying approaches.

Browning's distinctive style is apparent from the minute the curtain rises on Act I. The large grouping of pages and ladies-in-waiting surrounding the Princess Eboli are photographed with dramatic urgency, as the camera repeatedly zooms-in-and-out from the crowd. Close-ups are employed whenever a character sings, and there are frequent cuts from one position to the next in order to heighten the pacing. Brian Large, on the other hand, prefers a somewhat more stately point of view. The opening ensemble is revealed not through quick zooming but by a majestic camera pan, which sweeps in front of the crowd. Slow dissolves, rather than abrupt edits, are used to shift perspectives. Camera movement is kept to a minimum, as are close-ups. What emerges most clearly is Large's directorial feel for the integrity of stage space. Performers are often seen in dignified long shots, which sometimes last for thirty seconds before they dissolve to a shot with a tighter focus. Unlike Kirk Browning, who focuses primarily on main character action, Large tends to explore the vital relationship between characters and the settings that surround them. The prepossessing, high-ceilinged cloister of San Giusto plays a much greater role in his shooting of the second part of Act I than in Browning's version, where once it is introduced it seems to fade in the distant background. For Large, the cloister is as important as the singers, a fact he stresses by selecting long shots that prominently include its somber presence.

The differences between the two directors can also be seen in their perceptions concerning the camera's mission and scope. Kirk Browning's attention is centered on the story and the stars. He told Leslie Rubinstein of *Opera News*:

> I think you come out ahead if you concentrate on performances, so I sacrifice sets, lights, and character and the total look of the stage set at any given moment for the principal dynamic. . . . You'd be surprised how easy it is to get trapped into thinking that you have to register everything.
>
> I've always got to remember we're hitting a lot of people who are not opera-lovers. We've got to try to elicit their enthusiasm. That's why we use subtitles and focus on the stars. The opera fanatics only need a full shot of the stage and they're happy. I get hate mail all the time for those close-ups.[72]

While Brian Large rarely provides just a "full shot of the stage," there is little question that his sympathies lie somewhat closer to those "opera fanatics" Browning gently chides. His extensive musical background gives his directorial style a slower and surer rhythmic pulse. Large's approach is also more all-embracing, more concerned with bringing the "production" and not just the "performances" into television's narrower range. As John O'Connor reports, "Mr. Large interviews the singers, the stage directors, the designers and the conductors in an effort to be faithful to their intentions and to make the television 'presence' on the completed tape as unobtrusive as possible."[73] These careful techniques produced programs distinguished by their fidelity and by their feeling of scale.

Though Brian Large and Kirk Browning approached their work with different stylistic attitudes, both directors recognized that television's key role in an opera broadcast was to capture the "live" quality of the event. It was this ability—to transport viewers at home into direct contact with the world's greatest singers performing before a huge audience at one of the world's greatest opera houses—that made *Live from the Met* an enthralling experience. While the series was sometimes accused of being, in the words of George Hall, "little more than 'telecom peepholery' "[74] because of its reduction of grand opera to the not-so-grand small screen, the virtues of being a close witness to live stage proceedings offered numerous compensations. *Live from the Met* provided conclusive proof that the magic of opera is often best captured during the challenges of an actual performance. As Lloyd Schwartz observes, "There's never been anything better suited to television coverage than a live event,"[75] and sometimes the nature of that coverage can actually enhance the meaning of the event. Schwartz recalls the time during one telecast

> when Teresa Stratas, the star of *Lulu*, came down with the flu and her scarcely known replacement (Julia Migenes-Johnson) was called in at the last moment, [and] the camera was there to record her nervousness, her competence (she had sung the role at the Met earlier that week), and the astonishing moment, near the end of the scene of the first act, when Lulu wipes her husband's blood from her lover's hand, and Migenes-Johnson, her sexy half-smile filling the screen, suddenly took full possession of her role. Part of the thrill was that the camera could signal that moment by being there at the right time, the technical mastery allowing us to see something we could never fully experience in the theater, even from the best seats.[76]

The inherent drama of close-up cameras in the opera house was also underscored during a March 1983 telecast of *Tannhäuser*, directed by Brian Large. In the final act, one of the horrible hazards of live performing took place—tenor Richard Cassily momentarily lost his voice. John O'Connor describes what happened next: "Mr. Large, having to make a quick decision on how to treat it, decided to become a straightforward reporter and go in for a closeup that would capture the equivalent of a news event. It was the right decision. The feeling of the production remains live."[77]

The tensions and triumphs of live opera telecasting were not the sole province of *Live from the Met*; they were also to be found on the New York City Opera broadcasts presented every season on *Live from Lincoln Center*. Though without the large-scale resources of the Metropolitan, the New York City Opera's productions were often more stylistically daring and fanciful—qualities which came across surprisingly well on television. Among the many highlights were Sarah Caldwell's wittily allegorical interpretation of *The Barber of Seville*, a new 1979 staging of Kurt Weill's *Street Scene*, and an utterly beguiling broadcast of Janácek's *The Cunning Little Vixen*.

The Janacek opera, with its almost mystical celebration of farm and forest wildlife, would seem to defy TV treatment, since its aura is so far removed from the medium's traditional attachment to domestic reality. The City Opera's celebrated production, which depended on Maurice Sendak's fairy-tale sets and costumes and Frank Corsaro's inventive direction, would also be difficult to transpose to television's narrower focus and colder glare. But the TV version assembled by *Live from Lincoln Center*'s resident director, Kirk Browning, magically kept the work's spirit intact, a fact confirmed by Frank Corsaro, who noted that the TV translation "preserved and even enhanced the storybook quality and visual freshness of the piece."[78] Browning's decision to treat the opera differently from a typical stage telecast proved to be an important factor in the program's success. As he told the *New York Times*'s Tim Page prior to the broadcast, "We will approach 'Vixen' like a mime or a ballet, rather than a verismo thriller. . . . Too many close-ups would spoil the work's charm. At the same time, we can't retreat too far or we will lose the dramatic impetus."[79]

Rather than rely on his customary style of narrative urgency, Browning took a more restrained approach, using longer shots and less frequent cutting. His most expressive device was the slow dissolve, which he employed to not only gracefully shift from one plane of the stage to the next but also to approximate, on several occasions, the opera's evocative movements between the prosaic world of man and the enchanted realm of the forest. His work captured the unique flavor of *The Cunning Little Vixen* by focusing on both its story and its poetic atmosphere. Live opera telecasts have rarely cast such a spell.

In addition to their transmissions of complete productions, both *Live from Lincoln Center* and *Live from the Met* featured many operatic special events. Superstar recitals were a prime attraction, with the opera world's two leading tenors, Luciano Pavarotti and Placido Domingo, usually acting as the chief calling cards. Pavarotti appeared on three *Live from Lincoln Center* programs (the first with Joan Sutherland, the second as a soloist, and the third with Sutherland and Marilyn Horne); while Domingo appeared on two *Live from the Met* telecasts (one with Tatiana Troyanos, the other with Sherrill Milnes). Mezzo-soprano Marilyn Horne was the only artist to work both series—performing with Joan Sutherland in a concert with the New York Philharmonic and with Leontyne Price in a concert at the Metropolitan Opera.

If these recitals were distinguished by their concentrated artistic energy, the gala occasions broadcast by each series were marked by a sense of lavishness and festivity. Beverly Sills's final performance, which aired on *Live from Lincoln Center*, was staged like an enormous party/salute, with guests from every realm of the performing arts, ranging from Placido Domingo to Carol Burnett, Ethel Merman, Peter Martins, and Dinah Shore. An even grander event took place a few years later, when the Metropolitan Opera celebrated its centennial with a spectacular eight-hour display of musical talent. The gala concert, which took place from 2:00 to 6:00 P.M. and then resumed for another four-hour session at 8:00 P.M., was more than just a triumph of logistics (50 excerpts were performed, with singers flying in from all over the world to take part)—it was also a moving demonstration of the Metropolitan's tremendous artistic resources. *Live from the Met* broadcast the entire affair as it happened, giving millions of viewers the chance to share in the gala's excitement and sheer historical drama.

PBS's Other Opera Programs

Though the activities of the Met and the New York City Opera dominated PBS's opera schedule, the network did its best to represent productions from throughout the country. Its series *In Performance at Wolf Trap* offered four opera telecasts showcasing the repertoire of Beverly Sills, who was one of Wolf Trap's principal guest artists during the mid–1970s. The programs, taped at actual performances and then broadcast several months afterwards, featured Sills in lively, open-air presentations of *La Traviata*, *The Daughter of the Regiment*, *Roberto Deveraux*, and *The Merry Widow*.

A few years later, the network aired two operas recorded at the Spoleto Festival U.S.A. in Charleston, South Carolina. The first was a well-received production of Menotti's *The Consul*, directed, like the *Wolf Trap* shows, by Kirk Browning. As is true of most Menotti operas, the work's intense domestic focus lent itself particularly well to television. The performance, like the special telecasts from Covent Garden, was custom designed for television, "with," in Kirk Browning's words, "four cameras placed wherever we wanted to put them and with an invited audience that understood the ground rules."[80] This procedure was also observed the following year for a broadcast of the Spoleto Festival's revival of Samuel Barber's *Vanessa*.

The practice of televising performances direct from an opera house, which had once been seen as too difficult to control technically, had now become the chief means of putting opera on the air. Not only did viewers seem to prefer the thrill of a live event (or a taped live event), but production expenses, while high (a typical *Live from the Met* telecast costing upwards of $500,000), were still less than mounting a work in the expensive isolation of a TV studio. These factors, plus the increasing sophistication of remote TV technology, helped make "live" concert hall broadcasts the favored method for most PBS opera programs. By the early 1980s, productions had originated from almost every major stage in the nation. The Academy of Music in Philadelphia was the site of two memorable telecasts with the Opera Company of Philadelphia. The first was an earnest, sweet-tempered performance of *La Bohème*, with guest star Luciano Pavarotti and a supporting cast of young singers, which attracted a record TV opera audience of 22 million. The second was a broadcast of Gian-Carlo Menotti's new staging of Tchaikovsky's *The Queen of Spades*. Programs were also televised from the Kennedy Center in Washington, D.C., for a gala salute to George London; from Chicago's Civic Opera House, for a Chicago Lyric Opera Company production of Charles Gounod's *Faust*; and from the War Memorial Opera Hall in San Francisco, where the San Francisco Opera Company presented *Samson and Delilah* and *La Gioconda* (the latter was broadcast one act-at-a-time, during the course of a week, as part of a novel experiment in opera appreciation).

Despite the flood of live performance-in-the-theater telecasts, there were still a few experiments on PBS with opera assembled under more controlled conditions. Director Brian Large taped the Houston Grand Opera Company's production of Carlisle Floyd's *Willie Stark* without an audience, positioning his cameras throughout both the auditorium and the stage in order to capture the full effect of Hal Prince's opulent staging. For a 1982 broadcast of Lee Hoiby's and Lanford Wilson's *Summer and Smoke*, director Kirk Browning took the Chicago Opera Theater into the studio as a way to precisely regulate the opera's evocative atmosphere and lilting flashbacks.

One particularly ambitious production experiment was a taping of William Grant Still's little-known work, *A Bayou Legend*, which was recorded on a Mississippi bayou in the fall of 1979. Producer Curtis Davis had been waiting for almost 20 years for the opportunity to tape an opera "live" on location, but, as he observed, it had to be a piece "that could take us far from any highway and far from any airline traffic pattern"[81] in order to avoid any unintended background noise from civilization. Still's opera, with its remote southern setting, offered an ideal opportunity. The problem, however, was to figure out how to tape the performers live, without having to bring the accompanying orchestra out into a swamp for long hours under impossible conditions. Through a complicated technological process, a solution was reached which permitted the singers to hear a recording of the piano score and watch a videotape of the conductor at a previous rehearsal on monitors kept out of sight of the observing camera.

Sophisticated directional microphones recorded only their "live" voices, leaving the piano playback almost inaudible in the background. After matching computerized video and audio editing, the orchestra was brought back, and the accompaniment recorded, to be added to the soundtrack by a separate editing process, which assured that voices and orchestra would remain synchronized. (A similar procedure, suggested by this production, was used three years later for the Chicago Opera Theater's telecast of Lee Hoiby's *Summer and Smoke*.) The results were impressive, in terms of both sound and picture. Unlike the boxy, lifeless quality of many European TV operas (which were shot in appropriate settings but which featured singers lip-synching their prerecorded material with limited success), *A Bayou Legend* possessed an unexpected feeling of naturalness. Being able to hear the performers' live voices while seeing them in real locales made everything seem more vivid. With its haunting scenery, its atmospheric photography, and its vigorous cast from Opera South, the telecast captured the genuine folklorish spirit of Still's 1942 composition in a way impossible on the stage. The program suggested promising new approaches to on-location, opera telecasting—approaches which, unfortunately, no one in America has yet chosen to pursue.

No matter where they originated, domestic opera productions were an expensive commodity. Imported programs, usually of high quality and low cost, provided a much simpler solution to filling the vacancies in PBS's opera schedule. Beginning with *NET Opera Theater*, the network had regularly turned to foreign broadcasters for more affordable cooperative ventures or ready-made product. *Great Performances*, PBS's umbrella cultural series, continued this tradition, bringing, since the early 1970s, some of Europe's most imaginative TV operas to American home audiences. Among the program's many highlights were Jean-Pierre Ponnelle's celebrated productions of Monteverdi's *The Coronation of Poppea*, *Orpheus*, and *The Return of Ulysses*, as well as his handsome on-location version of Mozart's *The Marriage of Figaro*; a staging by Franco Zefferelli of *Carmen* with Placido Domingo; and a remarkable telecast of Wagner's *Tannhäuser*, recorded at Bayreuth and directed for television by Brian Large. Large also directed another, far grander Bayreuth project, the epic television version of Patrice Chereau's controversial production of *The Ring of the Nibelungen*. Taped live, but without an audience, Wagner's masterpiece came across powerfully on the small screen, due in part to Large's careful preparations and his sensitivity to Chereau's daring dramatic vision. Unfortunately, PBS, fearful that more than a dozen hours of Wagner would alienate their audience, chose to spread the broadcast of the four operas from January through April 1983, rather than broadcasting them one night after the next, as they were intended. This decision, which drew strong criticism in the press, inevitably diluted the work's impact; several months later, a few brave local affiliates, with strong opera constituencies, decided to make amends. Lucky viewers in New York and Boston were able to see *The Ring* repeated, this time in its proper form.

While PBS was concerned about its audience's appetite for Wagner, the network has had nothing but enthusiasm for any project involving either Luciano Pavarotti or Placido Domingo. Their frequent appearances on *Live from the Met*, *Live from Lincoln Center*, and various imported programs on *Great Performances* has given these two gifted tenors a visibility and prominence few opera stars have known before. (A measure of their popularity can be gauged by the interest they provoked on the commercial networks. Both were subjects of many news profiles and were accorded prime time's ultimate honor—their own specials. Pavarotti was seen on ABC in *Pavarotti and Friends*, a generally embarrassing hour, which included duets with country singer Loretta Lynn; while Domingo, with somewhat greater dignity, sang and clowned around with Carol Burnett in a 1983 CBS special. A few years later on ABC, he succumbed to the allure of the full-scale, lavish pop special, with *Placido Domingo Steppin' Out With the Ladies*, as he strolled around Manhattan with a curious assortment of female vocalists, including Leslie Uggams, Patti La Belle, Susan Anton, and Marilyn McCoo.)

PBS provided Domingo and Pavarotti with a wide range of opportunities to display their talent, sure in the knowledge that whatever they did would attract a large audience. Not only were there numerous telecasts of their American and European opera performances and recitals, but each was given a series of programs chronicling their master classes with young singers. "One-man specials" offered another type of exposure. For Pavarotti, this might mean a broadcast of one of his solo concerts given around the country. For Domingo, it took a more elaborate form—his 1983 program *Domingo Celebrates Seville* showed the tenor parading through various parts of the Spanish city, using its picturesque streets and courtyards as backdrops for appropriate arias from *Don Giovanni*, *Fidelio*, *Carmen*, and, obviously, *The Barber of Seville*.

Domingo and Pavarotti have also been prominent participants in PBS's annual fundraising/variety show, *Gala of Stars*, an event that has spotlighted dozens of opera luminaries since its premiere in 1980. Featured performers willing to sing an aria or two and demonstrate their support of public broadcasting have included Marilyn Horne, Renata Scotto, Samuel Ramey, Montserrat Caballe, Nicolai Gedda, Grace Bumbry, Carlo Bergonzi, and Jessye Norman.

Opera on the Commercial Networks During the 1970s and 1980s

As televised opera in various forms continued to grow and attract new audiences on PBS, it virtually disappeared from the commercial networks.

There was little room for an expensive, consistently low-rated, minority art form on the competitive, mass-oriented schedules of ABC, CBS, and NBC, especially since a sanctuary for cultural programming now existed on non-commercial channels.

After the demise of the *NBC Opera Theatre* in the mid–1960s, TV opera was largely relegated to the scarcely watched Sunday morning slot, where the networks clustered their shows devoted to religion or art. As it had since the 1950s, CBS's cultural series *Camera Three* proved to be a rare champion of non-prime-time endeavors, so long as the budget remained at rock bottom level. This meant that when the program focused on opera, there were few props or other vestiges of stagecraft. What remained, however, were often shows filled with committed artists and performers, excited to be on a TV series sensitive to their concerns.

Camera Three's customary opera format in the 1970s was the recital, which called for little more than a bare stage, an accompanying piano, and a singer (or singers). There were many such episodes, including concerts by Dorothy Kirsten, Marilyn Horne, Judith Blegen (in a show which also featured some documentary footage on her career), and a special salute to Richard Tucker on his 25th anniversary as an opera star. A 1977 program on "The Operas of Thomas Pasatieri" expanded the "in recital" studio method by mixing conversational scenes of the composer and four singers, chatting around the piano, with modestly staged and costumed excerpts from his works.

While Sunday morning shows had become opera's principal refuge on the commercial networks, there were still a few scattered attempts to bring the form to more popular time periods. In 1972, CBS presented a severely condensed version of the Metropolitan Opera's gala salute to Rudolph Bing in honor of his retirement. This one-hour prime-time program, sponsored by Texaco but with no formal commercials, was basically a series of rapid montages of the 43 singers who participated in the event, with some pauses for performances by Leontyne Price, Birgit Nilsson, and a duet by Joan Sutherland and Luciano Pavarotti.

Three years later, CBS telecast, as part of its *Festival of the Lively Arts for Young People*, "Danny Kaye's Look-In at the Met," a lively and informative view of the company's backstage operations. Thanks to the pressure of the Metropolitan's manager, Schuyler Chapin, the network "rescheduled the starting time of an NBA playoff game to give the Met prime Sunday-afternoon exposure."[82] Opera was also featured on another *Young People*'s program that same year, when Zero Mostel starred in a performance of Puccini's short comic work, *Gianni Schichi.*

CBS's only other opera efforts were a couple of prime-time specials starring Carol Burnett. In the first, Burnett appeared with Beverly Sills, who proved just as adept in comic turns and show-biz cheeriness as she was in playing Donizetti heroines. Burnett's second venture with an opera superstar, however, was not as successful, primarily because Placido Domingo, for all his charm and graciousness, seemed a trifle uncomfortable in the midst of the program's slick atmosphere. The show, plagued by poor pacing and writing, failed to do justice to either Domingo's talents or Burnett's.

Domingo was seen to much better advantage on a 1981 NBC program honoring Enrico Caruso. Resembling the format of a typical PBS concert presentation, this special *Live From Studio 8H* telecast featured Domingo and the New York Philharmonic, led by Zubin Mehta, in a selection of arias closely associated with the century's most legendary tenor. Aside from a few bits of documentary material recounting Caruso's career, the show consisted largely of exceptional music making, broadcast in a simple, straightforward fashion that suited the occasion perfectly.

A few years earlier, NBC, recalling its once annual yuletime tradition of televising Menotti's *Amahl and the Night Visitors*, decided it was time for a more lavish production. Instead of in-studio videotaping, which had been the customary method since the 1950s, filming was now to take place on appropriate exterior locations in Israel, with interiors to be shot in a studio in London. This new 1978 version of *Amahl* certainly had a more realistic feel, offering, in addition, a compelling performance by Teresa Stratas as Amahl's mother and intelligent direction by Arvin Brown. Still, as a reflection of changing times, the opera never resumed its role as a regular Christmas attraction. After a single, low-rated telecast on NBC, it moved to PBS for one airing and has not been repeated since.

If opera was not a regular attraction, it still received fairly frequent attention (for commercial television) on *The Tonight Show*. Through the years, host Johnny Carson, while hardly an opera enthusiast, has invited numerous opera luminaries to drop by for an aria and join him in conversation. Luciano Pavarotti was an early visitor, first appearing in 1974, and returning more than a dozen times. Placido Domingo has been on the show seven times, while soprano Judith Blegen (whose ebullience seems to particularly delight the usually cool Carson) holds *The Tonight Show* opera record with nearly two dozen appearances. Grace Bumbry and Renata Scotto have also been among many other opera stars to visit this last remaining outlet for variety programming on network television.

The Cable Networks and Opera

It was hoped that the creation of the full-scale cultural cable networks in the early 1980s, with their presumably large economic resources and their ambitious plans for new productions, would prove to be the salvation of the performing arts on television, especially since PBS was becoming increasingly strapped for funds. Services such as CBS Cable, The Entertainment Channel, ARTS, and Bravo seemed to be pointing the way to a bold new future for cultural programming, including that most expensive of projects, TV opera. However, with the collapse of the first two networks and the retrenchment of the two survivors, the vision of a sanctuary for the arts on cable had to be drastically revised.

Of the many domestic programs eventually produced by the four networks, opera was the least favored. The price was usually too high, and the country's major talent was already being seen for the most part on PBS. The only taped-from-the-stage, complete opera production done in America for cable was a program by the San Francisco Opera of *Aida* (starring Pavarotti and Margaret Price), which was paid for by The Entertainment Channel but ended up on The Arts and Entertainment Network (the successor to ARTS) after The Entertainment Channel folded.

But despite the paucity of home-grown products, full-length operas still played a prominent part in the schedules of most of the cultural networks, thanks to the abundance of inexpensive material available from overseas broadcasters. CBS Cable, ARTS, and Bravo were, like PBS, happy to broadcast the high-quality opera programs produced by the more culturally minded networks of England, Italy, and Germany. *Great Performances* was no longer the only place to see memorable telecasts from Covent Garden, La Scala, or Vienna.

However, while these imported productions were frequently thrilling, the promise of the cable TV networks to broaden the scope and nature of arts programming, particularly with respect to opera, lay largely unfulfilled. The remaining services—Bravo and The Arts and Entertainment Network—have been forced to sharply cut back on their original efforts, and there appears to be little sign that this policy will change. One of the best hopes is for more mutual ventures with foreign broadcasters, like Bravo's program, *A Day in the Life of the New York City Opera with Beverly Sills*, produced with German television, as a way of defraying the large costs inevitably associated with opera on television.

CONCLUSIONS

More than 30 years ago, Herbert Graf expressed the hopes of many when he wrote that television "promises to become opera's saving angel just as radio did in the 1930s."[83] While it's hard to prove convincingly that television has "saved" opera during the decades that followed (it can scarcely even match the durability and regularity of radio's Saturday afternoon Met broadcasts), it is true that television has often been remarkably successful in its efforts to bring opera's beauty and power to millions of home viewers.

In trying to squeeze one of the most theatrically grand forms into extremely narrow confines, American telecasters have encountered a series of formidable challenges. The foremost centers on scale. How can works created for the vast expanse of the opera house stage, with soaring vocal lines and surging orchestral accompaniment, ever fit comfortably on a 19–inch screen? How could a small electronic box convey the extremes of dramatic emotion and musical feeling that sweep across auditorium audiences witnessing a live performance?

Televising opera also posed problems of style and technique. What steps should be taken to make the form's grand manner—its larger-than-life actions and expressions—more meaningful in terms of television's intimate focus? How could opera, and its performers, appear less mannered and more natural when seen in close-up?

Broadcasters hoping to answer these questions were left with basically two approaches. The first, and seemingly the least complicated, involved television's abilities to document an on-going event. Rather than worry about reducing opera precisely to the medium's size, the cameras would simply go to the theater and record the proceedings as they take place live on stage. But, as ABC's coverage of the Metropolitan Opera's opening nights in the late 1940s demonstrated, it was not enough to just point the cameras and shoot. Careful coordination between stage action and electronic picture was essential, especially if viewers were to make any sense of activities declaimed in a foreign language. The difficulties which marred these first on-location opera telecasts (clumsy editing, poor lighting, bad camera placement) offered convincing proof that the success of future remote programs would depend not only on improved technical facilities but also on finding TV directors with some feeling for musical drama, who knew the most appropriate moment to cut from one singer to the next and when to accompany an aria with a close-up.

A second and far more common approach to televising opera (up until the mid–1970s) involved programs originating in the studio. Unlike the auditorium, the broadcast studio permitted complete technical control and the chance to shape the work directly for the cameras. Some of the earliest experiments with this method by NBC's Herbert Graf during World War II paved the way to a new conception of what TV opera could be like. Instead of using the studio as a small, remote theater and letting performers pretend they were on stage, Graf tailored his series of opera excerpts according to television's more realistic standards. Acting styles were toned down, recitatives were reworked, and English translations became the norm.

The innovations of the *NBC Opera Theatre* a few years later ushered in an exciting era of studio opera production. Artistic director Peter Herman Adler and producer Samuel Chotzinoff were committed to making opera on television accessible and immediate. Together with director Kirk Browning, they stripped away most of the form's distancing conventions (its tendency towards broad posturing and oversize emotions) and fashioned an approach that emphasized intimacy and naturalism. All programs were sung in clearly enunciated English by personable performers who looked their parts. Music and drama were at the service of television rather than the other way around—works were cut and sometimes reshaped to fit the demands of the medium.

Studio productions of opera, or at least the kind of productions offered by the *NBC Opera Theatre*, seemed to solve many of the basic issues concerning the form's presentation on television. When approached with inventiveness and flexibility, opera assumed a new life on the electronic medium, which in some cases proved to be every bit as moving as attendance at a live performance. Through clear English translations, a convincing naturalistic style, and attentive camerawork, television could lift the somewhat creaky veil of conventions draped around a good many operas and make them seem fresh and emotionally compelling.

Nevertheless, the methods so skillfully developed and practiced at NBC were not universal in their application. Only certain kinds of opera appeared to work well given the medium's restrictions. Television, as Adler observed back in 1952, "cannot at present handle successfully large, panoramic ensembles, and perhaps it will never be able to."[84] The grandiose sweep of *Aida* or most of Wagner would be difficult to capture on a screen which barely has room for more than two people. Instead, more direct melodramatic operas like *Carmen*, *La Bohème*, or *Tosca*, already couched in television's language of simple but vivid emotions and understandable domesticity were often the ones best equipped to make the transition to the small screen.

Given these limitations, studio opera productions still provided the most creative environment to test the form's theatrical challenges in TV terms. However, opera in the studio, despite its frequent aesthetic successes, was invariably an expensive and risky proposition. Costs were high, audiences were low, and advertising support (whenever opera appeared on NBC, CBS, or ABC) was virtually non-existent. Even after moving his ideas to the non-commercial realm of PBS in the late 1960s and setting up the *NET Opera Theater*, Peter Herman Adler continued to encounter the same kinds of financial difficulties and network pressures that marked the later part of his tenure at NBC.

The solution to many of televised opera's problems emerged, interestingly enough, with a triumphant return to live, from-the-stage broadcasts in the mid-1970s. New equipment and greater technical control in the auditorium now made it possible to capture the one crucial element missing from studio productions—the excitement and chemistry of singers facing an audience at a real performance. Unlike previous opera house telecasts, programs like *Live from Lincoln Center* and *Live from the Met* were planned in advance with enormous care to insure musical and dramatic coherence. Thanks to half-a-dozen strategically placed, light-sensitive cameras, the use of simultaneous English subtitles, FM stereo simulcasts, and the responsive TV direction of either Kirk Browning or Brian Large, audiences at home were offered an operatic experience that combined some of the best features of in-studio work with the compelling immediacy of a live event.

The strong, positive response from the public and the critics to the Met and Lincoln Center broadcasts suggests that American television has found, at least for now, an ideal approach to opera programming. While watching opera on a small screen inevitably deprives viewers, as John Rockwell notes, of "the spectacle that some think inherent in the operatic form, and certainly the communal experience of sitting in an expectant house for a live performance,"[85] the medium's ability to draw audiences into a close relationship with a work remains one of its greatest assets. More than 40 years of televised opera have demonstrated the happy conclusion that despite their apparent differences in size and scale, opera can emerge on television with a surprisingly large number of its virtues intact.

NOTES

1. Herbert Graf, *Opera for the People* (Minneapolis: University of Minnesota Press, 1951), p. 222–223.
2. Graf, *Opera*, p. 230.
3. Quaintance Eaton, "Television Audience Sees First Video Opera," *Musical America*, 15 December, 1948, p. 19.
4. Lilian E. Foerster, "Met Video," *Opera News*, 20 December, 1948, p. 8.
5. Jack Gould, "Matters of Record," *New York Times*, 5 December 1948, Section II, p. 15.
6. Gould, "Matters," p. 15.
7. Foerster, "Met Video," p. 29.
8. Gould, "Matters," p. 15.
9. Jack Gould, "The 'Met' on TV," *New York Times*, 27 November 1948, Section II, p. 9.
10. Quaintance Eaton, "The Occasion," *Musical America*, 6 November 1950, p. 6.
11. Peter Herman Adler, "A Cruel Medium," *Opera News*, 14 June 1969, p. 10.
12. Adler, "A Cruel Medium," p. 10.
13. Quaintance Eaton, "Great Opera Houses: NBC TV," *Opera News*, 8 February 1964, p. 30.
14. Quaintance Eaton, "Two Television Networks Give Opera," *Musical America*, 15 January 1950, p. 71.
15. Eaton, "Great Opera Houses," p. 30.
16. "NBC's Madame Butterfly," *Newsweek*, 20 February 1950, p. 44.
17. "Opera for Millions," *TIME*, 16 February 1953, p. 89.
18. Eaton, "Great Opera," p. 31.
19. Eaton, "Great Opera," p. 30.
20. Peter Herman Adler, "Opera on Television: The Beginning of an Era," *Musical America*, February 1952, p. 29.

21. Samuel Chotzinoff, "NBC Music Chief Discusses TV," *Musical America*, February 1953, p. 138.

22. Chotzinoff, p. 138.

23. Arthur Gelb, "The Future of Video Opera," *New York Times*, 28 December 1952, Section II, p. 10.

24. Adler, "Opera on Television," p. 29.

25. Olin Downes, "Menotti Opera, the First for TV, Has Its Premiere; Boy, 12, Is Star," *New York Times*, 25 December 1951, Section I, p. 1.

26. "Menotti and Television," *Newsweek*, 7 January 1952, p. 37.

27. Adler, "A Cruel Medium," p. 10.

28. Quaintance Eaton, "Billy's Bow," *Opera News*, 31 March 1979, p. 18.

29. Quoted in B.H. Haggin's "Music," *Nation*, 18 February 1956, p. 146.

30. Haggin, "Music," p. 146.

31. Chotzinoff, p. 138.

32. Eaton, "Great Opera," p. 31.

33. Olin Downes, " 'Billy Budd' Scores In Television Bow," *New York Times*, 20 October 1952, p. 18.

34. Downes, " 'Billy Budd,' " p. 18.

35. Downes, " 'Billy Budd,' " p. 18.

36. Ronald Eyer, "American Premiere of Billy Budd Launches NBC-TV Opera Season," *Musical America*, 15 November 1952, p. 17.

37. Irving Kolodin, "Billy Budd," *Saturday Review*, 8 November 1952, p. 36.

38. Adler, "A Cruel Medium," p. 10.

39. Robert Sabin, "TV Opera," *Musical America*, May 1953, p. 7.

40. Irving Kolodin, "NBC's Der Rosenkavalier," *Saturday Review*, 16 May 1953, p. 34.

41. Howard Taubman, " 'Boheme' Telecast Rewarding Work," *New York Times*, 23 February 1953, p. 20.

42. Graf, *Opera*, p. 231.

43. George Gent, "Good—But Not Grand," *New York Times*, 23 October 1955, Section II, p. 11.

44. Howard Taubman, "Televised Opera," *New York Times*, 24 April 1949, Section II, p. 13.

45. Lincoln Kirstein, "Television Opera in the USA," *Opera*, April 1952, p. 200.

46. Jack Gould, "New Age of Color," *New York Times*, 8 November 1953, Section II, p. 13.

47. Howard Taubman, "New Opera Techniques," *New York Times*, 16 May 1954, Section II, p. 7.

48. "Leontyne Price Heard in NBC *Tosca*," *Musical America*, 1 February 1955, p. 23.

49. Olin Downes, "Opera: Leontyne Price sings *Tosca*," *New York Times*, 24 January 1955, p. 19.

50. Howard Taubman, "Music: Magic Flute Sung on NBC," *New York Times*, 16 January 1956, p. 17.

51. Robert Sabin, "Review of 'The Magic Flute,' " *Musical America*, 1 February 1956, p. 12.

52. Haggin, p. 146.

53. Frank Merkling, "Opera Becomes Theater Via NBC-TV," *Musical America*, February 1957, p. 175.

54. Irving Kolodin, "NBC Fidelio," *Saturday Review*, 21 November 1959, p. 38.

55. Howard Taubman, "Opera: 'Maria Golovin'," *New York Times*, 9 March 1959, p. 34.

56. "Snubbing the Opera," *Newsweek*, 11 March 1957, p. 54.

57. Winthrop Sargeant, "Mozart's *Don Giovanni*," *New Yorker*, 16 April 1960, p. 168.

58. Ronald Eyer, "Siepi Sings in TV Don Giovanni," *Musical America*, May 1960, p. 25.

59. Irving Kolodin, "Tozzi as Boris," *Saturday Review*, 8 April 1966, p. 42.

60. "Four, Two, One . . . " *Newsweek*, 5 March 1962, p. 79.

61. Harold C. Schonberg, "Music: Menotti Opera," *New York Times*, 4 March 1963, (Western Edition), p. 8.

62. Peter Herman Adler, "Can TV Save Opera," *New York Times*, 13 September, 1970, section xi, p. 6.

63. Adler, "Can TV," p. 6.

64. Adler, "Can TV," p. 6.

65. Harold C. Schonberg, "TV: An Unusual and Important Opera," *New York Times*, 3 December 1969, p. 110.

66. Raymond Ericson, "TV: Mozart, Nicely Done," *New York Times*, 19 October 1969, p. 79.

67. Donal Henahan, "TV: 'Queen of Spades' in Miniature," *New York Times*, 1 March 1971, p. 59.

68. John J. O'Connor, "TV: 'Tales of Hoffmann'," *New York Times*, 14 December 1971, p. 90.

69. Irving Kolodin, "Opera, NET and Met," *Saturday Review*, 4 March 1972, p. 20.

70. Harold C. Schonberg, "The Met's Televised 'Boheme' Is A Harbinger of the Future," *New York Times*, 27 March 1977, Section II, p. 1.

71. John Rockwell, "The Impact of TV on Opera," *New York Times*, 25 January 1981, Section II, p. 1.

72. Quote by Kirk Browning in Leslie Rubinstein, "Live from the Met," *Opera News*, September 1979, p. 20.

73. John J. O'Connor, "Putting Life Into 'Live from the Met'," *New York Times*, 20 March 1983, Section II, p. 31.

74. George Hall, "Opera resists best attempts to televise," *Current*, 12 May 1980, p. 3.

75. Lloyd Schwartz, "Opera on Television," *Atlantic*, January 1983, p. 86.

76. Schwartz, p. 86.

77. O'Connor, "Putting Life," p. 31.

78. Tim Page, "City Opera's Very Special Fox Challenges the TV Cameras," *New York Times*, 6 November 1983, Section II, p. 35.

79. Page, p. 35.

80. Quote by Kirk Browning in Irving Kolodin, "Grand Opera on Television," *Saturday Review*, 8 July 1978, p. 25.

81. Curtis Davis, personal interview, 30 May 1984.

82. Rubinstein, "Live from the Met," p. 13.

83. Herbert Graf, " 'Saving Angel' Says Met Stage Director," *Musical America*, February 1953, p. 22.

84. Peter Herman Adler, "Opera on Television," p. 29.

85. John Rockwell, "The Impact of TV on Opera," p. 1.

REFERENCES

There is a wealth of material available on the history of opera on American television, particularly concerning the years from 1940 through the early 1960s. A useful place to start are two dissertations, Richard C. Burke's "A History of Televised Opera in the United States" and Edward J. Dwyer's "American Video Opera: An Introduction and Guidebook to its Production." Burke provides a thorough discussion of the form's development, with special attention to the growth of, and critical reaction to, the *NBC Opera Theatre*. Dwyer is a bit more general, concentrating on the styles and possibilities of TV opera production.

An informative account of the earliest radio experiments in opera broadcasting can be found in Erik Barnouw's *A Tower in Babel*. The optimism surrounding the early years of TV opera is well captured in the works of two authors who also worked in the field during its formative years. NBC Producer Herbert Graf provides an enthusiastic analysis of opera's future on television in several articles for *Musical America*, such as "Television . . . Its Potentialities for Grand Opera" and " 'Saving Angel' Says Met Stage Director" and in his book, *Opera for the People*, which contains an excellent chapter on opera telecasting during the 1940s. Producer John Gutman also presents a buoyant view in his 1953 essay for *Theatre Arts*, "The Case for Opera on Television."

The introduction of live telecasting from the Metropolitan Opera House in the late 1940s prompted numerous articles examining the significance and the potential of this TV opera breakthrough. These contemporary accounts are recommended for their detailed coverage: Lilian E. Foerster's "Met Video"; Quaintance Eaton's "Der Rosenkavalier is Viewed By Vast Television Audience," "The Occasion," and "Television Audience Sees First Video Opera"; *Newsweek*'s "Met's TV Venture," and "Met Closed Circuit"; and Val Adams's "Radio and TV." Jack Gould, TV critic of the *New York Times*, also offered enlightening comments on the technical quality of the Met programs ("Matters of Record," "The 'Met' on TV"), while the paper's music critics, Howard Taubman and Olin Downes, in their respective articles "Televised Opera" and "Music and the Networks," took a more philosophical, long-range view.

Both Taubman and Downes would, in the years that followed, write often about opera on television, especially the programs of the *NBC Opera Theater*. In a landmark review, Olin Downes thrust the series into national prominence when he praised its 1951 world premiere of *Amahl and the Night Visitors* on the front page of the *New York Times* ("Menotti Opera, the First for TV, Has Its Premiere"). His similar enthusiasm for the *Opera Theatre*'s version of *Billy Budd* (" 'Billy Budd' Scores in Television Bow"), which he preferred to the work's performance on stage, played a key role in establishing the company's artistic legitimacy. Howard Taubman was another fervent supporter of the series during the 1950s. His reviews and longer essays, such as "Future of Opera Looks Up," "New Opera Techniques," and "Something Grand," are among the most vivid documents recounting the *Opera Theatre*'s triumphs.

Taubman and Downes were not alone in their general acclaim of NBC's ambitious opera efforts. The series received favorable attention from the majority of the music press, including thoughtful appraisals from Irving Kolodin in the *Saturday Review*, Lincoln Kirstein in *Opera*, and from Quaintance Eaton and Ronald Eyer in *Musical America*. Many articles examined the *Opera Theatre*'s innovative approach and production techniques. Arthur Gelb's "The Future of Video Opera," Frank Merkling's "Opera Becomes Theater Via NBC-TV," George Gent's "Good—But Not Grand," Quaintance Eaton's "Great Opera Houses" and "Opera in the Camera's Eye," and B.H. Haggin's attack on the program's editing practices ("Music") are particularly instructive. NBC's efforts in making the *Opera Theatre* possible are explored and praised in Robert Sarnoff's "New Horizons for an Old Art"—Sarnoff's booster tone comes naturally since he was then president of the network. One other important source for information regarding the *Opera Theatre* are the various magazine articles by artistic director Peter Herman Adler, who wrote vigorously, and widely, on the series' aesthetic goals. See, for instance, his essays "A Cruel Medium," "TV in the Opera Picture," "Opera on Television: The Beginning of an Era," and "Music: The Silent Stepchild." For an overview of the company's history and activities, Richard C. Burke's, "The NBC Opera Theater," which summarizes material from his previously mentioned dissertation, is also particularly useful.

While the *NBC Opera Theatre* was by far the chief subject for writers discussing TV opera in the 1950s, a few additional programs attracted some degree of interest. CBS's 1950 broadcast of *Carmen* was one of many shows George A. Willey examined in his excellent survey, "Opera on Television." Robert Lewis Shayon discussed the state of TV opera and the efforts of CBS's *Omnibus* in "It's Opera, But Is It Grand?"; and the unfortunate forays of another CBS program, *The Ed Sullivan Show*, into the world of opera provided Jerry Bowles with lively anecdotes in his book *A Thousand Sundays*.

With the collapse of the *NBC Opera Theatre* in the mid–1960s (a condition predicted by *Newsweek* in a 1962 article, "Four, Two, One . . . "), televised opera was relegated largely to the little-viewed realms of Sunday mornings and the infrequent, and inexpensive offering, of National Educational Television. Richard T. Dasher's dissertation, "The Musical Programming of National Educational Television," provides detailed information on the diversity and the production costs of the network's opera telecasts. NET reached a more important position as an opera producer when Peter Herman Adler began the *NET Opera Theater* in the late 1960s. The *New York Times* proclaimed Adler's views on this new venture in a long essay, "Can TV Save Opera?" and in interviews conducted by Howard Taubman ("N.E.T. TV Project Seeks Young Audiences for Opera") and the paper's new TV critic, John J. O'Connor ("TV: 'Tales of Hoffman' "). The program's history and goals were explored by Curtis Davis's "Opera Box," Franzi Ascher-Nash's "Stop, Listen and Look," Raymond Ericson's "N.E.T. Hits More High C's," and John J. O'Connor's "Is Opera a Luxury for TV?" Irving Kolodin's "Opera, NET and Met," Harold C. Schonberg's "TV: An Unusual and Important Opera," Raymond Ericson's "TV: Saroyan Story Charms as Opera," and Donal

Henahan's "TV: 'Queen of Spades' in Miniature" offered some of the most perceptive reviews of the *NET Opera Theater*'s individual accomplishments.

PBS's chief contribution to televised opera, live broadcasts from the New York State Theatre and the Metropolitan Opera House on *Live from Lincoln Center* and *Live from the Met*, was examined in great detail. Recommended articles on the series' aesthetic importance include Harold Schonberg's "The Met's Televised 'Boheme' Is a Harbinger of the Future," Irving Kolodin's "Grand Opera on Television," John J. O'Connor's "TV: Opera and More From Lincoln Center," and George Hall's critical assessment "Opera resists best attempts to televise." Interesting discussions of the elaborate planning involved in each broadcast can be found in Leslie Rubinstein's "Live from the Met," Roland Gelatt's " 'La Boheme' by the Million," Christopher Porterfield's "The Met, The Moor, and the Eye," and Tim Page's "City Opera's Very Special Fox Challenges the TV Cameras." John J. O'Connor's "Putting Life Into 'Live from the Met' " and Jack Kuney's interview "Calling the Shots at the Metropolitan Opera" provide closer looks at the directorial styles of Brian Large and Kirk Browning, respectively.

There are several excellent theoretical overviews of televised opera in the 1970s and 1980s. The *New York Times*'s John Rockwell wrote frequently on the challenges television, and other media, posed to opera's theatrical traditions. His essays "The Impact of TV on Opera" and "Why Does Opera Lure Filmmakers?" are highly recommended. Readers searching for a broader historical analysis of TV opera during the past decade are well advised to turn to Samuel Lipman's "On the Air." Lloyd Schwartz's 1983 article for the *Atlantic*, "Opera on Television," covers similar ground but also offers an intriguing examination of the artistic power of live opera telecasting.

For brief but pointed discussions of commercial television's rare opera series and of regularly scheduled programs, such as *Voice of Firestone* and *The Bell Telephone Hour*, which featured opera selections, Tim Brooks and Earle Marsh's *The Complete Directory to Prime Time Network TV Shows* is highly recommended.

Books

Barnouw, Erik. *A Tower in Babel: A History of Broadcasting in the United States, 1933–1953*. New York: Oxford University Press, 1966.

Bowles, Jerry. *A Thousand Sundays*. New York: G.P. Putnam, 1980.

Brooks, Tim, and Earle Marsh. *The Complete Directory to Prime Time Network TV Shows. Rev. ed. New York: Ballantine Books, 1981.*

Graf, Herbert. Opera for the People. Minneapolis: University of Minnesota Press, 1951.

Articles

Adams, Val. "Radio and TV." *New York Times*, 2 December, 1948, p. 51.

———. "Streamlining Opera for Television." *New York Times*, 18 December 1949, Section II, p. 11.

Adler, Peter Herman. "Can TV Save Opera?" *New York Times*, 13 September 1970, Section XI, p. 6.

———. "A Cruel Medium." *Opera News*, 14 June 1969, pp. 9–12.

———. "Music: The Silent Stepchild." *Saturday Review*, 26 April 1969, pp. 22–24.

———. "Opera on Television: The Beginning of an Era." *Musical America*, February 1952, p. 29.

———. "TV in the Opera Picture." *Theatre Arts*, January 1956, p. 95.

Ascher-Nash, Franzi. "Stop, Listen and Look." *Opera News*, 27 January 1973, pp. 11–13.

Burke, Richard C. "The NBC Opera Theater." *Journal of Broadcasting*, Vol. X, no. 1, Winter 1965–66, pp. 13–26.

Chotzinoff, Samuel. "NBC Music Chief Discusses TV." *Musical America*, February 1953, p. 138.

Davis, Curtis W. "Opera Box." *Opera Journal*, Spring 1972, pp. 5–10.

Downes, Olin. " 'Billy Budd' Scores in Television Bow." *New York Times*, 20 October, 1952, p. 18.

———. "Martinu Opera Scores in TV Bow." *New York Times*, 8 February 1953, p. 78.

———. "Menotti Opera, the First for TV, Has Its Premiere; Boy, 12, Is Star." *New York Times*, 25 December 1951, p. 1.

———. "Music and the Networks." *New York Times*, 24 December 1950, Section II, p. 9.

———. "Television Operas." *New York Times*, 9 August 1953, Section II, p. 5.

Eaton, Quaintance. "Billy's Bow." *Opera News*, 31 March 1979, pp. 18–20.

———. "Great Opera Houses: NBC-TV." *Opera News*, 8 February 1964, pp. 29–32.

———. "The Occasion." *Musical America*, 6 November 1950, p. 6.

———. "Opera in the Camera's Eye." *Opera News*, 16 February 1953, pp. 13–15.

———. "Television Audience Sees First Video Opera." *Musical America*, 15 December 1948, p. 19.

———. "Two Television Networks Give Opera." *Musical America*, 15 January 1950, p. 71.

Ericson, Raymond. "N.E.T. Hits More High C's." *New York Times*, 26 June 1970, p. 13.

———. "TV: Mozart, Nicely Done." *New York Times*, 19 October 1969, p. 79.

———. "TV: Saroyan Story Charms as Opera." *New York Times*, 18 March 1970, p. 95.

Eyer, Ronald. "American Premiere of Billy Budd Launches NBC-TV Opera Season." *Musical America*, 15 November 1952, p. 17.

———. "Siepi Sings in TV Don Giovanni." *Musical America*, May 1960, p. 25.

Foerster, Lilian E. "Met Video." *Opera News*, 20 December 1948, p. 8.

"Four, Two, One . . ." *Newsweek*, 5 March 1962, p. 79.

Gelatt, Roland. " 'La Boheme' by the Million." *Saturday Review*, 19 March 1977, p. 42–43.

Gelb, Arthur. "The Future of Video Opera." *New York Times*, 28 December 1952, Section II, p. 10.

Gent, George. "Good—But Not Grand." *New York Times*, 23 October 1955, Section II, p. 11.

Gould, Jack. "Matters of Record." *New York Times*, 5 December 1948, Section II, p. 15.

———. "The 'Met' on TV." *New York Times*, 27 November, 1948, Section II, p. 9.

———. "New Age of Color." *New York Times*, 8 November 1953, Section II, p. 13.

Graf, Herbert. " 'Saving Angel' Says Met Stage Director." *Musical America*, February 1953, p. 22.

———. "Television . . . Its Potentialities for Grand Opera." *Musical America*, February 1949, p. 11.

Gutman, John. "The Case for Opera on Television." *Theatre Arts*, December 1953, pp. 74–75.

———. "The Future of Opera on TV." *Opera News*, 4 February 1961, p. 31.

Haggin, B.H. "Music." *Nation*, 18 February 1956, p. 146.

Hall, George. "Opera resists best attempts to televise." *Current*, 12 May 1980, p. 3.

Hamburger, Philip. "NBC's Abduction." *The New Yorker*, 13 November 1954, p. 150.

Henahan, Donal. "TV: 'Queen of Spades' in Miniature." *New York Times*, 1 March 1971, p. 59.

Hoffman, W.J. "Omnibus Opera." *Opera News*, 9 March 1953, p. 12.

Kirstein, Lincoln. "Television Opera in the USA." *Opera*, April 1952, p. 200.

Klein, Howard. "Opera on TV: 'Lucia.' " *New York Times*, 20 January 1964, p. 87.

Kolodin, Irving. "Billy Budd." *Saturday Review*, 8 November 1952, p. 36.

———. "Grand Opera on Television." *Saturday Review*, 8 July 1978, p. 25.

———. "NBC's Der Rosenkavalier." *Saturday Review*, 16 May 1953, p. 34.

———. "NBC Fidelio." *Saturday Review*, 21 November 1959, p. 34.

———. "Opera, NET and Met." *Saturday Review*, 4 March 1972, p. 20.

———. "Tozzi as Boris." *Saturday Review*, 8 April 1966, p. 42.

Kuney, Jack. "Calling the Shots at the Metropolitan Opera." *Television Quarterly*, No. IV, 1984, pp. 79–84.

Land, Barbara. "A Composer Serious About Television Music." *New York Times*, 10 February 1957, Section II, p. 11.

"Leontyne Price Heard in NBC *Tosca*." *Musical America*, 1 February 1955, p. 23.

Lipman, Samuel. "On The Air." *Commentary*, April 1980, pp. 75–81.

"Menotti and Television." *Newsweek*, 7 January 1952, p. 37.

Merkling, Frank. "Opera Becomes Theater Via NBC-TV." *Musical America*, February 1957, pp. 67, 175.

"Met Closed Circuit." *Newsweek*, 24 November 1954, p. 98.

"Met's TV Venture." *Newsweek*, 22 December 1952, p. 67.

"NBC's Madame Butterfly." *Newsweek*, 20 February 1950, p. 44.

"NBC-TV Opera Season." *Musical America*, 15 November 1952, p. 17.

O'Connor, John J. "Is Opera a Luxury for TV?" *New York Times*, 3 March 1974, Section III, p. 17.

———. "Public TV Finds The Gold in Opera." *New York Times*, 5 October 1977, Section III, p. 24.

———. "Putting Life Into 'Live from the Met.' " *New York Times*, 20 March 1980, Section II, p. 31.

———. " 'Tis the Season of Documentaries." *New York Times*, 22 December, 1978, Section III, 32.

———. "TV: 'La Traviata' and 'Baby Doe.' " *New York Times*, 22 February 1976, p. 70.

———. "TV: Opera and More From Lincoln Center." *New York Times*, 25 January 1979, Section III, p. 10.

———. "TV: 'Tales of Hoffman.' " *New York Times*, 14 December, 1971, p. 90.

"Opera—As It's Televised." *Newsweek*, 23 December 1957, p. 56.

"Opera for Millions." *TIME*, 16 February 1953, p. 89.

Page, Tim. "City Opera's Very Special Fox Challenges the TV Cameras." *New York Times*, 6 November 1983, Section II, p. 35.

Porterfield, Christopher. "The Met, The Moor, and the Eye." *TIME*, 8 October 1979, p. 108.

Rockwell, John. "The Impact of TV on Opera." *New York Times*, 25 January 1981, Section II, p. 1.

———. "Why Does Opera Lure Filmmakers?" *New York Times*, 8 May 1983, Section II, p. 1.

Rubinstein, Leslie. "Live from the Met." *Opera News*, September 1979, p. 13.

Sabin, Robert. "Review of 'The Magic Flute.' " *Musical America*, 1 February 1956, p. 12.

———. "TV Opera." *Musical America*, May 1953, p. 7.

Sargeant, Winthrop. "Mozart's *Don Giovanni*." *New Yorker*, 16 April 1960, p. 168.

Sarnoff, Robert W. "New Horizons for an Old Art." *Theatre Arts*, January 1957, pp. 37–38.

Schonberg, Harold C. "The Met's Televised 'Boheme' Is a Harbinger of the Future," *New York Times*, 27 March 1977, Section II, p. 1.

———. "Music: Menotti Opera." *New York Times*, 4 March 1963, (Western Edition), p. 8.

———. "TV: An Unusual and Important Opera." *New York Times*, 3 December 1969, p. 110.

Schwartz, Lloyd. "Opera on Television." *The Atlantic*, January 1983, p. 86.

Shayon, Robert Lewis. "It's Opera, But Is It Grand?" *Saturday Review*, 13 March 1954, p. 39.

Shepard, Richard F. "TV: Still's Opera of the Southland, 'A Bayou Legend.' " *New York Times*, 15 June 1981, Section III, p. 21.

"Snubbing the Opera." *Newsweek*, 11 March 1957, p. 64.

Taubman, Howard. " 'Boheme' Telecast Rewarding Work." *New York Times*, 23 February 1953, p. 20.

———. "Future of Opera Looks Up." *New York Times*, 13 December 1952, Section II, p. 18.

———. "Music: Magic Flute Sung on NBC." *New York Times*, 16 January 1956, p. 17.

———. "New Opera Techniques." *New York Times*, 16 May 1954, Section II, p. 7.

———. "Opera: 'Maria Golovin.' " *New York Times*, 9 March 1959, p. 34.

———. "Something Grand." *New York Times*, 15 December 1957, Section II, p. 11.
———. "Televised Opera." *New York Times*, 24 April 1949, Section II, p. 13.
———. "TV Opera Looks Up." *New York Times*, 14 September 1952, Section II, p. 7.
Trimble, Lester. "The Golden Child." *Nation*, 31 December 1960, p. 531.
Willey, George A. "Opera on Television." *The Music Review*, May 1959, pp. 150–158.

Dissertations

Burke, Richard C. "A History of Televised Opera in the United States." Ph.D. diss., University of Michigan, 1963.
Dasher, Richard T. "The Musical Programming of National Educational Television." Ph.D. diss., University of Michigan, 1968.
Dwyer, Edward J. "American Video Opera: An Introduction and Guidebook to Its Production." Ph.D. diss., Columbia University, 1963.
Willey, George A. "The Visualization of Music on Television, with Emphasis on the Standard Hour." Ph.D. diss., Stanford University, 1956.

VIDEOGRAPHY

Program: *Opera Television Theater*
Opera: *Carmen* by Georges Bizet
Network: CBS
Date: December 1, 1950
Performers: Gladys Swarthout, Robert Rounseville, Robert Merrill
Director: Byron Paul
Producer: Henry Souvaine

Program: *NBC Opera Theatre*
Opera: *Amahl and the Night Visitors* by Gian Carlo Menotti
Network: NBC
Date: December 24, 1950
Performers: Chet Allen, Rosemary Kuhlman
Director: Kirk Browning
Producer: Peter Herman Adler

Program: *NBC Opera Theatre*
Opera: *Billy Budd* by Benjamin Britten
Network: NBC
Date: October 19, 1952
Performers: Leo Lisher, Theodore Uppmann, Andrew McKinley
Director: Kirk Browning
Producer: Peter Herman Adler

Program: *NBC Opera Theatre*
Opera: *Trouble in Tahiti* by Leonard Bernstein
Network: NBC

Date: November 16, 1952
Performers: David Atkinson, Beverly Wolff
Director: Kirk Browning
Producer: Peter Herman Adler

Program: *Omnibus*
Opera: *Die Fledermaus* by Johann Strauss
Network: CBS
Date: February 1, 1953
Performers: Brenda Lewis, Jude Thompson, Charles Kullman
Director: Bob Banner
Producer: William Spier

Program: *NBC Opera Theatre*
Opera: *Dialogue of the Carmelites* by Francis Poulenc
Network: NBC
Date: December 8, 1956
Performers: Elaine Malbin, Patricia Newland, Leontyne Price
Director: Kirk Browning
Producer: Peter Herman Adler

Program: *NBC Opera Theatre*
Opera: *The Magic Flute* by W.A. Mozart
Network: NBC
Date: January 15, 1956
Performers: John Reardon, Leontyne Price
Director: Kirk Browning
Producer: Peter Herman Adler

Program: *NET Opera Theatre*
Opera: *Rachel, La Cubana* by Heinz Werner Henze
Network: PBS
Date: March 4, 1974
Performers: Lee Verona, Alan Titus, Robert Rounseville
Director: Kirk Browning
Producer: Peter Herman Adler

Program: *Live from the Met*
Opera: *La Boheme* by Giacomo Puccini
Network: PBS
Date: March 15, 1977
Performers: Luciano Pavarotti, Renata Scotto
Director: Kirk Browning
Producer: John Goberman

Program: *Live from the Met*
Opera: *The Rise and Fall of the City of Mahagonny* by Kurt Weil and Bertolt Brecht
Network: PBS
Date: November 27, 1979
Performers: Teresa Stratas, Richard Cassilly, Cornell MacNeil

Director: Brian Large
Producer: Michael Bronson

Program: *Live from Lincoln Center*
Opera: *The Cunning Little Vixen* by Leos Janácek
Network: PBS
Date: November 9, 1983
Performers: Richard Cross, Gianna Rolandi
Director: Kirk Browning
Producer: John Goberman

5

Theater on Television

Of all the performing arts, theater has made the transition to television with the greatest ease and success. Unlike dance, opera, or classical music, most dramatic works taken from the stage are not plagued with abstract movement, foreign languages, or generally static visual material. The theater's naturalistic base and mass appeal automatically guaranteed it a primacy on a medium eager to reach the same audiences that flocked to movies and listened to the radio. Hollywood and network radio's reliance on the stage—for plays, performers, writers, and producers—would be duplicated by television, which frequently turned to Broadway as an important source of talent and material during its early years.

The movement from large theater to small screen, however, often proved troublesome, particularly when dramatic works came up against television's chief constraints—time, budget, and varying degrees of censorship. Very few plays survived a TV production without cutting and reshaping, sometimes to the point where virtually nothing was left of the original but the skeleton. In the late 1940s, five-act Shakespearean dramas would be trimmed to one-hour versions; throughout the 1950s plays which ran two hours or more in the theater were lucky to be given 75 minutes of air time. Scenes and characters were excised not only to "improve" the pace and keep costs down but also to avoid any suggestion of controversy, which might upset viewers and alienate the sponsors who played such an important role in most TV theatrical productions.

Despite these problems, television has offered theater an unusually sympathetic forum. Because of their more popular appeal, stage play telecasts were not immediately relegated to the little watched, cultural "ghetto" areas of Sunday mornings and afternoons, where most ballet and opera programs found themselves scheduled. More importantly, the medium's techniques, particularly the use of fluid camera movements and the concentrated gaze of the close-up lens, opened new avenues for dramatic emphasis and expression. Theatrical works thoughtfully recast in TV terms often gained a sense of power and directness that compensated for the textual abridgements. TV's ability, as George Schaeffer once remarked, "to catch that glowing, growing kind of performance you might see on stage if you were a bumblebee buzzing around everywhere you wanted to be,"[1] was probably its greatest asset when translating proscenium drama to its more intimate range.

The large number of Broadway and classic plays broadcast during the past four-and-a-half decades testifies to the strong affinity the medium has felt for productions drawn from the stage. Though television has not always been respectful of specific dramatic intentions, it has, through its closer focus and broader reach, brought theater to life in interesting and surprising ways. Examining its varying treatment of theatrical material provides a revealing view of TV's artistic methods and priorities.

HISTORICAL DEVELOPMENT

Theater Experiments Through 1945

Stage plays were a frequent feature throughout the beginning years of TV programming in America. During the medium's hectic experimental period from the late 1920s up until the late 1930s, efforts to present some type of imaginative fare to capture public attention often centered on dramatic productions. One of the earliest telecasts, heralded by a front-page report in the *New York Times*, was J. Hartley Manners's espionage melodrama, *The Queen's Messenger*, which aired over General Electric's station in Schenectady, New York, in September 1928. The 40–minute adaptation took place in a small, crude studio, with a cast of two actors and equipment consisting of three cameras and one microphone.

In the decade that followed, experimental stations frequently offered short dramatic scenes during their brief broadcast hours. New York City's first TV station, W2XCR, inaugurated its schedule with excerpts from Broadway plays featuring Lionel Atwill, Gertrude Lawrence, and Louis Calhern. Broadway highlights were also the policy of NBC's station W2XBS, which went to considerable efforts to boost program production values. There were extensive rehearsals and a great deal of attention paid to sets and props. A 22–minute broadcast in 1938 of scenes from Rachel Crother's *Susan and God*, for example, not only starred Gertrude Lawrence and the original Broadway cast but also showcased the original costumes and duplicated the settings. After the official public premiere of television at the New York World's Fair in April 1939, W2XBS continued to present approximately two plays a week for the next 15 months. "The actors and actresses were often," as William Hawes notes, "prominent personalities, and the plays were mostly adaptations of the works of famous playwrights."[2] The period was characterized by technical and dramatic experimentation. Unburdened by the strict time scheduling of network radio, programs would usually run more than an hour and utilize an assortment of special effects. A production of Frank Elser and Marc Connelly's *The Farmer Takes a Wife* contained filmed inserts, miniature models, authentic period costumes, and sound effects ranging from train whistles to insect noises. A 1940 modern dress telecast of *Julius Caesar* employed electronic superimpositions to provide a vision of Caesar's "ghost" and brought the medium itself into the action, with the conspirators watching Caesar's entry into Rome on a TV set.

Always an ambitious programmer, General Electric's Schenectady station WRGB broadcast 14 full-length plays during the early 1940s. Typical was a 1943 telecast of *The Taming of the Shrew*, performed by the Russell Sage College Dramatic Students that lasted two hours and 25 minutes. The program's producer watched several stage rehearsals in order to plan studio shooting and to decide what elements needed to be adjusted for television. "The cuts and changes," wrote Judy Dupuy, "involved tightening the greatly dispersed business so that a camera could hold two or more performers during a scene. Broadway gestures and long speeches were eliminated when unnecessary to advancement of the plot."[3] Other productions included Richard Sheridan's *The Rivals*, Noel Coward's *Hay Fever*, and, in 1943, the first uncut presentation of William Shakespeare on American television, a telecast of *Twelfth Night* performed by the Mountebanks of Unison College.

After the slowdown imposed by the war, NBC's efforts to utilize stage works for its TV programming continued in 1945 with the unusual scheduling of Robert Sherwood's *Abe Lincoln in Illinois*, presented in separate act-by-act installments over the course of a month. A few months later, the network introduced its unsponsored series, *Classic Plays on Television*, featuring full-length performances of George S. Kaufman and Moss Hart's *You Can't Take It With You*, Ben Hecht and Charles Macarthur's *Front Page*, Maxwell Anderson's *Winterset*, and Moliere's *Le Bourgeois Gentilhomme*.

Works drawn from the theater had, by this point, proved to be a valuable source of material for the networks and some independent stations. Since production was based largely in New York, drama, as Francis Sturcken notes, was "a ready made form of entertainment that could easily fill the programming void. Many plays of past Broadway seasons were available and actors and directors were trained in the techniques of performing them."[4] Problems remained, however, about the best way to mount something originally intended for the stage on television. Most plays were simply placed in front of the cameras and, after some cutting, dutifully and unimaginatively photographed. New methods needed to be developed to exploit the medium's dramatic strengths and limitations. John Reich's advice to TV professionals in 1946 suggested several promising avenues. Reich wrote in *Televiser:* "In selecting his material from the vast storehouse of the dramatic stage, the program director may well follow his instinct for the video art rather than any artificial set of rules. He should be guided, however, by three characteristics of television, namely: *immediacy*, *fluidity*, and *emphasis* on objects."[5]

By the conclusion of the war, the difficulties affecting one area of TV play production—time limits—were beginning to be resolved. Though there had been many 90–minute plus presentations in the early 1940s, the half-hour and one-hour program length was fast becoming an industry standard. Within a few years, most three-act dramas would need to be even more drastically shortened to accommodate the kind of rigid scheduling practices commercial television adopted from network radio.

Postwar TV Theatrical Production

In 1946, the majority of the dramatic activity in television was taking place at NBC's New York station, WNBT. The station had assembled a distinguished staff, including writer and director Fred Coe, theater designer Robert Wade, and producer Edward Sobol, to mount a variety of full-length productions. Sobol's widely praised series of Sunday night Broadway revivals provides an interesting example of the station's early drama programs. In preparing for a telecast of Noel Coward's *Blithe Spirit*, Sobol spent two weeks writing the "tele-adaptation," two weeks rehearsing (including 15 hours of camera rehearsals), and had three sets constructed, instead of the play's one, in order to "keep the story flowing and to keep the passage of time—an important play factor—clearly established for the viewing audience."[6] The result was hailed in *Variety* as proof that "video . . . can equal the best of stage and screen. . . . This is television as it should be."[7]

In 1947, NBC continued to lead the way in innovative dramatic productions. In April its series, *Television Theatre*, which generally featured three-act plays produced and directed by Fred Coe, presented the first network Shakespearean broadcast—a 70–minute version of *Twelfth Night*, with commercials appearing only at the beginning and end of the show. In May, the first hour-long dramatic series, *Kraft Television Theatre* premiered, offering a diverse showcase for play adaptations and original works throughout the next decade. Later in the fall, NBC reached an agreement with two Broadway theatrical companies to co-produce a series of dramas. The Theatre Guild presented six, one-hour programs, including versions of *The Late George Apley*, *Stage Door*, and George Bernard Shaw's *The Great Catherine* but failed to find a sponsor willing to underwrite future costs. *Television Playhouse*, the series produced by the American National Theatre and Academy, met a similar fate, after televising a half-dozen, 30–minute dramas.

CBS, meanwhile, was barely functioning as a dramatic producer because of a budgetary decision in mid–1947 to shut down its studio operations for a year in favor of old films and remote pickups. One of its few theatrical experiments during this period consisted of taking TV cameras into major New York theaters for a series of live excerpts from current plays. *Tonight on Broadway*, which also featured commentary from critic John Mason Brown and interviews with performers, lasted for six shows beginning in April 1948 and returned for a brief run in October 1949.

The 1948–49 season marked one of the most creative periods for all three networks in TV theatrical production. ABC's *Actors Studio* was a 30–minute series of realistic plays, adapted from both the stage and classic short stories and produced live by the Actors Studio. Performers associated with the studio, such as Jessica Tandy, Martin Balsam, Kim Hunter, and Julie Harris, worked for "low salaries in order to achieve experience in the television medium."[8] Innovative and dramatically ambitious, *Actors Studio* was the first TV program ever to win a Peabody Award.

Premiering in October 1948, NBC's *Philco TV Playhouse* offered a series of distinguished Broadway revivals, often with the original casts, in generally lavish, one-hour productions. The most expensive TV program up until that time (costs ranged from $10,000 to $20,000 per installment), *Philco TV Playhouse* was co-produced in its first season by MCA, which provided the plays, and the Actors Equity Association, which provided the performers. A great critical and popular success, the series' first year highlights included star-studded versions of Elmer Rice's *Counsellor at Law* and Sidney Howard's *The Late Christopher Bean* (both with Paul Muni) and an elaborate *Cyrano de Bergerac*, that used seven complete sets, street scenes, and a large supporting cast, headlined by Jose Ferrer.

CBS returned to studio production in the fall of 1948 with two theatrically based series. The first, *Ford Theatre*, used leading Broadway actors, such as Eva Le Gallienne, Raymond Massey, and Burgess Meredith, in one-hour play adaptations. The network's second dramatic series, *Studio One*, proved to be a genuine landmark in early TV history. Under the executive supervision of veteran Broadway producer and director Worthington Miner, the program became an influential testing ground for new approaches and techniques to studio drama.

Studio One's first triumph was a one-hour, March 1949 production of *Julius Caesar*, performed in modern dress (the costuming, according to Tim Brooks and Earle Marsh, was the result of a strapped budget[9]). From its opening moments, it was clear that this was truly a TV version of the play and not just a reshaped proscenium stage performance. The camera, acting more like a participant in a crowd rather than a detached spectator, glided through the set's evocatively lit arches and streets, as soldiers, dressed in vaguely fascistic uniforms, paraded by. The screen was constantly filled with movement. Spectators swarmed in front of the lens to make way for Caesar; telling close-ups revealed an assassin flicking a switchblade or a guard wielding a gun. Characters were framed with a dramatic sense of perspective and depth. While Brutus delivered his funeral oration, his head visible in the far left of the frame as the crowd listened on, Antony was seen on the right in close-up, smirking, with a cigarette dangling from his lips. Even soliloquies were given a forceful emphasis. Cassius's Act I speech after leaving Brutus was delivered as a voice-over, the camera gradually moving in on a tight shot of his eyes as the scene concluded.

The reaction to this TV *Julius Caesar* was extraordinarily enthusiastic. *Variety* acclaimed it as "a big step forward in mastering television techniques . . . which gave breadth and intensity to an exciting version of Shakespeare."[10] Jack Gould of the *New York Times* went even further, praising Miner's production as

> the most exciting television yet seen on the home screen—a magnificently bold, imaginative and independent achievement that stands as an event of the season. . . . [Miner] imbued the Shakespearean tragedy with a visual power and vitality that lifted television to the status of a glorious art.[11]

Singling out the program's technical achievements—its "brilliant concept of setting," its fluid direction (by the unmentioned Paul Nickell), its "delicate shadings"—Gould ended his paean by noting:

> Cumulatively, in short, "Julius Caesar" provided a new insight into what television can be: the perfect integration of a host of older arts into a new form which stands on its own. It had the elusive quality of kaleidoscopic oneness, with its appeal being rooted in the unorthodox use of the orthodox tools of stage craft.[12]

The critical acclaim forced the series to embark on what was then a rare TV occurrence. In the days before the wonder of videotape repeats, cast and crew of *Julius Caesar* were all assembled later that spring to perform the program once again before the live cameras.

Studio One's venture into Shakespeare was matched by NBC, which presented two Shakespearean productions a few months afterwards. The first, a one-hour version of *Macbeth*, opted for a more traditional approach, without any modern updates or inferences, but with some nods to TV technology to enhance the atmosphere. Electronic superimpositions made the three witches (played in this case by men) seem to fly through the air and caused Macbeth's imaginary dagger to glow mysteriously in front of him. Film inserts helped set the stage for the opening thunderous storm. Striking, silhouetted lighting was also effectively used in the battle scenes and in Lady Macbeth's vivid stabbing of Duncan. Unfortunately, the production was marred by a pervasive "hamminess," ranging from Walter Hampden's far too broad performance in the title role to a throbbing musical score underlining most of the program's key scenes.

The network adopted a different method three weeks later with an unusual telecast of *Romeo and Juliet*, directed by Albert McCleery in an "arena-style" format. The elaborately costumed actors performed on a central platform, surrounded by cameras, that filmed them from all sides and angles, often in tight close-ups. The effect was intriguing and the generally favorable reviews prompted McCleery to refine his techniques still further in his ambitious *Cameo Theatre* programs the following summer.

NBC's willingness to experiment can also be seen in one other sustaining dramatic program from this period. Rather than rely solely on its traditional show business suppliers, the network ventured out in the summer of 1949 to the halls of academia. Curtis Canfield, a professor of drama at Amherst College, was hired to produce an eight-week series of live, half-hour plays, which went under the title *Academy Theatre*. The programs focused on poetic and obscure works by dramatists such as Thorton Wilder and Edna St. Vincent Millay.

By the end of the decade, the commercial networks had made great strides in adapting stage plays to TV terms. The medium's chief asset, as Jack Gould noted in a 1948 article, was its intimacy and immediacy.

> The camera lifts the television viewer out of the usual orchestra or balcony seat and takes him directly into the group upon the stage. Unlike the 'canned' Hollywood film, however, this is done without sacrifice of the qualities of spontaneity and sustained performance, which are the heart of true theatre.[13]

Removing the proscenium barrier in a production like *Studio One*'s *Julius Caesar* opened new possibilities for expressive camera movements and emotional involvement.

While television continued to make advances in the presentation of drama, it also began to rely less and less on stage plays as a source of programming material. Television's inherent restrictions at this point—its cramped studio space, its inability to clearly register more than two or three people on the screen at the same time, its need to set most action indoors with a bare minimum of sets—limited the number of plays suitable for adaptation. More pressingly, the supply of plays which did fit the medium's physical, budgetary, and censorship confines had, for the most part, been exhausted. Broadway was no longer a ready goldmine for live, 30- and 60-minute dramatic shows. Increasingly, series were turning to the larger dramatic realms of the short story, the novel, and to what would soon be the small screen's chief staple—the original script, custom-tailored to television's methods and techniques.

The Advances of the Early 1950s

By the time network television finally linked the country from coast-to-coast in 1951, a variety of methods had emerged for adapting stage plays to television. The most common involved pruning a three-act drama of all superfluous characters and activities, squeezing it into an hour-long format (or less) and generally placing the cameras in a front-row auditorium situation. Though the live audience and footlights were no longer present, the rigid conventions of the proscenium stage were all too frequently observed.

Programs like *Studio One* and *Philco TV Playhouse* utilized a more imaginative approach, combining the flexibility of movies (shifting viewpoints, fluid camerawork) with the intensity of a continuous stage performance. Theatrical works were often boldly reconceived in TV terms, offering the home audience the chance to experience a play from a fresh and intimate perspective.

An impressive experiment along these lines was NBC's 1950 summer series *Cameo Theatre*, produced and directed by Albert McCleery. Like his earlier telecast of *Romeo and Juliet*, most of the half-hour programs were staged in the round, relying on tight close-ups, varied camera angles from all sides, and minimal props. Often, the only set consisted of stools set up on a bare platform. *Cameo Theatre*'s style, which McCleery once described as "the destruction of the proscenium arch in an effort to achieve fluidity," struck some critics as too severe, but it drew high praise from many who were intrigued by its distinctive, designed-for-TV approach.[14] As Philip Hamburger noted in the *New Yorker*:

> The average television drama is often a mere photographing of a stage show performed on a traditional set. . . . Now along comes Cameo Theater with the simple rather obvious notion that it is possible to photograph television actors from many angles and that the audience can be taken anywhere the cameras want to take it.[15]

The series returned intermittently during the next few seasons with productions of the musical *Dark of the Moon*, an ambitious three-part condensation of Henrik Ibsen's *Peer Gynt*, and several original works.

A few months after the premiere of *Cameo Theatre*, NBC launched another interesting dramatic program, *Masterpiece Playhouse*, which presented one-hour adaptations of the classics, produced by Fred Coe, Curtis Canfield, or Albert McCleery. Selections included Luigi Pirandello's *Six Characters in Search of an Author* (*Studio One* had mounted his *Henry IV* a year earlier), Ibsen's *Hedda Gabler* (starring Jessica Tandy and Walter Abel), Sheridan's *The Rivals*, and two Shakespearean works, *Richard III* and *Othello*. The latter received an unusual production that took great liberties with the text in the hopes of finding a new TV equivalent to the bard's dramatic methods. Asserting the somewhat dubious similarities between the techniques of the Elizabethan stage (which "forced Shakespeare to explain through dialogue the time of day, the weather, the place") and "the style many of us have set for ourselves in televising a play," producer

Fred Coe felt the challenge of his TV version was to make the play understandable and exciting for the broadest possible audience.[16] This process not only involved chopping *Othello* down to a one-hour format but, in a rather unconventional move, adding a new prologue and connecting dialogue. As Coe explained:

> We cut the play to the basic scenes of the story; we re-arranged them to suit our studio and equipment, and then we composed enough dialogue and action to unite the scenes we wished to retain. We also knew that we had little time to set the background of action and characters, so instead of using Shakespeare's expository scenes, we wrote a complete narrative in Elizabethan-style dialogue to introduce the characters and the situation confronting them.[17]

While *Studio One* never attempted the textual freedom characteristic of Fred Coe's version of *Othello*, executive producer Worthington Miner also believed that television could open fresh and stimulating avenues to Shakespeare. In an article discussing his 1951 modern-dress production of *Coriolanus*, which marked the play's first professional presentation in the United States, Miner championed television's ability to lend immediacy and psychological effectiveness to an unfamiliar classic. The medium's fluid techniques made it possible, he argued, to offer a *Coriolanus* stripped of excess and, as a result, more dramatically compelling.

> One of the greatest handicaps to a good production of Shakespeare in the theatre is our insistence upon costume and scenery, both of which take time to change. Even though intervals be reduced to a minimum, they rock the flow of the original as badly as a flat wheel. In television, there are no pauses. Shakespeare's superb juxtaposition of scenes can be retained, therefore, and with the added impact of immediate transitions. To this extent, our production of Coriolanus may come closer to the original intention than a more elaborate theatrical production could hope to achieve.[18]

Despite his difficult to prove claims, Miner's telecast of *Coriolanus* was an intriguing effort to try another contemporary-costumed Shakespeare in the spirit of his earlier success with *Julius Caesar*. Directed once again by Paul Nickell, the production boasted the same kind of abstract set and lighting design, TV techniques (shifting camerawork, voice-over soliloquies), and ominous military emphasis. If anything, the efforts to link the play's original Roman setting with modern-day fascism were more tellingly made. Yet, possibly because of a weaker cast and less easy to compress material, *Studio One*'s *Coriolanus* never quite achieved the quality of daring that made the program's *Julius Caesar* such a TV watershed.

In October 1951, Worthington Miner attempted a different Shakespearean approach with the fourth network appearance of *Macbeth* in just two years. (NBC had broadcast a one-hour adaptation in 1949, followed a year later by a production on *Kraft Television Theatre* starring E.G. Marshall and Uta Hagen; CBS offered a futuristic interpretation on its program *Sure as Fate* in January 1951.) Setting aside his interest in modern day versions, Miner's *Macbeth* was performed in traditional period costumes but with the producer's customary insistence on contemporary techniques. Prerecorded audio soliloquies were used whenever possible; the lighting and sets were dramatically conceived; and the camera was a deliberately active observer. The program's heightened artfulness, however, struck *New York Times* critic Jack Gould as far too self-conscious. "As it evolved on the home screen," he wrote, " 'Macbeth' often seemed more a tour de force of production than of drama. There was a pre-occupation with techniques that intruded on the audience's concentration."[19] Nevertheless, he concluded by noting that "Once again, 'Studio One' has had the common sense and venturesome spirit to depart from the norm and tackle Shakespeare according to its own lights."[20] That spirit would characterize the program's experiments for many years to come, even after Worthington Miner left in 1952, following a contract dispute with CBS.

Though the supply of suitable stage material was becoming harder to find, the numerous live dramatic series of this period still turned frequently to Broadway and theater classics for their weekly presentations. ABC's *Pulitzer Prize Playhouse* was a showcase for both Pulitzer Prize-winning dramas and for other works by playwrights cited by the Pulitzer committee. NBC's *Robert Montgomery Presents*, while devoted primarily to original teleplays and adaptations of novels and Hollywood films, broadcast several distinguished stage productions, including a one-hour version of *Victoria Regina*, with Helen Hayes repeating her original theatrical role. The same network's *Kraft Television Theatre* continued to be the premiere forum for TV theater. By the conclusion of its sixth season in 1953, the series had presented a total of 169 plays from Broadway, 23 adaptations from the London stage, and 22 classics.

One of the most notable stage-to-TV efforts was ABC's 1951 *Celanese Theater*, put together by the William Morris talent agency. Obtaining the rights to a number of prominent Broadway hits from past seasons, such as S.N. Behrman's *No Time for Comedy*, Robert Sherwood's *The Petrified Forest,* Eugene O'Neill's *Anna Christie* and *Ah, Wilderness*, and Elmer Rice's *Street Scene*, the agency hired producer/director Alex Segal, who mounted the one-hour versions with unusual care and dramatic fidelity. Script editor, Mabel Anderson, wife of playwright Maxwell Anderson, insisted on keeping the adaptations theatrically faithful. In contrast to prevailing TV practices, the original dramatists were given a large amount of control, either working directly on the TV scripts or consulted frequently as their works were adapted. Mrs. Anderson's policy, as reported by *TIME* magazine, was that "no deletions, changes or shifts of emphasis may be made without the playwright's consent."[21] Enthusiastically praised, the series included a wide range of acting talent (from Jean-Pierre Aumont, Lillian Gish, and David Niven to Alfred Drake, Veronica Lake, and Mickey Rooney) and was awarded the Peabody Award at the conclusion of its brief, one-season appearance.

Theatrical telecasts were not the exclusive province of the commercial networks during this period. Local television also got in the act of live drama. Station WOR in New York City made the most ambitious attempt with its *Broadway Television Theater*. Every night for a week, the same vintage play was broadcast, virtually uncut, with commercials placed at the end of each act. The repeat scheduling allowed audiences the option of either watching the show later if they missed it the first time or, as some letters to producer Warren Wade suggested, re-viewing it night after night.[22] The first program, *The Trial of Mary Dugan* by Bayard Veiller, attracted high ratings, with audience size continuing to grow throughout the week. *Three Men on a Horse* by John Cecil Holm and George Abbott and *The Jazz Singer* by Samson Raphaelson were among the other plays the series telecast during its two local seasons.

Live drama was also an attraction on the Dumont network's New York station, WABD, which offered a curious program in 1952 called *One Man's Experience*. Featuring just a solo performer, the series presented a serialized version of *Hamlet*, broadcast in 15–minute segments over the course of two weeks. Producer Larry Menkin justified this "As the World Turns" approach by noting, "I think all great stories are just as corny as soap operas, only more so."[23]

The Hallmark Hall of Fame—The Maurice Evans Years

After enduring one-hour condensations, abbreviated modern-dress interpretations, and the indignity of serialization, Shakespearean drama on television took a turn for the better with *The Hallmark Hall of Fame*'s celebrated broadcast in 1953 of *Hamlet*. The two-hour program, starring Maurice Evans in his TV debut, marked an unusually large commitment by a network and an advertiser to bring quality drama to the small screen. Employing a cast of 28 (most of whom worked at minimum union scale) and five cameras and utilizing three weeks of rehearsals, the show's final cost for NBC was a huge $180,000—Hallmark Greeting Cards contributed $100,000 as sole sponsor.

Serving in the dual capacity of both producer and lead actor, Maurice Evans's main concern was "to protect the full values of the play"—a difficult task given the fact that *Hamlet* runs four hours uncut in the theater.[24] Whole scenes were excised; characters, including the gravediggers and Fortinbras, were eliminated; and one soliloquy was chopped out, "in an effort," Evans maintained, "to keep the play taut and swift."[25] Accustomed to the broad dynamics of the stage, Evans encountered other problems in adapting to television's reduced performing area. "I found it excruciatingly difficult," he confessed in a memoir, "to deliver certain passages with the requisite vehemence without looking ridiculous at such close quarters."[26] Having an assistant hold a piece of cardboard in front of him during rehearsals, cut to the exact dimensions of the screen, made it easier to understand the small scale he was working in.

Executive director Albert McCleery and George Schaeffer, who served as stage director, brought a vivid theatrical charge to the production. Close-ups were used for psychological emphasis in connecting the home viewer with Hamlet's inner turmoil. Camera movements propelled the action with emotional directness. The result of their close collaboration with Evans was greeted with widespread enthusiasm. Jack Gould called the program "memorable and exciting viewing" and "superbly arresting theater."[27] *TIME* magazine hailed it as "one of the best TV shows ever."[28] Writing in the *Quarterly of Film, Radio and Television*, Flora Rheta Schreiber went even further, praising the telecast for its originality and its reaffirmation "of this medium's artistic potentialities. . . . The televised *Hamlet* was no photographed stage play, no miniature movie, no radio play with sight," she proclaimed, "but an experience belonging uniquely and indigenously to television itself. It was a production which showed that television, despite the fact that it derives from theater and movies, actually has an aesthetic all its own."[29]

Taking great pride in the quality of its special dramatic presentations, *The Hallmark Hall of Fame* would continue to turn to Shakespeare and other classic playwrights as a signature of its high standards in the years that followed. At the same time, the series' production methods grew increasingly more elaborate. For Maurice Evans's next TV Shakespeare project, a two-hour version of *Richard II* in 1954, enormous studio sets were constructed, featuring 40–foot castle walls, vast exteriors, and a huge, baroque-designed chamber hall. The screen was literally stuffed with ornamentation and props, ranging from a burning fireplace, a full assortment of Elizabethan antiques, and an animal menagerie, highlighted by a troupe of black-and-white live horses, assembled primarily for decorative effect.

Similar production complexity characterized a telecast of *Macbeth* later in the year, which was aswirl with series director George Schaeffer's typically intricate camera movements and unusual angles. The program's most notorious feature was its emphasis on bloodshed, opening with an extreme close-up of Macbeth's blood-soaked hands, followed by comparable shots of Lady Macbeth and later of the returned-from-the-grave Banquo, his face still covered with the marks of violence. Broadcast in vivid color, the effect was, in those comparatively innocent times, shocking and gruesome. "Even an NBC vice president," according to *Newsweek*, "confessed that his young daughter ran from the set and hid her face."[30] Dame Judith Anderson performed Lady Macbeth, with the lead role once again played by Maurice Evans, a position he would continue to perform on all of *The Hall of Fame*'s productions of Shakespeare and Shaw throughout the decade.

Beginning in the 1955–56 season, *The Hall of Fame* introduced a series of carefully produced, full-length Broadway revivals. Attractions included Eva Le Gallienne in *Alice in Wonderland* and *The Corn is Green*, Cyril Ritchard and Julie Harris in Ferenc Molnar's *The Good Fairy*, Siobhan McKenna and Judith Anderson in *The Cradle Song*, and Hume Cronyn, Christopher Plummer, and Julie Harris in *A Doll's House*. During the next few years, programs such as Jean Anouilh's *The Lark*, starring Julie Harris, *Ah, Wilderness* with Helen Hayes and Burgess Meredith, and an eloquent realization of Marc Connelly's *The Green Pastures*, with William Warfield and Earle Hyman, clearly established *The Hall of Fame*'s reputation as commercial television's foremost showcase for tasteful, handsomely mounted, attractively cast dramatic specials.

Maurice Evans's Shakespeare productions for the series, meanwhile, were adopting a much lighter, freer approach. A bouncy 1956 *Taming of the Shrew* was staged in the commedia del l'arte style, with very few sets (mostly defined in brief outline strokes), an abundance of clowns, and a surprising sense of playfulness, as demonstrated by its placement of the opening sparring match between Kate and Petruchio in a boxing arena. Evans's Petruchio comes across as appropriately genial and spry, with a perfect opponent in Lilli Palmer's rompish Kate.

A telecast of *Twelfth Night* a year and a half later set the work as a lyrical fantasy, the majority of its action appearing to take place in a dream, imagined by the fool, Feste. The atmosphere was suggestively whimsical. Rouben Ter-Arutunian's props and settings were the merest hints of objects, and soft music played as a constant accompaniment to the proceedings. The program, however, was not as successful as *The Hall of Fame*'s similar stylization with *The Taming of the Shrew*, primarily because the show's erratic performance style, with its sudden moves into broad vaudeville, was frequently at odds with the drama's prevailing poetic mood.

Nineteen sixty marked Maurice Evans's last year on the series as its chief Shakespearean actor, and his final roles reflected the strengths and weaknesses of his TV approach. More than any other stage performer of the period, Evans was committed to bringing classic plays to home audiences in a direct and unstuffy fashion. While his own acting was frequently a bit fulsome and overblown, he proved to be an eager advocate, along with *The Hall of Fame*'s chief director George Schaeffer, of using the medium's techniques to explore new dramatic avenues. Sometimes this might take the form of an overelaborate interest in camera angles and effects (as in the 1954 *Macbeth*, when several soliloquies were marred by front projections or tricky mirror shots), but it was also reflected in a more fluid and open style of TV staging, as demonstrated by *Hallmark*'s cycle of Shakespeare comedies in the mid–1950s.

The February 1960 telecast of *The Tempest* was another example of the inventive production methods and mixed acting styles that typified the series' previous versions of *The Taming of the Shrew* and *Twelfth Night*. Rouben Ter-Arutunian's set designs were once again fanciful suggestions of objects and locales that complimented the program's other hints of magic and mystery, ranging from sudden bursts of ethereal music to a superimposed image of the sprite Ariel that constantly changed in size. The efforts at visual and oral enchantment were only fitfully matched, however, by the contrasting qualities of the cast. Screen star Lee Remick was a beautiful, but somewhat ill-defined Miranda; TV comedian Tom Poston was an uneasy Trinculo; and Maurice Evans, typical of his Broadway stage turns, played Prospero as an avuncular, eye-twinkling magician. Only Richard Burton, in a spellbinding performance as Caliban, managed to find the proper tone of wonder, charm, and mournfulness.

Evans's final Shakespearean appearance for *The Hallmark Hall of Fame* took place nine months later, when he and Judith Anderson returned to the roles they had originally performed together in a 1954 special broadcast of *Macbeth*, the series' first program in color. This new production also established a precedent as *The Hall of Fame*'s first presentation done entirely on film. Director George Schaeffer was eager for the challenge since it meant the opportunity to leave the confines of the studio and set the play on location in the fields and castles of Scotland. Because the program was viewed more as a motion picture than a standard TV show (it was designed to be shown in theaters after its TV run), production values were kept unusually high, complete with a supporting cast of distinguished British actors and the deployment of hundreds of extras in the battle scenes. The show/movie went on to receive high critical reviews and the Emmy award as "The Program of the Year."

Whatever his merits as an actor, Maurice Evans's association with *The Hallmark Hall of Fame* did play an important role in promoting the cause of classical theater on television. His contributions, and those of producer Mildred Alberg and George Schaeffer, helped make Shakespeare a surprisingly popular TV attraction throughout the 1950s. The series' *Taming of the Shrew* was watched by 19 million viewers; *The Tempest* drew an audience of 21 million. Though his Shakespearean performances received most of the attention, Evans also participated in numerous other *Hallmark* attractions. After his well-received portrayals of Hamlet and Richard II, he went on to star in a 1955 production of Shaw's *The Devil's Disciple*, a 1956 telecast of *Man and Superman*, as well as appearances in 1958 with Rosemary Harris in *Dial M for Murder* and with Carol Channing, Cyril Ritchard, and Jessica Tandy in *The Christmas Tree*. For his last *Hall of Fame* broadcast in 1967 he returned to Shaw, performing in *Saint Joan*, with Genevieve Bujold in the title role.

Omnibus* and *Producers' Showcase

If *The Hallmark Hall of Fame* was noted for its stately, occasionally overdecorous mountings of the classics and Broadway, CBS's *Omnibus* made its reputation as a cultural iconoclast, dedicated to pursuing the ambitious and the adventurous in all the arts. Supported by a large grant from the Ford Foundation, the series surveyed the varied forms of drama with the same innovative spirit that characterized its explorations of music and dance. Its opening show, featuring the premiere of two one-act plays by Maxwell Anderson and William Saroyan, was typical of the program's interest in expanding TV's boundaries by enlisting top-notch talent from other fields. Throughout its nine seasons on the air, original theater for television remained an *Omnibus* priority, as the series presented works by authors not usually drawn to the medium, such as James Agee, Tennessee Williams, and William Inge.

Restagings of the classics also played a part in the *Omnibus* format, with Peter Brook's 90–minute version of *King Lear* in 1953 serving as a prominent example. Offered without commercial interruptions, the telecast starred Orson Welles in his TV debut as Lear, with a score composed and conducted by Virgil Thomson. Brook's production, directed for television by Andrew McCullough, began on a striking note—as the darkness lifts, a map of England fills the screen, only to be ripped to pieces by the massive form of Lear, standing behind it. The black backgrounds of the studio were used as the primary settings; characters existed in a kind of spacelessness, defined by small, surrounding pools of light. There was little sharp cutting; the cameras instead seemed to glide through the proceedings, capturing the movements of Brook's blunt stage choreography. Throughout the program, the TV frame's small playing area was employed for maximum effect, with the actors grouped carefully around the edges of its boundaries to heighten the play's spatial tensions. The shadowy illuminations and lack of props provided an unusual feeling of depth, underscoring the prevailing mood of emotional distance, coldness, and gloom. Anticipating his later existential version with Paul Scofield in the early-1960s, Brook concluded this bleak TV *King Lear* in the blackness with which it began; the only thing left visible on the screen was the fallen figure of Lear, dimly lit, as the camera pulled away.

While not as avowedly experimental as *Omnibus*, NBC's *Producers' Showcase* offered a wide range of productions, noted for their elaborate style. Part of network president Sylvester (Pat) Weaver's "spectaculars," the once-a-month series sought to captivate viewers with star performers, fresh stagings, and lavish effects. Its opening program in 1954 was Noel Coward's *Tonight at 8:30*, featuring Ginger Rogers. Other presentations that season included a topically updated version of Howard Lindsay and

Russell Crouse's *State of the Union* (directed by Arthur Penn), Claire Booth Luce's *The Women*, and what would be one of the most celebrated and beloved shows in TV history, James M. Barrie's *Peter Pan*, imported right after its closing on Broadway. Starring Mary Martin and Cyril Ritchard, staged by Jerome Robbins, and produced by Fred Coe, the program, like *Amahl and the Night Visitors*, was an instant phenomenon—unanimously acclaimed by the critics, watched by an enormous audience of 65 million, and repeated, with the same cast brought back live, ten months later. For the still young medium, *Peter Pan* ranked as a genuine musical and dramatic triumph, honored by an Emmy as best program of the year and demonstrating, with great verve, television's powers to transform theatrical excitement in its own terms. To Jack Gould, the broadcast represented "a sublime fusion of skill and inspiration," mixing Broadway energy with television's magical intimacy. He wrote:

> The greatness of the 'Peter Pan' telecast, stemmed from a marriage of media under ideal circumstances. The advantages of "live" television and the advantages of living theatre were merged as one. Alone neither medium could have offered the miracle of Monday evening.[31]

For its second season opener, *Producers' Showcase* turned to a play which had already been televised three times in the past seven years (twice on NBC, once on ABC). However, unlike previous TV and stage versions of Thornton Wilder's *Our Town*, the series, given its mission to be out of the ordinary, converted the drama into a musical, complete with an original score by Jimmy Van Heusen and Sammy Cahn and a cast headed by Frank Sinatra, Eva Marie Saint, and Paul Newman. Smoothly directed by Delbert Mann, the program began with a lovely, semi-expressionistic set, that gradually became more detailed and conventionally theatrical as the play unfolded. Sinatra, pipe in hand, and obviously uncomfortable with the folksy trappings of his role, walked through the open staging somewhat warily, only seeming at ease when he could stand back and deliver the show's big hit, "Love and Marriage," as the silhouetted figures of Saint and Newman were seen rocking on a swing behind him. Though often sweet and earnestly conceived, the production ranks more as a TV curiosity than a successful dramatic reinterpretation.

Producers' Showcase may have lacked *Omnibus*'s appetite for the offbeat, but its theater programs were invariably presented with a sense of excitement and lavishness the Ford Foundation series could rarely match. This was partially the result of star power in its casting and of the care exercised by its first-rate staff of producers and directors, many of whom went on to fruitful careers in Hollywood. Memorable attractions during the program's three-year run included an adaptation of *The Petrified Forest*, with Henry Fonda, Lauren Bacall, and Humphrey Bogart, re-creating his original stage and screen role; *Cyrano de Bergerac* with Jose Ferrer and Claire Bloom; *The Barretts of Wimpole Street* with Katherine Cornell and Anthony Quayle; a witty *Caesar and Cleopatra* starring Sir Cedric Hardwicke, Judith Anderson, and Claire Bloom; an opulent version of *Mayerling*, featuring Audrey Hepburn and Mel Ferrer, directed by Anatole Litvak, and costing more than any TV program up to that time; and a 1957 Old Vic production of *Romeo and Juliet* with John Neville and Claire Bloom that provoked great press attention because of its low ratings.

Dramatic Transitions in the Mid–1950s

Like *Producers' Showcase*, CBS's *The Best of Broadway* was an effort to mount glamorous "spectaculars," filled with glittering stars and elegant production values. The 1954–55 series, the network's first in color, sought to preserve the atmosphere and perspective of a New York stage event. Theatricality was emphasized, rather than ignored; the proscenium arch was largely left intact. A responsive studio audience and camera viewpoints, suggesting the illusion of a comfortable orchestra seat, made home viewers feel like they were participating in a special performance. The stellar cast of Helen Hayes, Claudette Colbert, and Fredric March appearing in the series' opening telecast of *The Royal Family* was not atypical. Later programs offered Monty Wooley, Merle Oberon, and Joan Bennett in *The Man Who Came to Dinner*; Boris Karloff, Peter Lorre, and Helen Hayes in *Arsenic and Old Lace*; and Ethel Merman in the title role of *Panama Hattie*.

Ford Star Jubilee, broadcast the following year on CBS, pursued a similar once-a-month, "spectaculars" approach, this time with a line-up of musical programs as well as drama. For its premiere, the series presented *The Caine Mutiny Court Martial*, featuring Lloyd Nolan as Captain Queeg. Later in the season, Noel Coward appeared in two of his plays—*Blithe Spirit* and *This Happy Breed*; Jack Lemmon, Charles Laughton, and Lillian Gish starred in *The Day Lincoln Was Shot*; and Orson Welles and Betty Grable performed in *Twentieth Century*. High expenses, low ratings, and controversy surrounding casting decisions finally led Ford to withdraw its support from the series in November 1956.

Increasingly during this period, the types of problems which led to the cancellation of programs like the *Ford Star Jubilee* were being felt by all forms of live dramatic programming, whether they were of the "spectacular" format or the weekly New York-based anthologies. Though a renaissance of sorts occurred with the flurry of original teleplays commissioned for programs such as *Philco TV Playhouse*, *Kraft Television Theatre*, *Goodyear TV Playhouse*, and *Armstrong Circle Theatre*, a variety of considerations began to limit the amount of one-shot drama television in favor of comedy and actions series, produced on film in Hollywood. Economics was clearly the chief factor. Filmed series were not only cheaper but more useful, lending themselves to endless replays and, because of their continuing characters, to easier audience identification. Suitable theatrical material also posed a major difficulty. Broadway stage plays, classic theater works, and even celebrated tele-dramatists like Rod Serling, Paddy Chayefsky, and Reginald Rose could no longer satisfy the medium's insatiable demand for broadly popular, non-controversial programming. Faced with troublesome content and declining ratings for live TV drama, the advertisers and the networks threw their support to the more crowd-pleasing, commercially satisfying product manufactured so smoothly by the Hollywood factory system.

By the end 1957–58 TV season, most of the New York drama programs which had provided a ready forum for stage revivals were off the air. After 650 installments, the *Kraft Television Theatre* changed its focus to mysteries in June 1958. Westinghouse closed down *Studio One* a few months later, deciding to replace it with a Hollywood series. The remaining non-film anthologies, shows like *Armstrong Circle Theatre* and *Playhouse 90*, tended to concentrate their efforts on original scripts based on novels or documentary material. Televised stage plays would, from now on, be largely restricted to the "special events" category, presented by programs such as *The Hallmark Hall of Fame*, where sponsor support was generous enough to underwrite the high cost of individual theatrical production.

If prime-time commercial television was becoming less and less open to the concept of TV theater, there was one area of the broadcast schedule which still welcomed some degree of dramatic experimentation. This was on Sunday mornings, when the networks turned over their unsold, unrated time periods to their religious and cultural affairs departments. Stage adaptations were a frequent attraction on sustaining programs like *Look Up and Live*, *Lamp Unto My Feet*, and *Camera Three*. The latter show in particular offered many unusual and ambitious presentations, performed in its characteristic setting of a mostly bare, dark studio, with just a few scattered stools and ladders and a couple of spotlights. Robert Herridge, who produced the series from its beginnings on local television in 1953 to its full CBS network pickup in 1956, pioneered the concept of television as an "open theater," where fluid staging and camerawork was combined with a sparse, symbolic setting, a narrator who addressed the audience, and a small group of actors.[32] The technique was especially well suited to *Camera Three*'s multi-episode serializations of *Moby Dick*, *The Red Badge of Courage*, and *Crime and Punishment* and its dramatized short stories and biographies; but more traditional theater works were also televised as well, including a half-hour version of *Othello* and a three-part reading of *Hamlet*, featuring black actor Earle Hyman. Herridge's successor, Lewis Freedman, adopted a more flexible approach that veered from studies of Elizabethan playwright Ben Jonson and the acting methods of Konstantin

Stanislavsky to demonstrations of Japanese Noh theater, four-part explorations of the Shakespeare history plays, adaptations of Moliere's *The Misanthrope* and Sophocles's *Philotectes*, and an imaginative juxtaposition of Samuel Beckett's *Waiting for Godot* with George Herriman's cartoon "Krazy Kat." The series' free-wheeling diversity continued when John McGiffert took over as producer in 1958. Drama shows during his tenure included TV essays on the performing style of Richard Mansfield, the challenges of acting, and a profile of Circle-in-the-Square.

By the conclusion of the 1950s, *Camera Three* was the only regularly scheduled program on the commercial networks that still looked, in even a small way, towards the stage. This was in sharp contrast to circumstances at the start of the decade, when the New York theater world served as a central resource for TV talent and material. Shows as varied as *Philco TV Playhouse*, *Studio One*, *Kraft Television Theatre*, and *Producers' Showcase* had often relied on Broadway and the classics for programming, with viewers treated to the works of playwrights from Shakespeare to Kaufmann and Hart and George Bernard Shaw during the course of a single season.

Unfortunately at the very time in the mid–1950s that TV techniques in bringing theater to the small screen were growing more sophisticated, there were fewer and fewer places to apply them. The move to filmed series production eliminated the need for the innovative matching of camerawork and dramatic impulse that typified many of the live New York anthology programs. Broadcasts like *Peter Pan* or *Omnibus*'s *King Lear*, which provided audiences at home with a compelling combination of theatrical energy, brilliant stagecraft, and front row intimacy, were simply not as attractive to advertisers or networks on a long-term basis when compared with the advantages of cheaper, more predictable, and more popular Westerns and comedies. The low ratings garnered by several of the prestige theater specials of the period only confirmed American television's rapid shift away from the stage to the slickly produced series of Hollywood.

Independent Efforts in the 1960s

While theater was losing its place in commercial prime time, stage telecasts did appear on various broadcast outlets that were not as concerned with the pressures of satisfying the largest possible audiences and the broad demands of sponsors. The most ambitious of these independent drama endeavors was *Play of the Week*, produced on a local station in New York City, WNTA-TV, owned by National Telefilm Associates. The series' mission, as defined by company chairman Ely Landau, was to raise the station's ratings with weekly programs of prominent theater attractions. A bargain basement budget of about $45,000 per two-hour production made it impossible to stage recent hits and well-known fare; instead, *Play of the Week* turned, in the words of producer Lewis Freedman, "to shows that nobody else would touch."[33] These included everything from Beckett's *Waiting for Godot*, starring Zero Mostel and Burgess Meredith, to Jean Anouilh's *Waltz of the Toreadors*, with Hugh Griffith and Mildred Natwick; Ivan Turgenev's *A Month in the Country*, featuring Uta Hagen and Luther Adler; Jean Giradoux's *Tiger at the Gates*, as well as plays by Anton Chekhov, August Strindberg, and Ben Jonson. Premiering in October 1959 with Robinson Jeffers's adaptation of *Medea*, starring Judith Anderson, the series televised more than 50 plays during its two seasons on the air, an unprecedented feat considering its limited rehearsal period (two weeks a production) and cramped resources (performers such as Helen Hayes were paid only $500 an appearance).

From the start, *Play of the Week* was the subject of unusually enthusiastic critical attention. When precarious finances threatened to end the series' run after just a few months, *New York Times* critic Jack Gould led a personal campaign to save this "new cultural asset of the community, a heaven-sent means of extending the riches of adult theatre into countless homes"[34] and urged viewers to write to the station to proclaim their feelings. Less than two weeks later, 22,000 letters were received—a response that prompted Standard Oil of New Jersey to assume a beneficent, noninterfering sponsorship for the remainder of the season. Under executive producer David Susskind and his successor Worthington Miner, *Play of the Week* was widely regarded, in the words of *Newsweek*, as "Little TV's Glory Road,"[35] one of the last places left where those in front of and behind the camera could test their limits with challenging dramatic material.

Of its many celebrated offerings, the series' highlight was unquestionably its uncut, four-hour presentation of Eugene O'Neill's *The Iceman Cometh*. Television proved to be an eloquent medium for the playwright's expansive and poetic vision of despair. Director Sidney Lumet's restless camerawork and fondness for tense close-ups helped viewers feel the mood and rhythm of flophouse life in a way difficult to duplicate from even the best proscenium theater seat. The program's unrelenting intimacy, when combined with its strong supporting cast (including Myron McCormick, Farrell Pelly, and a young Robert Redford) and the brilliant lead performance by Jason Robards, Jr., helped make this TV version of *The Iceman Cometh* exceptionally compelling.

Realizing that they were dealing with adult fare, *Play of the Week*'s senior staff took several steps to minimize any potential audience outcry concerning the program. Unwilling to tamper with O'Neill's language—according to producer Lewis Freedman, "we changed a few sons-of-bitches to bastards because some people thought that bastard was less likely to offend, I'm not sure why. Nobody seemed to be bothered by whore or tart"[36]—the two-hour, two-part broadcast was scheduled at the late hour of 10:30 P.M. To further warn unsuspecting viewers of the play's nature, an introduction was made before the drama began, noting that this was one show not intended for everyone.

Always in strapped financial circumstances, even after its productions began to be syndicated to independent stations around the country, *Play of the Week* finally expired in June 1961, once WNTA-TV was sold to a group committed to non-commercial, educational broadcasting. The new station that resulted, WNET-TV, would later become one of the most important production sources for NET and PBS.

A little more than a year following the suspension of *Play of the Week*, the Westinghouse Broadcasting Company mounted its own alternative effort to present theater in prime time. In August 1962, the company revealed plans to televise, on a tape-delay basis, the opening night premieres of six new Theatre Guild productions on its five stations. The announcement drew immediate attacks from practically everyone connected with the New York stage. In a typical reaction, Billy Rose decried the TV theater broadcasts for being "as good a way of turning the fabulous invalid into the fabulous corpse as any I've ever seen."[37] With pressures rising from the Broadway business community, who feared television would destroy future box office revenues, Theatre Guild backed out of the arrangement a month later. Nevertheless, Westinghouse persevered, and in October 1963 they transmitted a previously recorded tape of Robert Noah's *The Advocate* on the same night that it opened in New York. Continued opposition, high costs, and controversy, however, eventually led to the abandonment of future Broadway telecasts altogether.

Off-Broadway proved to be a more hospitable TV environment, at least in the experience of a New York City station, during this same period. Because it was young, enterprising, and non-profit, the New York Shakespeare Festival, run by Joseph Papp, was far more willing to have its activities televised than its theatrical counterparts on Schubert Alley. Beginning in 1962, the festival's "Shakespeare in the Park" summer presentations became an annual event on WCBS-TV, with the station transporting its equipment into Central Park to videotape the performances. The first program starred George C. Scott in *The Merchant of Venice*; this was followed a year later with *Antony and Cleopatra*, featuring Michael Higgins and Colleen Dewhurst. The third and final show, a production of *Hamlet*, with Alfred Ryder and Julie Harris, aired in the summer of 1964.

The 1960s also saw one other non-network dramatic series worth noting. This was *Esso Repertory Theater*, produced by David Susskind, who had emerged as one of the medium's chief cultural impressarios and sharpest critics. A successor to the oil company's previous sponsorship of *Play of the Week* and of a syndicated group of specials entitled *Festival of the Performing Arts*, the 60–minute weekly series was designed to showcase experimental and classical drama, performed by the country's leading regional theaters. For the first time, TV viewers were exposed to productions drawn from outside the familiar orbit of New York and Los Angeles. During its one season on the air, *Esso Repertory Theater* taped programs by groups such as Cincinnati's Playhouse in the Park, the Seattle Repertory Theater, and the Cleveland Playhouse, which were then broadcast over an assortment of independent stations on the east coast.

Network Specials

With the cancellation of most of the remaining anthology drama series by the early 1960s, televised stage plays on the three commercial networks now appeared only as occasional special events. The chief forum for theater on television continued to be *The Hallmark Hall of Fame*, which usually presented five "television spectaculars" a season. *The Hall of Fame*'s attractions ranged from Broadway standards (*Arsenic and Old Lace*, *Inherit the Wind*, *The Teahouse of the August Moon*, *The Magnificent Yankee*) and the classics (*Cyrano de Bergerac*, *Pygmalion*, *Saint Joan*) to colorful costume epics, like *Anastasia*, *Elizabeth the Queen*, and *Victoria Regina*, that served as the embodiment of the series' careful displays of "good taste" and glossy production values. Possibly its chief distinction was the extraordinary talent who appeared in its programs. Starring performers included Julie Harris, Dame Judith Anderson, Christopher Plummer, Trevor Howard, Richard Burton, Dirk Bogarde, Jason Robards, Jr., Alfred Lunt, Lynn Fontanne, Rosemary Harris, and Paul Scofield.

Like most of the dramatic shows of the 1940s and 1950s, *The Hallmark Hall of Fame* took a flexible approach when adapting stage material to the small screen. Even though they were generally allotted 90 minutes for their specials, this was still not long enough to present a full-length play. Key scenes and characters were often abruptly eliminated to accommodate the limited time period and the occasional worries of sponsor and network over questionable content. The results varied, depending on the work's original length, the scope of its action, and the sharpness of its themes. Inevitably, those who valued allegiance to the text and theatrical integrity were disappointed at the transformations prompted by the medium's commercial demands. Playwright Arthur Miller spoke for many when he attacked *The Hall of Fame* for its severely truncated version of Ibsen's *A Doll's House*, arguing that "you cannot cut it in half without cutting in half its emotional, philosophical and human value. . . . The justification that half is better than nothing does not hold when one knows the humanizing power of the original."[38]

The perils of condensation were, however, readily acknowledged by its practitioners. *The Hallmark Hall of Fame*'s associate producer and chief selector of scripts, Robert Hartung, provided this example of what happens when strict TV scheduling comes up against a multi-act stage classic.

I had to condense "Cyrano de Bergerac," a three-hour drama, into 74 minutes. That was my most difficult assignment. The lesson learned from that production was that unless one has a long time to present a long play, it shouldn't be done. Forget it. Get something else. If we do "Hamlet" again, we'll take more than two hours.[39]

Though the series tried to preserve as much of the author's intentions as possible, its primary emphasis was understandably on TV "playability." Adapters like Robert Hartung and the team of Audrey Gellen and Jacqueline Babbin considered their task as one governed more by technical factors than any effort to match a playwright's dramatic style. Producing and directing, according to Hartung, provided him with "a theatrical objectivity in preparing a play for the home screen that a writer might lack."[40] Jacqueline Babbin was equally frank about the importance of specific television skills in reshaping stage material. "An adapter should know technical problems, camera angles, set arrangements," she remarked. "We're basically producers and editors."[41]

Unfortunately, this workmanlike approach to the process of adaptation on *The Hallmark Hall of Fame* sometimes led to questionable "creative" liberties. An extra scene, inspired by "indications in the text," was added to Terence Rattigan's *The Browning Version* to help make the program last longer. James M. Barrie's stage directions were used for additional dialogue in a broadcast of *What Every Woman Knows*. And to provide time for the lead players to change their costumes, a new character functioning as a narrator was created for a telecast of Jan de Hartog's *The Fourposter*.

These kind of problems were avoided in a series of drama programs produced by David Susskind for CBS in the mid–1960s. In each of these special events, the playwrights themselves had an active role in shaping the TV text. Tennessee Williams approved all of the cuts necessary to fit *The Glass Menagerie* into a two-hour time slot. Arthur Miller went even further, writing the adaptations of both *Death of a Salesman* and *The Crucible* to insure their fidelity to his intentions.

Of the three broadcasts, *Death of a Salesman* came across with the greatest forcefulness. The play's fluid flashback structure, intermittent dreamlike atmosphere, and intense domestic focus proved to be ideally suited to television's dramatic scale—a fact director Alex Segal emphasized with imaginative camerawork that mixed realism and poetry. Wrenching close-ups of the anguish of the Willy Loman family alternated with gliding camera movements which made the various scenes blend lyrically into one another. This interior style offered an appropriate environment for the towering performances of Lee J. Cobb and Mildred Dunnock. The small TV screen, rather than reducing the theatrical charge of Cobb's defeated rage and Dunnock's sad domesticity, actually served to strengthen their emotional range. As Jack Gould noted in his enthusiastic review, "By subtly softening the brash dominance of Willy and bringing up the gentle influence of his wife the tragedy gained in its enveloping totality."[42]

Arthur Miller's TV adaptation of *The Crucible* a year later proved less sucessful, primarily because of the work's more sprawling structure and didacticism. Though the program was directed once again by Alex Segal, it failed to find a consistent tone, especially after its frenzied "voodoo" opening. The scene, featuring a group of young women "sporting" in a foggy forest at night, "may have been intended to 'hook' the fickle television viewer," as the *Saturday Review*'s Robert Lewis Shayon points out, "but it had the Hollywood, not the Miller touch."[43] Subsequent action veered unsteadily in mood between an overly impassioned judicial atmosphere and the more intimate domestic scenes, well performed by George C. Scott and Colleen Dewhurst. In keeping with the play's moral fervor, Miller added a special epilogue to the TV version, reminding viewers of the timelessness of his themes.

In addition to these playwright-supervised telecasts on CBS, David Susskind, working usually with his partner Daniel Melnick, produced a number of other special theater telecasts during the decade. In 1962, he arranged the American TV premiere of Ingrid Bergman in a 90–minute version of Ibsen's *Hedda Gabler*. Five years later, on the same night CBS aired his production of *The Crucible*, Susskind presented Miss Bergman again, this time on ABC, in Jean Cocteau's tour de force monologue, *La Voix Humaine*. He also produced, among other events, CBS's Emmy-award winning broadcast in 1966 of John Gielgud's *The Ages of Man* and a 1968 tribute to Chekhov, *To Chekhov with Love*, starring Gielgud and Irene Worth and directed by Jonathan Miller.

Throughout the 1960s, the remaining stage specials the commercial networks aired once or twice a year provided a diverse range of theater attractions. CBS, with its reputation for classy showmanship, often seemed to select programs for their promotional prestige. These included events like *The Ages of Man*, a well-received broadcast of Hal Holbrook's *Mark Twain Tonight*, and a revival of *Ivanov*, starring John Gielgud and Claire Bloom. In a rare triumph for the bard, the network also offered a virtually complete, filmed version of *A Midsummer Night's Dream*, produced by the Royal Shakespeare Company and broadcast during prime time on a Sunday night. ABC stuck more closely to Broadway, with revivals of vehicles like *Dial M for Murder*, *Arsenic and Old Lace*, and *The Diary of Anne Frank*, as well as broadcasts of John Osborne's *Luther* and of Michael V. Gazzo's powerful drama *A Hatful of Rain*. NBC, meanwhile, relied primarily on *The Hallmark Hall of Fame* for its stage events, but it did televise a few musicals and a well-received 90–minute adaption of Peter Weiss's *The Investigation*, directed by Ulu Grossbard. As its title indicates, the network's Sunday afternoon series *Experiment in Television* was a chance to try something different. Examples of the varied theatrical fare included *Pinter People*; a British program of five Harold Pinter revue sketches; a revival of a short play by Emanuel Peluso, *Good Day*, starring Frank Langella and Jo Van Fleet; and a program on the National Theater of the Deaf.

A more frequent forum for unusual theater could be found on CBS's *Camera Three*, which focused on experimental stage offerings many times during the 1960s. A 1964 program presented a commedia del l'arte version of *Hamlet*. Other broadcasts featured a performance of Lanford Wilson's *This is Rill Speaking*, selections from Carson McCuller's *Ballad of the Sad Cafe*, profiles of the Actor's Studio and Lee Strasberg, an interview with Andre Gregory, and repertory highlights from the Chinese Classical Theater, the Little Theater of the Deaf, and the Living Theater.

Educational Television and Theater

Camera Three's low budget, off-the-mainstream approach was not that far removed from the orientation of the typical educational TV station in the early 1960s. Like CBS's Sunday morning cultural series, financing and limitations in programming were the chief problems of non-commercial television. The formation of National Educational Television (NET) in 1959 helped establish a central distribution network, but a good many of the productions bicycled from station to station suffered from strapped resources and an overly academic tone. An ambitious exception was a 1961 series called *Playwright at Work*, which broadcast excerpts from unfinished scripts by dramatists like Lorraine Hansberry, Michael V. Gazzo, and the still Off-Broadway Edward Albee, directed by theater luminaries such as Alan Schneider and Lloyd Richards, with Frank Perry serving as general producer.

When the Ford Foundation stepped up its funding of NET from $1 million to $6 million a year in the mid–1960s, the network was able to expand its dramatic programming in significant ways. This not only included occasional looks at theater personalities in its programs *The Creative Person* and *ARTS: USA* but the introduction in October 1966 of *NET Playhouse*, which would emerge as one of the network's most distinguished presentations during its seven-year run. Like many of NET's efforts, the series often relied on low-cost, high-quality imported programs to help fill its schedule. *NET Playhouse*'s signature, however, was its commitment to modern American drama. During its first year, more than half of its $1.3 million budget was allocated for domestic productions—six in all, covering the diversity of contemporary theater. These included Ronald Ribman's

Journey of the Fifth Horseman, with the then unknown Dustin Hoffman; Tennessee Williams's *Ten Blocks on Camino Real*; Arthur Miller's version of Ibsen's *Enemy of the People*; Maxwell Anderson's *Star Wagon*; and three short works by the "La Mama Playwrights": Jean Claude van Italie, Sam Shephard, and Paul Foster.

In the years that followed, *NET Playhouse* pursued a deliberately innovative course, mounting the kind of stage works commercial television would never have considered, even in its more freewheeling days. The program's repertory was drawn largely from Off- and Off-Off-Broadway, with many of the period's major avant-garde playwrights and theater troupes receiving some form of exposure. In addition to productions of Jack Richardson's *The Prodigal*, Lanford Wilson's *The Sad Castle*, and Ronald Ribman's *The Ceremony of Innocence*, the series presented the Open Theater in a 90–minute version of *The Serpent*, a sampler entitled *Theater America: New Theater for Now*, and the La Mama Troupe in Paul Foster's *!Heimskringla! Or the Stoned Angels*. The latter proved to be *NET Playhouse*'s most unusual and visually audacious enterprise, an hour-and-a-half program combining advanced video imagery with a rambling drama about, among other things, Leif Eriksson's discovery of America, the arms race, and current sexual mores. Tom O'Horgan, who was well known for his calculated theatrical anarchy, brought this same quality to his TV direction. The program's tone veered wildly from expressionistic myth to hip comedy, with dramatic scenes constantly shifting into sudden bursts of psychedelic colors and waves (thanks to a technology dubbed "videospace," developed at KQED). Though often difficult to follow, *!Heimskringla!* provided an interesting TV approximation of the more frantic qualities of Off-Off-Broadway experimentation.

During its last few years, *NET Playhouse* occasionally turned towards a more unified, serieslike approach, grouping programs around a collection of themes. The 1970–71 season featured a look at the 1930s, with new productions of Clifford Odets's *Paradise Lost* and Arthur Miller's *A Memory of Two Mondays*, in addition to a film revival and a documentary about the period. *NET Playhouse*'s *Biography* was a larger umbrella title, which departed from the show's stage focus in favor of old and new material from the BBC and a few domestic film productions.

While *NET Playhouse* reflected an east coast theatrical bias, *Hollywood Television Theater* attempted to present a greater variety of newer dramatic works, with more "star" power. Created by Lewis Freedman, funded by the Ford Foundation, and produced by PBS affiliate KCET-TV in Los Angeles, the series premiered in the spring of 1970 with a telecast of Saul Levitt's *The Andersonville Trial*, directed by George C. Scott and starring William Shatner, Buddy Ebsen, and Richard Basehart. The Civil War drama, written as a reflection on the theme of responsibility in the Nuremberg war trials, received new currency in the light of the controversial

My Lai massacre trial, which was just about to take place. Highly praised, the show won both a Peabody Award and the Emmy as the best single program of the year. The participation of George C. Scott (who was then at the height of his career), combined with the critical acclaim, helped establish *Hollywood Television Theater*'s reputation as one of the select TV environments where screen and TV performers were willing to work for scale (then about $600). Through the years, actors such as Walter Matthau, Gene Wilder, Richard Chamberlain, Patty Duke, and Andy Griffith were among the many who made their PBS debut on the series' often enterprising productions.

Hollywood Television Theater's first season reflected the program's philosophy of enticing viewers to watch little-known works by casting well-known (or at least semi-well-known) Hollywood personalities. Popular TV actor Bill Bixby appeared in Hugh Wheeler's *Big Fish, Little Fish*; a dramatization of John Dos Passos's novel *U.S.A.* featured singer John Denver, along with James Farentino and Michele Lee; Hurd Hatfield and New York stage veterans Rip Torn and Geraldine Page appeared in Lillian Hellman's *Montserrat*. The series continued to mount several full-length productions during its second year, but its main focus now shifted to shorter plays, requiring smaller casts and less costly technical budgets. Thirteen one-hour dramas were presented in all, mostly drawn from Off-Broadway. Programs ranged from Murray Schisgal's comedy *The Typists*, with Anne Jackson and Eli Wallach re-creating their original stage roles, to Leonard Melfi's offbeat melodrama *Birdbath*, starring Patty Duke and James Farentino, to Jack MacGowran's celebrated readings from Samuel Beckett, *Beginning to End*, performed in an appropriately striking desert locale.

Perhaps the highlight of *Hollywood Television Theater*'s third season was its notorious production of Bruce Jay Friedman's *Steambath*. In contrast to the generally safe and predictable tone of previous telecasts, *Steambath* was a dramatic departure in content and style. Friedman's black comedy was not only funnier than most TV stage works, but also coarser and more profane. The play's frequent use of four-letter words and its casual sexual references would have traditionally made it off-limits for broadcasting. *Hollywood Television Theater*, however, decided to present the work intact, including the brief glimpses of male and female nudity that characterized the stage version. The resulting telecast prompted immediate controversy from PBS and its affiliates. The network found the production inappropriate for national distribution under its auspices, and an alternative arrangement had to be worked out. Many local PBS stations, when confronted by the show's profanity and its occasional topless and bottomlessness, either delayed it until late at night or simply refused to air it. Despite the show's crisp direction (by Burt Brinkerhoff), generally good cast (featuring Bill Bixby, Stephen Elliott, Jose Perez, and Valerie Perrine), and praise from the critics, it would be several years before any domestic PBS dramatic series attempted to once again test the limits of contemporary TV obscenity standards. (Imported BBC programs, which sometimes displayed sporadic nudity, seemed exempt from these problems, possibly because British accents made everything appear inherently classier.)

Though none of *Hollywood Television Theater*'s offerings proved as daring as *Steambath* in the seasons that followed, the series was still committed, up until its cancellation in 1977, to giving lesser-known plays greater exposure. Newer works presented included Enid Bagnold's *The Chinese Prime Minister*, George Kelly's *The Fatal Weakness*, Steve Tesich's *Nourish the Beast*, Phillip Hayes's *Story of the Blind Pig*, and Edward Bond's English version of Ibsen's *The Master Builder*, starring Burt Lancaster. The program also mounted various theatrical revivals, such as Arthur Miller's *Incident at Vichy* and Christopher Fry's *The Lady's Not for Burning*. The most imaginative of these was an adaptation by Paul Avila Mayer of Pirandello's *Six Characters in Search of an Author*, which switched the play from its original setting in a theater to a TV studio. Substituting TV terminology for the work's original stage vocabulary and combining familiar rehearsal elements with intricate views of the action on TV monitors, the program avoided the pitfalls of most radical transpositions. Instead of too much flash and cleverness, this TV version employed a concentrated approach that actually revitalized Pirandello's existential and self-reflexive themes. The many implicit connections and parallels between the play's "theatrical" metaphors and the electronic "realities" of the TV screen were underscored not only by Mayer's careful reworking but also by Stacy Keach's direction, with its emphasis on the medium's multiple viewpoints. The show's strong cast was headed by John Houseman and Andy Griffith (whose years as a TV star brought its own resonance to the production).

Theater in America/Great Performances

In 1973, WNET-TV in New York introduced one of non-commercial television's most adventurous dramatic series, *Theater in America*. Recognizing that TV theater needed to extend its boundaries away from just New York or Los Angeles, executive producer Jac Venza hoped to capture the often exciting developments emerging from the country's varied regional theater companies. "Our aim," as Venza put it, was "to bring to a national audience those unique talents and outstanding productions which have proven so successful in their own communities."[44] The process involved not only a great deal of travelling to sample the repertory of groups like San Francisco's American Conservatory Theatre or Louisville's Actors Theatre or Cincinnati's Playhouse in the Park, but also an unusual willingness, once a play had been selected, to work closely with the theater company in the process of electronic adaptation. Whether the program was taped in New York or co-produced with a local public TV station in the theater's community, the series employed, in Venza's words, "the best television people," to help the stage director, designer, and actors in the difficult task of re-creating a theatrical vision to the small screen.[45]

Theater in America's first year budget was $2 million, a small sum by commercial network standards (where a single made-for-TV movie at that time could cost over a million dollars to produce), but one which WNET was able to stretch to include 18 weekly programs. To fill the schedule, several installments were actually reruns from previous series such as *Playhouse New York* and were not the product of any theater company, regional or otherwise. The majority, however, originated as separate stage presentations, which were then carefully rethought and transformed to television's more fluid and intimate dimensions. The Repertory Theater of Lincoln Center was the first ensemble to be featured, and the telecast of their production of Maxim Gorky's *Enemies* offered an example of *Theater in America*'s methods. Like most of the series' new programs, the work was a collaborative effort between the original stage director (Ellis Rabb) and an experienced TV director (Kirk Browning). Rather than confine the play to the restrictions of a studio, the setting was moved to a picturesque mansion in Tarrytown, New York—a decision that opened the production up to a more lyrical and reflective atmosphere. What critic Stephen Koch had attacked in the theater as a "stupefying thing" was now transformed into "something positively interesting. . . . Television sometimes vastly improves a work," Koch noted, "The camera has given *Enemies* texture, rhythm, air—saved it."[46]

Other productions during the series' first season spanned a wide range of styles and approaches. There were sturdy classical revivals (the American Conservatory Theatre's *Cyrano de Bergerac* and the New York Shakespeare Festival's *King Lear* with James Earl Jones); a little known play by D.H. Lawrence (*The Widowing of Mrs. Holroyd*, performed by the Long Wharf Theatre); a modernized Georges Feydeau farce (*In Fashion*, staged by the Actors Theatre of Louisville); David Storey's contemporary work *The Contractor*, with the Chelsea Theater Center; and an extraordinary poetic drama about the life and imprisonment of Oscar Wilde, *Feasting With Panthers*. Written by Richard Cumming and Adrian Hall and produced by the Trinity Square Repertory Company, *Feasting With Panthers* was an imaginative merger of experimental theater and television. Wilde's career and his years in Reading Gaol were dramatized in a fashion that took advantage of the electronic medium's freedom of movement, its close-range intensity, and its technology. Time and scenery changes flowed into one another; soft-focus camerawork, echo chambers, and jarring superimpositions created a vivid feeling of claustrophobia and social repression. Next to Richard Cumming's stirring performance as the embattled Wilde, the highlight of the production was designer Eugene Lee's transformation of an old Rhode Island textile mill into a haunted theatrical playground.

With its curious layout, distinctive architecture, and structural decay, the mill served as both a versatile dramatic locale and an evocative symbol. As Adrian Hall, who co-directed the play with Rick Hauser, observed:

> It was not a set in conventional stage terms. It was a hundred sets. We used every nook and corner of the old mill—hallways, metal staircases, concrete dye vats that had long been discarded, crumbling and peeling walls. It was an atmosphere. Far more important, it was everything that we had been experimenting with for years about space and its relationship to actors. It was not a stage, it was an environment.[47]

While none of the plays presented by *Theater in America* during its second season was as avowedly experimental as *Feasting with Panthers*, the series pursued a stimulating course between attractive revivals (Sheridan's *The School for Scandal*, with the Guthrie Theater; Pirandello's *Rules of the Game*, staged by Phoenix Theatre; an open-air version of Chekhov's *The Seagull*, performed by the Williamstown Theatre Festival) and newer works, such as Frank Chin's *The Year of the Dragon*, Peter Nichols's *Forget Me Not Lane*, and Elie Wiesel's *Zalmen or the Madness of God*. Problems still remained in transposing many of these dramas to television. Acting styles and rhythms that worked well on the large stage sometimes seemed cramped and overly stylized when seen in close-up, but the program's belief in matching original theater directors with skilled TV counterparts proved to be an important asset in bridging the gap (both technical and aesthetic) between the two media.

Though collaboration might appear to be a difficult task, the stage and television directors who worked together on the series generally found the process stimulating and rewarding. As Arvin Brown of the Long Wharf Theater remarked, *Theater in America*'s specialized atmosphere—its "fairly substantial rehearsal periods, producer pressure at a relative minimum, and slightly looser scheduling"—helped make the process of co-directing much easier.[48] For the most part, the television directors brought in to translate from theater to the home screen followed a philosophy similar to that of TV director Nick Havinga, who commented:

> Whenever a stage production is presented on television in the manner of *Theater in America*, the stage director's voice is the one to listen to carefully. It was probably his or her vision that caused the stage production to have been chosen in the first place. The chances are that, as co-director for television, if one listens carefully, most of the work will have been done.[49]

Havinga's co-direction with Michael Langham in *The School for Scandal* was a model of the series' efforts to creatively combine theater and TV talent. In mounting the Guthrie Theater production, Havinga was committed, as he told original director Langham, to serving the interests of the stage version. "I suggested that, short of being merely a camera director, I saw my function as one devoted to seeing that *his* work and the work of his company was well presented in a new medium."[50] Langham, for his part, was eager to adapt the play to the differing requirements of television. "It was quickly established between Nick, producer David Griffiths and myself," he stated, "that our job was not to photograph a stage production; least of all to record on video-tape the energy and range of a performance scaled for a totally different medium."[51] New sets were designed to accommodate the reshaping of the TV studio; and together the two co-directors carefully preblocked the entire production prior to taping, a project which, Havinga reports,

> enabled us to understand each other's problems quickly. Langham grasped the difficulties in adding cameras, television lighting and audio pick-up to the play while losing the important live audience factor. I worked to preserve the style and form he had created for *The School for Scandal*.[52]

The result was a program characterized by a refreshing briskness and clarity, with little sense of its origins as a stage production.

During its third season, *Theater in America* continued to expand the scope of its offerings and the diversity of its producing theaters. Programs were drawn from the McCarther Theatre Company of Princeton (Eugene O'Neill's *Beyond the Horizon*), the Negro Ensemble Company (Leslie Lee's *The First Breeze of Summer*), the Asolo State Theater (Sidney Kingsley's *The Patriots*), as well as from The Acting Company, the Circle Repertory Company, the Hartford Stage Company, and the Manhattan Theatre Club. A highlight was an evocative staging of Tennessee Williams's *Eccentricities of a Nightingale*, produced in collaboration with the Old Globe Theatre of San Diego. This chamber drama, depicting the anguished longings of a small town southern spinster, is one of the playwright's most romantic and fragile works. Its delicate moods of reverie, passion, and plaintiveness can easily be trampled by just the slightest touch of overemphasis or self-conscious stylization. Fortunately, the performances of Blythe Danner and Frank Langella and the direction of Glenn Jordan were attuned to Williams's lyric tempos. The musical coloring to Danner and Langella's voices and their ardent approach to acting gave their roles a quality of tenderness rarely found in the intense, close-up scrutiny of televison. Glenn Jordan's restrained camera work, with its simple, gliding movements and deep focus shots, played an equally important role in capturing the drama's hazy, poignant spirit.

Theater in America's fourth season began with a wonderful production of Eugene O'Neill's *Ah, Wilderness*, a play just as infused with memory tones as *Eccentricities of a Nightingale*. But where Williams looked to the past with a feeling for life's losers, O'Neill, at least in this work, provides an affectionate and cheerful view of upper-middle-class America at the turn-of-the century—a dramatic environment realized with unsentimental charm in the staging by the Long Wharf Theater. In a departure from customary series practice, the program was directed solely by its original theater director, Arvin Brown, who skillfully matched the medium's intimate demands with the more expansive rhythms of the stage. Taping the play inside and outside of a large, Victorian-style mansion, Brown approached O'Neill's warm comedy with restraint and seriousness. His fluid shifts of perspective, crisp pacing, and expert handling of his cast, headed by Geraldine Fitzgerald and Richard Backus, were crucial factors in making this production a first-rate example of intelligent theatrical translation to television.

Theater in America's other programs during its fourth season offered a varied menu of traditional fare with revivals of less well-known works. The American Conservatory Theatre performed a commedia del l'arte version of Shakespeare's *The Taming of the Shrew* that featured large doses of horseplay, wrestling, and a free-for-all treatment of the text. The Phoenix Theatre presented a respectful mounting of William Gillette's ancient melodrama *Secret Service*, with a cast comprised of Meryl Streep, John Lithgow, and Mary Beth Hurt. There were also productions of Heinrich Kleist's *The Prince of Homburg*, starring Frank Langella; S.N. Behrman's *End of Summer*, with Helen Hayes and Lois Nettleton; and Beckett's *Waiting for Godot*, performed by Dana Elcar, Donald Moffat, and Ralph Waite.

As part of *Great Performances*, PBS's umbrella showcase of drama, music, and ballet, *Theater in America* underwent a transformation during its fifth year. Rather than highlight the latter's regional theater focus, WNET-TV, which produced *Great Performances*, adopted a more thematic approach to all of its dramatic programming. Promotable, descriptive categories were applied to a diverse collection of plays and films. Three of the station's co-productions (Tom Stoppard's *Professional Foul* and David Mercer's *Shooting the Chandelier*, both made in association with the BBC; and Daniel A. Stein's *The Trial of the Moke*, a collaboration with WQLN in Erie, Pennsylvania) were advertised as "Human Rights Dramas." Another series, comprised of two imported shows, one domestic play, and an original film adaptation of Paul Gallico's *Verna: USO Girl*, was announced as "Off Stage Dramas." In the midst of this regrouping, only two new *Theater in America* programs were offered (Wendy Wasserstein's *Uncommon Women and Others*, performed by the Phoenix Theatre, and Circle-in-the-Square's version of Moliere's *Tartuffe*), as the station shifted its emphasis away from regional theater to New York-based projects, less costly imported acquisitions and co-productions.

By its sixth year, *Theater in America* had become simply a small part in the realm of *Great Performances*' drama presentations—presentations that tended to be dominated by the large number of classy English theatrical programs filling the schedule. The 1978–79 season saw only three domestic productions. One of these, however, ranked as the most ambitious, and expensive, televised play in PBS history. This was *Mourning Becomes Electra*, Eugene O'Neill's epic recasting of Aeschylus's *Oresteia*, set during the American Civil War. Budgeted at $1 million, the long work was divided into five, one-hour episodes that seemed especially well suited to TV serialization. Co-producer Jac Venza noted, "When I first read it, I realized that the form, the relationship of the family and their activity, was very much like television drama. In form, at least, *Mourning Becomes Electra* is not much different than a soap opera."[53] Director Nick Havinga faced a sizable challenge in making sure the play's occasionally overwrought atmosphere did not upset the smaller emotional scale of the TV screen. By keeping "what could be highly stylized . . . as natural as possible" (as the *New York Times*'s John J. O'Connor points out), Havinga avoided the pitfalls of O'Neill's passionate theatricality, while preserving the drama's "haunting and at times awesome power."[54] He was assisted by a strong cast, including Joan Hackett and Roberta Maxwell, an effective adaptation that eliminated many minor characters in the cause of clarity, and exceptionally handsome photography and production design.

Theater works played a less important role on subsequent seasons of *Great Performances*. The program instead began to rely more on assorted literary adaptations and imported, multi-part series. During the 1979–80 season, only three domestic stage productions were scheduled: an energetic version of David Mamet's *A Life in the Theatre*; Cocteau's *The Human Voice*, directed by Jose Quintero and starring Liv Ullmann; and a surprisingly lively telecast of Samuel Beckett's *Happy Days*, which, despite the fact that its lead character was imprisoned up to her waist in a sand hill, still seemed to move with the speed and sharpness of an acrobatic display. (The program, based on Andrei Serban's original New York Shakespeare Festival production, featured a triumphant performance by Irene Worth and was inventively directed for television by David Heeley.) By the next season, American theater had disappeared entirely from *Great Performances*, replaced by Mark Twain, Dorothy Parker, and Irwin Shaw short story dramatizations, a BBC mini-series (John le Carre's *Tinker, Tailor, Soldier, Spy*), and the third year of the BBC's Shakespeare plays cycle. Founded in 1973 as a self-proclaimed "showcase for distinguished American regional theater companies,"[55] the series would now follow a dramatic path far removed from the varied stage repertory of its past.

Theater on the Commercial Networks in the 1970s

PBS's enterprising approach to televised theater throughout the 1970s could hardly be matched by ABC, CBS, or NBC, where there was little willingness, given the emphasis on mass programming, to tackle dramatic projects too far off the beaten path. Still, the networks did broadcast several specials during the decade that proved interesting and ambitious in their own right. NBC's *The Hallmark Hall of Fame* continued to be the premier forum for "prestige" stage events. Its five or six "television spectaculars" a year spanned a wide theatrical range, from productions of *Hamlet* (starring Richard Chamberlain and Margaret Leighton) and Shaw's *Caesar and Cleopatra* (with Genevieve Bujold and Alec Guinness) to more recent works such as Paddy Chayefsky's *Gideon* (starring Peter Ustinov and Jose Ferrer), Tad Mosel's *All the Way Home*, and Arthur Miller's *The Price* (with George C. Scott and Colleen Dewhurst). Other presentations included a disastrously received updating of Kaufmann and Hart's *The Man Who Came to Dinner*, featuring Orson Welles as "TV personality" Sheridan Whiteside; a restaging of *Peter Pan* with Mia Farrow and Danny Kaye; James Stewart and Helen Hayes in *Harvey*; and Greer Garson in the costume drama *Crown Matrimonial*. Towards the end of the decade, *The Hallmark Hall of Fame*, like *Great Performances*, shifted its focus away from stage works to literary adaptations and to original made-for-TV dramas.

The refined tone that distinguished both the *Hallmark* series and Hallmark's long relationship with NBC was in sharp contrast to the most explosive episode in network theater production of the 1970s—CBS's ill-fated alliance with the New York Shakespeare Festival's Joseph Papp. Announced with great fanfare in the fall of 1972, Papp was signed to do a minimum of 13 full-length plays for broadcast during the next four years, at a cost of more than $7 million. His reputation for theatrical controversy was, oddly enough, welcomed by CBS, with no less a figure than Fred Silverman, then the network's vice-president of programming, declaring: "The problem of TV drama is that it's been like musical chairs—the same creators year in and year out doing the same thing. Papp always ends up doing what nobody expects. The medium can use new vitality."[56]

Papp himself was eager for the opportunity to expand his activities, as well as broaden the terms of commercially televised theater. He told a reporter from *Newsweek*:

> Our aim is to engage the audience, not alienate it. We are interested in family viewing as well as controversial adult material. We will try not to offend gratuitously, but we will risk offending if the theme is meaningful and serious.[57]

Aware that he was proposing a distinctly different idea about the nature of TV drama, neither Papp nor CBS approached their collaboration with any illusion that it would make the network rich. "I wish CBS could make money on this," Papp announced at a news conference, but "I think they plan to lose money."[58] Network president Robert Wood acknowledged that the project "is not going to be looked at as a profit center for CBS."[59]

For his first production, Papp chose to televise the New York Shakespeare Festival's current Broadway hit, a turn-of-the-century version of

Shakespeare's *Much Ado About Nothing*, directed by A.J. Antoon. With the assistance of Nick Havinga, Antoon preserved the assets and the limitations of his stage approach on television. The program was a brassy, bouncy, good-natured, but rather one-noted comic affair. For all of its lovely costume design and scenery, the show's occasionally frantic pulse tended to obscure the stylish, elegant wit of the play—a fact which was probably more obvious in the restricted space of the TV screen than in the theater's larger surroundings. Nevertheless, Papp did take some risk in televising an event still playing to packed houses on Broadway, and unfortunately, the results appear not to have been worth it. Not only did he lose money on the program ($60,000 in his own production costs by Papp's estimate), but the 15 million viewers who watched on television effectively robbed him of his stage audience. Following the telecast, *Much Ado*'s theater attendance dropped from the previous week's 25,000 to a disastrous 9,000. The show was forced to close.

Papp's financial troubles with *Much Ado* were nothing compared with what happened with his next CBS project. Moving from the non-controversial waters of Shakespeare, he chose to present David Rabe's *Sticks and Bones*, a harsh drama of a blind Vietnam veteran's return home to his seemingly oblivious family. Winner of the Tony Award for best play of 1972, *Sticks and Bones* was, as John J. O'Connor noted, "unusually strong for television, whether commercial or public."[60] Selecting underground filmmaker Robert Downey to direct the TV version did little to lessen the work's sting or soften its jarring dramatic elements. If anything, Downey's expressionistic camera devices and unconventional pacing made the program appear even more unsettling and abrasive.

After a closed-circuit screening for its affiliates, in which more than a third stated they would not air the show, CBS announced, just three days before the scheduled March 9, 1973, telecast, that it would postpone Papp's production indefinitely. *Sticks and Bones*, the network claimed, might be "unnecessarily abrasive" for viewers at a time when tremendous attention was being focused on the return of former P.O.W.'s and other veterans from Vietnam.[61]

Denunciations of the decision followed immediately. Papp attacked CBS's ruling as "cowardly," a "politicization of the play" and "presumptuous."[62] "It is frightening that this monster corporation has decided to put its tail between its legs and back away from this program because some affiliates find it too strong stuff," he proclaimed.[63] The American Civil Liberties Union decried the network for its "corporate cowardice."[64] In an impassioned essay in the *New York Times*, John J. O'Connor lambasted CBS's shabby treatment of the producer:

> Papp did not choose the air date. That was done by the network at a time when it should have been obvious that the returning P.O.W.'s would be in the news.

Papp was willing to compromise on certain elements in the play, some of the language and even some of the situations. Working closely with the network, he delivered a production only to be told in the final days before broadcast that it might be unnecessarily abrasive.[65]

"The medium can be more than a lulling narcotic," O'Connor concluded. "It is essential that CBS and its stations carry 'Sticks and Bones.' "[66]

The program was eventually broadcast, but in a fashion that was not really satisfying to anyone concerned. Hidden on the schedule in mid-August, when viewing levels are traditionally at their lowest, *Sticks and Bones* was shown on only half of CBS's affiliates. Ninety-four stations refused to air it, and no advertiser was willing to sponsor it. Papp ended his relationship with the network shortly thereafter.

CBS avoided further controversy in its later dramatic specials. Though it did broadcast Ingmar Bergman's adult TV play, *The Lie*, and briefly revived its *Playhouse 90* series of new works, the network, for the most part, preferred to showcase prime-time theater events that either guaranteed predictability (such as Carol Burnett's featured role in George Furth's *Twigs*) or prestige.

ABC and NBC employed a similar policy, but with some degree of variation. In contrast to its counterparts, ABC televised numerous imported drama specials. Magnificent English telecasts of *Long Day's Journey into Night* and *The Merchant of Venice*, both starring Laurence Olivier, provided the network with an inexpensive and, at the time, much needed shot of distinction. ABC's domestic drama programs were, somewhat surprisingly, of equally high quality. Katherine Hepburn and Sam Waterston appeared in a polished film version of *The Glass Menagerie* in 1973. The Negro Ensemble Company offered an impressive production of Lonnie Elder's *Ceremonies and Dark Old Men* in 1975. Possibly the network's chief stage event during the decade was a broadcast of the 1974 Broadway revival of Eugene O'Neill's *Moon for the Misbegotten*. Produced by David Susskind and directed by Jose Quintero, this stirring, two-and-a-half-hour program captured the spirit of O'Neill's tortured romanticism. Though clearly taped in a studio, the TV version sought to give the work a realistic feel (there were live pigs in the barnyard and the set looked like a Depression artifact), while still softening its edges with poetic lighting effects. At the show's center was a trio of masterful performances by Colleen Dewhurst, Jason Robards, Jr., and Ed Flanders, that, despite some traces of theatrical stylization, came across with unusual power in close-up. *Moon for the Misbegotten* proved to be yet another example of how well O'Neill's dramas play when thoughtfully translated to television.

In addition to its *Hallmark Hall of Fame* "spectaculars," NBC presented a varied menu of contemporary theater attractions. Arthur Miller's *After the Fall*, adapted and revised by the playwright, was broadcast in 1974. A radically altered version of John Osborne's *The Entertainer* was televised in 1976, which not only switched locales (England to California) and time periods (1950s to 1944) but also added eight original songs by Marvin Hamlish. In the same year, the network introduced its "Tribute to American Theatre" with an English production of Tennessee Williams's *Cat on a Hot Tin Roof*. Even with the bravura hamminess of Laurence Olivier's Big Daddy, the program was marred by its soap opera style (intense closeups, cramped direction, excessive musical underlining) and the weak performances of Robert Wagner and Natalie Wood, who, try as they might, never skimmed below the surfaces of their roles.

A more successful stage event was an NBC telecast of *Our Town* in 1977. Produced and directed by George Schaeffer, the show found an interesting strategy to convert Thorton Wilder's artful theatrical techniques to television. The dramatic magic of the play, which depends so much on its apparent simplicity and direct stagecraft, was carefully rethought in TV terms. Instead of relying on the closure of the proscenium arch, the performing area was now a bare rehearsal studio, seen from all angles. The fluid movements of the cameras added an appropriate sense of openness and intimacy, as viewers were able to glide through the constantly shifting locales. Other TV practices helped enhance the work's modest, poetic mood. Simple chroma-keyed backgrounds, which electronically projected a picture behind the actors, were used to suggest the artificial quality of the sets. Since there were few real props, sound effects, such as the clatter of imaginary plates being put away or the swish of invisible water from a faucet, added another note of indirect reality. The much abused techniques of freeze frames and superimpositions were also employed for telling effect during the play's most emotional moments. With accomplished performances by Barbara Bel Geddes, Sada Thompson, Hal Holbrook, and Ned Beatty, this TV version of *Our Town* was often as persuasive and moving as the best productions on stage.

CBS's *Camera Three* continued to be the primary forum for network TV drama outside of prime time. Until its cancellation in 1979, the series was an active promoter of the avant-garde theater, frequently venturing into areas even PBS had abandoned as too unconventional. Executive producer Merrill Brockway's programs in the early to mid–1970s offered nothing less than an international catalogue of experimental plays, playwrights, and directors. From Paris, the Theatre Labatoire Vicinal performed excerpts from Frederic Baal's *Real Reel*. Germany's Peter Handke discussed "Theater and Ideas." English director Peter Brook, who had recently started a new troupe in France, was profiled in two different, two-part episodes. American theater was also well represented. The Open Theater Ensemble appeared in a 30–minute version of *Terminal*, their chilling, ritualistic drama about death and dying. Directed in a choreographic style by Brockway, matching the rhythm of the work's incantory phrases with precise cutting from camera to camera, the program provoked one of the series' largest responses, mostly from viewers upset by its theme and the harshness of its tone. The Open Theater returned in 1974 with a production of their final piece as an ensemble, *Nightwalk*. Later in the year, Brockway also mounted an extraordinary television version of the La Mama Theater Company's *Three Greek Plays*, based on Andrei Serban's original direction. The highlights from *Medea*, *Electra*, and *The Trojan Women*, though performed in ancient Greek and Latin, came across with a power that was startling, thanks to a fiery cast, evocative staging and lighting, the occasional use of masks, and Elizabeth Swados's eerie music.

After Merrill Brockway's departure, the series took a less radical turn. There were programs on American playwrights at Joseph Papp's Public Theater, Circle-in-the-Square's 25th Anniversary with tributes from Dustin Hoffman and George C. Scott, and the directorial experiments of playwright David Mamet.

The Commercial Networks and the Stage in the 1980s

Despite the virtual absence of prime-time drama specials in the late 1970s, theater on television did make a comeback of sorts in the 1980s. NBC proved to be the most enterprising network with their new once-a-year event, *NBC Live Theatre*. Hoping to capture the excitement of 25 years ago, when all drama was televised live, the program premiered in April 1980 with a performance of Preston Jones's *The Oldest Living Graduate*, starring Henry Fonda. The broadcast, originating from the Bob Hope Theater at Southern Methodist University, went smoothly but was rather uninvolving—the result of a sometimes overly mannered play, the limitations of a strict proscenium perspective, and the uncomfortable collision between the intimacy of the small screen and the broad activities being enacted on stage. Similar problems plagued *NBC Live Theatre*'s future telecasts. The second, Tad Mosel's *All the Way Home*, while a better drama, seemed just as emotionally inert. The flat camerawork, the somewhat boomy miking from the theater at the University of Southern California, and the distracting presence of a large audience made it difficult for viewers to feel like anything more than distant eavesdroppers. Carson McCuller's *A Member of the Wedding*, televised in 1982, succeeded a bit better, thanks to the performances of Dana Hill and Pearl Bailey, which seemed more scaled to TV dimensions. The 1984 broadcast of Joshua Logan's *Mister Roberts*, however, was by far the series' weakest installment—an out-of-date play, with a cast of lightweight comic actors, most of whom were unable to dramatize their roles. As John J. O'Connor fittingly observed, "About the only thing live was the transmission, and that just isn't enough. It never was."[67] No future productions of *NBC Live Theatre* have been planned.

While NBC explored telecasts from the stage, ABC, in its chief theater program since the new decade began, turned to the attractions of superstar power as an audience lure. Its revival of Tennessee Williams's *A Streetcar Named Desire* was headlined by Ann-Margret, who was recommended for the role of Blanche DuBois by the playwright. Her performance prompted sharply divided opinions, with some critics praising the actress for her courage and ability to make the part her own, while others condemned her portrayal as "feebly shrill" and an "empty mess."[68] There was considerably less controversy about the weakness of her co-star, Treat Williams, and the production's misguided efforts at "frankness." In keeping with prime-time television's current infatuation with steaminess, the play's sexual currents were played very explicitly. Innuendoes were underlined and the rape scene was graphic in a way impossible to do in the 1951 film version by Elia Kazan. Yet the updating actually added little other than a few choice moments for the network to use in its promotions. Director John Erman's excessively sweaty atmosphere and fondness for gaudy, dark orange filters was typical of a production characterized by Tom Shales of the *Washington Post* as "utterly nuance-less."[69]

Public Broadcasting and the Stage in the 1980s

With the virtual disappearance of *Theater in America* into the broad cultural folds of *Great Performances*, the most regular outlet for stage events on PBS was its new series, *American Playhouse*, premiering in 1982. Produced by a consortium of the network's chief stations (WNET in New York, KCET in Los Angeles, WGBH in Boston, and South Carolina Educational Television), the program was designed as a domestic alternative to *Masterpiece Theater* and other British imports. Though it did present several original TV dramas by non-mainstream writers, like PBS's earlier series, *Visions*, the scope of *American Playhouse* was substantially wider. The show offered an eclectic menu ranging from a commissioned teleplay by John Cheever to unusual literary adaptations, a documentary on Carl Sandburg, a revived Broadway musical (Studs Terkel's *Working*) and a half-dozen stage dramas reworked for television. The two plays televised during the first season—*Medal of Honor Rag* and *For Colored Girls Who Have Considered Suicide/When the Rainbow is Enuf*—were both strong theater works that unfortunately lost a fair share of their power in the transfer to the small screen. The former suffered from an unfocused production that strained too hard for intensity; the latter, noted John J. O'Connor, "turned too visually literal in its television treatment, jarring the poetic flow of images that made the Joseph Papp stage version extraordinary."[70]

TV theater productions fared somewhat better in *American Playhouse*'s second year. The season opened from San Diego's Old Globe Theater with a live telecast of Thornton Wilder's *The Skin of Our Teeth*, starring Sada Thompson and Harold Gould. Trying to break the mould of traditional from-the-stage programs, the show added some introductory mock newsreel footage as well as a flashy news report (anchored by John Houseman) to open Act II. Under Jack O'Brien's direction, the broadcast had little of playing-to-the-rafters quality that made *NBC Live Theatre* seem so stagey. A presentation of Arthur Kopit's *Wings* four months later utilized various electronic technologies, such as repeat actions and fancy dissolves, to heighten the drama's emotional study of a woman (portrayed by Constance Cummings, in a re-creation of her Tony award-winning role) suffering from aphasia. The series' final theater program of 1983 was one of the earliest of PBS's co-productions with the pay-cable channel, Showtime. Under the arrangement, Lanford Wilson's *Fifth of July* had its TV premiere on Showtime, in a complete and uncut version. By the time it reached *American Playhouse*, however, 20 minutes of colorful situations and language had been excised—Public Television, for all of its adventurousness, still lacked the freedom of cable. Despite a fine performance by Richard Thomas, there were other problems with this TV presentation of *Fifth of July*, notably co-director Kirk Browning's fondness for severe close-ups and quick cutting, which made it almost impossible to grasp spatial relationships or the work's important ensemble spirit.

American Playhouse's most successful theater adaptation was its production of Sam Shepard's *True West*, televised in January 1984. In contrast to the frantic, situation-comedy techniques of *Fifth of July*, TV director Allan Goldstein employed a creative approach that sharpened the drama of the stage. To reproduce the intensity of Shepard's unsettling portrait of two warring brothers, Goldstein relied on a concentrated style with few noticeable edits, shots which often lasted a minute or longer, and camerawork every bit as restless as the play's leading characters. The effect was thrilling, particularly during the climax of Act II when a hand-held video camera mirrors John Malkovich's extended, circling dance around the seated figure of Gary Sinise. This edgy ballet holds an additional TV surprise. Near the end of the camera's first 360 degree rotation, the show's suburban kitchen set, which has been seen all along as a traditional, three-walled proscenium stage, is suddenly revealed to be a fully enclosed room. As Tom Carson of the *Village Voice* noted, "It's a dazzling switch: when you see paneling and a den where you're subconsciously come to think an audience has been sitting, it's as if the last possible escape route for both brothers has been shut off."[71] The shrewdly contrasting performances of Sinise (who directed the Chicago stage revival on which the show was based) and Malkovich—the former preppy, shaky and bewildered; the latter slovenly, explosive, and wickedly funny—made *True West* one of the few stage-to-TV adaptations that delivered genuine theatrical energy.

Though *American Playhouse* was the principal forum for theater works on PBS, plays did occasionally air on a few of the network's other series during the 1980s. *Great Performances* presented three recent New York attractions that were all restaged in one way or another for television. The first was Eva Le Gallienne's ill-fated 1982 revival of *Alice in Wonderland*, which bombed on Broadway, after WNET-TV had invested a considerable sum of money in its production. Hoping to balance its losses, the station offered a dramatically transformed TV version, with new cast members (including Richard Burton) and an array of special effects. Most critics agreed that the result, as directed by Kirk Browning, possessed considerably more charm than what was seen in the theater. Browning also co-directed, along with Ellis Rabb, a telecast of *You Can't Take It With You*, which Rabb had recently mounted in New York with great success. A co-production with Showtime, the program was taped before a live audience at the Royale Theater, right after the show completed its Broadway run. Like the Kaufman and Hart work itself, the TV version was a warm and sunny affair, highlighted by Jason Robards, Jr.'s affectionate performance, and the star turns of Colleen Dewhurst and George Rose. The series also presented A.R. Gurney, Jr.'s *The Dining Room*—an Off-Broadway tour-de-force, using six actors to impersonate more than 50 characters during the course of five decades. Despite the fact that all the action takes place on one set, the play rarely seemed stagebound, thanks to its brief scenes, its varied assortment of personalities, and director Allan Goldstein's flexible pacing and camerawork.

One other PBS drama program is worthy of note. In 1983, *Kennedy Center Tonight*, a program usually focusing on taped-from-the-stage music and dance events, televised Robinson Jeffers's adaptation of *Medea*, starring Zoe Caldwell and Judith Anderson. Based on the 1982 Broadway revival by Robert Whitehead, the broadcast effectively captured the work's fury and violence, while enhancing the range of the stage production. As John Corry of the *New York Times* remarked, where Zoe Caldwell was a "magnetic field" in the theater, "the camera changes the focus," offering greater perspectives of the other actors, while adding more shading to Miss Caldwell's portrait in the title role, "deepening what already was a memorable performance."[72] This studio TV version was directed by Mark Cullingham and originally produced for CBS Cable.

The Cable TV Theater Explosion

Like the early days of commercial television, many of the major cable services springing up in the 1970s and early 1980s turned to the stage as the kind of prestigious event that would lure potential customer/viewers. The two pay-movie companies—Home Box Office (HBO) and Showtime—both offered taped theatrical attractions in a conscious effort "to broaden the appeal of the service and to add what is called 'perceived ticket value.' "[73] Showtime was by far the most ambitious with its still running series *Broadway on Showtime*. Premiering in September 1979, the program has presented a surprisingly diverse collection of nearly 50 recent or revived dramas, with a scattered sampling of musical and dance productions (such as the Peking Opera, the American Dance Machine, and John Curry's Icedancing) included for variety. The range of theater has remained fairly consistent through the years—light Broadway comedies, strong melodramas, and a small number of unusual contemporary efforts—but there has been a pronounced shift towards "more recognizable stars and properties," prompted by a demand from Showtime's audience for "better programming."[74] Early, less promotable events, with few recognizable performers, like the Goodspeed Opera House's revival of George M. Cohan's *Little Johnny Jones* in 1980 or Eric Bentley's dramatization of the House Un-American Activities Committee meetings, *Are You Now Or Have You Ever Been*, gave way to shows with at least a couple of movie or TV stars. A production of Clifford Odets's *The Country Girl* in 1982 featured Dick Van Dyke and Faye Dunaway. During the same year TV personality Scott Baio led the cast of Albert Inaurato's *Gemini* and Madeleine Kahn appeared with the original members of the musical revue *Scrambled Feet*.

Still, even with its more "commercial" emphasis, *Broadway on Showtime* continued to be among the last American TV outlets willing to make a strong commitment to televised theater. Its programs, financed and produced with an assortment of companies, such as PBS's *Great Performances* and *American Playhouse*, Lorimar Pay Television, and Group W Cable, have not been locked into one standard approach. Some have used the standard proscenium method, taping in front of live audiences at an actual theater performance; some have moved the drama outdoors to exterior locations; and some have been taped in the carefully controlled environment of a TV studio. One, Ed Graczyk's *Come Back to the Five & Dime, Jimmy Dean, Jimmy Dean*, was shot on film by its Broadway director Robert Altman and released to movie theaters, to great acclaim.

In recent times, *Broadway on Showtime* has presented several well-received studio theater programs. Jessica Lange headlined a new production of Tennessee Williams's *Cat on a Hot Tin Roof*, complete with dialogue considered too racy for the 1958 film version or the 1976 telecast with Laurence Olivier. Athol Fugard's *Master Harold . . . and the Boys*, a drama whose bitter examination of South African racism would seem to be outside the series' usual focus, aired in November 1984, largely because the rising young stage and screen actor Matthew Broderick was willing to appear in a leading role. To help maintain a "crispness of pacing that has become customary for television," the show's producers cut about 15 minutes of "mostly expository material, mostly at the top of the play," with the approval of the playwright, who also made changes of his own.[75] These minor alterations and the shift from stage to television's closer quarters led the *Washington Post*'s David Richards to observe that though the work now carried less of a theatrical "wallop," it "seems a far more intimate, reflective piece on the small screen. . . . What 'Master Harold' has lost in fury, it may have gained in poignancy."[76] (Like *Cat on a Hot Tin Roof*, when the program was broadcast a year later on PBS, some of its strong language was exorcised to avoid upsetting public standards.)

Showtime's other major project of the period was a mildly controversial telecast of the recent Broadway revival of Shaw's *Heartbreak House*, starring Rex Harrison. Though praised for its performances, the stage production had been sharply attacked for its textual abridgements. Even greater liberties were taken, however, with the TV version, in order to cut the play down from four hours to two. Adopting the traditional knowing pose of a commercial network programmer from the 1950s, co-producer John H. Williams justified the approach by noting, "The original running length was just more than a television audience would stand for. There were places that called out for some editing, and this makes it more accessible to a modern audience—in terms of what the average movie-going audience is used to today."[77] Less alarming changes included some rearrangement of the action, moving scenes which used to take place inside Captain Shotover's house to the outside rear garden, "to open up the feel of things, and give it more variety."[78]

HBO's theater programming was of a more limited scope. Its *Standing Room Only* series was designed to offer one stage production a month, beginning with its premiere in March 1981 of Jack Heifer's *Vanities*. Like most of the program's presentations, *Vanities* was a light, vaguely sentimental drama, taped during an actual theater performance, with a cast largely comprised of TV veterans. Later telecasts included a mixture of such dinner theater perennials as *Barefoot in the Park*, *Plaza Suite*, and *Wait Until Dark*, along with more interesting fare like Terence Ratigan's *Separate Tables*, *Bus Stop*, and *The Rainmaker* and James Lapine's *Table Settings*. Ironically, HBO's biggest theater event—a lavish, $3 million production of *Camelot*, starring Richard Harris—helped to signal a shift in programming priorities. As ex-director of theatrical development Arthur Whitelaw noted, while stage plays brought prestige, for about half a million dollars less than it took to mount *Camelot*, the network could produce a new made-for-TV movie, "And that's what the viewers say they want to see."[79] By the end of 1982, HBO would move away from televised theater to original films and teleplays.

In contrast to the "star personalities, star properties" orientation of both Showtime and HBO, the cable service ARTS (a co-venture of ABC and

Hearst) chose a different route for its stage events. ARTS's drama productions were far more experimental and willing to take chances. A typical example was a program of two one-act, two-character plays by David Mamet, strikingly directed by Lamont Johnson. The first, *Dark Pony*, was essentially a rambling monologue, delivered in a moving car at night, that gained considerable power from the natural confinement of the TV screen and from Johnson's mannered editing rhythms. Heavily shadowed shots were held much longer than on conventional TV dramas, creating an appropriately odd and uneasy effect. *Reunion*, the second short work, was a compelling, one-set mood piece, featuring the same skillful performers as *Dark Pony*—Michael Higgins and Lindsay Crouse.

Off-Broadway proved to be ARTS's most fertile theatrical territory. Two plays by Frank South, *Rattlesnake in a Cooler* and *Precious Blood*, were transferred to television by their director Robert Altman, soon after they closed in the theater. Working on videotape, Altman adapted his usually fluid cinematic style to South's more jagged, ornery pace, with highly effective results. A telecast of David Henry Hwang's *The Dance and the Railroad*, originally produced by Joseph Papp at the Public Theater, was equally successful in matching TV methods with stage techniques. Director Emile Ardolino, who had worked for many years with PBS's *Dance in America*, brought a choreographic approach to the program that was perfect for Hwang's intriguing study of two Chinese workers on the California railroad in the late 1860s. Rarely has a studio setting—in this case, a half-completed wooden bridge in the middle of a fog-bound forest—appeared more open and expansive, thanks to Ardolino's fleet camerawork. The spiritual "dance"/quest of the character played by John Lone found a meaningful TV equivalent in the program's dynamic cutting and in the special effects sequence near the end, where a dream version of Chinese opera is performed in colorful costumes against a blinding white background.

ARTS also presented Geraldine Page's celebrated all-black production of *Long Day's Journey Into Night*, highlighted by Ruby Dee's stirring performance, and an original video work, *Stations*, by avant-garde theater wizard Robert Wilson. Rising costs and lack of advertising, however, have led to an almost total elimination of domestic drama programming since 1982. The service, rechristened the Arts and Entertainment Network in 1984, now relies on imported efforts, mostly from the BBC, for any new stage events.

The two other cable networks that provided televised theater are, unfortunately, no longer in operation. CBS Cable, launched with much fanfare in October 1981 and extinguished by CBS less than a year later, offered several ambitious plays, including Athol Fugard's *Sizwe Banzie is Dead* (starring the original cast of John Kani and Winston Ntshona), David Storey's *Early Days* (with Sir Ralph Richardson and a supporting ensemble from England's National Theatre), Robert Patrick's *Kennedy's Children*, and Elizabeth Swados's *Songs of Innocence and Experience*. The Entertainment Channel, during its short, costly life, opted for a more popular course, hoping to present a recent Broadway attraction each month. One of the few original shows that aired before the pay service's demise was a highly acclaimed, rescaled version of Stephen Sondheim's musical, *Sweeney Todd*, featuring George Hearn and Angela Lansbury, and taped, without an audience, at the Dorothy Chandler Theater in Los Angeles.

While once seen as a promising avenue for TV theater—a place to recapture the excitement of televised drama of the 1950s or showcase plays with less than mass appeal—cable television has largely opted for the tactics of its commercial broadcast competitors. Of the three more innovative ventures of the early 1980s, only one (Arts and Entertainment) is still on the air, and it no longer experiments with domestic stage productions. Home Box Office, the giant of the industry, has similarly stopped its theater programming. Its chief adversary, Showtime, provides one of the few rays of hope for new theater on American television. The network's long-running series, *Broadway on Showtime*, though mostly devoted to mainstream attractions, has shown a willingness to try different types of plays. By co-producing and co-financing stage programs with various companies, particularly with PBS, Showtime has made it possible to keep TV theater alive at a time when interest in the form has greatly decreased.

CONCLUSIONS

Though interest in stage plays on television may presently be at a low ebb, the significance and influence televised theater exerted during the medium's first decades should not be forgotten. Unlike opera, ballet, or concerts, theatrical works on television were often tremendously popular and the methods used in their production helped develop a distinctive TV aesthetic.

By the late 1940s, it was already clear that stage plays brought to the small screen functioned best when they were not simple proscenium reproductions. The different dramatic environment of television demanded a different approach, combining the intensity of the theater with the flexibility of film. What television offered was the chance to capture the dynamics of live performance, shaped by the intimacy and the visual power of the camera. Breakthrough programs like *Studio One*'s 1949 telecast of *Julius Caesar* revealed how the medium, through innovative production design, exciting camera movement, and controlled acting, could create a theatrical experience uniquely its own.

The bounty of stage plays flooding the airwaves up until the mid–1950s—reflecting the industry's then New York orientation and its insatiable demand for material—led producers and directors to formulate an assortment of methods for transferring works from theater to television. An inevitable common denominator in practically every stage-based program was the need to strip a play of "excess" padding, sometimes down to the very bone. Characters, dialogue, entire scenes were often discarded in the effort to tailor a work to the strict time and propriety limits of commercial television.

Yet despite numerous artistic travesties, theater condensed for television was often surprisingly effective. The streamlining techniques of skillful adaptors hoping, in Paul Gardner's words, to "satisfy knowledgeable theatergoers who do not like clamps and sutures left on their drama" and to preserve "the author's intent and personality—if he has one," frequently produced programs with an impressive impact.[80] Many playwrights, though harshly critical at first of television's careless theatrical excisions, began to recognize the scope of the medium's power and undertook the task of adaptation themselves. (The most prominent was Arthur Miller, who after denouncing TV dramas in 1959 for offering predigested, cut-rate versions of full-length works, carefully rewrote and reshaped all of the TV productions based on his plays.)

By its narrower visual focus and its more concentrated emotional range, television provided viewers with a fresh perspective on theater. The absence of the boundaries of the stage removed, to a degree, the distance and the occasional artifice in attending a live event. Dramatic scale was revised. Spectacles and bravura which might impress in an auditorium appeared hopelessly hammy on the small screen. Instead, the intimacy of character relationships loomed as the medium's natural attraction, a fact that helped foster the rise of the naturalistic, "Golden Age" original teleplays of Paddy Chayefsky and Rod Serling, among others, during the 1950s.

Where TV theater excelled was in its capturing of performances. Even in programs otherwise flawed by dull direction, poor design, or complacent camera positioning, watching an actor at the peak of his or her form in close-up produced the kind of stage thrill previously available only to those with expensive front row seats.

Pioneering directors like Alex Segal, Paul Nickell, and George Schaeffer, however, went much further than showcasing bravura acting. They delighted in the freedom of a proscenium-less stage and of the possibilities in intricate camera arrangements. Instead of relying solely on the intensity of the close-up, their productions employed a fluid sense of television space, imaginatively reshaping a drama in TV terms.

Though there were fewer and fewer opportunities to experiment with TV theater as the commercial networks filled their schedules with Hollywood series, the rise of educational television in the 1960s presented a valuable new arena. Ambitious programs such as *NET Playhouse* were deliberately designed to challenge the conventional types of stage telecasts on ABC, CBS, and NBC. A few years later, the series *Theater in America* left the standard TV centers of New York and Los Angeles and focused on the country's diverse regional companies, offering a wide range of productions distinguished by their loyalty to the text (most plays were shown virtually uncut), their high standards of performance, and their unusually responsive direction.

The enterprise of programs like PBS's *Theater in America* and *American Playhouse*, the short revival of live, from-the-stage telecasts on NBC, and the various dramatic ventures of the cable networks may not have led to any long-range renewal of TV theater in the 1980s, but they did demonstrate the flexibility of drama on television and how it can be refashioned to current demands. It's a testament to the form's importance that its possibilities, after more than four decades, are still very much worth exploring.

NOTES

1. "Dialogue—George Schaeffer and Lewis Freedman," *Television Quarterly*, Vol. 1, no. 2, May 1962, p. 10.
2. Williams Hawes, "Television Drama: The First Twenty Years," *Today's Speech*, September 1963, p. 22.
3. Judy Dupuy, *Television Show Business* (Schenectady: General Electric, 1945), p. 24.
4. Francis W. Sturcken, "An Historical Analysis of Live Network Television Drama from 1938 to 1958," Ph.D. diss., University of Minnesota, 1960, p. 14.
5. John Reich, "Stage Plays for Television," *Televiser*, January/February 1946, p. 11.
6. " 'Blithe Spirit,' NBC's Top Show, Was Much Hard Work: Sobol," *Televiser*, July/August 1946, p. 20.
7. "Blithe Spirit," *Variety*, 15 May 1946, p. 35.
8. Sturcken, "An Historical," p. 53.
9. Tim Brooks and Earle Marsh, *The Complete Directory to Prime Time Network TV Shows 1946–Present* (New York: Ballantine Books, 1981), p. 723.
10. George Rosen, "Julius Caesar," *Variety*, 9 March 1949, p. 33.
11. Jack Gould, " 'Julius Caesar'," *New York Times*, 13 March 1948, Section II, p. 11.
12. Gould, " 'Julius Caesar,' " p. 11.
13. Jack Gould, "A Matter of Form," *New York Times*, 31 October 1948, Section II, p. 11.
14. Sturcken, "An Historical," p. 83.
15. Philip Hamburger, "Television," *New Yorker*, 22 July 1950, p. 46.
16. Fred Coe, "Televising Shakespeare," *Theatre Arts*, April 1951, p. 56.
17. Coe, p. 96.
18. Worthington Miner, "Shakespeare for the Millions," *Theatre Arts*, June 1951, p. 94.
19. Jack Gould, "Radio and Television," *New York Times*, 24 October 1951, p. 43.
20. Gould, "Radio and Television," p. 43.

21. "Drama for an Hour," *TIME*, 5 May, 1952, p. 88.

22. Harriet Van Horne, "Old Plays in the Newest Bottle," *Theatre Arts*, August 1952, p. 38.

23. "Shakespeare," *New York Times*, 20 December, 1952, p. 22.

24. Arthur Oppenheimer, "Shakespeare on Television," *Electronic Age*, Autumn 1964, p. 20.

25. Oppenheimer, p. 20.

26. Oppenheimer, p. 20.

27. Jack Gould, "Television in Review," *New York Times*, 27 April 1953, p. 29.

28. "Through the Time Barrier," *TIME*, 4 May 1953, p. 59.

29. Flora Rheta Schreiber, "Television's *Hamlet*," *Quarterly of Film, Radio, and Television*, Vol. VIII, no. 2, Winter 1952, p. 150.

30. "Muggs to Macbeth," *Newsweek*, 13 December 1954, p. 62.

31. Jack Gould, "Delightful 'Peter Pan,' " *New York Times*, 15 March 1955, Section II," p. 15.

32. Raymond J. Schneider, "A Study of the Television Program *Camera Three*," Ph.D. diss., University of Michigan, 1965, p. 105–106.

33. Russell Lynes, "After Hours," *Harper's*, February 1961, p. 30.

34. Jack Gould, "TV: Madison Avenue Case Study," *New York Times*, 29 December 1959, p. 49.

35. "Little TV's Glory Road," *Newsweek*, 23 November 1959, p. 81.

36. Lynes, "After Hours," p. 30.

37. George Eells, "Riches or Rain for Theatre," *Theatre Arts*, November 1963, p. 28.

38. "Mailbag—Arthur Miller on Adaptations," *New York Times*, 29 November, 1959, Section II, p. 12.

39. Paul Gardner, "Cutting Plays Down to TV's Size," *New York Times*, 8 December 1963, Section II, p. 17.

40. Gardner, p. 17.

41. Gardner, p. 17.

42. Jack Gould, "TV: 'Death of a Salesman,' " *New York Times*, 9 May 1966, p. 95.

43. Robert Lewis Shayon, "From anxiety to identity: Arthur Miller's The Crucible," *Saturday Review*, 27 May 1967, p. 48.

44. "*Theater in America*: Can Directors Co-Direct?" *Action*, July/August 1975, p. 7.

45. *Great Performances—10th Anniversary* (New York: Educational Broadcasting Corporation, 1982), p. 8.

46. Stephen Koch, "Theater on the Tube," *Saturday Review/World*, 23 March 1974, p. 54.

47. Adrian Hall, "Television and the Stage," in *Promise and Performance: ACT's Guide to TV Programming for Children*, ed. Maureen Harmonay (Cambridge: Ballinger Publishers, 1979), p. 51.

48. "*Theater in America*," p. 17.

49. "*Theater in America*," p. 13.

50. "*Theater in America*," p. 13.

51. "*Theater in America*," p. 12.

52. "*Theater in America*," p. 13.

53. Leah D. Frank, "Turning O'Neill's Electra into a TV Mini Series," *New York Times*, 3 December 1978, Section II, p. 1.

54. John J. O'Connor, "Mourning Becomes Electra Begins on WNET," *New York Times*, 6 December 1978, Section III, p. 26.

55. *Great Performances*, p. 4.

56. "Theater in the Home," *Newsweek*, 20 November 1972, p. 86.

57. "Theater for Everyman," *Newsweek*, 14 August 1972, p. 47.

58. "CBS-TV gets Papp for 13 Plays over 4 years," *Broadcasting*, 7 August 1972, p. 22.

59. "CBS-TV gets Papp," p. 22.

60. John J. O'Connor, "How About Some Backbone?," *New York Times*, 18 March 1973, Section II, p. 19.

61. O'Connor, "How About," p. 19.

62. "Papp cools some, CBS stays quiet," *Broadcasting*, 19 March 1973, p. 121.

63. "Papp, Sweet and Sour," *TIME*, 19 March 1973, p. 60.

64. Albin Krebs, "ACLU Decries CBS over Play," *New York Times*, 9 March, 1973, p. 75.

65. O'Connor, "How About," p. 19.

66. O'Connor, "How About," p. 19.

67. John J. O'Connor, " 'Mister Roberts,' a Live Broadcast," *New York Times*, 21 March 1984, Section III, p. 22.

68. O'Connor, " 'Mister Roberts,' " p. 22. For a thoughtful, positive evaluation of her performance, see Tom Carson, "Stellar," *Village Voice*, 6 March 1984, p. 58.

69. Tom Shales, " 'Streetcar': Much to Be Desired," *Washington Post*, 3 March 1984, Section III, p. 1.

70. Tom Shales, " 'Streetcar,' " p. 4.

71. Tom Carson, "True Best," *Village Voice*, 24 January 1984, p. 63.

72. John Corry, "TV: Zoe Caldwell Stars in 'Medea,' " *New York Times*, 20 April 1983, Section III, p. 27.

73. Kirsten Beck, *Cultivating the Wasteland* (New York: American Council for the Arts, 1983), p. 56.

74. Beck, p. 58.

75. Steve Schneider, "Restaging Fugard for the Home Screen," *New York Times*, 11 November 1984, Section II, p. 29.

76. David Richards, "The Breaking of Bonds in Fugard's 'Master Harold,' " *Washington Post*, 12 November 1984, Section III, p. 1.

77. Steve Schneider, "Shrinking 'Heartbreak House' for TV," *New York Times*, 23 December, 1984, Section II, p. 26.

78. Schneider, "Shrinking," p. 26.

79. Kirsten Beck, *Cultivating*, p. 57.

80. Gardner, p. 17.

REFERENCES

From the very beginnings of American television, stage plays were seen as an important programming element. Newspapers, trade magazines, and books were filled with discussions of the methods and the exciting potential of TV theater.

Contemporary accounts such as John Reich's "Stage Plays for Television," Judy Dupuy's *Television Show Business*, Orrin E. Dunlap, Jr.'s *The Future of Television*, and Thomas H. Hutchinson's *Here is Television* not only capture the enthusiasm surrounding the form but catalog the variety of techniques already in use by the mid–1940s in translating drama to the small screen. A more historical overview of this early period is provided by William Hawes's 1963 essay, "Television Drama: The First Twenty Years," and by the dissertations of Albert W. Bluehm and Francis W. Sturcken, which also trace, in thorough detail, the development of TV drama until the end of the 1950s, particularly the initial efforts of NBC and CBS.

Theater on television expanded rapidly in the years following World War II, with the networks and local stations turning more and more to Broadway to fill their schedule. Moving plays to television, however, was not always an easy or successful process, and several articles appeared examining the problems. Among the more interesting are those by Marc Daniels, actress Judith Evelyn, TV writer Edmund Rice, and by the *New York Times*'s perceptive TV critic Jack Gould ("A Matter of Form"). Yet the medium's limitations could be overcome, sometimes triumphantly, as demonstrated by Worthington Miner's 1949 telecast of *Julius Caesar* on *Studio One*. The program received tremendous acclaim, particularly from Jack Gould (see his review " 'Julius Caesar' ") and helped establish, once and for all, television's theatrical legitimacy.

The flurry of drama series like *Kraft Television Theatre*, *The Hallmark Hall of Fame*, and *Philco Playhouse* in the early 1950s led to a period of great creativity and experimentation. Unusual and innovative productions of Shakespeare proved to be surprisingly popular—a development that prompted a great deal of attention. *Theatre Arts* commissioned two of the decade's foremost producers, Fred Coe and Worthington Miner, to write about their approaches to the bard. The style and techniques of Maurice Evans's 1953 landmark broadcast of *Hamlet* were extensively discussed by Byron Bentley, Arthur Oppenheimer, Flora Rheta Schreiber (in one of the first academic celebrations of TV theater), and in the pages of *TIME* ("Through the Time Barrier"). Paul Denis's "Shakespeare Makes The Grade" describes the popularity of *The Hallmark Hall of Fame*'s Shakespearean telecasts as well as the technical details of the series' 1960 film version of *Macbeth*.

In addition to famous telecasts like *Peter Pan* and the theatrical spectaculars of *The Hallmark Hall of Fame* (which are thoroughly described in a useful booklet published by the Museum of Broadcasting, *Hallmark Hall of Fame—A Tradition of Excellence*), the 1950s also saw the rise and the fall of original, written-for-TV drama, commonly and somewhat hazily referred to as television's "Golden Age." The teleplays of Rod Serling, Horton Foote, and Paddy Chayefsky, among others, took many of their cues from the best stage-to-small screen adaptations of the time, focusing on the small dramatic scale and character intimacy in which TV theater seemed to be most effective. For illuminating examinations of what these programs were like, Michael Kerbel's "The Golden Age of TV Drama" and Kenneth Tynan's "The Electronic Theater" are highly recommended. Also recommended is Tim Brooks and Earle Marsh's invaluable reference guide, *The Complete Directory to Prime Time Network TV Shows 1946–Present*. Surveying every single drama series, both original and stage based, broadcast by the three commercial networks, the book provides useful information on production styles, range of material, and some cast credits.

Even as stage telecasts were being replaced by less expensive and easier to produce series from Hollywood concern about the methods of TV drama continued to grow. Jack Gould's articles, "Artistic Problems" and "Scenery and Props," explore how close-ups and set designs are frequently mishandled. Theater director Robert Whitehead's "From Stage to TV Screen" laments the medium's lack of rehearsal time and its demand for stars. Tyrone Guthrie's "Theater and Television" discusses, in broad terms, the difficulties and challenges of moving stage plays to the small screen. Both Martin Mayer's "How Good is TV at its Best?" and the pseudonymously penned "Oedipus, Schnedipus" (by "Mr. Harper") take a harsh view of television's ability to tackle the classics.

More than any other issue, the thorny question of adaptation provoked the most controversy. To playwright Arthur Miller, reducing a work down to a few major incidents was nothing less than an artistic travesty—a position he expressed in a letter to the *New York Times*. He was answered a week later by dramatist Dale Wasserman, who defended his TV version of *Don Quixote*. Paul Gardner's "Cutting Plays Down to TV's Size" provides another view on the pressures of tele-adaptation, as explained by those who practice this admittedly difficult craft. (Readers looking for a more detailed study of the problems of adaptation are urged to consult Robert Hilliard's dissertation, which closely compares three tele-versions of three different stage plays to see what changes were made and why.)

One of the highlights of televised theater in the 1960s was *Play of the Week*—a syndicated series that garnered immediate praise for its challenging repertory and distinguished acting. When the show was threatened with cancellation a few months after its premiere because of low ratings, Jack Gould, in a rare instance of advocacy, urged his readers to write to the station to express their support ("TV: Madison Avenue Case Study"). Twenty-two thousand did, and the program was saved. Interesting reviews of *Play of the Week*'s approach and of its most honored production, Eugene O'Neill's *The Iceman Cometh*, can be found in Louis Celta's "TV Dramas in Relay," Russell Lynes's "After Hours," *Newsweek*'s "Little TV's Glory Road," and Jack Gould's "TV: Unequaled Standard" and "A Welcome for 'The Iceman.' "

Building on the foundation of its earlier series, *NET Playhouse*, PBS presented *Theater in America* in the early 1970s—a program widely applauded for its celebration of the country's diverse repertory theater companies. (See Frank Getlein's "The Theater on Television," Stephen Koch's "Theater on the Tube," and John J. O'Connor's "For $2–Million, It Looks Like a Bargain.") In 1975, the trade magazine *Action* devoted almost half an issue to a discussion of the program's most novel feature—its philosophy of "translation," which paired the original stage director with an experienced TV director in bringing the play to television. The various sections by executive producer Jac Venza and directors Michael Langham, Nick Havinga, Kirk Browning, and others, collected in the article "Can Directors Co-Direct," make fascinating reading. Adrian Hall's "Television and the Stage" is an equally intriguing account of a theater director's experiences with the series. WNET-TV's booklet *Great Performances—10th Anniversary* contains useful information on *Theater in America*'s development and production credits.

By way of contrast, PBS's other stage series of the period, *Hollywood Television Theater*, took a more traditional approach, featuring well-known actors and actresses whenever possible. John J. O'Connor's articles " 'Updating' Can Be Downright Silly" and "Is It the Tube's Answer to Off Broadway?" provide a general discussion of the show's methods. In her provocative essay, "A Semiotic Approach to Television as Ideological Apparatus," Teresa de Lauretis offers a more closely argued analysis of one of the series' most unusual presentations, Paul Avila Mayer's updated adaptation of Pirandello's *Six Characters in Search of an Author*.

In addition to the activities of PBS, the other major TV theater event of the 1970s was CBS's notorious cancellation of Joseph Papp's production of *Sticks and Bones*, three days before its scheduled broadcast. The decision prompted a tremendous outcry. The best accounts of the controversy are *TIME*'s "Papp, Sweet and Sour," *Broadcasting*'s "Papp cools some," and the impassioned comments of the *New York Time*'s TV critic, John J. O'Connor, ("TV: 'Sticks and Bones,' " and "How About Some Backbone?"). An earlier Papp telecast of *Much Ado About Nothing* ran into a different set of problems. Michael Knight's " 'Much Ado' of TV Dooms Stage Version" recounts how the show's popularity led to the closing of the production on Broadway a week later.

The rapidly changing nature of televised theater in the 1980s has been well documented, especially in Kirsten Beck's book, *Cultivating the Wasteland*, which examines the promise and the pitfalls of cable television. Other recommended articles include Richard Corliss's 1982 paean "Broadway Comes to Cable," written when it seemed theater might be cable's greatest attraction; Steve Schneider's "Restaging Fugard for the Home Screen" and "Shrinking 'Heartbreak House,' " which look at the production methods of the longest-running cable stage series, *Showtime on Broadway*; Leslie Bennetts's account of an *NBC Live Theatre* program, "Refloating 'Mister Roberts' for TV"; and John J. O'Connor's observations on PBS's *American Playhouse*, "When Public TV Excels."

A final bibliographic note: because the form is inherently "dramatic" and accessible, televised theater has understandably inspired much greater enthusiasm and interest from TV critics than broadcasts of opera, ballet, or symphonic concerts. Gifted journalists like Jack Gould and John J. O'Connor of the *New York Times*, Tom Shales of the *Washington Post*, and Tom Carson of the *Village Voice* reach a level of passion and insight when writing about TV drama one rarely encounters in their occasional discussions of the other arts. Reading their often exciting reviews of memorable and not-so-memorable theater telecasts proved to be among the chief pleasures in researching this chapter.

Books

Beck, Kirsten. *Cultivating the Wasteland*. New York: American Council for the Arts, 1983.

Brooks, Tim and Earle Marsh. *The Complete Directory to Prime Time Network TV Shows 1946–Present*. Rev. ed. New York: Ballantine Books, 1981.

Dunlap, Orrin E., Jr. *The Future of Television*. New York: Harper and Row, 1947.

Dupuy, Judy. *Television Show Business*. Schenectady: General Electric, 1945.

Hutchinson, Thomas H. *Here is Television*. New York: Hastings House, 1946.

Booklets

Great Performances—10th Anniversary. New York: WNET/Thirteen, 1982.

Hallmark Hall of Fame—A Tradition of Excellence. New York: Museum of Broadcasting, 1985.

Articles

Bennetts, Leslie. "Refloating 'Mister Roberts' for TV." *New York Times*, 18 March 1984, Section II, p. 32.

Bentley, Byron. "No Time for Playwrights." *Theatre Arts*, December 1955, pp. 30–32, 195–196.

Can Directors Co-Direct?" *Action*, July/August 1975, pp. 7–18.

Carson, Tom. "Stellar." *Village Voice*, 6 March 1984, p. 58.

———. "True Best." *Village Voice*, 24 January 1984, p. 94.

Celta, Louis. "TV Dramas in Relay." *New York Times*, 24 April 1960, Section II, p. 15.

Coe, Fred. "Televising Shakespeare." *Theatre Arts*, April 1951, pp. 56, 96.

Corliss, Richard. "Broadway Comes to Cable." *TIME*, 20 September 1982, pp. 72–73.

Daniels, Marc. "Always the First Time." *Theatre Arts*, February 1950, pp. 46–48.

de Lauretis, Teresa. "A Semiotic Approach to Television as Ideological Apparatus." In *Television: The Critical View*. ed. Horace Newcomb. 2d ed. New York: Oxford University Press, 1979, pp. 107–117.

Denis, Paul. "Shakespeare Makes The Grade." *New York Herald Tribune*, 20 November, 1969, Section IV, p. 3.

"Dialogue—George Schaeffer and Lewis Freedman." *Television Quarterly*, Vol. 1, no. 2, May 1962, pp. 6–16.

Evelyn, Judith. "Player's Vantage." *New York Times*, 13 June 1948, Section II, p. 8.

Gardner, Paul. "Cutting Plays Down to TV's Size." *New York Times*, 8 December 1953, Section II, p. 17.

Getlein, Frank. "The Theater on Television." *Commonweal*, 14 March 1975, pp. 58–59.

Gould, Jack. "Artistic Problems." *New York Times*, 18 September 1955, Section II, p. 13.

———. " 'Julius Caesar.' " *New York Times*, 13 March 1948, Section II, p. 11.

———. "A Matter of Form." *New York Times*, 31 October 1948, Section II, p. 11.

———. "Scenery and Props." *New York Times*, 31 January 1959, Section II, p. 13.

———. "Significant Step." *New York Times*, 17 January 1960, Section II, p. 13.

———. "TV: 'Death of a Salesman.' " *New York Times*, 9 May, 1966, p. 95.

———. "TV: Madison Avenue Case Study." *New York Times*, 29 December 1959, p. 49.

———. "TV: Unequaled Standard." *New York Times*, 16 November 1960, p. 83.

———. "A Welcome for 'The Iceman.' " *New York Times*, 20 November 1960, Section II, p. 19.

Guthrie, Tyrone. "Theater and Television." In *The Eighth Art*. New York: Holt, Rinehart, and Winston, 1962, pp. 91–99.

Hall, Adrian. "Television and the Stage." In *Promise and Performance: ACT's Guide to TV Programming for Children*. Ed. Maureen Harmonay. Cambridge: Ballinger Publishers, 1979, pp. 49–53.

Harper, Mr. [pseud.] "Oedipus, Schnedipus." *Harper's*, November 1956, p. 80.

Hawes, William. "Television Drama: The First Twenty Years." *Today's Speech*, September 1963, pp. 22–23.

Kerbel, Michael. "The Golden Age of TV Drama." *Film Comment*, July-August 1979, pp. 12–19.

Knight, Michael. " 'Much Ado' of TV Dooms Stage Version." *New York Times*, 7 February 1973, p. 30.

Koch, Stephen. "Theater on the Tube." *Saturday Review/World*, 23 March, 1974, pp. 54–55.

"Little TV's Glory Road." *Newsweek*, 23 November 1959, p. 81.

Lynes, Russell. "After Hours." *Harper's*, February 1961, pp. 28–30.

Mayer, Martin. "How Good is TV at its Best?" *Harper's*, September 1960, pp. 86–90.

Miller, Arthur. "Mailbag—Arthur Miller on Adaptations." *New York Times*, 29 November 1959, Section II, p. 12.

Miner, Worthington. "Shakespeare for the Millions." *Theatre Arts*, June 1951, pp. 58, 94–95.

O'Connor, John. J. "For $2–Million, It Looks Like a Bargain." *New York Times*, 7 April 1974, Section II, p. 19.

———. "How About Some Backbone?" *New York Times*, 18 March 1973, Section II, p. 19.

———. "Is It the Tube's Answer To Off Broadway?" *New York Times*, 3 October 1971, Section II, p. 17.

———. "TV: 'Sticks and Bones.' " *New York Times*, 9 March 1973, p. 74.

———. " 'Updating' Can Be Downright Silly." *New York Times*, 10 December 1972, Section II, p. 23.

———. "When Public TV Excels." *New York Times*, 27 June 1982, Section II, p. 27.

Oppenheimer, Arthur. "Shakespeare on Television." *Electronic Age*, Autumn 1964, pp. 19–21.

"Papp cools some, CBS stays quiet." *Broadcasting*, 19 March 1973, p. 121–122.

"Papp, Sweet and Sour." *TIME*, 19 March 1973, p. 60.

Reich, John. "Stage Plays for Television." *Televiser*, Jan./Feb. 1946, pp. 11–12.

Rice, Edmund. "Writing for Television." *New York Times*, 13 June 1948, Section II, p. 8.

Schreiber, Flora Rheta. "Television's *Hamlet*." *Quarterly of Film, Radio, and Television*. Vol. III, no. 2, Winter 1952, pp. 150–155.

Schneider, Steve. "Restaging Fugard for the Home Screen." *New York Times*, 11 November 1984, Section II, p. 29.

———. "Shrinking 'Heartbreak House' for TV." *New York Times*, 23 December 1984, Section II, p. 26.

Shales, Tom. " 'Streetcar': Much To Be Desired." *Washington Post*, 3 March 1984, Section III, p. 1.

"Through the Time Barrier." *TIME*, 4 May 1953, p. 82–83.

Tynan, Kenneth. "The Electronic Theater." *Holiday*, August 1960, pp. 83–91.

Wasserman, Dale. "Mailbag: Writers Reply to Arthur Miller." *New York Times*, 6 December 1959, Section II, p. 15.

Whitehead, Robert. "From Stage to TV Screen." *Theatre Arts*, October 1956, pp. 69–70.

Dissertations

Bluehm, Albert W. "The Influence of Medium upon Dramaturgical Method in Selected Television Plays." Ph.D. diss., Ohio State University, 1959.

Hilliard, Robert L. "Concepts of Dramaturgical Technique as Developed in Television Adaptations of Stage Plays." Ph.D. diss., Columbia University, 1959.

Sturcken, Francis W. "An Historical Analysis of Live Network Television Drama from 1938 to 1958." Ph.D. diss., University of Minnesota, 1960.

VIDEOGRAPHY

Play: *Julius Caesar* by William Shakespeare
Program: *Studio One*
Network: CBS
Date: March 6, 1949
Cast: Philip Bourneuf, Robert Keith, John O'Shaughnessy
Director: Paul Nickell
Producer: Worthington Miner

Play: *Hamlet* by William Shakespeare
Program: *Hallmark Hall of Fame*
Network: NBC
Date: April 26, 1953
Cast: Maurice Evans, Sarah Churchill
Director: George Schaeffer
Producer: Albert McCleery

Play: *King Lear* by William Shakespeare
Program: *Omnibus*
Network: CBS
Date: October 18, 1953
Cast: Orson Welles
Director: Andrew McCullough
Producer: Fred Rickey

Play: *Peter Pan* by Sir James Barrie
Program: *Producers' Showcase*
Network: NBC
Date: March 7, 1955
Cast: Mary Martin, Cyril Ritchard
Director: Vincent Donehue
Producer: Fred Coe

Play: *Macbeth* by William Shakespeare
Program: *Hallmark Hall of Fame*
Network: NBC

Date: November 20, 1960
Cast: Maurice Evans, Dame Judith Anderson
Director: George Schaeffer
Producer: George Schaeffer

Play: *The Iceman Cometh* by Eugene O'Neill
Program: *The Play of the Week*
Network: syndicated by National Telefilm Associates
Date: November 15, 1960
Cast: Jason Robards, Jr., Myron McCormick
Director: Sidney Lumet
Producer: Lewis Freedman

Play: *Death of a Salesman* by Arthur Miller
Program: CBS Special
Network: CBS
Date: May 8, 1966
Cast: Lee J. Cobb, Mildred Dunnock
Director: Alex Segal
Producers: David Susskind and Daniel Melnick

Play: *Sticks and Bones* by David Rabe
Program: CBS Special
Network: CBS
Date: August 1973
Cast: Tom Aldredge
Director: Robert Downey
Producer: Joseph Papp

Play: *Six Characters in Search of an Author* by Luigi Pirandello, adapted by Paul Avila Mayer
Program: *Hollywood Television Theater*
Network: PBS
Date: 1974
Cast: Andy Griffith, John Houseman
Director: Stacy Keach
Producer: Norman Lloyd

Play: *Feasting with Panthers* by Adrian Hall and Richard Cummings
Program: *Theater in America*
Network: PBS
Date: March 27, 1974
Cast: Richard Kneeland, Richard Kavanaugh
Director: Adrian Hall and Rick Hauser
Producer: Ken Campbell

Play: *Eccentricities of a Nightingale* by Tennessee Williams
Program: *Theater in America*
Network: PBS
Date: June 16, 1976
Cast: Frank Langella, Blythe Danner

Director: Glenn Jordan
Producers: Glenn Jordan and Lindsay Law

Play: *Our Town* by Thornton Wilder
Program: NBC Special
Network: NBC
Date: March 30, 1977
Cast: Sada Thompson, Hal Holbrook, Ned Beatty
Director: George Schaeffer
Producer: George Schaeffer

Play: *The Dance and the Railroad*
Program: ARTS Special
Network: ARTS Cable
Date: 1982
Cast: John Lone
Director: Emile Ardolino
Producer: Joseph Papp

Play: *True West* by Sam Shepard
Program: *American Playhouse*
Network: PBS
Date: January 31, 1984
Cast: John Malkovich, Gary Sinise
Director: Allan Goldstein
Producer: Lindsay Law

Index

About the Author

BRIAN G. ROSE, Assistant Professor, Fordham University at Lincoln Center, is the author of *Narrative Structures in the Social Films of Frank Capra*. He edited *TV Genres: A Handbook and Reference Guide* (Greenwood Press, 1985) and his articles have appeared in *The International Encyclopedia of Dance*, *The Journal of Popular Film and Television*, and *The Journal of Communication*.